A NOTICE TO THE READER

The prices of all products listed in this book have been omitted primarily because they are subject to frequent change. This would make the book outdated before the next edition could be printed. The publisher does, however, maintain a printed list of current prices. This may be obtained by sending two (2) first class stamps along with your name and address to: The Great Outdoors Trading Company, 24759 Shoreline Highway, Marshall, California 94940

The Complete Outfitting & Source Book for
BIRD WATCHING

The products, services and firms listed herein are for
reference only; no endorsement is implied. While every
effort has been made to insure the accuracy of information
included, neither the author or publisher can be held
responsible for errors or for changes that occurred after
the book went to press.

Printed in the United States of America

First Printing: November 1978

Published by The Great Outdoors Trading Company
24759 Shoreline Highway, Marshall, California 94940

Distributed to the book trade by
Holt, Rinehart and Winston
383 Madison Avenue, New York 10017

Art Director: Marja Wicker

Cover Photography: Hal Lauritzen

Typography: Graffic Jam

Library of Congress Cataloging in Publication Data

Scofield, Michael.

   The complete outfitting & source book for
bird watching.

   (A Holt Great Outdoors book)

   1. Bird watching. 2. Bird watching—
Equipment and supplies. II. Great Outdoors
Trading Company. II. Title

QL677.5.S36   589.2'073   78-56578

ISBN title number: 0-03-045616-9

The Complete Outfitting & Source Book for
BIRD WATCHING

Compiled By
The Staff of the Great Outdoors Trading Company

Written and Edited By
Michael Scofield

Published By
The Great Outdoors Trading Company

DEDICATION

To Elizabeth, Mary Ellen, and Sandy, with love.

ACKNOWLEDGMENTS

To Christine Wilkins for tackling the hundreds of odd jobs needed to see this
book through; to Sandy Johnson and Biney Willcutt for their typing skills;
to Frank Allen, Laurence Binford, Ted Chandik, Doug Cheeseman,
Glenn Christiansen, Frank Farran, and Marie Mans for their technical
expertise; to Susan Roney Drennan of *American Birds* for helping with the
History section; to the American Birding Association, Johan Kooy of the
California Academy of Sciences, Connie Major, Jim Pope, for their generosity
in supplying photographs and illustrations; to Les Taylor for the chance to do
this book, to my parents for their encouragement, to
Holt, Rinehart & Winston's Leslie Rowe for his enthusiasm,
and to Pierre Mornell for seeing me through all this.

PHOTO CREDITS

All product photographs were furnished by their respective manufacturers.
American Birding Association: pages 13, 14, 35, 36, 37, 123, 128, 133, 152,
154, 157, and 158; Audio-technica, U.S., Inc.: page 81; Bancroft Library at the
University of California, Berkeley: page 33; Bushnell Optical Co.: page 41;
California Academy of Sciences: pages 20, 21, 22, 23, 26, 27, 28, 29, 30, 32, 34,
35, 143, and 185; Paul Covel: page 16; Ken W. Gardiner: pages 10 and 11;
National Audubon Society: page 24; Nature Expeditions International:
pages 134, 137, and 173; Connie Major: pages 112, 115, 116, 161, 162, 165, and 166;
Jim Pope: pages 9, 17, 38, 55, 65, 72, 86, 121, 124, and 171; Arnold Small: page 12;
Smithsonian Institution: pages 18, 31, 32, and 33; Society Expeditions: page 151;
U.S. Fish & Wildlife Services: pages 15, 130, 140, 148, and 187;
Wilderness Southeast: pages 145 and 147.

Table of Contents

Introduction

Why bother with birds?

A 1974 Department of Agriculture study discovered bird watching to be the fastest growing sport in America. Roger Tory Peterson, the grand old man of birding, estimates that upwards of 20 million Americans—or at least one out of ten—seriously watch birds.

The craze is not confined to the United States. In terms of the percentage of citizens who watch, England ranks number one. America ranks number two followed by Australia, Scandinavia, Holland, Belgium and West Germany. No figures are in for the rest of the world, but you can bet that where leisure exists, so also exist ever-growing legions of zealots bearing spotting scopes, field guides and binoculars.

Why do they do it?

Perhaps the easiest answer is that birds are evident everywhere. Ornithologist Joel Carl Welty reports that over one trillion birds live in the world today. 7,600,000,000 of those breed in

the United States, 120,000,000 breed in the British Isles. Sheer numbers, of course, can satiate, but birds come in dizzying variety, too, thanks to mutation. The world boasts nearly 8,700 species of birds, from the Bee Hummingbird (*Mellisuga helenae*) of Cuba, whose body measures less than an inch long, to the Andean Condor (*Vultur gryphus*) whose 11-foot wingspan makes it the world's largest flying bird. Of the 8,700 species of birds extant, 840 exist in the United States.

Birds are evident. But so are many forms of life. What causes our enchantment with birds? In the 19th century language of naturalist Thomas Nuttall, "Of all the classes of animals by which we are surrounded in the ample field of Nature, there are none more remarkable in their appearance and habits than the feathered inhabitants of the air. They play around us like fairy spirits, dart like meteors in the sunshine of summer or seek the solitary recesses of the forest and waters."

Brown Pelican *(Pelecanus occidentalis)*, photographed by amateur Ken W. Gardiner with a Topcon Super-D camera and 500mm motor-driven lens, at Seacliff State Park, Monterey Bay, Northern California. Senior research engineer Gardiner works at SRI International, has been photographing birds —mostly in black and white—since 1971. Although usually the Brown Pelican dives for it's food as shown, flocks have been known to beat their wings violently while swimming in arcs towards shallow water, where they scoop up driven fish.

Birds, unless they're squawking, make us feel good. They remind us all—the rushed businessman, the jaded housewife, even the love-sick adolescent—that life has it joys. As engineer-turned-naturalist Frank Farran says, "Birds offer the watcher beauty, grace, majesty, and the thrill of being in on a unique performance. Whoever has seen a Peregrine Falcon dive or Anna's Hummer mate will never forget it."

There is, too, the fact that birds resemble people in curious ways. We both can sing. Magpies, jays, and parrots are the only animals besides chimpanzees that can also talk. Birds and men are the sole creatures that regularly walk upright. Like the birds, and like no other vertebrate except bats, man has learned to fly, however artificial the performance.

But the 150,000 membership in Britain's Royal Society for the Protection of Birds, and the 350,000 membership in America's Audubon Society, testifies to more, and that is, alarm concerning what Buckminister Fuller calls, "This Spaceship, Earth." Birds have as much right to be here as do we. Yet, fifty-one species of birds are on the World Endangered Species List. Because of DDT, because of skyscrapers and housing tracts, we are at fault, and beginning to admit it. Many of us are not so much watching birds as attempting to watch over them.

American Birding Association president Arnold Small, shown here in New Guinea, says that birding is the best way he knows to turn strangers into lifelong friends.

The conservationist's zeal is matched by that of the 'lister,' he who leaps from bed before midnight to track down a Flammulated Owl, adding birds heard or sighted until the sun goes down, in hopes that he can vaunt to fellow listers the number of species noted in one day. "The lure of the list" is what Roger Tory Peterson calls it. This kind of birder is both sportsman and competitor, driven by an obsession called collectomania. Yet he harms nothing, content merely to see or hear, and add names to his list.

A shadowy Australian named Steuart Stokes, by the way, may be the unofficial world champion lister. A retired naval officer and former director of the World Bank, Stokes spends nine months a year birding. He's been doing it since 1945. Of the 8,700 species in the world, Steuart Stokes has seen or heard over 5,600.

Joining the conservationist's and the lister's fascination with birds is that of the field ornithologist. Often an amateur, he—or she—is the one who increases our knowledge of bird traits through observation and publishing. Such classics by amateurs as *The Life of the Robin* by Britain's David Lack, following four years of watching, and *The Life History Studies of the Song Sparrow* by America's Margaret Morse Nice, following eight years of watching, tell us not only about birds but once again make us ponder the philosophical question, "Why are any of us here at all?."

In 1874, field ornithologist Elliott Coues felt he must write in his *Manual of Instruction,* "The cane-gun should be mentioned. It is a single-barrel, easily mistaken for a cane. My own experience with it is very unsatisfactory; the handle always hit me in the face and I generally missed my bird. [But] if you approve of shooting on Sunday and yet scruple to shock popular prejudice, [with a cane gun] you can slip out of town unsuspected."

No longer need the close observer of birds shoot them, unless of course it is the corpse about which he is curious: dissection remains necessary to discover nuances of anatomy or to find levels of pesticide poisoning. Armed only with binoculars, the ability to scrutinize, and much patience, today's field ornithologist has many lifetimes of study before him.

Still one may ask, why bother with birds?, and still the answers roll on. Zoologist/lister Arnold Small, president of the American Birding Association, finds it difficult to conceive of another pursuit in which total strangers so quickly become lifelong friends. Naturalist John Muir often used birds to excuse his need for long walks and fresh air. Henry David Thoreau used birds to build, with Emerson, the philosophy of Transcendentalism. Roger Tory Peterson is sure that what attracted him to birds as a boy is their apparent freedom to fly *where* they want to *when* they want to—free-spirit Peterson has always chafed under regimentation.

What brings you to the pastime, sport, obsession of bird watching, call it what you will? Others have named the never-ending quest for something new to see, the allure of courtship antics such as those of the Western Grebe, the mystery of migration, the sweetness of bird song,

On the left, Roger Tory Peterson, author of **Field Guide to the Birds**. On the right, Chandler S. Robbins, co-author of **Birds of North America**. Shown birding together in North Dakota. These men have penned two of America's most-used field guides.

the brilliancy of plumage, the chance to travel, the chance to make good friends (both avian and *Homo sapiens*), the joys of communing with nature on one's own. It may be simply that you are depressed, bored or bedridden, and look to birds to bring you, if not mirth, at least diversion.

But whatever your reason, know that you can start any place, any season. There are no dues to pay, no permissions needed. All you really have to do is open your eyes.

Ways You Can Get Involved

Before deciding which phase of bird watching appeals most, you want to get your feet wet. We'll assume you've poured through the sections in this book on Equipment, Publications, and Sites, purchased a pair of binoculars, a field guide, and

chosen where to go. Bringing someone with you sounded pleasant until you happened to read in Gilbert Pearson's 1919 *Birds of America:* "When one is in the company of others, nature never completely enthralls him. His attention is more or less distracted by his companions—they talk, laugh, even shout with a loud voice, swing their arms, and move about, pointing, gesticulating, and assuming attitudes. Even such students will see birds, for many of our feathered friends have become used to strange sounds and antics. But the expert who sees all the birds has taken lessons from the fox—he hunts alone."

You intend to be that expert. What do you do now?

First of all, dress in colors that harmonize with nature—no blacks and whites, no fluorescent

"The expert who sees all the birds has taken lessons from the fox—he hunts alone"—from Gilbert Pearson's **Birds of America**. *Taking a bead on a Seaside Sparrow (Ammospiza maritima) near Beaumont, Texas.*

knits. Wear boots with crepe or rubber soles; at the least, tennis shoes, so you won't make loud noises when crossing concrete or rocks. A field jacket whose upright pockets keep your field guide and notebook from slipping out is useful. Fill one of your pockets with raisins or the birder's k-ration, Crunchy Granola™ bars—you'll get hungry sooner than you think. A billed cap helps in bright sun. Be sure it's not too tight; you'll want to push it back when using binoculars.

Frank Farran offers these tips for beginning birders at the site itself:

1) "Find an ecotone, a spot where two or more biotic communities meet, such as a field and chaparral, or woods and a marsh. Posted picnic areas are excellent, too. Any 'island' habitat is good for spotting unusual birds—a tree where there aren't many trees, brush where there isn't much brush. Soaring birds can best be seen riding updrafts along the brows of hills.

2) "Keep your binoculars focused for mid-range (25 yards). Once you've seen the bird, keep your eyes on him while raising your binoculars. Adjust for clarity. Pay particular attention to how the bird sits, how he moves his wings and tail, the shape of his beak, unusual marks, the sounds he makes. Coloration can be deceptive, so can size.

3) "Try to find the bird in your field guide while he's still there. And don't be discouraged if you draw a blank on your first try, that is unless he was a male Cardinal or Steller's Jay. They're pretty hard to miss."

Once you become expert, even without binoculars you'll be able to recognize many birds. The legendary Ludlow Griscom, prime mover in the Massachusetts Audubon Society, could identify 502 species by their calls alone. In 1937 Harold Wood produced the following chart. Its data still hold true.

Visual Distance for Unaided Eyesight Identification

Species	Visual Distance
Hummingbird	100 feet, on wire
Swallow	250 feet, on wire
American Goldfinch	200 feet, flying
American Robin	250 feet, identified by shape
American Crow	Can be seen twice the distance of the American Robin
Broad-winged Hawk	Recognized as Hawk at one-half mile

*Source: "How Far Can a Bird Be Seen?" Auk, 54:96-97

Whether or not on your first excursion you can name the birds you see, you're intrigued, you want to know more. The Clubs and Associations section of this book can help. The American Birding Association, 4,000 members strong, caters mainly to listers. The Cooper and Wilson Ornithological Societies, and the American Ornithologists' Union—each with its own national publication—welcome those who wish to study birds from a scientific point of view. So does Cornell's Laboratory of Ornithology which will send you for a fee a course-by-mail in ornithology.

Perhaps your best first step, however, is to join a local Audubon chapter or affiliate, where you'll meet bird watchers of all levels of skill. You'll receive the monthly magazine, *Audubon,* dealing with wild life conservation, and for another ten dollars, get the bi-monthly *American Birds.* But be prepared: a year ago July, National Audubon decided to withhold local chapter telephone numbers and addresses. If you can't find the data here or in your telephone book, you'll have to write National Audubon and wait six-seven weeks for a reply.

With the necessary funds and time, you can take tours that specialize in wildlife and birds. Many are listed in this book. Some go to exotic places and cost thousands of dollars; others, like the American Birding Association's "Weekends" on the East Coast, cost under $100.

Enticing birds to come to you is a hobby to which many bird watchers gravitate. You can do this merely by sitting still. As T. Gilbert Pearson puts it, again from *Birds of America,* "All wood birds, both shy and rare, may be out-generaled by the quiet sitter. They seem to wonder what manner of thing this is that looks so like a man, but neither smokes nor swears, talks, laughs, nor tramps about. Slowly they draw near and peer at the curiosity."

The stationary watcher speeds the process of bringing birds to him by using an artificial bird call, by creating a smack-kiss sound by sucking the back of his hand, by playing a tape recording of bird calls, or—most effective—by learning to imitate the sounds of birds himself. But poor W. Dan Quattlebaum (that was his real name). Quattlebaum could imitate over one hundred songs and gave performances in the Arcadia, California Arboretum in the early 1950's to prove it. The birds came flocking but so did the children. Their taunts drove him first to silence, at last to long vacations.

Surrounding yourself with birds can be most elegantly done by creating a bird garden. Books are written telling what fruit, berries, ground-cover and shrubbery to plant for what species. Others give plans for bird houses and feeders, counsel the inclusion of baths, or better, pools with dripping water. One (*The Hungry Bird Book* by Arbib and Soper) gives the four recipes birds like most: mealworm culture, anti-sparrow pudding, bird cake, and basic pud. You may even

wish to hook up a transmittal system to your stereo set in order to pipe outside bird sounds indoors. The volume may be turned low if by chance a sparrow allergic to anti-sparrow pudding should mistake it for basic pud.

In your garden or in the field, the use of electronic gear is growing. Tape recorders serve two purposes. You can record bird sounds and your own field notes for later identification. Or you can pre-record a particular sound, using the phonograph records distributed by Dover and Houghton Mifflin, take the recorder outside and use the sound to 'chum' birds hither. The sound of a Screech Owl will bring song birds out in protest. But vocal chumming can be abused. Beseiged by cassette-carrying birders at the Audubon Sonoita Creek Sanctuary in Arizona, the rare Black Hawk (*Buteogallus anthracinus*) became so neurasthenic that it was unable to fledge its young for three years.

Photography offers the bird watcher a different diversion. You'll need a lens with a focal length of 200 mm or more, and a tripod or shoulder mount with which to steady it. The new teleconverters, selling for under $100, double or triple the power of the lens you have. Bird photography requires money, patience, and a strong back for lugging

*This male Cardinal (**Richmondina cardinalis**) is pretty hard to mistake, even for a beginner. Photographed at College Park, Maryland.*

equipment around. But sometimes the results are worth it, as in the photo of the Brown Pelican by amateur Ken W. Gardiner, shown on page 10.

You may want to get into banding. Bird banding is no joke; it's regulated by the Fish and Wildlife Service's Office of Migratory Bird Management, Laurel, Maryland 20811. You must furnish the names of three licensed banders or recognized ornithologists who know you can identify the birds you handle, and know, too, that you can keep thorough, accurate and legible records of what you do.

The birds are trapped in black so-called mist nets, one leg banded with coded aluminum strips, then they are let go, hopefully to be found dead or alive in a different location. Banding has proven that some Arctic Terns, the world champs of migration, fly 11,000 miles and back from Labrador to South Africa. All banding data in this country is sent to Maryland where it's converted to magnetic computer tape for use by ornithologists and wildlife technicians around the globe.

Cornell's Laboratory of Ornithology (159 Sapsucker Woods Road, Ithaca, New York 14853) offers a pursuit easier to get into: its Nest Record-Card Program. What you do is send for the cards, search for the nests, and fill in the blanks—recording such data as how many eggs or young are in the nest, how high the nest is above the ground, and what supports it. Of course you also have to be able to identify the bird that's nesting.

The Cornell Lab now has 250,000 nest records on file; participants get a semi-annual newsletter free.

Maybe you're wondering, of what use is all this data? Besides helping researchers know when to sound the alarm on pollution and pesticide problems, such information—available to amateurs and professionals—aids studies undertaken for their own sake. Toiling to answer the questions What? How? and Why? has always given man a sort of visceral satisfaction.

Many mysteries in the bird world exist. Who knows? You yourself may unravel one. According to Palo Alto, California, naturalist Theodore Chandik, the biggest mystery is the 'how' of bird navigation. To navigate during migration, birds use genetic cues plus the sun, stars, wind, and the earth's magnetism—but how, we don't know.

Observation of grounded migrants, banding, radar, special orientation cages, and radio transmitters are being employed to find out.

Wisconsin ornithologist Joseph Hickey in his *Guide To Bird Watching* urges the amateur to catalogue bird tracks—no complete identification guide by tracks has ever been done. Hickey, too, prints a 15-page outline for a choose-your-own-songbird life-history study, much of which you can undertake in your back yard.

If the idea of headwork tires you before you start, and it's fellowship in open fields you crave, don't despair. Join 19,000 others in the National Audubon Society's Christmas Bird Count. Each Christmas since 1900, groups of locals have risen before dawn to march about the countryside—in carefully designated areas—counting birds. The results get published in Audubon's *American Birds* in the July issue. Or, form your own group any time of the year for a bird-

Banding a Canvasback (Aythya valisineria), a diving duck, at the Lake Merritt Wildlife Refuge, Oakland, California. Note special pliers needed for this exacting work.

Julie Lemoine of California's Oakland Museum records bird sounds at Point Reyes National Seashore, using a Uher #400 portable recorder and homemade parabolic reflector. Note earphones around neck.

watching Big Day. You start at midnight hooting up as many species of owls as you can muster, proceed through a day and much of the next night amassing additional species. Sight identification always counts, sound is counting more and more, since for *every* bird seen ten others will be heard. The American record for numbers of species identified in 24 hours by a group of birders (no more than four) is 203, set in California in 1976. Texas follows with 192. The American Birding Association's journal, *Birding,* prints Big Day results in the February issue.

You can see that the ways to get involved with

birds are about as numerous as the birds themselves. Just look at the lists you can compile: a Christmas Count list, a Big Day list, your own back yard list (divide that into birds seen *in* your back yard and *from* your back yard), a bedroom window list, a list of birds identified from a moving car, birds seen on television, birds seen in your dreams, a county list, state and national lists, and the big one, the lifetime world list. For all these lists, you can start over each week, each month or every year. The list of lists goes on and on. But whether you prefer to list birds, study birds or simply to enjoy birds, the book you hold in your hands gives you all the information you need to get started.

How To Use This Book

The Complete Outfitting and Source Book for Bird Watching is designed as your basic access tool to the sport. Even experienced birders now have a complete reference guide for getting the most out of their adventures.

You'll note that the book has a glossary at the back, but no index. That's because the book's design, with its unique 'information blocks,' allows you to find the data you need fast, without strain, simply by referring to the Table of Contents. The sections on Equipment, Publications, Organizations, and Sites, are prefaced by guides showing how best to use the information blocks that follow, with a little history thrown in.

Suppose you plan to travel next summer to Europe. This book, we think, contains the most exhaustive list of birding tours in and leaving the United States, now in print. To discover which tours go to Europe, turn to Tours in Other Countries-Europe. To discover which organizations to contact there (many will send you helpful hints before you leave), turn to Organizations In Other Countries-Europe. Suppose you decide to treat yourself to a portable tape recorder before you go. Turn to Equipment-Tape Recorders. And, of course you want to experiment with the recorder in the field first. If you live in Maine, turn to Bird Watching Sites-Maine. The sites are organized alphabetically by state, then by nearest town.

We tried to keep the layout of this book simple. That's because we hope you spend most of your time, not with this book, but with all those birds and bird watchers out there waiting to welcome you. Happy birding.

History

The first representation of a bird we know anything about appears in a cave in Spain, in the Upper Pyrenees. Probably the Common, or European Crane *(Grus grus),* the drawing was scratched on the wall in Paleolithic times, about 10,000 B.C.

Colonel Willoughby Verner and his friend, the Abbe' Breuil, also saw, in 1913, Neolithic cave drawings (6,000-8,000 B.C.) in the Spanish province of Cadiz. The twelve species identified, still native to Spain, include flamingos and wild ducks. Pictured in pursuit are hungry men armed with bows and arrows.

Birds became so important to the Egyptians of 3,000 B.C. that they gave their divinities birds' heads. Horus, the supreme sun god, looked down with the eyes of a hawk; Thoth, the moon god of magic and wisdom, spoke with an ibis' bill. Many birds, like their human counterparts, were preserved whole, as mummies.

The Greek comic playwright, Aristophanes, was an acute observer of birds. In 414 B.C. he molded a satire, called *The Birds,* around their habits. But most of the ancient Athenians, like the Romans who conquered them, got used to watching birds, depending on their flight and feeding patterns for omens. Our word "auspicious," in fact, comes from the Latin *avi-spez.* It means bird observer.

Fifty years after Aristophanes, Aristotle tried to systematize what was known (and suspected) of birds. A determined naturalist, in his *History of Animals* he wrote, "We must not recoil from examination of the humbler creatures. Some may not charm the senses, even though they give pleasure to those inclined to philosophy, but every realm of nature is marvellous. . ."

Aristotle's greatness, unfortunately, extended to guillibility. With his own observations he mixed accounts from birdcatchers, farmers and fishermen, even accounts from Aristophanes' plays. Who knows where he heard the following: "When a hen has vanquished a rooster, she crows, imitating him, too, by pouncing on other hens. This change in behavior results in the hen growing rooster feathers."

Aristophanes (448-380 B.C.) taking a break between bird watching sorties.

For 2000 years—through the Roman conquest, the Dark and Middle Ages, the Renaissance—scholars clung to Aristotle's preference for systematics over accuracy. In the first century after Christ, Pliny the Elder wrote 37 books about animals, including birds. Willy-nilly he arranged fantasy, heresay, and observations in an air-tight, orderly manner. As late as 1250 A.D., the Dominican Thomas de Cantimpre, studying Aristotle and Pliny but refusing to see for himself, could write about storks, "They murder their wives when they have had sex with another, nor do they wash up after the crime. It has often been noted."

Outnumbered by the scholastics as they were, keen observers still left their marks. On our own continent, near the Ohio River around 500 A.D., the Hopewellian Indians carved birds in the form of stone pipes. So accurate were their representations that ornithologists have been able to identify them as the Common Raven *(Corvus coras)*, the Carolina Paroquet (now extinct), the Cardinal (one of America's few crested birds), and the Sparrow Hawk or American Kestrel *(Falco sparverius*, our smallest falcon).

Two hundred and fifty years later—750 A.D.—the Polynesians had learned enough about birds to risk following, in huge sailing canoes, the American Golden Plover's spring migration north from Tahiti. Thus those brown-skinned explorers discovered the Hawaiian Islands, or so some authorities believe. Polynesian tradition tells us that wherever they sailed, the ancients took the frigatebird (often called Man-o'-war) with them as a good luck charm. They knew that this rapacious soarer-over-seas, with his small body and seven-foot wing span, has to find land in order to rest—he will drown if he touches water.

While primitives plied the waves and scholars studied their Aristotle and Pliny the Elder, a learned eccentric took Europe by storm between 1,194 to 1,250 A.D., the Italian emporer, Frederick II. Between sieges on Germany and Jerusalem—it was the era of the Crusades—and between three marriages, Frederick II amused himself with falcons.

The sport of hunting game with falcons got its start in China around 2,000 B.C., advancing to Persia in 1,700 B.C., thence to Europe a few hundred years before Christ. By Frederick's day falconry had become a high art, pursued by royalty and commoners alike. But Frederick, clad in Arabic robes and attended by Moorish slaves,

Aristotle (384-332 B.C.) and his students on the trail of a Red-rumped Swallow.

used falconry as pretext to pen one of the world's great treatises on ornithology. He called his seven volumes *De Arte Venandi Cum Avibus*, the Art of Hunting with Birds, writing in Latin, as did all medievalists, to secure the work's prestige. On flight, for instance, only watchers in the 20th century such as Crawford Greenewalt and Konrad Lorenz have surpassed Frederick's ability to see. He analyzed the relation of body weight and wing surface to the number of wing beats and feather structure, correlating air speed to the size of the pectoral muscles of falcons and eagles.

Although Dante placed the excommunicated Frederick II in the sixth circle of Hell, this "amazement of the world," as a contemporary called him, loved nothing better than to meander in his private menagerie of pelicans, cranes, wild geese and herons.

*In order to write his **Natural History in Thirty-Seven Books,** Pliny the Elder (A.D. 24-79) used to rise before dawn, and take a cold bath each noon.*

Five hundred years before Frederick II, plovers may have guided the Polynesians to Hawaii. Two hundred years later in the far north the squawking, Black Guillemots (related to auks and puffins) no doubt let Eric the Red know he had discovered Greenland. And from the daybook of Christopher Columbus, Oct. 8 and 9, 1492, we read, "There were many small land-birds. [The crew] took one which was flying southwest. There were jays, ducks, and a pelican. All night the men heard birds passing."

Unwittingly, Columbus had sailed into a fall migration heading south toward Bermuda. His hopes soared; scurvy had sickened the crew. Three days later he landed on the island of Guadahani. "The songs of birds were so pleasant," he wrote, "That it seemed as if a man could never wish to leave this place." After recuperating in the West Indies, he sailed with a cage of parrots—not such sweet singers—back to the king and queen of Spain. Though the *Santa Maria* had sunk and

many men had died, he told his Majesties, "Always the land was of the same beauty. Even the pigeons had their crops full of flowers sweeter than orange blossom."

Columbus' penchant for hyperbole was matched by that of a Frenchman named Pierre Belon, born sixty-six years later in 1517. Columbus' interest in birds took second place to his interest in gold; Belon was a naturalist first. Self-taught, Belon wandered through England, Europe, and the mideast, making sketches, taking notes. While the Swiss scholar, Conrad Gesner, was ransacking previous works— including those old favorites by Aristotle and Pliny the Elder—to come up with his own 806-page treatise on birds, Belon watched bee-eaters (Meropidae) atop Crete's Mount Ida, pelicans along the Nile, the Blue Rock Thrush in Corfu, and Africa's exuberant Red-billed Chough (pronounced chef). He also dissected and was first to describe homologies between avian and human bones. One hundred and forty-four paintings by a not-too-adept friend illustrate Belon's great work, *"L'histoire de la Nature des Oyseaux.* In 1564 Belon should have kept his eyes off birds, for bandits stabbed him to death in Paris' 2500 acre park, the Bois de Boulogne.

*The flight of the Magnificent Frigatebird, or Man-o'-War **(Fregata magnificens)** is more rapid than any other sea bird. Frigatebirds are robbers. Once they have badgered a sea gull into dropping its prey, they dive down and overtake it in mid-air, sometimes flipping the fish in flight in order to swallow it headfirst.*

Columbus' crew may have seen the Brown Pelican **(Pelecanus occidentalis)** *or one of these magnificent White Pelicans* **(Pelecanus erythrorhynchos),** *whose wings span 10 feet and whose bill is over two feet long.*

Unlike Columbus, Belon never reached America. But many foreign naturalists did. From the second expedition to Virginia in 1584, the Englishman Thomas Hariot reported back to Sir Walter Raleigh, "[We have seen] turkey cocks and turkey hens, partridges, cranes and herons. I have noted in the native [Indian] language the names of 86 kinds of fowl. . .Besides those named, we have caught and eaten, as well as made pictures of, several [other birds]."

In terms of the percentage of citizens that watches birds today, England ranks number one, followed by the United States. Such Pan-Atlantic zeal got its start during the 16th and early 17th centuries. "I have seen them fly," writes the English colonist William Wood of passenger pigeons in 1634, "as if the ayerie regiment had been pigeons, [with] neither beginning nor ending, length or breadth of these millions of millions." And in 1621 the Englishman Thomas Morton writes of the American wild turkey, "divers times [these birds] in great flocks have sallied by our doors."

Yet even before Mark Catesby's, Alexander Wilson's, and John James Audubon's illustrated works boosted enthusiasm for New World natural history, the passenger pigeons, turkeys and other natives were being wiped out. Says John Josselyn of the pigeon in 1674, "of late they are much diminished, the English taking them

with nets." And of the turkey, "I have seen three-score broods of young turkies on the side of a marsh, sunning themselves. But this was thirty years since, the English and the Indians having now destroyed much of the breed."

Wholesale slaughter of American birds had to wait for the late nineteenth century. Meanwhile, those Hardy Boys of English ornithology, Francis Willughby and John Ray, reconnoitered Europe between 1663 and 1666, tramping fields and poking into birdcatchers' stalls to obtain specimens for dissection. They planned nothing less than to describe the whole of nature. Willughby was the perfectionist and Ray the wordsmith, boiling down, after Willughby's death at age 37, the latter's observations. "At times," writes Ray, "he seems to us too painstaking in the description of the colors of individual feathers."

But the Willughby-Ray *Ornithologiae*, penned in both Latin and English, scrapped the 2000 year old Aristotelian systematics at last. Aristotle had classed birds according to whether they lived on land, at the edge of land, or on water. Willughby and Ray based their pigeon-holing on form: beak shape, body size, foot structure. Even the boastful Swede, Carl Linnaeus, who sixty years later fathered today's genus/species system of scientific names, acknowledged his debt to the *Ornithologiae*.

*(Clockwise) Conrad Gesner (1516-65), sometimes called the German Pliny, is best known as a naturalist, yet he once published a book in which he translated the Lord's Prayer into 22 languages, then described 108 more. Naturalist John Ray (1627-1705) completed Willughby's **Ornithologiae** after the older man died, garnering ideas for his own **Collection of English Proverbs** as he did so. Britain's Ray Society was formed in Ray's honor in 1844. Carl Linnaeus (1707-1778), the Swedish botanist and ornithologist, enjoyed posing in his Lapland dress. A compulsive worker, he published 180 books in his lifetime.*

24

*The Gannet **(Morus bassanus)** was in the 17th century called a Solon Goose. John Ray got some ideas for his **English Proverbs** by studying Gannets' kamikaze attacks on baited boards in Wales.*

Francis Willughby died before he could sail to America. John Ray got sidetracked with gannets (goose-sized seabirds related to boobies), writing from Padstow, "[the Welch] have a strange way of catching them. They tie a fish on a board so that the bird may see it, who then comes down with so great swiftness that he breakes his neck on the wood."

Mark Catesby, however, America's first painter/naturalist, managed to sail to the New World in 1710, financed by an inheritance from his father.

Driven by his own curiosity and a growing appetite on both sides of the Atlantic for mounted specimens, and colored prints of specimens, Catesby roamed south from the Carolinas, stalking birds, shooting, preserving, painting them. Like so many of his counterparts, he was also a botanist, took pressed flowers back to England to be purchased by the rich. He spent 17 years describing mammals, birds, plants and fish in a two-volume work entitled, *"The Natural History of the Carolinas, Florida, and the Bahama Islands,* engraving and coloring the illustrations himself. Although a Quaker merchant lent him funds, he died a pauper, some say in London, some say in California.

Mark Catesby may have believed that passenger pigeons roosted on one another's backs, even that the scarcity of American birds was due to their remoteness from Noah's Ark, but he pioneered the combining of birds and plants in a single print, whetting drawing room appetites for more.

In the fever that gripped 18th century minds to catalogue Nature, no one outdid France's Compte de Buffon. Starting with eighty stuffed, insect-riddled birds in the Cabinet de Roi Museum, he expanded his research to include all wildlife, minerals, and plants, packing forty-four volumes with words and illustrations within fifty years. His *Natural History* contains 844 colored plates of birds, often drawn from specimens brought him by adventurers hired for the task. At the age of 72, Buffon is rumored to have cried, "Oh, these boring water birds—one does not know what to say about them, and their number is overwhelming," forthwith passing the writing baton to an assistant, who finished up as best he could.

Rare was the educated 18th century man who did not know his Buffon nor have something of his own to say about birds. In 1784 in his *Notes on the State of Virginia*, Thomas Jefferson catalogued ninety-three Virginia birds under the Buffon, the Mark Catesby, and the Linnean Taxonomic systems. In that year Ben Franklin wrote to his daughter:

"I wish the bald eagle had not been chosen as the representative of our country; he is a bird of bad moral character; he does not get his living honestly. Too lazy to fish for himself, he watches

William Bartram, who befriended Alexander Wilson, published in 1791 his illustrated **Catalogue** *of 215 species of birds, the most accurate ornithological listing prior to Wilson's.*

the labor of the fishing-hawk [*Pandion haliaetus*, American Osprey]; and, when that diligent bird has at length taken a fish, and is bearing it to his nest, the bald eagle pursues him and takes it from him. For in truth the turkey is a much more respectable bird. Eagles have been found in all countries, but the turkey was peculiar to ours. He is, besides (though a little vain and silly) a bird of courage."

In America and England the movement grew to portray birds as they are, but a French adventurer named Francois Levaillant turned European ornithology upside down. Given money to collect South African rarities by the German ornithologist Jacob Temminck, Levaillant traveled among the Hottentots for three years, picking up a girl friend named Narina. He returned alone with 2000 bird skins and enough notes to write and illustrate the six-volume *Oiseaux d'Afrique*, a book which made him famous. Two subsequent books brought him wealth as well, wealth that he soon squandered. He died poor in a Parisian apartment in 1818. Only later did ornithologists discover that much of what Levaillant wrote were lies. He had gone so far as to glue feathers from three birds onto the skin of a fourth in order to claim a new species. Even though he had been first to record

Alexander Wilson (1766-1813), called the Father of American Ornithology, emigrated from Scotland to America in 1794, carrying only a gun and the clothes on his back.

the Rosy-faced Lovebird (*Agapornis roseicollis*, not a fake) the public scoffed. Was this the naturalist who had praised himself as an accurate observer and truth lover? "I have never let myself be deceived," he wrote. "Never."

Ten years after Levaillant sailed for Africa, Alexander Wilson—often called the father of American ornithology—sailed for America. He had fled in disgrace from Scotland. Although his love poem, *Watty & Meg,* had sold 100,000 copies and had been praised by Robert Burns, he later wrote satires on textile manufacturers (Wilson was a weaver). One manufacturer sued him, forcing Wilson to recant in public and to burn his poetry at the town cross.

Once in America, spurned by three Philadelphia women in succession, Wilson turned introvert until he met the rich Philadelphia naturalist, William Bartram. Wilson started drawing birds. Inflamed by the praise of Bartram and an engraver, Alex Lawson, Wilson determined to secure fame not through poetry or love, but through bird watching. As he wrote the engraver Lawson in 1804:

"I am most earnestly bent on pursuing my plan of making a Collection of all the Birds of this part

Our third president, Thomas Jefferson (1743-1826), as portrayed by Gilbert Stuart. Jefferson acquired his life-long love of natural history at William and Mary College. He once asked that a stuffed moose be sent the Compte de Buffon, to disprove Buffon's theory that Europe produced more robust animal specimens than the United States.

Georges Luis Leclerc (1707-1788) tacked Buffon onto his name at the age of 25 to give it a more euphonious sound. The Compte de Buffon, as he preferred being called, became in his own time the world's most famous naturalist. His son, whom he hoped would succeed him, died a wastrel and drunkard at the age of 30.

Great-crested Flycatcher **(Myiarchus crintus)**, common in the southern states which Audubon tramped looking for birds to paint. No other eastern flycatcher has the long, rusty tail. He cannot harm the gall-fly grub secure in the gall shown.

"This majestic and formidable species stands at the head of the whole class of woodpeckers hitherto discovered. His eye is brilliant and daring; and his whole frame so admirably adapted for his mode of life, and method of procuring subsistence, as to impress on the mind of the examiner the most reverential ideas of the Creator. . .The sound and healthy tree is the least object of his attention. The diseased, infested with insects, and hastening to putre-faction, are his favorites; there the deadly crawling enemy have formed a lodgement between the bark and tender wood, to drink up the vital part of the tree. . ."

Like Audubon after him, Wilson had to solicit subscriptions to his work himself. At $120 for the nine volume set, including 400 life histories and 76 full-page water-colored plates, that seems a bargain today. But the effort cost Wilson his health; he died of dysentery at the age of 48. The

Ivory-billed Woodpecker, as portrayed by John James Audubon. A crow-sized bird, its single-note, high-pitched call was last heard in 1964. It may well now be extinct.

of North America. Now I don't want you to throw 'cold water,' as Shakespeare says, on this notion, Quixotic as it may appear. I have been so long accustomed to the building of Airy Castles and brain Windmills that it has become one of my comforts in life, a sort of rough Bone that amuses me when sated with [life's] dull drudgery."

Off he went into the woods, a pack on his back, a sketch book in his hand. Of the 262 species he portrayed, 39 were new (a record for new American species discovered, before his time or since), including five birds that still bear his name—the Wilson's Petrel, Wilson's Phalarope, Wilson's Plover, Wilson's (Common) Snipe, and the Wilson's Warbler.

In Savannah he shot, in order to color it in detail, the crow-sized, Ivory-billed Woodpecker, *Campephilus principalis*, a bird now believed extinct. The gusto Wilson exhibits in the following excerpt about the bird shows why his nine-volume *American Ornithology* gave him the fame he sought.

international ornithologist, Charles Lucien Bonaparte—mild-mannered nephew to Napoleon—completed the two final volumes of Wilson's *American Ornithology.*

America's patron saint of bird watching, John James Audubon, once met Alexander Wilson in a Kentucky tavern. What Audubon wrote later tells the story:

"One fair morning I was surprised by the sudden entrance of Mr. Alexander Wilson, the celebrated author of the *American Ornithology.* This happened in March, 1810. How well do I remember him! His long, rather hooked nose, the keenness of his eyes, and his prominent cheekbones, stamped his countenance with a peculiar character. His stature was not above the middle size. He had two volumes under his arm, and as he approached the table at which I was working [perhaps painting a spring migrant like the Great Crested Flycatcher from a recently-shot specimen] I thought I discovered something like astonishment in his countenance. He, however, opened his books, explained the nature of his occupations, and requested my [subscription]."

Audubon had no money. He was 25 years old at the time, Wilson was 44. Audubon had four decades to live, Wilson only a few years. Audubon, who had not yet thought of publishing his own paintings, loaned several to Wilson on Wilson's request, later heard the Scot playing sad tunes on his flute alone in his room. Wilson realized he had stumbled across an unknown but already formidable rival. Audubon's watercolors were far more real than his own.

Born a bastard in Haiti, packed off to France to be reared by his seaman father's long-suffering wife, Audubon was packed off again to the United States at the age of twenty in order to escape the French draft. Near Philadelphia, on his father's estate, he shot birds and courted the 15-year old Lucy Bakeman. Three years later they married. As far as we know Lucy stayed faithful to him, and he to her, though he spent most of his time in the woods, alone or with his two sons, shooting, mounting, drawing birds; or in European salons seeking $1,000 subscriptions to his own masterpiece, *The Birds of America.*

Issued in 4 volumes over a period of eleven years, *The Birds of America* contained 435 hand-colored plates with 1,065 individual birds. Unlike Wilson, Audubon painted all his birds life-

John James Audubon (1785-1851) was often in a bad mood. With his sons Victor and John he spent 13 years between America and Europe struggling with the preparation of obtaining finances for his 4-volume **Birds of America.**

size, making the page size of his book a whopping 27" x 40". But while the book made Audubon's fortune, scholars have puzzled over some of the birds portrayed. Did John Audubon have Francois Levaillant's penchant for chicanery? The Townsend Bunting has never been seen outside Audubon's painting. Nor has the Carbonated Warbler, nor the Cuvier's Regulus (akin to the real kinglet, *Regulus calendula),* nor what Audubon calls a Bemaculated—'besmirched'—Duck.

Alongside *The Birds of America,* Audubon published a 5-volume description of bird and human habits, dubbing it *Ornithological Biography.* The occasional vehemence of its sixty "Delineations of American Scenery and Manners" may be judged from a letter he sent Lucy:

"Such a steamer as we have come in from Louisville—the very filthiest of all filthy old rat-traps I ever travelled in. Our *compagnons de voyage*, about one hundred and fifty, were composed of Buckeyes, Wolverines, Suckers, Hoosiers, and gamblers, with drunkards of each and every denomination, their ladies and babies of the same nature and specifically the dirtiest of the dirty. We had to dip the water for washing from the river in tin basins, soap ourselves all from the same cake, and wipe the one hundred and fifty with the same solitary towel."

Even with his attacks on potential bird watchers, Audubon in the 19th century, like the Compte de Buffon in the 18th century and Roger Tory Peterson in our own, turned bird watching

Thomas Nuttall (1786-1859), was a printer before he became a naturalist. Of delicate features, he braved the western frontier in search of botanical and ornithological specimens.

into a craze. He was as eagerly sought by ornithologists elsewhere as by Lucy at home. His mind finally went soft towards the end of his 66 years, wrecked by last-ditch efforts to add a work on mammals to his work on bird. The final volume of his *Quadrupeds of North America* saw light in 1854, three years after his demise.

Spurred by the influence of Thomas Jefferson in the early 1800's, and by Audubon thirty years later, exploring parties to the American West

started taking scientists with them, men formally educated in botany, mammology, and ornithology. Two of the most avid of these professionals were John Townsend and Thomas Nuttall. The ebullient Townsend was primarily a bird man; Nuttall—so shy that at Harvard he had cut a slot through his door through which meals were to be passed—was a botanist. Yet in his *Manual of the Ornithology of the United States and Canada,* published in 1832, Nuttall was the first to accurately describe birds by their voices. Thus of Baltimore Orioles he wrote: "The mellow whistled notes which they are heard to trumpet from the high branches of our gigantic elms resemble, at times, 'tshippe-tshayia too too, and sometimes 'tshippee 'tshippee (lispingly), too too, with the last syllables loud and full."

Townsend and Nuttall became one expedition's Odd Couple after they joined Captain Nathaniel Wyeth on his way west to Vancouver, B.C. As Townsend wrote in connection with the Nebraska prairie,

"Flowers of every hue were growing—more than one of our matter-of-fact people exclaimed, 'beautiful, beautiful'! Mr. Nuttall was here in glory."

*Townsend's Solitaire (**Myadestes townsendi**), one of the birds discovered by John Townsend during the Wyeth Expedition to British Columbia. Unlike other thrushes, this builds his nest on the ground.*

He rode on ahead of the company, and cleared the passage with a trembling hand, looking anxiously back at the approaching party, as though he feared it would come ere he had finished [collecting botanical specimens], and tread his lovely prizes under foot."

Townsend is best known for the Townsend's Warbler and Townsend's Solitaire (a thrush), discovered by him on this trek—two of 70 specimens carried back for Audubon to paint. There might also have been a Townsend's Owl, but Nuttall and Captain Wyeth cooked for breakfast the bird Townsend had shot, during a hunger fit on the banks of Columbia River. The usually talkative Townsend would not speak to either man for two days.

*First edition of Darwin's classic, **On the Origin of Species**, 1859.*

John Townsend died in obscurity; Thomas Nuttall died with his boots on. His heart gave out at the age of 73, when, in his keeness to open a packing case of rhododendrons, he overstrained himself at the family estate in England—Nut Grove Hall.

The year Nuttall died, 1859, Charles Darwin published *On the Origin of Species by Means of Natural Selection, or the Preservation of Favored Races in the Struggle for Life*. London licked its lips—the entire edition of 1,250 copies sold out in one day.

A whole subfamily of finches, the Geospizinai, containing 10-13 species, is named after Charles Darwin. In 1835, during his five-year voyage as naturalist on the H.M.S. "Beagle," he stopped 500 miles west of Equador at the Galapagos

*The retiring disposition of Charles Robert Darwin (1802-82) kept him out of the battles fought over his **On the Origin of Species**. Towards the end of his life he thought as much about God as about natural history, writing in 1880, "My theology has become simply a muddle."*

Archepelago. There, among the stub-winged cormorants and four-eyed fish, he discovered each island occupied by its own species of finch, apparently evolved from a single species blown long ago from the mainland. Some of the birds fed in trees, some on the ground, one fed on cactus, another—now called the Woodpecker Finch— clamped a cactus thorn in its bill to scare insects from their crevices. Darwin credits these Darwin's (or Galapagos) Finches with firing his first thoughts on the possibility of natural selection.

Three years after returning to England, his health ruined, Darwin married a mothering cousin. He spent the brunt of his remaining years thinking about what he'd seen, then writing and vindicating *On the Origin of Species*. He died an agnostic in 1882.

Charles Darwin symbolises a change in man's attitude towards himself and towards the world he finds himself in—that is, that man may not have Divine sanction to do what he wants. He may have no more elevated place than a piece of granite, a bull thistle, a Trumpeter Swan.

*Elliott Coues (1842-1899) was trained as a surgeon. At the age of 30 he published his **Key to North American Birds,** bringing him fame and an Army commission to explore this country's northern boundary.*

At first Darwin used a gun to collect specimens; later he kept them alive close at hand, resulting in his *The Variation of Animals and Plants Under Domestication,* an expansion of his *Origin of Species'* chapter one. Henry David Thoreau took a different tack; in 1845 he gave up his gun to move to Walden Pond, building a shack on three acres lent him by Ralph Waldo Emerson.

The drive behind earlier naturalists had been to collect, systematize, describe, display. What we may call the Darwinian drive was to link the world of nature to ourselves. No one succeeded better in this than Thoreau. Though he died from tuberculosis at the age of 45, he left a million words unpublished in his diaries, linking man with nature. Read what Thoreau writes of the Great Blue Heron: "John Garfield brought me this morning [Sept. 6, 1852] a young great heron. It measured four feet, nine inches, from bill to toe, and belongs to a different race from myself. [But] I am glad to recognize him for a native of America —why not an American citizen?"

"Is not the bird," writes Thoreau's successor, John Burroughs, from his own retreat in New York's woods, "the original type and teacher of the poet? The beautiful vagabonds, masters of all climes—how many human aspirations are realized in their free, holiday-lives?"

And from out west, in 1894, the walker and foremost guide of the Sierra, John Muir, writes, "I suddenly heard the well-known whir of an Ouzel's [Dipper, *Cinclus mexicanus*] wings, and, looking up, saw my little comforter coming straight across the ice from the shore. In a second or two he was with me, flying three times round my head with a happy salute, as if saying, "Cheer up, old friend; you see I'm here, and all's well.""

Thoreau, Burroughs, and Muir were not professionals, yet even so august a scholar as Dr. Elliott Coues can plead in his 1874 *Field Ornithology, A Manual for Procuring, Preparing and Preserving Birds,* "The true ornithologist goes out to study birds alive, and destroys some of them simply because that is the only way of learning their structure and technical characters. The man who only gathers birds, as a miser, money to swell his cabinet, and that other man who gloats, as miser-like, over the same hoard, both work on a plane far beneath that of the enlightened naturalist."

Coue's plea for life, incidentally, did not extend to his own. Renowned as founder of the American Ornithological Union, but let down by Theosophy, what he later called "Mme Blavatsky's Famous Hoax," at the end of his life he sat up suddenly in bed at his Washington D.C. home and cried, "Welcome, oh welcome, beloved death!"

Those who began to feel it wrong to shoot birds, but still wished to study or portray them, were helped in the early 19th century by the French invention of the camera (1822), and in the latter part of the century by the appearance of field glasses, later refined by prisms into binoculars. Yet the slaughter of birds increased. The American journalist LeGrand T. Meyer, writing in 1889, explains why:

"What is the cause of this extermination? Let me enumerate:

"First, the 'Pot-Hunters.' Those human fiends that tramp the happy feeding grounds of game birds. The Pinneated Grouse [Eastern Pinnated Grouse or Heath Hen, now extinct] was once one of the most common game birds east of the

John Burroughs (1837-1921, left) and John Muir (1838-1914, right) the best of friends. Although living on separate coasts, they periodically met for long walks and conversation.

Mississippi River. For a market supported by bloated epicures and sensualists, they [the 'pot,' or game, hunters] have done their work thoroughly.

"Second, for Fashion. Those ladies(?) [sic] that from their illconcealed vanity yearly sign death warrants of millions of birds. Recently an item in an exchange read 'Lady Gemini appeared in the reception room with a dress decorated with patches of 3,000 Brazillian Hummingbirds!' [probably Gould's Heavenly Sylph, *Aglaiocercus coelestis*].

"Third, our Amateur Naturalists. Many of the present embryonic Ornithologists believe that in order to become Audubons or Bairds [Spencer Fullerton Baird, in 1878 made head of Washington D.C.'s Smithsonian Institution, had by the time he was 27 collected 3,500 bird skins], they must slaughter indiscriminately every species met, and every nest must be robbed, under the veil of science."

With no formal education past high school, Frank Michler Chapman (1864-1945) became Curator of Ornithology at New York's prestigious American Museum of Natural History at the age of 44. He was awarded both the Theodore Roosevelt and John Burroughs' medals for helping to save birds.

33

One of those most concerned was Frank M. Chapman. During a stroll through Manhatten in 1886, Chapman counted 700 hats, 542 of which were decorated with bird corpses. This short, hot-tempered but dedicated bird man, recognized 40 dead species on that stroll, including Wilson's Warblers, Pileated Woodpeckers, Saw-whet Owls, Ruffed Grouses, kingfishers, and a Northern Shrike. Incensed, he quit his job as banker the next year, seeking employment at New York's American Museum of Natural History. Eventually he became its Curator of Ornithology, a post he held from 1908 until his retirement in 1942.

Some found Chapman pompous, but he helped pioneer bird protection laws, and in 1899 founded the magazine *Bird-Lore,* whose motto read, "A Bird in the Bush is Worth Two in the Hand." State Audubon societies (they did not unite as a national group until six years later) adopted Chapman's *Bird-Lore* as their official publication.

The Pinnated Grouse or Heath Hen **(Cupidonia cupido)** *was a favorite target of game hunters. It is now extinct.*

The magazine changed its name to *Audubon* in 1941. From a circulation of under 5,000 it has grown to a circulation of over 350,000.

Frank M. Chapman loved live birds but he loved ornithology more. Thanks to his impetus, The American Museum of Natural History now has 800,000 bird skins, matched by no other institution in the world except the British Museum. Chapman's prize was the so-called Rothchild Collection—230,000 bird skins stuffed with cotton—bought from England's Tring Museum in 1932. Ornithologist Erwin Stresemann

describes the Tring curator's desolation when he got the news that his collection had been sold:

"I can never forget how, on a grey February morning, he came staggering in to me with an envelope in his fingertips, and sank into a chair. 'My collection! My collection!' he stammered out, his chest heaving and his clear eyes swimming with tears."*

Twenty months later the Tring curator was dead.

Chapman's close friend Theodore Roosevelt was both avid bird watcher and conservationist. During his presidency from 1901 to 1909 he increased the area of national forests from 43 to 194 million acres, over cries of impeachment by loggers. He also established fifty-three national bird reserves.

In 1909 Roosevelt carried to Africa a request from his friend John Burroughs. The naturalist found hard to believe legends surrounding a short-billed relative of the woodpecker called a Greater Honey-guide *(Indicator indicator).* Would Roosevelt pause long enough in his pursuit of mountable trophies to observe the bird live?

Roosevelt did; the legends were true. The little bird starts chattering to attract a man's attention, then leads that man to a hive of wild bees, scolding if the man won't follow. When the man extracts the hive's contents—up to fifteen pounds of honey—he is expected to leave the Honey-guide its portion. The natives cut off the ears of anyone found killing the bird. But what the bird likes most, said Roosevelt, is not honey but the wax, and the bee grubs left behind.

Through the efforts of men like Chapman and Teddy Roosevelt, birds got protected and publitected. In America the Audubon Societies pushed for the passage of the Lacy Act in 1900, the first comprehensive federal law to save birds; in England, the Royal Society for the Protection of Birds guided similar legislation. The year 1906 saw the first American pocket-sized field guide, Chester Reed's *Bird Guide to Land Birds East of the Rockies* (reissued in 1951). Frank Chapman's friend Louis Fuertes painted 106 plates for the neo classic, 832-page, *Birds of America* (not related to Audubon's book of the same name).

*Ornithology from Aristotle to the Present, page 268. See Bibliography, entry (7).

And then along came Roger Tory Peterson, born of Swedish father and German mother in Jamestown, New York on the 28th of August, 1908. Claiming to be the fifth grader most often spanked in the history of his school, by the age of 17 Peterson was an adept enough artist to have two watercolors—a kingbird and a hummingbird—hung in the American Ornithological Union's national exhibition of 1925.

Until that time he was self-trained, having spent a boyhood obsessed by birds, insects, and flowers, but especially birds. Teachers say the print in his history and math books was overwhelmed by bird sketches of eagles, owls, and hawks.

Working as a decorator of chests of drawers, he spent a while at New York's Art Students League (seeing his first naked woman there, a model), and as nature counselor at Camp Chewonki in Maine. Later in Boston, at the Rivers

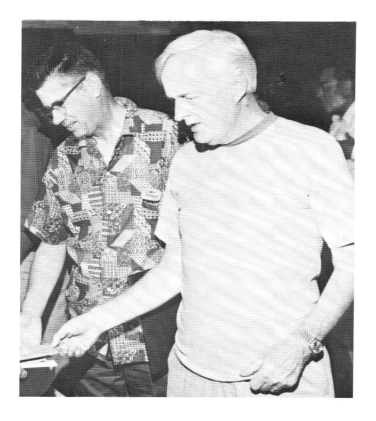

(Clockwise) Theodore Roosevelt (1858-1919), our 26th President and champion of preserving millions of acres for birds and other wildlife. In 1909 the Smithsonian Institution sent him and his son Kermit to Africa to collect specimens.

Greater Honey-guide. Primitive Africans still believe that the gods will make sick whoever injures this bird. It can lead a native as far as five miles to a hive.

*Roger Tory Peterson (1908-), at the 1973 American Birding Association Convention, Kenmare, North Dakota. The man on Peterson's right is Chandler S. Robbins, coauthor of **Birds of North America**.*

Current American Birding Association president Arnold Small has photographed 1,007 species of birds.

School where he taught natural history, he shared a room with a Burrowing Owl.

It was in this room that Peterson worked in secrecy on his pocket-sized *Field Guide to the Birds,* the book whose first edition in 1934 sold out almost as fast as Darwin's *On the Origin of Species*—2,000 copies snapped up in five days.

Revised and expanded, *Field Guide to the Birds* through 1977 had gone through 2,000,000 copies, or 100,000 a year. What makes *Field Guide* so popular is Peterson's friendly, self-assured style, plus the use of field marks—those parts of birds, highlighted by arrows, that distinguish one species from another.

Back in the 1930's other bird watchers were on their way to making names for themselves. An Ohio housewife, Margaret Morse Nice, wrote her pioneer *Studies in the Life History of the Song Sparrow (Passerella melodia).* By using colored bands on their legs, she was first in this country to follow the fate of individual birds from birth to

dealth. Arthur Allen and Peter Paul Kellogg of Cornell decided to record bird sounds for posterity, beginning with birds about to become extinct like the Ivory-billed Woodpecker. Arthur Bent quit as a textile manufacturer to compile his 23-volume life history series. Charles Broley, a banker, retired to start a new life, banding Bald Eagles in the tops of Florida pines.

But Dr. Roger Tory Peterson is the name the world knows. And no wonder. He has authored, illustrated or edited more than 20 field guides. He left his job as the Audubon Society's art director in 1943 to free-lance write and paint, which he has been doing every since. A master still photographer, he has four movies to his credit, ten books other than field guides, eight honorary degrees—the list goes on and on.

Peterson's love affair with both nature and fame has led to a fluctuating home life. He and his first wife parted after six years. His second wife, Barbara, bore him two sons and spent 35 years

Standing tall at the 1976 American Birding Association Convention, Beaumont, Texas, is G. Stuart Keith, official world record holder for number of bird species (5,340) seen. The former president of the American Birding Association may have just seen species number 5,341.

In 330 B.C., Aristotle toted up 155 different birds. Seven hundred years later, those arch rivals, the Frenchman Pierre Belon and the Swiss Conrad Gesner, were able to come up with only 65 more, or 220 different bird forms apiece. In 1758 Linnaeus boosted that to 564. Then the numbers of different bird forms classified, including subspecies (so-called 'races'), began to take off. By 1946 the ornithologist Ernst Mayr had catalogued 28,500 forms of birdlife.

Yet the history of bird watching is not so much about numbers as about man's fascination with, and impact on, the world into which he finds himself thrown. It's a story of killing—for food, laughs, and plumage—a story of love, of curiosity and greed, of the craving to simplify what keeps getting more and more complicated, and finally, of respect for life. For we realize how dreary our own lives would be if there were no longer any birds around.

Bibliography

(1) *Birds and Men* by Robert Henry Welker, Belnap Press, Cambridge, 1955.

(2) *A Dictionary of Birds* "Introduction," by Alfred Newton, Adam and Charles Black, London, 1896.

(3) *Early Annals of Ornithology* by J.H. Gurney, H.F. & G. Witherby, London, 1921.

(4) *Field Ornithology* by Dr. Elliott Coues, Naturalists Agency, Salem, 1874.

(5) *A Gathering of Birds* by Donald Culross Peattie, Dodd, Mead & Company, New York, 1939.

(6) *Men, Birds & Adventure* by Virginia S. Eifert, Dodd, Mead & Company, New York, 1962.

(7) *Ornithology from Aristotle to the Present* by Erwin Stresemann, Harvard University Press, Cambridge, 1975.

(8) *A Treasury of Birdlore* by Joseph Wood Krutch and Paul S. Eriksson, Vermont, 1962.

(9) *The World of Roger Tory Peterson* by John C. Devlin and Grace Naismith, Times Books, New York, 1977.

orienting her life around his. In 1976 Barbara moved out. A few months later Peterson married a former biochemical researcher and mother of two daughters. The Petersons live now in a sprawling house in Old Lyme, Connecticut.

During his 70 years, Roger Tory Peterson has seen many kinds of birds, but does not hold the official, all-time-high record. That distinction belongs to G. Stuart Keith. Research associate at the American Museum of Natural History, Keith has spent more than 30 years spotting 5,340+ out of 8,650+ species. The Californian, Arnold Small, former infantryman and now president of the American Birding Association, has tallied 4,410+ species. He has photographed 1007 of these. As diminutive as his name says but with a tough, self-assured look, Small scours the world for birds when he is not teaching biology at Long Beach's Harbor College. "It's an obsession," he admits. "I picked up the fever as a Boy Scout and haven't been able to shake it since."

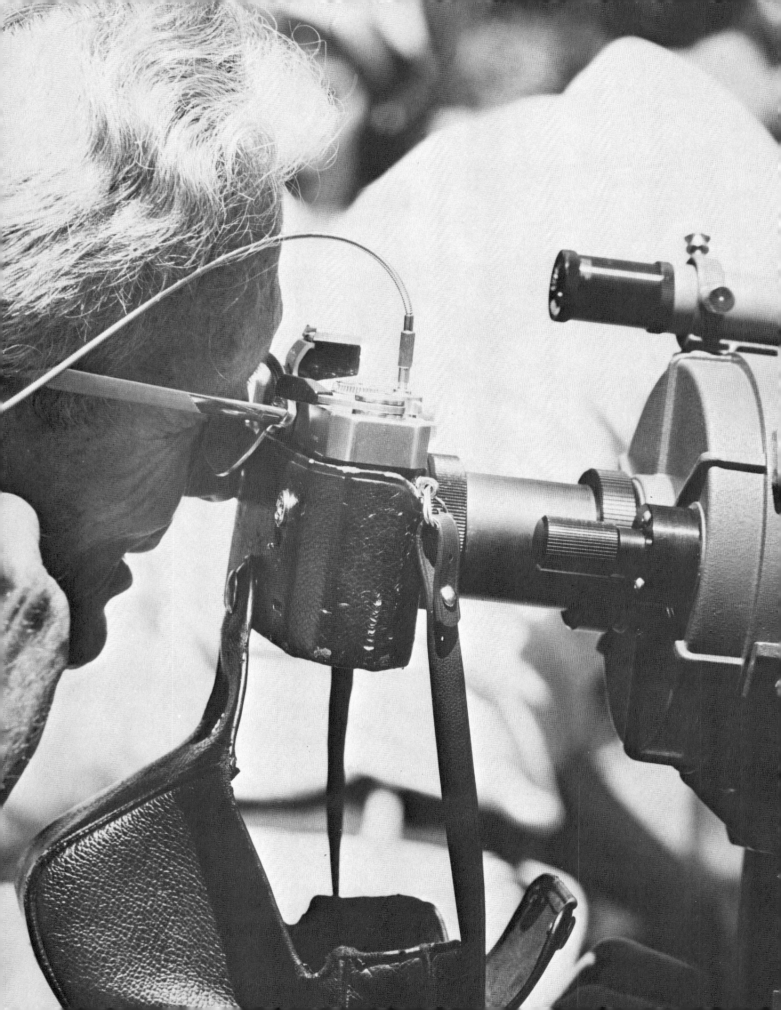

Basic Equipment

In the pages that follow you will find the most complete array of major birding equipment ever assembled—that's our belief. We tried to contact every U.S. manufacturer and distributor of binoculars, spotting scopes, tripods, telephoto lenses, portable tape recorders, and microphones. We did it twice. All who responded are represented here.

Had this book sought, in addition, to incorporate still and movie cameras, it would have been so heavy you could not have picked it up. Nor did we seek out manufacturers of bird feeders and houses, thinking that, with the excellent books in print that show plans, you can save money and have a good time constructing your own.

Remember as you thumb through these pages that whatever equipment you eventually buy should be your friend. Get acquainted on a personal basis first. Don't pay too much attention to what you read, or to what a salesperson tells you, until you have tried that piece of equipment out yourself. See if you can bring it home for the night for probable purchase on the morrow. Or join a group of birdwatchers for a weekend jaunt —a fine way to try out various brands and models that others own.

You will pretty much get what you pay for. But until you're sure you want to spend years recording bird calls, or gazing at the shapes of water birds through a high-resolution scope, think about buying inexpensive equipment first. There is really no such thing as a once-in-a lifetime buy. Technology changes; the uncoated optics of pre-World War II binoculars make them seem down-right tarnished compared with the optics of today.

On the other hand, if you've been in birding awhile, and are sure it's photography, for instance, you want to branch into, spend as much money as you can afford. The more you pay—provided the equipment is manufactured by a name you trust—the more quality you get.

It is always a good investment to obtain a grime-proof case for what you buy; nothing destroys a tape recorder faster than leaving it exposed to dust. Optical equipment requires extra care. Clean the lenses regularly with liquid detergent, water, and toilet paper that's single ply (the double-ply leaves too much lint). Instead of detergent and water, try rubbing alcohol for stubborn smears.

Remember that most birds won't wait around while you get used to your equipment. That's why it's best to get the bugs out before you venture into the field. A word of caution: don't leave anything, including an empty carrying case, on the seat or floor of your parked car, even though you lock that car up tight. Windows are easy to break, especially if what's inside looks like it might just be a telephoto lens or a $400 pair of binoculars.

The data in the listings themselves come directly from the manufacturers. We have not verified their figures, but it is well to keep in mind that they are not likely to underestimate the advantages and performance of their products. For explanations of terminology, the reader is referred to the Buying Guide preceding each section on equipment, or to the Glossary at the back of the book.

Binocular Buying Guide

In addition to a field guide and a sturdy pair of walkers, binoculars are your best friend. No other piece of birding equipment is lightweight enough to carry along no matter how far you go on foot, yet powerful enough to bring distant birds within range for study or identification. Yet trying to find, from the dozens of models available, exactly what you need, can reduce you to tears.

The photo diagram on the opposite page shows better than words the general components of a pair of binoculars. Let's take a look at what options are available, then at how you can best determine binocular quality.

Options

Conventional Versus Straightline—Two general types of binoculars are on the market today: Offset (or conventional) and straightline. In the offset type, the 90° (Porro) prisms bend the light rays four times between their entrance and their exit. In the straightline type, the so-called roof prisms bend the light rays five times. This means that if other factors are equal, the light emerging from the eye-pieces of the offset type will be brighter than the light emerging from straightline binoculars. It also means that offset binoculars are less expensive to make, and will probably cost you less, than straightline binoculars—other factors being equal. On the other hand, straightline binoculars can be built smaller—and thus lighter—than offset. What's most important is up to you.

Central Focus Versus Individual Focus—most birders prefer—and most binoculars are built with—central focus, even though the term central focus can be misleading. *All* binoculars have an individual focus knob for the right eyepiece. That's because, for most of us, our left and right eyes have differing abilities to see the same object clearly. By focusing the right eye-piece first, you adjust for that difference.

The advantage of having central focus (the notched wheel, or lever, on the hinge between the two barrels) is that, once right focus is set, you can adjust for distance fast. It takes only seconds to move from an Anna's Hummingbird hovering 20 feet in front of you to a Great Blue Heron flap-ping to its nest 200 feet away. If your binoculars have individual focus, each time you sight a new bird you must focus the right eyepiece, then the left eyepiece. This takes time; the bird may have gone. But individual focus lends itself better to keeping the internal mechanism clean and water-tight. That's why, if you intend to bird watch much aboard ship, you may want your binoculars to have individual focus.

Tripod Adapter—Many binoculars, even some of the smaller ones, have a built-in tripod adapter, which for some reason you hear little about. Ask the salesperson to show you—often the adapter is a covered hole on the end of the hinge opposite the central focus wheel. Securing your binoculars to a tripod or car window mount allows you to keep them steady.

Magnification—Somewhere on the hinge between the two eyepiece barrels you will see a number, an X and another number—thus 7X35 (or, more correct but less frequent: 7X,35). The the first number and the X refer to the power of the binoculars. A pair rated 7X means a bird looks 7 times larger, or 7 times closer, than he does when you look at him unaided. The common degrees of magnification for binoculars meant for birding are 7X, 8X, 9X and 10X. One manufacturer—Tasco—also makes zoom binoculars. Zoom means that you have a range of magnification, 7X to 15X or 8X to 16X.

Why don't birders automatically go for the higher-power binoculars? There are three reasons. The higher the power the heavier the equipment—that's one (10X binoculars can weigh three pounds). The second reason is that the higher the power, the more the image tends to jump; not only is the image magnified, but also magnified is the tremor in your hands.

The main reason birders do not automatically choose a high powered pair of binoculars is that the greater the magnification, the more restricted the area—called field of view—you can see. Field of view is engraved on your binoculars in terms of feet, or in terms of degrees, using a distance of 1,000 yards as gauge. The term "Field 420," for instance, means that through your binoculars you can encompass an area 420 feet across at 1,000 yards away. The term 8° means the same thing. Multiply 8°—or any field of view expressed as an angle in degrees—by the cabalistic number 52.5, and you get the field of view expressed in feet. Thus, 8 x 52.5 = 420 feet.

One of the hottest debates in birding is whether or not to wear glasses when using binoculars. The problem is that the barrier of glasses moves the eyes away from the eyepiece lenses, in effect narrowing the area you can see, the field of view. If you take off your glasses, you can push your eyes close to the eyepiece lenses, and see as wide a field of view as the binoculars intend you to see. But taking off your glasses takes time— that Spotted-breasted Thrush you thought you spied may have flow. What to do?

Everyone has an opinion, the binocular manufacturers and the author included. Manufacturers have said, in effect, "Leave your glasses on." These firms have added retractable eyecups to the ends of the binoculars you look through. Either these eyecups are made of fold-down rubber, or can be screwed out or in. Their stated purpose is to allow the eyeglass-wearer the same distance from the eyepiece lenses as the person blessed with perfect vision: those with glasses fold the rubber down or screw the eyecup in; those blessed with perfect vision screw out or leave the rubber extended.

But sometimes, eyecups or not, the closer you can push your eyeballs to the eyepiece lenses, the more area you can see. The author's suggestion is this: if you wear glasses and get serious about birding, switch to contact lenses. Or, take your glasses, drill a hole through the end of each ear-piece, attach twine or a jewelers chain, string it in back of your neck and practice pulling your glasses off your nose just before raising your binoculars. Use one hand only for both steps (leave the other hand free to hold or leaf through your field guide). The cord securing your glasses should be short; that securing your binoculars, longer.

Ability to Gather Light—The number engraved into your binoculars following the X signifies the width of the lens furthest from your eye. That lens is called the objective lens (as opposed to the eyepiece lens), and its width is given in millimeters (mm). One millimeter = 1/25"; one inch = 25 millimeters. The common widths for objective lenses in binoculars useful for birding are 35mm, 40mm and 50mm.

Thus, the designation on the binoculars, 7X50, or (more precise) 7X,50 means those binoculars will make a Pink-sided Junco look seven times larger, through an objective lens 50 millimeters (2") wide.

The width of the objective lens (the lens furthest from your eye) is important. It determins how much light your binoculars bring in. The wider the objective lens, the more light your binoculars have to work with. Of course, the bigger the lens, the more your binoculars will weigh, too.

Exit Pupil—Point a pair of binoculars towards

Most Conventional and Straightline binoculars have same general components. These include (1) the eyepiece lens system, (2) central-focus knob, (3) a prism system for folding up the light rays, and (4) an objective lens. The binoculars pictured are of a Conventional design.

a well-lighted surface or clear sky, as though you wished to sight through them. Only this time hold the binoculars a foot away from your eyes. See the little circle of light in the middle of each eyepiece lens? That's called the exit pupil. Its width is the width of the beam of light that comes through each barrel into your eyes. You can determine its width by using a ruler—or, more simply, by dividing magnification into objective lens width. If the numbers on the binoculars you hold read 8X40 (or 8X,40), the width of the exit pupil is 40÷8, or 5 millimeters, 1/5 of an inch.

Your eyes can gather no more light than the exit pupil's width allows. At midday, the pupils of your own eyes measure 2mm to 3mm across. So any binoculars whose exit pupils measure that, or more, will give you as much light as if you were looking out unaided. But near dawn, or dusk, when most of the birds are out, the natural light is less. This causes your own pupils to expand, up to 6mm across. Now if the binoculars' exit pupils are only 5mm (such as with binoculars marked 7X35, 8X40, or 10X50), you won't receive quite as much light as when you put the binoculars down. That gull you think may be a stray Glaucous Gull won't look as bright through the binoculars as through your naked eyes. Even though magnified, his subtle markings will be harder to spot.

To have an exit pupil of over 5mm, however, you will need to buy binoculars marked 7X50 (exit pupil = 7.1mm), or 8X56 (exit pupil = 7mm). Both models are heavy. Binoculars marked 7X42 (exit pupil = 6mm) would seem an ideal compromise, but to the author's knowledge only one manufacturer—E. Leitz—makes them. You can also buy binoculars with exit pupils of less than 5mm. Unless you plan to bird mostly in blazing sunlight, stay away from these. Their designations run from 6X15 (exit pupil = 2.5mm) to 9X35 (exit pupil = 3.9mm).

Close Focus—It's important in birding to be able to focus your binoculars on objects close by as well as far away. This is especially true for the smaller land birds. Thirty-two species of sparrow exist in North America. Except for a few with distinguishing marks of red, yellow or black about the head, these birds look pretty much alike. They will remain within 50 feet of you, but often half obscured by foliage. To identify them, you need to bring them closer. Your binoculars should provide a clear image down to at least 20 feet.

How to Test for Quality

Before buying any pair of binoculars, ask the following questions. If your answers are all Yes, you know you have made a good buy for bird watching.

1. Is the magnification at least 7X?
2. Is the Exit Pupil at least 5mm?
3. Are the binoculars light-weight enough for me to carry and use at least three hours in the field?
4. Is the central hinge not too tight, not too loose? Is the same true of the focusing levers or wheels?
5. Held at a slant, do the objective lenses (those furthest from your eyes) reflect a colored tinge? (This colored coating minimizes internal glare, increasing the amount of light that reaches your eyes.)
6. Are both exit pupils clear, free of blotches, specks, and gray areas at the edges?
7. Can I bring both barrels close enough together so that the image seen through each merges into a single, clear image within a single perfect circle? (This test is important. If you don't get a clear image in a circle, your eyes and head will soon begin to ache.)
8. Are my hands steady enough to keep an image a block away from jiggling?
9. Do the binoculars provide a clear image of an object 20 feet away?
10. When I look through the barrels at a telephone pole less than fifty feet away, keeping the pole in the center of my field of view, do I see only the color of the pole? Do I see only the color of the pole when I move it to the edge of my field of view? (Good binoculars will shoe no chromatism—a rainbow colored fringe—on the pole when it is in the center of your field of view; only a slight color fringe when you move it to the edge.)
11. Does that same telephone pole appear to be as straight up and down as it really is when I move it close to the edge of my field of view? (Be warned: all binoculars will show some distortion. The less the distortion the better their quality.)
12. When I focus on a brick wall or hedge that fills my field of view, is the image sharp in both the center and at the edges?
13. When I focus on a license plate two blocks away, are the numbers clear?

Binoculars

Swift

NIGHTHAWK

Magnification: 8X. Objective Lens: 40mm. Exit Pupil: 5mm. Field of View: 499 feet. Weight: 28 oz. Height: 5.4". Focus: central. Shape: Offset. Special features: All lenses hard amber coated. Objective lens ultra violet coated for protection from sun and glare. Roll away eyecups. Cowhide grain case. Focuses to 18 feet.

E 1001. Swift Instruments, Inc.

AUDUBON

Magnification: 8.5X. Objective Lens: 44mm. Exit Pupil: 5.18mm. Field of View: 445 feet. Weight: 38.4 oz. Height: 5.9". Focus: central. Shape: Offset. Special features: Focuses down to 13 feet. Sunproof, glare-free viewing with hard amber lens coating and ultraviolet ray inhibitor. Black cow hide grain case. Retractable eyecups.

E 1002. Swift Instruments, Inc.

7X35 TRILYTE

Magnification: 7X. Objective Lens: 35mm. Exit Pupil: 5mm. Field of View: 393 feet. Weight: 18.6 oz. Height: 5.8". Focus: central. Shape: Straightline. Special

features: Ultraviolet coated objective lenses. Lightweight magnesium body. Air-to-glass surfaces coated with magenta to boost brilliance. Rubber retractable eyecups. Metal-reinforced bullhide grained case with straps.

E 1003. Swift Instruments, Inc.

SKIPPER

Magnification: 7X. Objective Lens: 50mm. Exit Pupil: 7.14mm. Field of View: 376 feet. Weight: 38 oz. Height: 7". Focus: central. Shape: Offset. Special features: Amber and ultraviolet coatings for protection against sun and glare. Sealed against moisture and dust. Cowhide grain case. Retractable eyecups. Tripod adapter. Close focuses to 24 feet.

E 1004. Swift Instruments, Inc.

AEROLITE

Magnification: 8X. Objective Lens: 40mm.

Exit Pupil: 5mm. Field of View: 525 feet. Weight: 24 oz. Height: 5.1". Focus: central. Shape: Offset. Special features: Four lens modified Erfle optical system. Cowhide-grain case. Retractable rubber eyecups. Close focuses to 21 feet.

E 1005. Swift Instruments, Inc.

COMMODORE

Magnification: 7X. Objective Lens: 50mm. Exit Pupil: 7.14mm. Field of View: 372 feet. Weight: 38.6 oz. Height: 7.0". Focus: central. Shape: Offset. Special features: Slotted prisms, coated lenses and ultraviolet ray inhibitor provide sun and glare proof viewing. Close focuses to 24 feet. Cowhide grain black case. Tripod adapter. Retractable eyecups.

E 1006. Swift Instruments, Inc.

TRITON

Magnification: 7X. Objective Lens: 35mm. Exit Pupil: 5mm Field of View: 376 feet. Weight: 22 oz. Height: 5". Focus: central. Shape: Offset. Special features: Air-to-glass surfaces coated with amber to boost brilliance. Ultraviolet coating blocks harmful sun rays. Lined black cowhide grain case. Center post tripod adapter.

E 1007. Swift Instruments, Inc.

8X40 TRILYTE

Magnification: 8X. Objective Lens: 40mm. Exit Pupil: 5mm. Field of View: 341 feet. Weight: 20.4 oz. Height: 6.7″. Focus: central. Shape: Straightline. Special features: All air-to-glass surfaces have hard magenta coating to enhance light transmission. 5 lens Erfle-type ocular cell. The body is light-weight magnesium. Rubber retractable eyecups. Plush-lined, metal reinforced Bullhide grained carrying case.

E 1008. Swift Instruments, Inc.

NEPTUNE

Magnification: 7X. Objective Lens: 35mm. Exit Pupil: 5mm. Field of View: 240 feet. Weight: 20 oz. Height: 5.5″. Focus: central. Shape: Offset. Special features: Amber coating on all air-to-glass surfaces. Ultraviolet coating on objective lenses for glare proof viewing. Black pig skin case. Retract-

able eyecups for eyeglass viewing. Tripod adapter. Lightweight magnesium body.

E 1009. Swift Instruments, Inc.

Celestron

7X 35

Magnification: 7X. Objective Lens: 35mm. Exit Pupil: 5mm. Field of View: 576 feet. Weight: 2.2. lbs. Height: not given. Focus: central. Shape: Offset. Special features: low light level binoculars.

E 1010. Celestron International.

7X 50

Magnification: 7X. Objective Lens: 50mm. Exit Pupil: 7.1mm. Field of View: 393 feet. Weight: 2.6 lbs. Height: not given. Focus: central. Shape: Offset. Special features: Low light level binoculars.

E 1012. Celestron International.

11 X 80

Magnification: 11X. Objective Lens: 80mm. Exit Pupil: 7.2mm. Field of View: 235 feet. Weight: 5.10 lbs. Height: not given. Focus: central. Shape: Offset. Special features: Low light level binoculars.

E 1011. Celestron International.

Nikon

7 X 50 STANDARD/TROPICAL

Magnification: 7X. Objective Lens: 50mm. Exit Pupil: 5mm. Field of View: 385 feet. Weight: 50 oz. Height: 7.2″. Focus: individual. Shape: Offset. Special features: Sealed against humidity. Hard leather case.

E 1015. Nikon, Inc.

10 X 70 WIDE FIELD

Magnification: 10X. Objective Lens: 70mm. Exit Pupil: 7mm. Field of View: 342 feet. Weight: 88.2 oz. Height: 10.2″. Focus: individual. Shape: Offset. Special features: Roofprism optics. Leather case.

E 1013. Nikon, Inc.

Zeiss

8X56

Magnification: 8X. Objective Lens: 56mm. Exit Pupil: 7mm. Field of View: 330 feet. Weight: 36.30 oz. Height: 8¾". Focus: central. Shape: Straightline. Special features: Rubber armored. Corrosion proof. Leather case. Rubber eyecups.

E 1017. Carl Zeiss, Inc.

7X50

Magnification: 7X. Objective Lens: 50mm. Exit Pupil: 7.14mm. Field of View: 390 feet. Weight: 41.30 oz. Height: 5". Focus: individual. Shape: Offset. Special features: Corrosion proof. Rubber armored. Self-sealing lens guards. Rubber eyecups.

E 1018. Carl Zeiss, Inc.

Bushnell

7X50 FEATHERLIGHT

Magnification: 7X. Objective Lens: 50mm. Exit Pupil: 7.1mm. Field of View: 375 feet. Weight: 39 oz. Height: 7⅜". Focus: central. Shape: Offset. Special features: Insta-Focus—keeps action in focus—at any speed. Rubber eyecups.

E 1019. Bushnell Optical Co.

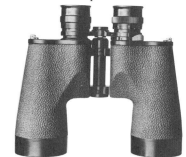

CUSTOM

Magnification: 7X. Objective Lens: 35mm. Exit Pupil: 5mm. Field of View: 578 feet. Weight: 36 oz. Height: 5". Focus: central. Shape: Offset. Special features: All air to glass optical surfaces amber coated to prevent internal light loss. Built in Tripod Socket. Nylon eyecups. Case.

E 1020. Bushnell Optical Co.

7X35 FEATHERLIGHT

Magnification: 7X. Objective Lens: 35mm. Exit Pupil: 5mm. Field of View: 420 feet. Weight: 21½ oz. Height: 5⅝". Focus: central. Shape: Offset. Special features: Insta-Focus device keeps action in focus at any speed. Rubber eyecups.

E 1021. Bushnell Optical Co.

7X35 EXPLORER

Magnification: 7X. Objective Lens: 35mm. Exit Pupil: 5mm. Field of View: 578 feet. Weight: 27 oz. Height: 4⅞". Focus: central. Shape: Offset. Special features: Insta-Focus —keeps action in focus—at any speed. Air-to-glass surfaces coated with magnesium floride. Ultraviolet filters on objective lenses. Rubber roll-down eyecups. Case included.

E 1022. Bushnell Optical Co.

Photo not available.

7X50 EXPLORER

Magnification: 7X. Objective Lens: 50mm. Exit Pupil: 7.1mm. Field of View: 420 feet. Weight: 38 oz. Height: 6⅛". Focus: central. Shape: Offset. Special features: Insta-Focus —keeps action in focus—at any speed. Air-to-glass surfaces coated with magnesium floride. Ultraviolet filters on objective lenses. Rubber roll-down eyecups. Case included.

E 1023. Bushnell Optical Co.

10X50 EXPLORER

Magnification: 10X. Objective Lens: 50mm. Exit Pupil: 5mm. Field of View: 368 feet. Weight: 38 oz. Height: 6⅛". Focus: central. Shape: Offset. Special features: Insta-Focus —keeps action in focus—at any speed. Air-to-glass surfaces coated with magnesium floride. Ultraviolet filters on objective lenses. Rubber roll-down eyecups. Case included.

E 1024. Bushnell Optical

Tasco

7X50 RZ

Magnification: 7X. Objective Lens: 50mm. Exit Pupil: 7.1mm. Field of View: 520 feet. Weight: 44 oz. Height: 6". Focus: central. Shape: Offset. Special features: Fully coated a chromatic lenses for glare protection. Rubber armored body. BK-7. Porro Prisms. Case included.

E 1025. Tasco Sales, Inc.

INTERNATIONAL

Magnification: 7X. Objective Lens: 35mm. Exit Pupil: 5mm. Field of View: 578 feet. Weight: 27 oz. Height: 4½". Focus: central. Shape: Offset. Special features: Gold and magenta combination coating on lenses for bright glare free viewing. Tripod adapter. Shock resistant rubberized objective rims. Rubber eyecups. Case included.

E 1026. Tasco Sales, Inc.

VIENNA

Magnification: 7X. Objective Lens: 50mm. Exit Pupil: 7.1mm. Field of View: 400 feet. Weight: 38 oz. Height: 7". Focus: central. Shape: Offset. Special features: Gold and magenta coated lenses for bright glare free viewing. Kellner type eyelens. Porro prisms. Fold down rubber eyecups. Case included.

E 1027. Tasco Sales, Inc.

10X50 ZIP

Magnification: 10X. Objective Lens: 50mm. Exit Pupil: 5mm. Field of View: 367 feet. Weight: 32.5 oz. Height: 7". Focus: central. Shape: Offset. Special features: Fast focus adjustment. Fully coated optics and prisms for glare free viewing. Camera tripod adapter.

E 1028. Tasco Sales, Inc.

BOLD VENTURE

Magnification: 7X. Objective Lens: 35mm. Exit Pupil: 5mm. Field of View: 551 feet. Weight: 26 oz. Height: 4½". Focus: central. Shape: Offset. Special features: Coated porro prisms for glare protection. Camera tripod adapter. Rubber bumperized objective rims. Fold down rubber eyecups. Case included.

E 1029. Tasco Sales, Inc.

ADVENTURER

Magnification: 7X. Objective Lens: 50mm. Exit Pupil: 7.1mm. Field of View: 372 feet. Weight: 32.5 oz. Height: 7". Focus: central. Shape: Offset. Special features: Coated optics and prisms for glare free viewing. Camera tripod adapter. Fold down rubber eyecups. Case included.

E 1030. Tasco Sales, Inc.

MARINE

Magnification: 7X. Objective Lens: 50mm. Exit Pupil: 7.1mm. Field of View: 385 feet. Weight: 55 oz. Height: 7¼". Focus: central. Shape: Offset. Special features: Nitrogen filled fog and water proof body. Non reflective rubber armored. Water resistant vinyl case. Fully coated chromatic lenses.

E 1031. Tasco Sales, Inc.

RUBBER ARMORED

Magnification: 8X. Objective Lens: 40mm. Exit Pupil: 5mm. Field of View: 341 feet. Weight 27 oz. Height: 5¾". Focus: central. Shape: Offset. Special features: Rubber armored body. Coated chromatic Kellner lenses and ultraviolet coated objective lenses for glare protection. Rubberized. Case included.

E 1032. Tasco Sales, Inc.

SUPER SPOTTER

Magnification: 12X. Objective Lens: 80mm. Exit Pupil: 6.6mm. Field of View: 236 feet. Weight: 91 oz. Height: 12". Focus: central. Shape: Offset. Special features: Fully coated lenses for glare protection. Camera tripod adapter. Case included.

E 1034. Tasco Sales, Inc.

8X40 ZIP

Magnification: 8X. Objective Lens: 40mm. Exit Pupil: 5mm. Field of View: 341 feet. Weight: 21 oz. Height: 4½". Focus: central. Shape: Offset. Special features: Coated lenses for glare protection. Fold down rubber eyecups.

E 1033. Tasco Sales, Inc.

SAFARI V

Magnification: 7X. Objective Lens: 35mm. Exit Pupil: 5mm. Field of View: 431 feet. Weight: 18 oz. Height: not given. Focus: central. Shape: Straightline. Special features: Includes case. Roll-down rubber eyecups.

E 1035. Tasco Sales, Inc.

MARINER

Magnification: 10X. Objective Lens: 50mm. Exit Pupil: 7.1mm. Field of View: 367 feet. Weight: 32.5 oz. Height: 7". Focus: central. Shape: Offset. Special features: Coated optics and prisms for glare free viewing. Camera tripod adapter. Fold down rubber eyecups. Case included.

E 1036. Tasco Sales, Inc.

7X35 ZOOM

Magnification: 7X to 15X. Objective Lens: 35mm. Exit Pupil: 5 @ 7X. Field of View: 330 feet @ 7X. Weight: 32.5 oz. Height: 6½". Focus: central. Shape: Offset. Special features: Fully coated optics and Porro prisms. Camera tripod adapter. Case included.

E 1037. Tasco Sales, Inc.

EXECUTIVE ELECTRIC ZOOM

Magnification: 7X to 15X. Objective Lens: 35mm. Exit Pupil: 5mm @ 7X. Field of View: 330 feet @ 7X. Weight: 38 oz. Height: 5½". Focus: central. Shape: Offset. Special features: Battery powered zoom control. Batteries included. Fully coated optics and Porro prisms. Rubber eyecups, objective rims. Camera tripod adapter. Case.

E 1038. Tasco Sales, Inc.

8X40 ZOOM (109)

Magnification: 8X to 16X. Objective lens: 40mm. Exit Pupil: 5mm @ 8X. Field of View: 280 feet @ 8X. Weight: 31¼ oz. Height: 8¾". Focus: central. Shape: Offset. Special features: Fully coated optics. Achromatic objective lenses. Fold down rubber eyecups. Case included.

E 1040. Tasco Sales, Inc.

8X50 ZOOM (106)

Magnification: 8X to 16X. Objective Lens: 40mm. Exit Pupil: 5mm @ 8X. Field of View: 280 feet @ 8X. Weight: 28 oz. Height: 6½". Focus: central. Shape: Offset. Special features: Tripod adapter. Rubber fold down eyecups. Case included.

E 1039. Tasco Sales, Inc.

8X50 ZOOM

Magnification: 8X to 15X. Objective Lens: 50mm. Exit Pupil: 6.2mm @ 8X. Field of View: 314 feet @ 8X. Weight: 30 oz. Height: 6". Focus: central. Shape: Offset. Special features: Fully coated optics and Porro prisms. Finger tip Zoom lever. Rubber bumperized objective lenses, fold down eyecups. Case included.

E 1041. Tasco Sales, Inc.

Bausch & Lomb

7X35 STRAIGHTLINE

Magnification: 7X. Objective Lens: 35mm. Exit Pupil: 5mm. Field of View: 446 feet. Weight: 18.6 oz. Height: 5". Focus: central. Shape: Straightline. Special features: Focus adjustment internal for weather resistance. Lined black vinyl case.

E 1042. Bushnell Optical Co.

7X35 OFFSET

Magnification: 7X. Objective Lens: 35mm. Exit Pupil: 5mm. Field of View: 382 feet. Weight: 22 oz. Height: 5⅜". Focus: central. Shape: Offset. Special features: Has about the same field of view as 7X, 50 binoculars. Case included.

E 1043. Bushnell Optical Co.

7X50

Magnification: 7X. Objective Lens: 50mm. Exit Pupil: 7.1mm. Field of View: 381 feet. Weight: 46 oz. Height: 7⅛". Focus: central. Shape: Offset. Special features: Highest useable brightness of any Bausch & Lamb binocular. Case included.

E 1044. Bushnell Optical Co.

Leitz

8X40 TRINOVID

Magnification: 8X. Objective Lens: 40mm. Exit Pupil: 5mm. Field of View: 384 feet. Weight: 21 oz. Height: 5.4". Focus: central. Shape: Straightline. Special features: Water resistant. Retractable rubber eyecups.

E 1045. E. Leitz, Inc.

7X42 TRINOVID

Magnification: 7X. Objective Lens: 42mm. Exit Pupil: 6mm. Field of View: 420 feet. Weight: 23 oz. Height: 6.5". Focus: central. Shape: Straightline. Special features: Large exit pupil for dawn and twilight viewing. Water resistant. Retractable rubber eyecups.

E 1046. E. Leitz, Inc.

Scope Buying Guide

Sometimes a pair of binoculars does not do the job. If it's shorebirds you're after—the sandpipers, plovers, avocets, and phalaropes—a scope allows you to scan that half mile of mudflat you can't get to. Or you may want to study the haunts of eagles and hawks, or search the winter seas for the Common Murre. A subsport some birders take up is searching a flock of well-known migrants for the unusual stray. Keeping track of the action in a rookery or nest diverts other birders for hours.

A spotting scope allows you to enjoy the above activities. Binoculars bring birds up to 15 times closer; a spotting scope brings them from 15 to 60 times closer (makes them 15 to 60 times larger than they seem with the naked eye).

You can, of course, buy telescopes with greater magnifications than 60X. But the higher the magnification, the less sharp the image looks (its 'resolution' suffers). Even scopes with 60X produce a fuzzy image, especially if you are trying to sight a bird on a line parallel to the ground; that's because of atmospheric interference. Too, the greater the magnification, the more restircted your field of view.

The main problem with scopes is that most of them are long and all are heavy. This makes them hard to hold steady unless you give them artificial support. Such support comes in a variety of forms. All scopes have a tripod adapter (see Tripods Buying Guide for further discussion). Like the tripod, a monopod—a one-legged device that doubles as a walking stick or prodder—will support the scope on the ground. Lighter than tripods, monopods are useful in brush or where a crowd of watchers has gathered shoulder-to-shoulder. Most scope manufacturers also make a mount for cars that goes up and down with the window. Or, for no money, you can roll the window all the way down, and support your scope on a bean bag or pillow.

Serious 'scopers' often abandon fixed mounts for the shoulder mount. This is a rifle stock modified to hold a scope instead of a gun barrel. For searching the skies instead of the shore, marsh, or prairie, shoulder mounts are handy.

You can give your scope added support by using the fork of a tree.

Most spotting scopes today are made to double as telephoto lenses in order to save camera buffs money. For still shots, you need a single lens reflex (SLR)-type camera and a so-called T-adapter (T for telephoto); for movies you need a so-called C-adapter. There is a disadvantage to using scopes as camera lenses, however. You have no choice of f/stops. See the Telephoto Lenses Buying Guide for details.

It's true that a spotting scope can turn you into a birdlife peeping tom. And that's fun. But besides weight to be lugged around (one to four pounds, exclusive of support and protective case), other disadvantages exist when compared to binoculars. Because you have only one tube to look through, you get little sense of depth. You also get a narrower field of view (40 feet to 160 feet across, at 1,000 yards' distance, rather than 250 feet to 450 feet across with binoculars). Narrow field of view means you have to work harder to find, and to hold, your bird if he's moving. Spreading out and collapsing a tripod is both time-consuming and wearisome, unless you plan to leave your scope alone for days behind a blind (camouflage set up to keep the birds from spotting you). Finally, the higher the magnification the scope has, the less light it often takes in. Those Semipalmated Sandpipers you wanted to spy on at dusk may blend into the sand until they've vanished.

With all its drawbacks, however, chances are you'll want a spotting scope if you get serious about bird watching. You have two general types to choose from, both invented over 300 years ago. These types are described below.

Refractive Scope

The Refractive Scope most resembles binoculars. A long tube, it employs lenses, and sometimes prisms, to gather light, to magnify, and to pop the clear image in front of your eye. This is the scope that can most easily be mounted on a rifle stock. It's the one pictured on this book's

With refractive scopes you have two further

options. You can buy a fixed power refractive. This means that to change the magnification you have to unscrew one eyepiece, and screw another back on. Or you can buy a zoom refractive scope. The zoom has a magnification range which you alter by twisting a ring. It takes you but a second to go from 15X or 20X to 60X—especially useful for pinpointing field marks that will help you distinguish, say, the Long-billed Dowitcher from the Short-billed Dowitcher before it takes off. Zoom scopes generally are less expensive than fixed power scopes. What's the disadvantage? Often the image gets distorted in zooms at the edges of the field of view.

Both kinds of refractive scopes—the fixed power and the zoom—cost less, and have lower magnification options than the type of scope to be described next.

The Reflective Scope

The Reflective Scope (called a catadioptric lens, a mirror lens, or a mirror reflex lens —an MRL—when described by photographic buffs), uses the same principle employed in high-power astronomy telescopes. Incoming light rays are folded twice, by two mirrors, before reaching your eye. This is shown in the diagram. The result and advantage is that reflective scopes need be only one-half as long as refractive scopes (8″ versus 15″). Reflective scopes sometimes have a low power (usually 5X) finder scope mounted on top of them. Certain manufacturers claim (although they do not recommend) that by pushing your elbow against your rib cage, you can hold reflective scopes steady without artificial support because of their short length. Depending on the eyepiece you use, reflective scopes' magnification ranges from 20X to 300X. No zoom models exist.

Although reflective scopes make marvelous instruments for viewing the heavens as well as birds, they cost two to four times as much as refractive scopes.

How to Buy

When contemplating purchase of a spotting scope you have only two real factors to consider. These factors apply to binoculars and telephoto lenses as well. For all the driving over rough roads, and hiking, you are going to do as your fascination with birds grows, you must have rugged equipment. Ruggedness is hard to test beforehand—you'll need to rely on what other birders tell you and on the reputation of the manu-

facturer. The other factor, the factor that mostly determines what price you pay—as explained at the end of the Binoculars Buying Guide—is the quality of the optics. This quality can be tested. When comparing scopes, ask yourself the following questions:

1. Focused two blocks away, at equal magnification, which scope gives me the sharpest image?

2. How far away do I need to look before I get a sharp image? (the nearer to you the better).

3. When I look at a telephone pole less than fifty feet away, keeping the pole in the center of my field of view, do I see only the color of the pole? Do I see only the color of the pole when I move it to the edge of my field of view? (Good scopes will show no chromatism—a rainbow colored fringe—on the pole when it is in the center of your field of view; only a slight color fringe when you move it to the edge.)

4. Does that same telephone pole appear to be as straight up and down as it really is when I move it close to the edge of my field of view? (Be warned: all scopes will show some distortion. The less the distortion the better their quality.)

5. When I focus on a brick wall or hedge that fills my field of view, is the image sharp in both the center and at the edges?

Unlike binocular and telephoto lens specifications, those for spotting scopes are a mishmash. Perhaps this is because manufacturers think of their scopes as hybirds, not quite binoculars, not quite lenses, and mix the technical jargon of each. What we hope will result from the brand rundown that follows—to our knowledge the most complete ever done—is an agreement among manufacturers on what data customers need, and what language to employ. For example, if you are buying a spotting scope to use both as a scope and as a telephoto lens, you need to know its magnification, exit pupil, and field of view (discussed in Binoculars Buying Guide), and its focal length and f/stop, (discussed in Telephoto Lens Buying Guide). You want to know its physical length and weight. You also want to know how, even why, magnification and focal length are related (roughly $IX = 50mm$).

Scopes

Questar

3½-INCH

Magnification: 28X, 50X, 80X. Objective lens: 89mm. Exit Pupil: 3.1mm @ 28X, 1.8mm @ 50X, 1.2mm @ 80X. Focal length: 1400mm. f/stop: f/16. Type: reflective. Length: 10". Weight: 48 oz. Special features: Focuses down to 10 feet. Includes 4X and 8X mounted finder scope. Fits camera tripods. Adapts to single lens reflex cameras. Optional eyepieces raise magnification as high as 250X.

E 1047. Questar Corp.

Celestron

C90

Magnification: 20X, 55X, 140X, 200X. Objective lens: 90mm. Exit Pupil: 4.5mm @ 20X, 1.6mm @ 55X, 0.6mm @ 140X, 0.45mm @ 200X. Focal length: 1000mm. f/stop: f/11. Type: reflective. Length: 8". Weight: 48 oz. Special features: Focuses down to 15 feet. Includes 5X mounted finder scope and swivel base. Fits camera tripods. Adapts to single lens reflect cameras.

E 1048. Celestron International.

C5

Magnification: 50X, 100X. Objective lens: 125mm. Exit Pupil: 2.5mm @ 50X, 1.25mm @ 100X. Focal length: 1,250mm. f/stop: f/10. Type: reflective. Length: 11". Weight: 4½ lbs. Special features: Focuses down to 15 feet. Includes 5X mounted finder scope and swivel base. Fits camera tripods. Adapts to single lens reflex cameras. Eyepieces up to 300X available.

E 1049. Celestron International.

Bausch & Lomb

DISCOVERER BALSCOPE ZOOM

Magnification: 15X to 60X. Objective lens: 60mm. Exit pupil: 4mm @ 15X to 1mm @ 60X. Field of View: 156 feet @ 15X to 40 feet @ 60X. Focal length: 750 @ 15X to 3000mm @ 60X. f/stop: f/16. Type: refractive. Length: 17.5". Weight: 48.5 oz. Special features: Fits camera tripods. Adapts to single lens reflex cameras.

E 1050. Bushnell Optical Co.

Bushnell

SENTRY

Magnification: 20X. Objective lens: 50mm. Exit Pupil: 2.5mm. Field of View: 120 feet. Type: refractive. Length: 12½". Weight: 25 oz. Special features: 32X, 48X eyepieces available. Sealed against moisture and dust. Fits camera tripods or Bushnell model.

E 1051. Bushnell Optical Co.

SPACEMASTER ZOOM

Magnification: 20X to 45X. Objective lens: 60mm. Exit Pupil: 3mm @ 20X to 1.3mm @ 45X. Field of View: 120 feet @ 20X to 72 feet @ 45X. Type: refractive. Length: 11½". Weight: 36 oz. Special features: optional accessories include cushioned case, car window mount.

E 1052. Bushnell Optical Co.

SPACEMASTER II

Magnification: 15X. Objective lens: 60mm. Exit Pupil: 4mm. Field of View: 158 feet. Focal length: 750mm. f/stop: f/11. Type: refractive. Length: 11½". Weight: 36 oz. Special features: optional eyepieces include 20X, 25X, 40X, 60X; optional T-mount turns scope into telephoto lens.

E 1053. Bushnell Optical Co.

Unitron

80mm QC

Magnification: 20X, 30X, 40X, 60X. Objective lens: 80mm. Exit Pupil: 4mm @ 20X, 2.6mm @ 30X, 2mm @ 40X, 1.3mm @

60X. Field of View: 91 feet @ 20X, 48 feet @ 30X, 35 feet @ 40X, 26 feet @ 60X. Type: refractive. Length: 20". Weight: 3 lbs. Special features: closest focusing distance @ 20X is 35 feet. Table top or field model tripods, wooden carrying case available as accessories.

E 1054. Unitron Instruments, Inc.

Swift

TELEMASTER, JR. ZOOM

Magnification: 25X to 50X. Objective lens: 50mm. Exit Pupil: 2mm @ 25X to 1mm @ 50X. Field of View: 95 feet @ 25X to 50 feet @ 50X. Focal length: 1700mm @ 25X to 3400mm @ 50X. f/stop: f/28. Type: refractive. Length: 15". Weight: 2 lbs. Special features: Fits camera tripods, or Swift tripod. Adapts to single lens reflex cameras.

E 1055. Swift Instruments, Inc.

TELEMASTER MARK II ZOOM

Magnification: 15X to 60X. Objective lens: 60mm. Exit Pupil: 4mm @ 15X to 1mm @ 60X. Field of View: 160 feet @ 15X to 40 feet @ 60X. Focal length: 1000mm @ 15X to 4000mm @ 60X. f/stop: f/16. Type: refractive. Special features: Fits camera tripods, or Swift model. Adapts to single lens reflex cameras. Optics cell is waterproof.

E 1056. Swift Instruments, Inc.

Tasco

ZOOM 15

Magnification: 15X to 45X. Objective lens: 40mm. Exit Pupil: 2.7mm @ 15X to 0.9mm @ 45X. Type: refractive. Length: 16½". Weight: 15½ oz. Special features: 8" tabletop tripod included, but will adapt to camera tripod.

E 1057. Tasco Sales, Inc.

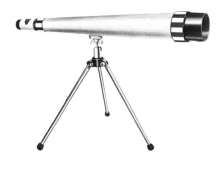

SPOTTING 60.

Magnification: 15X, 30X, 40X, 60X. Objective lens: 60mm. Exit Pupil: 4mm @ 15X, 2mm @ 30X, 1.7mm @ 40x, 1mm @ 60X. Type: refractive. Length: 16½". Weight: 64 oz. Special features: Revolving turret for eyepieces. Adapts to camera tripods.

E 1058. Tasco Sales, Inc.

ZOOM 20

Magnification: 20X to 60X. Objective lens: 60mm. Exit Pupil: 3mm @ 20X to 1mm @ 60X. Type: refractive. Length: 16". Weight: 64 oz. Special features: Comes with metal tabletop tripod. Adapts to camera tripods.

E 1059. Tasco Sales, Inc.

ANGLE VIEW

Magnification: 25X. Objective lens: 60mm. Exit Pupil: 2.3mm. Type: refractive: Length: 16½". Special features: Sideview eyepiece. Comes with metal tabletop tripod. Adapts to camera tripods.

E 1060. Tasco Sales, Inc.

Lens Buying Guide

Why is photography among birders growing at such a clip? Two reasons stand out. With a photograph the beauty and habits of the bird, and the grace of its flight, can be yours and your friends' to marvel at again and again. Too, there is a special thrill not only in spotting something rare, but in bringing proof back home. Few will believe you've seen a White-faced Ibis, for instance, unless it shows itself on film. Best of all, no matter what your trophy, you bag it without ending its life.

Bird photographers group in two camps: the sitters and the stalkers. A sitter named Frank M. Chapman, introduced bird photography to America. Using a self-designed reflex camera and a blind, he produced the 1900 classic, *Bird Studies with a Camera*. Ninety percent of his photos, however, like those of his disciples, show birds incubating or feeding their young. That's because the equipment was heavy and the film speeds slow. It took 30 years before stalkers like Arthur Allen (also a pioneer in recording bird sounds) could preserve on film birds foraging, mating, and chasing through the skies.

Some Photographic Generalities

Were we to give photography, even the photography of birds, its due, this section would soar to thousands of pages. Five monthly magazines alone are published on the subject. The accessories seem limitless: equipment cases; extension tubes; filters; electronic flash; motor drives; a raft of types of film; not to mention the still cameras (automatics, range-finders, single and twin-lens reflexes); the movie cameras; the soft-focus, macro, fish-eye, wide-angle, zoom, and telephoto lenses. So we've decided to limit discussion and product rundown to lenses, specifically to those most used in bird photography—telephoto lenses, of which there are five varieties.

First, some generalities for those to whom photography is a foreign language. Telephoto lenses today are manufactured mainly for use on so-called single-lens-reflex (SLR) 35mm still cameras. Of all still cameras available, the SLR is the easiest to use. You focus and compose your shot through a fully-open lens, thus maximizing

chances that what you see is what you get. On most models you are free to interchange lenses.

With a single lens reflex (SLR) camera you have three controls with which to obtain a crisp picture: the shutter speed ring (on the camera body itself), the focusing ring (on the lens), and the f/stop ring (on the lens also—refractive lenses only). We'll treat each in turn, saving the f/stop for last because it's the most confusing.

First, think of the shutter as an eyelid. The longer it stays open, the longer time the light has to come in. In the case of a camera, the longer the shutter stays open, the more exposure the film gets. But also, the more blurred the image is if the bird moves. So, it's important to have that shutter able to open and close fast: on some SLR cameras; shutter speed goes up to 1/2000 of a second. You control shutter speed by twisting a dial.

The focusing ring's importance is obvious. Focusing on a Belted Kingfisher at rest is simple, focusing on him diving takes more skill. Two lens manufacturers, Novoflex and Leitz, have developed a sliding device that speeds the focusing process.

Now for the f/stop ring. All refractive lenses have iris diaphragms that open and shut like the iris of your eye. The diaphragm controls the strength of the light that enters. When it's wide open lots of light can enter; when it's a pinprick, only a little light can enter. The width of the diaphragm opening is measured in an optical ratio called an f/stop. When the f/stop number is low (say f/4), lots of light can enter. When the f/stop number is high (say f/16), the diaphragm is closed to a pinprick and only a little light can enter. On refractive lenses the f/stop opening is controlled by twisting a ring. On reflective (mirror) lenses, the f/stop opening cannot be changed: it's fixed.

The lower the f/stop possibility on your lens and the faster the shutter speed on your camera, the more money you'll have to pay, but the better picture you'll get. Why? Birds move, even if they're just sitting on a wire wondering what to do next. A fast shutter speed freezes that movement, preventing blur. But the faster the shutter clicks, the less light that comes in. That's why most of the time your lens should be wide open (set at the lowest f/stop number possible, like f/4).

We're not out of the wood yet. You want a lens with the lowest f/stop number possible (the lower the number, sadly, the 'faster' your lens and the more you have to pay), but you don't always want your lens set at that low number—don't always want your lens wide open. Here's why: it's an optical law that pictures taken through the center of the lens have greater "depth of field" than pictures taken through a lens more fully open. That's because lenses are more optically perfect towards the center than towards the edges. Greater depth of field means that a greater area in front of the bird and in back of him stays in focus—crucial if the bird is flapping towards you or away. Example: suppose you buy a lens with a open-wide rating of f/4, but close it to f/5.6 in order to freeze a Black-backed Three-toed Woodpecker (Picoides tridactylus) as he swoops towards you. Assuming the same magnification and shutter speed, you have a better chance of keeping him in focus with your f/4 lens closed to f/5.6 than if you use a 'slower', less expensive lens wide open at f/5.6.

Now that you're thoroughly muddled, let's move on to the telephoto lenses themselves.

Types of Telephoto Lenses

The term 'telephoto lens' means a lens system designed to produce an image on film larger than the object appears as seen by the unaided eye. In bird photography the assumption is that a telephoto lens has at least a 4X magnification. Lens "focal length" (the distance from the optical fulcrum of the lens system, where the image gets inverted, to the film itself) is the term used in photography to describe magnification. Since 50mm = 1X, a lens with a magnification of at least 4X is a lens with a focal length of at least 200mm. It's called a 200mm lens.

As explained in the Spotting Scopes Buying Guide, many scopes can be used as single-lens-reflex camera lenses by attaching a so-called T-adaptor. With ingenuity, in fact, you can take any scope or pair of binoculars, wire or band them to your camera, wrap the joint to seal out the light, and come up with a working telephoto lens. It's been done. How well it's been done is another

question. You can't say such a device has ruggedness. Nor is its versatility high. Even scopes manufactured to fit SLR cameras have a disadvantage: they have no iris diaphragm built into them no range of f/stop numbers. Capturing a bird flying towards you or away without f/stop flexibility is tough.

All photographic lenses, including telephoto lenses, are described by their focal length and the f/stop number where the lens is wide open. A 300mm f/5.6 lens is one whose focal length is 300mm (6X magnification) and whose focal ratio (f/stop number) when wide open is f/5.6. The greater the focal length, by the way, the higher the wide-open f/stop number usually is (the less light the lens can let in). It's also true that the greater the focal length, the less depth-of-field the lens can have.

While on the subject of depth-of-field we should say that sometimes you'd just as soon keep background and foreground out of focus. This helps isolate the bird himself amidst environmental distractions. The ideal is a choice; multiple f/stops give you that choice. To get background and foreground in focus, because you want them pictured or because the bird is flying away or towards you, move to a higher f/stop number. To blur background and foreground, in order to concentrate on the bird (the non-flying bird), move to a lower f/stop number. The choice gives you flexibility.

Of the five types of telephoto lenses, three operate like refractive telescopes—convex and concave lens elements are grouped inside a tube. The first is called a single-focal-length lens. Each has one fixed focal length (magnification) but several f/stop numbers (indicating the width of the aperture in the lens through which light passes). One advantage of single-focal-length lenses is f/stop flexibility. The good ones also offer the best possible photo quality: sharpness, truest color, lowest f/stop number for whatever focal length (magnification) you buy. Above 600mm (12X), they have two drawbacks, their length (and thus weight), and the fact that often they cannot focus as close to you as a comparable reflective, or mirror-type, lens. Also, unlike the 'zoom' lens we're about to describe, a single-focal-length lens must be removed from the camera, and replaced by another, If you wish to change magnification. If that 4" Bahama Honeycreeper turns out to be not 25 yards from you, but 35 yards, you may want to change from a 400mm

lens to a 600mm lens in order to fill your film frame with him. By that time, he could well have had his fill of honeysuckle, and crept into a thicket.

The second type of refractive lens is the zoom. As with binoculars, and scopes, zoom camera lenses have multiple focal lengths. Different than binoculars and scopes, zoom lenses have several f/stop numbers, too. Thus, like the single-focal-length lenses discussed above, zooms have f/stop flexibility. The added focal-length flexibility makes them ideal for filming birds that are doing a lot of hopping around, like sea birds landing at and

taking off from their rookery. Zooms are excellent, too, for sitting rather than stalking. The disadvantages are length and weight, and the fact that their wide-open f/stop number is often higher (photography buffs say 'slower') than a comparable single-focal-length lens. Nor can their photo sharpness match that of the single-focal-length lens, especially at their shortest and longest lengths.

Teleconverters (sometimes called extenders) are the third, and last, type of refractive lens. They can double or triple a lens' focal length (its magnification) without adding much to length or weight. You will pay less for a 2X teleconverter to turn your 200mm lens, say, into a 400mm lens than you will for a 400mm lens.

Like everything, teleconverters have short-comings. The biggest complaint concerns the quality of their optics—distortion and fuzziness are common. Always test teleconverters on your primary lens before purchase. A 2X teleconverter also cuts your lens' maximum aperture in half. A 300mm f/4 primary lens becomes a 600mm f/5.6 lens. But this is little different than were you to buy the 600mm lens itself.

Those are the three types of refractive lenses: Single-focal-length, zoom, and teleconverter. A mirror lens (also called a reflex lens, a mirror reflex lens, or a catadioptric lens) is reflective—light rays get folded twice, against two mirrors, before they're focused. A mirror lens, like its sister, the mirror scope, resembles a coffee can in appearance. It's two to three times shorter, and usually lighter in weight, than its single-focal-length and zoom cousins. One mirror lens model focuses as close as eight feet.

You can use a rifle stock to support a mirror lens, although some photographers manage to support it by hand. But because mirror lenses have a fixed f/stop, you have no control over depth of field. The out-of-focus background becomes fuzzy concentric circles—these can sometimes be distracting. Mirror lenses, too, have a fixed focal length. On the other hand, you can buy additional eyepieces to increase magnification without increasing physical length or weight.

The last, and newest type of telephoto lens is the solid-mirror lens. It combines mirrors and lens elements into a nearly solid glass construction. Because of the compactness of components, rough roads can't easily jar them out of alignment. A 600mm solid-mirror lens is only 3.3 inches long, even less than a mirror lens. Tested in outer space, this lens is too new to know its faults as applied to bird watching. Like the mirror lens, it has a fixed f/stop.

How to Spend Your Money
We've said it before—here it is again: what you mainly pay for is optical quality. Color accuracy, freedom from distortion, and image sharpness can all be tested by asking the same five questions posed at the end of the Spotting Scope Buying Guide. You already know that among lenses of equal focal lengths (equal magnification) the one with the lowest f/stop number will cost the most. At equal shutter speed, that's the one that gives you the most light. A zoom lens will cost less than several single-focal length lenses in the zoom range. But zooms can't give you the others' optical excellence.

A Last Stab at Definitions
Understanding its vocabulary is three-fourths of understanding what an activity is all about. Lenses are rated by their focal length (magnification) in millimeters (mm). Remember that 50mm = 1X. Remember, too, that for single-focal-length and zoom lenses, 50mm often equals 2" long. Lenses are also rated by the f/stop number at which the lens is wide open.

In the product rundown that follows, you'll come up against these additional terms:

Angle of View—If you multiply this by the magic constant, 52.5, you'll get field of view—the number of feet across you can see through your lens at 1,000 yards. Field of view is the term used when discussing binoculars and scopes.

Filter Size—We haven't touched on filters, but the more sophisticated you get the more important they become. You'll want to know if the filters you own fit the lens you plan to buy.

Macro (or Close Focus)—Some telephoto zoom lenses have the so-called macro (close focus) capability of focusing on an object inches from your nose. Most birds won't let you get that close; some, like the Blue-footed Booby will (thus his name). The macro capability is great for phenomena like flowers and drops of rain. If may be, however, that adding macro causes optical quality to suffer.

Minimum Aperture—This gives the highest f/stop number your lens will go. The range between the maximum or wide-open aperture (the lowest f/stop number) and the minimum or pinprick aperture (highest f/stop number) tells you how flexible in f/stops your lens is.

Minimum Focusing Distance—By knowing this you know how close you can get to your bird while keeping him in focus. For macro (or close-focus) zoom lenses, you get the macro focusing distance as well as the normal zoom distance. Happy browsing.

Telephoto Lenses

Questar

FIELD MODEL MIRROR

Magnification: 28X. Minimum focusing distance: 10 feet. Angle of view: 1½°. Diameter: 110mm. Length: 10 inches. Weight: 48 oz. Special features: carrying case. Combination 50X/80X eyepiece. T-mount adapts to 95% of SLR cameras. Optional: eyepieces raising magnification as high as 250X, accessories to convert to spotting scope.

E 1061. Questar Corp.

700mm f/8 MIRROR

Magnification: 14X. Minimum focusing distance: 10 feet. Angle of view: 3½°. Filter size: 35mm. Diameter: 110mm. Length: 8 inches. Weight: 64 oz. Special features: T-mount adapts to 95% of SLR cameras. Optional: leather carrying case, accessories to convert to spotting scope.

E 1062. Questar Corp.

Celestron

1250mm f/10 MIRROR

Magnification: 25X. Minimum focusing distance: 20 feet. Diameter: 137mm.

Length: 11 inches. Weight: 64 oz. Special features: T-mount camera adaptor. Photo tripod adaptor. Foam-lined carrying case. Will fit the following cameras: Nikon, Canon, Pentax, Olympus, Minolta, Miranda, Exacta, Konica, Alpa, and Petri. Optional eyepieces to increas magnification: 50X, 69X, 104X, 139X, 208X, 250X, 312X. Optional accessories convert to spotting scope.

E 1063. Celestron International.

750mm f/6 MIRROR

Magnification: 15X. Minimum focusing distance: 15 feet. Diameter: 137mm. Length: 10 inches. Weight: 64 oz. Special features: T-mount camera adaptor. Photo tripod adaptor. Foam-lined carrying case. Will fit the following cameras: Nikon, Canon, Pentax, Olympus, Minolta, Miranda, Exacta, Konica, Alpa, and Petri. Optional eyepieces to increase magnification: 30X, 42X, 62X, 83X, 125X, 150X, 187X. Optional accessories convert lens to spotting scope.

E 1064. Celestron International.

Rokkor-X

500mm f/8 SOLID MIRROR

Magnification: 10X. Secondary aperture: f/16. Minimum focusing distance: 13 feet. Angle of view: 5°. Diameter: 83mm. Length: 4 inches. Weight: 25 oz.

E 1065. Minolta Corp.

2X TELECONVERTER

Especially designed for the Rokkor-X 400mm f/5.6 single focal length lens, converting it into a 800mm f/11 lens.

E 1066. Minolta Corp.

300mm f/4.5 SINGLE FOCAL LENGTH

Magnification: 6X. Minimum aperture: f/22. Minimum focusing distance: 15 feet. Angle of view: 8°. Filter size: 72mm. Diameter: 80mm. Length: 8 inches. Weight: 41 oz.

E 1068. Minolta Corp.

75-200mm f/4.5 ZOOM

Magnification: 1.5X—4X. Minimum aperture: f/32. Minimum focusing distance: 6 feet. Angle of view: 30°—12°. Filter size:

55mm. Diameter: 74mm. Length: 6 inches. Weight: 24 oz.

E 1069. Minolta Corp.

Fujinon

54-270mm f/4.5 ZOOM

Magnification: 1X—5.4X. Minimum aperture: f/22. Minimum focusing distance: 8 feet. Angle of view: 44°—8°. Filter size: 82mm. Diameter: 90mm. Length: 9 inches. Weight: 47 oz. Special features: Carrying case. Built-in lens hood.

E 1073. Fuji Photo Film U.S.A., Inc.

600mm f/5.6 SINGLE FOCAL LENGTH

Magnification: 12X. Minimum aperture: f/45. Minimum focusing distance: 41 feet. Angle of view: 4°. Filter size: 49mm. Diameter: 121mm. Length: 17½ inches. Weight: 107 oz. (6½ pounds). Special features: Carrying case. Built-in lens hood.

E 1074. Fuji Photo Film U.S.A., Inc.

400mm f/4.5 SINGLE FOCAL LENGTH

Magnification: 8X. Minimum aperture: f/54. Minimum focusing distance: 26 feet. Angle of view: 6°. Filter size: 49mm. Diameter: 101mm. Length: 11½ inches. Weight: 68 oz. Special features: Carrying case. Built-in lens hood.

E 1075. Fuji Photo Film U.S.A., Inc.

200mm f/4.5 SINGLE FOCAL LENGTH

Magnification: 4X. Minimum aperture: f/22. Minimum focusing distance: 8 feet. Angle of view: 12.5°. Filter size: 49mm. Diameter: 63mm. Length: 5 inches. Weight: 17 oz. Special features: Carrying case. Built-in lens hood.

E 1076. Fuji Photo Film U.S.A., Inc.

Novoflex

500mm f/6.3 SINGLE FOCAL LENGTH

Magnification: 10Z. Minimum aperture: f/32. Minimum focusing distance: 44 feet. Angle of view: 8°. Filter size: 49mm. Length: 17 inches. Weight: 96 oz. (6 pounds). Special features: lens hood. Optional follow-focus pistol grip (as shown) allows rapid focusing.

E 1078. Burleigh Brooks Optics, Inc.

400mm f/5.6 SINGLE FOCAL LENGTH

Magnification: 8X. Minimum aperture: f/32. Minimum focusing distance: 6 feet. Angle of view: 6°. Filter size: 75mm. Diameter: 90mm. Length: 6½ inches. Weight: 29 oz. Special features: lens hood. Optional follow-focus pistol grip (as shown) allows rapid focusing.

E 1079. Burleigh Brooks Optics, Inc.

Yashica

70-210mm f/4 ZOOM

Magnification: 1.4X—4.2X. Minimum aperture: f/22. Minimum focusing distance: 9 feet. Angle of view: 34°—12°. Filter size: 58mm. Diameter: 65mm. Length: 6½ inches. Weight: 24 oz. Special features: retractable lens hood.

E 1083. Yashica, Inc.

200mm f/4 SINGLE FOCAL LENGTH

Magnification: 4X. Minimum aperture: f/22. Minimum focusing distance: 8 feet. Angle of view: 12½°. Filter size: 58mm. Diameter: 64mm. Length: 4½ inches. Weight: 19 oz. Special features: retractable lens hood.

E 1084. Yashica, Inc.

Rolleinar

200mm f/3.5 SINGLE FOCAL LENGTH

Magnification: 4X. Minimum aperture: f/22. Minimum focusing distance: 7½ feet. Angle of view: 12°. Filter size: 58mm. Diameter: 71mm. Length: 6 inches. Weight: 20½ oz. Special feature: retractable lens hood.

E 1087. Rollei of America, Inc.

Tamron

200-500mm f/6.9 ZOOM

Magnification: 4X—10X. Minimum aperture: f/22. Minimum focusing distance: 10 feet. Angle of view: 12°—5°. Filter size: 82mm. Diameter: 89mm. Length: 14½ inches. Weight: 97 oz. (6 pounds). Special features: Built-in lens hood. Rotating tripod socket.

E 1088. Berkey Marketing Companies.

80-250mm f/3.8-4.5 MACRO ZOOM

Magnification: 1.6X—5X. Minimum aperture: f/22. Minimum focusing distance: 8 feet zoom. Angle of view: 30°—10°. Filter size: 62mm. Diameter: 71mm. Length: 7 inches. Weight: 33 oz. Special features: Retractable lens hood. Carrying case.

E 1089. Berkey Marketing Companies.

85-210mm f/4.5 MACRO ZOOM

Magnification: 1.6X—4.2X. Minimum aperture: f/22. Minimum focusing distance: 6½ feet zoom, 8 inches macro. Angle of view: 28°—12°. Filter size: 55mm. Diameter: 65mm. Length: 5½ inches. Weight: 22 oz. Special features: Retractable lens hood. Carrying case.

E 1090. Berkey Marketing Companies.

300mm f/5.6 SINGLE FOCAL LENGTH

Magnification: 6X. Minimum aperture: f/22. Minimum focusing distance: 8 feet. Angle of view: 8°. Filter size: 58mm. Diameter: 67mm. Length: 6 inches. Weight: 20½ oz. Special features: Retractable lens hood. Carrying case. Intra-red index.

E 1091. Berkey Marketing Companies.

200mm f/3.5 SINGLE FOCAL LENGTH

Magnification: 4X. Minimum aperture: f/22. Minimum focusing distance: 8 feet. Angle of view: 12°. Filter size: 62mm. Diameter: 69mm. Length: 4½ inches. Weight: 18 oz. Special features: Retractable lens hood. Carrying case.

E 1092. Berkey Marketing Companies.

70-350mm f/4.5 ZOOM

Magnification: 1.4X—7X. Minimum aperture: f/22. Minimum focusing distance: 8 feet. Angle of view: 34°—7°. Filter size: 82mm. Diameter: 91mm. Length: 11 inches. Weight: 65 oz. Special features: rotating tripod socket. Built-in lens hood. Carrying case.

E 1093. Berkey Marketing Companies.

Hanimex

80-200mm f/3.5 MACRO ZOOM

Magnification: 1.6X—4X. Minimum aperture: f/22. Minimum focusing distance: 6½ feet zoom. Angle of view: 30°—12°. Diameter: 70mm. Length: 7 inches. Weight: 36 oz. Special features: Carrying case. Will fit the following SLR cameras: Pentax, Minolta, Nikon, Canon, Konica, Olympus.

E 1094. Hanimex, Inc.

Nikkor

600mm f/5.6 SINGLE FOCAL LENGTH

Magnification: 12X. Minimum aperture: f/22. Minimum focusing distance: 20 feet. Angle of view: 4°. Filter size: 39mm.

Diameter: 134mm. Length: 15 inches. Weight: 95 oz. (6 pounds). Special features: rotating tripod socket. Telescopic lens hood. Pre-set focusing ring.

E 1100. Nikon, Inc.

400mm f/5.6 SINGLE FOCAL LENGTH

Magnification: 8X. Minimum aperture: f/32. Minimum focusing distance: 16 feet. Angle of view: 6°. Filter size: 72mm. Diameter: 83mm. Length: 10½ inches. Weight: 50 oz. Special features: rotating tripod socket. Telescopic lens hood.

E 1101. Nikon, Inc.

400mm f/3.5 SINGLE FOCAL LENGTH

Magnification: 8X. Minimum aperture: f/22. Minimum focusing distance: 15 feet. Angle of view: 6°. Filter size: 39mm. Diameter: 134mm. Length: 12 inches. Weight: 99 oz. (6 pounds). Special features: rotating tripod socket. Telescopic lens hood. Pre-set focusing ring.

E 1102. Nikon, Inc.

300mm f/2.8 SINGLE FOCAL LENGTH

Magnification: 6X. Minimum aperture: f/22. Minimum focusing distance: 13 feet. Angle of view: 12°. Filter size: 39mm. Diameter: 138mm. Length: 10 inches. Weight: 88 oz. Special features: built in lens hood. Rotating collar with tripod socket. Click-stopped ring facilitates fast refocusing.

E 1103. Nikon, Inc.

300mm f/4.5 SINGLE FOCAL LENGTH

Magnification: 6X. Minimum aperture: f/22. Minimum focusing distance: 13 feet. Angle of view: 8°. Filter size: 72mm. Diameter: 78mm. Length: 8 inches. Special features: built-in lens hood. Rotating collar with tripod socket.

E 1104. Nikon, Inc.

200mm f/4 SINGLE FOCAL LENGTH

Magnification: 4X. Minimum aperture: f/32. Minimum focusing distance: 7 feet. Angle of view: 12°. Filter size: 52mm. Diameter: 68mm. Length: 5 inches. Weight: 19 oz. Special feature: telescopic lens hood.

E 1105. Nikon, Inc.

800mm f/8 SINGLE FOCAL LENGTH

Magnification: 16X. Minimum aperture: f/22. Minimum focusing distance: 70 feet. Angle of view: 3°. Filter size: 122mm. Diameter: 135mm. Length: 28 inches. Weight: 81 oz. Special feature: requires separate focusing unit.

E 1106. Nikon, Inc.

600mm f/5.6 SINGLE FOCAL LENGTH

Magnification: 12X. Minimum aperture: f/22. Minimum focusing distance: 40 feet. Angle of view: 4°. Filter size: 122mm. Diameter: 135mm. Length: 11½ inches. Weight: 85 oz. Special feature: requires separate focusing unit.

E 1107. Nikon, Inc.

400mm f/4.5 SINGLE FOCAL LENGTH

Magnification: 8X. Minimum aperture: f/22. Minimum focusing distance: 18 feet. Angle of view: 6°. Filter size: 122mm. Diameter: 135mm. Length: 11 inches. Weight: 67 oz. Special feature: requires separate focusing unit.

E 1108. Nikon, Inc.

1200mm f/11 SINGLE FOCAL LENGTH

Magnification: 24X. Minimum aperture: f/64. Minimum focusing distance: 150 feet. Angle of view: 2°. Filter size: 122mm. Diameter: 133mm. Length: 35½ inches. Weight: 215 oz. (13½ pounds).

E 1109. Nikon, Inc.

2X TELECONVERTER TC-300

For single-focal-length lenses 300mm and more. Doubles magnification of the lens in use. Aperture range: f/5.6—f/64. Depth of field: ½ that of lens in use. Minimum focusing distance: same as that of lens in use. Diameter: 64mm. Length: 4½ inches. Weight: 10 oz.

E 1110. Nikon, Inc.

2X TELECONVERTER TC-200

For single-focal-length lenses up to 200mm focal length. Doubles magnification of the lens in use. Aperture range: f/4—f/64. Depth of field: ½ that of lens in use. Minimum focusing distance: same as that of lens in use. Diameter: 64mm. Length: 2 inches. Weight: 8 oz.

E 1111. Nikon, Inc.

2000mm f/11 MIRROR

Magnification: 40X. Minimum focusing distance: 60 feet. Angle of view: 1°. Filter size: built-in. Diameter: 262mm. Length: 23½ inches. Weight: 618 oz. (38½ pounds). Special features. four built-in filters on a rotating turret. Carrying handle incorporates a peepsight. Optional mounting platform.

E 1112. Nikon, Inc.

1000mm f/11 MIRROR

Magnification: 20X. Minimum focusing distance: 25 feet. Angle of view: 2½°. Filter size: 39mm. Diameter: 119mm. Length: 9½ inches. Weight: 67 oz.

E 1113. Nikon, Inc.

500mm f/8 MIRROR

Magnification: 10X. Minimum focusing distance: 13 feet. Angle of view: 5°. Filter size: 39mm. Diameter: 93mm. Length: 5½ inches. Weight: 35 oz. Special feature: may be hand held at high shutter speeds.

E 1114. Nikon, Inc.

360-1200 f/11 ZOOM

Magnification: 7.2X—24X. Minimum aperture: f/32. Minimum focusing distance: 20 feet. Angle of view: 7°—2°. Filter size: 122mm. Diameter: 125mm. Length: 27

inches. Weight: 250 oz. (15½ pounds). Special features: automatic diaphragm (f/stop) mechanism. Single focusing/zooming ring. Rotating tripod socket.

E 1115. Nikon, Inc.

200-600mm f/9.5 ZOOM

Magnification: 4X—12X. Minimum aperture: f/32. Minimum focusing distance: 13 feet. Angle of view: 12°—4°. Diameter: 89mm. Length: 15 inches. Weight: 84 oz. Special features: automatic diaphragm (f/stop) mechanism. Single focusing/zooming ring. Rotating tripod socket. Optional close-focus attachment reduces minimum focusing distance to 7½ feet.

E 1116. Nikon, Inc.

180-600mm f/8 ZOOM

Magnification: 3.6X—12X. Minimum aperture: f/32. Minimum focusing distance: 8½ feet. Angle of view: 14°—4°. Filter size: 95mm. Diameter: 105mm. Length: 16 inches. Weight: 120 oz. (7½ pounds). Special features: automatic diaphragm (f/stop) mechanism. Single focusing/zooming rings. Rotating tripod socket.

E 1117. Nikon, Inc.

Photo not available.

80-200mm f/4.5 ZOOM

Magnification: 1.6X—4X. Minimum aperture: f/32. Minimum focusing distance: 6 feet. Angle of view: 30°—12°. Filter size: 52mm. Diameter: 73mm. Length: 6½ inches. Weight: 26½ oz.

E 1118. Nikon, Inc.

50-300mm f/4.5 ZOOM

Magnification: 1X—6X. Minimum aperture: f/22. Minimum focusing distance: 8½ feet.

Angle of view: 56°—8°. Filter size: 95mm. Diameter: 98mm. Length: 11½ inches. Weight: 81 oz. Special features: built-in rotatable tripod socket. Separate zooming and focusing rings.

E 1119. Nikon, Inc.

Zuiko

1000mm f/11 SINGLE FOCAL LENGTH

Magnification: 20X. Minimum aperture: f/45. Minimum focusing distance: 98 feet. Angle of view: 2.5°. Filter size: 100mm. Diameter: 110mm. Length: 26½ inches. Weight: 141 oz. (9 pounds). Special features: retractable lens hood. Tripod mount ring can be removed.

E 1120. Olympus Camera Corp.

600mm f/6.5 SINGLE FOCAL LENGTH

Magnification: 12X. Minimum aperture: f/32. Minimum focusing distance: 36 feet. Angle of view: 4°. Filter size: 100mm. Diameter: 110mm. Length: 15 inches. Weight: 99 oz. (6 pounds). Special features: retractable lens hood. Tripod mount ring can be removed.

E 1121. Olympus Camera Corp.

400mm f/6.3 SINGLE FOCAL LENGTH

Magnification: 8X. Minimum aperture: f/32. Minimum focusing distance: 16½ feet. Angle of view: 6°. Filter size: 72mm. Diameter: 80mm. Length: 10 inches. Weight: 46 oz. Special features: retractable lens hood. Tripod mount ring can be removed.

E 1122. Olympus Camera Corp.

300mm f/4.5 SINGLE FOCAL LENGTH

Magnification: 6X. Minimum aperture: f/32. Minimum focusing distance: 11½ feet. Angle of view: 8°. Filter size: 72mm. Diameter:

80mm. Length: 7 inches. Weight: 38½ oz. Special features: retractable lens hood. Tripod mount ring can be removed.

E 1123. Olympus Camera Corp.

200mm f/4 SINGLE FOCAL LENGTH

Magnification: 4X. Minimum aperture: f/32. Minimum focusing distance: 8 feet. Angle of view: 12°. Filter size: 55mm. Diameter: 67mm. Length: 5 inches. Weight: 17½ oz. Special feature: retractable lens hood.

E 1124. Olympus Camera Corp.

Canon

800mm f/8 SINGLE FOCAL LENGTH

Magnification: 16X. Minimum aperture: f/32. Minimum focusing distance. 60 feet. Angle of view: 3.1°. Filter size: 48mm. Length: 20 inches. Weight: 189 oz. (11 lbs. 13 oz.).

E 1126. Canon U.S.A., Inc.

600mm f/5.6 SINGLE FOCAL LENGTH

Magnification: 12X. Minimum aperture: f/32. Minimum focusing distance: 18 feet. Angle of view: 4.1°. Filter sites: 48mm. Length: 17½ inches. Weight: 176 oz. (11 pounds).

E 1127. Canon U.S.A., Inc.

400mm f/4.5 SINGLE FOCAL LENGTH

Magnification: 8X. Minimum aperture: f/22. Minimum focusing distance: 13 feet. Angle of view: 6°. Filter site: 34mm. Length: 11 inches. Weight: 46 oz. Special features:

internal cam focusing keeps lens-length constant no matter what the focusing distance.

E 1128. Canon U.S.A., Inc.

300mm f/2.8 SINGLE FOCAL LENGTH

Magnification: 6X. Minimum aperture: f/22. Minimum focusing distance: 12 feet. Angle of view: 8°. Filter size: 34mm. Length: 9 inches. Weight: 67 oz. Special features: fluorite coated. Optional 2X Extender designed for this lens turns it into an 600mm (12X) f/5.6 lens.

E 1129. Canon U.S.A., Inc.

85-300mm f/4.5 ZOOM

Magnification: 1.7X—6X. Minimum aperture: f/22. Minimum focusing distance: 8 feet. Angle of view: 29°z-8°. Length: 9½ inches. Weight: 55½ oz.

E 1130. Canon U.S.A., Inc.

200 f/2.8 SINGLE FOCAL LENGTH

Magnification: 4X. Minimum aperture: f/22. Minimum focusing distance: 6 feet. Angle of view: 12°. Filter size: 72mm. Length: 5½ inches. Weight: 24 oz.

E 1131. Canon U.S.A., Inc.

Soligor

3X TELECONVERTER

Triples the focal length (magnification) of whatever single-focal-length lens you attach

it to. Available in Miranda, Pentax, Nikon, Canon, Minolta, Konica, Olympus mounts. Automatic diaphragm (f/stop) control. Multicoating to reduce glare available.

E 1136. AIC Photo, Inc.

2X TELECONVERTER

Doubles the focal length (magnification) of whatever single-focal-length lens you attach it to. Available in Miranda, Pentax, Nikon, Canon, Minolta, Konica, Olympus mounts. Automatic diaphragm (f/stop) control. Multicoating to reduce glare available.

E 1137. AIC Photo, Inc.

200mm f/2.8 SINGLE FOCAL LENGTH

Magnification: 4X. Minimum aperture: f/22. Minimum focusing distance: 7 feet. Angle of view: 12°. Filter size: 77mm. Diameter: 78mm. Length: 5 inches. Weight: 18 oz.

E 1138. AIC Photo, Inc.

400mm f/6.3 SINGLE FOCAL LENGTH

Magnification: 8X. Minimum aperture: f/22. Minimum focusing distance: 21 feet. Angle of view: 6°. Filter size: 72mm. Length: 11½ inches. Weight: 39 oz. Special features: will fit the following SLR cameras: Pentax, Mamiya-Sekor, Praktica, Canon, Miranda,

Nikon, Konica, Ricoh, Fujica, Minolta, Olympus.

E 1139. AIC Photo, Inc.

300mm f/5.5 SINGLE FOCAL LENGTH

Magnification: 6X. Minimum aperture: f/22. Minimum focusing distance: 19 feet. Angle of view: 8°. Filter size: 62mm. Length: 6½ inches. Weight: 28 oz. Special features: will fit the following SLR cameras: Pentax, Mamiya-Sekor, Praktica, Canon, Miranda, Nikon, Konica, Ricoh, Fujica, Minolta, Olympus.

E 1140. AIC Photo, Inc.

90-230mm f/4.5 ZOOM

Magnification: 1.8X—4.6X. Minimum aperture: f/22. Minimum focusing distance: 8 feet. Angle of view: 27°—12°. Filter size: 58mm. Length: 8 inches. Weight: 32 oz.

E 1141. AIC Photo, Inc.

75-260mm f/4.5 ZOOM

Magnification: 1.5X—5.2X. Minimum aperture: f/22. Minimum focusing distance: 5 feet. Angle of view: 33°—9°. Filter size: 67mm. Length: 7½ inches. Weight: 40 oz.

E 1142. AIC Photo, Inc.

200mm f/3.5 SINGLE FOCAL LENGTH

Magnification: 4X. Minimum aperture: f/22. Minimum focusing distance: 8 feet. Angle of view: 12°. Filter size: 58mm. Diameter: 65mm. Length: 4½ inches. Weight: 18 oz. Special features: will fit the following SLR cameras: Pentax, Nikon, Minolta, Canon, Konica, Olympus, Fujica.

E 1143. AIC Photo, Inc.

70-220mm f/3.5 MACRO ZOOM

Magnification: 1.4X—4.25X. Minimum aperture: f/22. Minimum focusing distance: 4.9 fet zoom, 10 inches macro. Angle of view: 34°—11°. Filter size: 72mm. Diameter: 82mm. Length: 7 inches. Weight: 46 oz. Special features: comes with leather case and built-in hood.

E 1144. AIC Photo, Inc.

70-210mm f/3.5 MACRO ZOOM

Magnification: 1.4X—4.2X. Minimum aperture: f/22. Minimum focusing distance: 4.9 feet zoom, 15 inches macro. Angle of view: 34°—11°. Filter size: 67mm. Diameter: 74mm. Length: 6½ inches. Weight: 36 oz. Special features: comes with leather case and built-in hood.

E 1145. AIC Photo, Inc.

100-300mm f/5 MACRO ZOOM

Magnification: 2X—6X. Minimum aperture: f/22. Minimum focusing distance: 6.6 feet zoom, 16½ inches macro. Angle of view: 24°—8°. Filter size: 62mm. Diameter: 68mm. Length: 6½ inches. Weight: 31½ oz. Special features: will fit the following SLR cameras: Pentax, Nikon, Minolta, Canon, Konica, Olympus. Comes with leather case and built-in hood.

E 1146. AIC Photo, Inc.

90-230mm f/4.5 MACRO ZOOM

Magnification: 1.8X—4.6X. Minimum aperture: f/22. Minimum focusing distance: 6.6 feet zoom, 8 inches macro. Angle of view: 27°—12°. Filter size: 62mm. Diameter: 68mm. Length: 7½ inches. Weight: 31 oz. Special features: will fit the following SLR cameras: Pentax, Nikon, Minolta, Canon, Konica, Olympus.

E 1147. AIC Photo, Inc.

85-210mm f/3.8 MACRO ZOOM

Magnification: 1.65X—4.2X. Minimum aperture: f/22. Minimum focusing distance: 5 feet zoom, 15 inches macro. Angle of view: 28°—12°. Filter size: 62mm. Diameter: 70mm. Length: 7 inches. Weight: 28 oz. Special features: will fit the following SLR cameras: Pentax, Nikon, Minolta, Canon, Konica, Olympus.

E 1148. AIC Photo, Inc.

80-210mm f/3.8 ZOOM

Magnification: 1.6X—4.2X. Minimum aperture: f/22. Minimum focusing distance: 7 feet. Angle of view: 30°—12°. Filter size: 62mm. Diameter: 73mm. Length: 7 inches. Weight: 33 oz. Special features: will fit the following SLR cameras: Pentax, Nikon, Minolta, Canon, Konica, Olympus, Miranda.

E 1149. AIC Photo, Inc.

80-200mm f/3.5 MACRO ZOOM

Magnification: 1.6X—4X. Minimum aperture: f/22. Minimum focusing distance: 8 feet zoom, 31.5 inches macro. Angle of view: 28°—12°. Filter size: 62mm. Diameter: 73mm. Length: 7 inches. Weight: 33.5 oz. Special features: will fit the following SLR cameras: Pentax, Nikon, Minolta, Canon, Konica, Olympus. Comes with leather case and built-in hood.

E 1150. AIC Photo, Inc.

75-260mm f/4.5 MACRO ZOOM

Magnification: 1.5X—5.2X. Minimum aperture: f/22. Minimum focusing distance: 6.6 feet zoom, 8.3 inches macro. Angle of view: 31°—9.5°. Filter size: 62mm. Diameter: 68mm. Length: 7.4 inches. Weight: 31 oz. Special features: will fit the following SLR cameras: Pentax, Nikon, Minolta, Canon, Konica, Olympus.

E 1151. AIC Photo, Inc.

Vivitar

2X TELECONVERTER

Doubles the focal length (magnification) of whatever single-focal-length lens you attach it to. Available in Universal Thread, Nikon, Canon, Minolta, Konica, Pentax, and Olympus mounts. Automatic diaphragm (f/stop) control.

E 1156. Vivitar Corp.

70-210mm f/3.5 MACRO ZOOM

Magnification: 1.4X—4.2X. Minimum aperture: f/22. Minimum focusing distance: 6.5 feet zoom, 11.5 inches macro. Angle of view: 32°—11°. Filter size: 67mm. Diameter: 76mm. Length: 6 inches. Weight: 31 oz. Special features: Collapsible rubber lens hood. Same ring controls focusing and focal length.

E 1157. Vivitar Corp.

100-300mm f/5 CLOSE FOCUS ZOOM

Magnification: 2X—6X. Minimum aperture: f/22. Minimum focusing distance: 6.5 feet zoom, 17 inches close focus. Angle of view: 24°—8°. Filter size: 62mm. Diameter: 68mm. Length: 6.5 inches. Weight: 28 oz. Special features: Switch from zoom to close focus by twisting a ring. Remains in focus throughout entire zoom range. Will adapt to following SLR cameras: Pentax, Mamiya, Olympus, Nikon, Canon, Minolta, Konica, Fujica.

E 1158. Vivitar Corp.

600mm f/8 SOLID MIRROR

Magnification: 12X. Minimum focusing distance: 23 feet. Angle of view: 4°. Filter size: 35.5mm. Diameter: 106mm. Length: 3.3 inches. Weight: 48 oz. Special features: screw-in lens hood, case, four filters—Neutral Density, Ultra Violet, Red, Yellow. Rotates 360° inside the tripod mounting ring.

E 1161. Vivitar Corp.

800mm f/11 SOLID MIRROR

Magnification: 16X. Minimum focusing distance: 25 feet. Angle of view: 3°. Filter size: 35.5mm. Diameter: 108mm. Length: 3.3 inches. Weight: 48 oz. Special features: screw-in lens hood, case, four filters—Neutral Density, Ultra Violet, Red, Yellow. Fits following SLR cameras: Olympus, Konica, Minolta, Canon, Nikon.

E 1160. Vivitar Corp.

90-230mm f/4.5 CLOSE FOCUS ZOOM

Magnification: 1.8X—4.6X. Minimum aperture: f/22. Minimum focusing distance: 6.5 feet zoom, 17 inches close focus. Angle of view: 27°—11°. Filter size: 62mm. Diameter: 68mm. Length: 6.5 inches. Weight: 28 oz. Special features: remains in focus throughout entire zoom range. Close focus control coupled to zoom ring. Built-in lens hood.

E 1159. Vivitar Corp.

100-300mm f/5 CLOSE FOCUS ZOOM

Magnification: 2X—6X. Minimum aperture: f/22. Minimum focusing distance: 6.5 feet zoom, 17 inches close focus. Length: 6.5 inches. Weight: 28 oz.

E 1162. Vivitar Corp.

300mm f/5.6 SINGLE FOCAL LENGTH

Magnification: 6X. Minimum aperture: f/22. Length: 7 inches. Weight: 26.5 oz. Special features: retractable lens hood. Can be hand held.

E 1163. Vivitar Corp.

OTHER LENSES OF INTEREST TO BIRD WATCHERS FOR WHICH PHOTOS NOT AVAILABLE:

75-260mm f/4.5 zoom, 200mm f/5.6 single focal length, 3X teleconverter.

E 1164, E 1165, E 1166. Vivitar Corp.

Chinon

200mm f/3.5 SINGLE FOCAL LENGTH

Magnification: 4X. Minimum aperture: f/22. Minimum focusing distance: 8 feet. Angle of view: 12°. Filter size: 62mm. Diameter: 70mm. Length: 5 inches. Weight: 18 oz. Special features: instant depth-of-field preview. Non-slip rubber surfaces on control rings. Bult-in lens hood. Fits following SLR cameras: Canon, Konica, Minolta, Nikon, Olympus, Pentax/Praktica.

E 1167. Chinon Corp. of America, Inc.

300mm f/5.6 SINGLE FOCAL LENGTH

Magnification: 6X. Minimum aperture: f/22. Minimum focusing distance: 8 feet. Angle of view: 8°. Filter size: 58mm. Diameter: 70mm. Length: 7 inches. Weight: 23 oz. Special features: Instant dept-of-field preview. Non-slip rubber surfaces on control rings. Built-on lens hood. Fits following SLR cameras: Canon, Konica, Minolta, Nikon, Olympus, Pentax/Praktica.

E 1168. Chinon Corp. of America, Inc.

OTHER LENSES OF INTEREST TO BIRD WATCHERS FOR WHICH PHOTOS NOT AVAILABLE:

85-210mm f/4.5 zoom, 85-210mm f/4.5 macro zoom.

E 1169, E 1170. Chinon Corp. of America, Inc.

Tripod Buying Guide

Spotting scopes, telephoto lenses, even binoculars, aren't much use unless you can hold them steady. The heavier they are or the greater the magnification, the more of a problem steadiness becomes. Tripods solve this problem best.

Most spotting scope manufacturers sell tripods although only one furnished us with photos. Scope tripods adapt to cameras as well. But the majority of tripods are made by companies who make nothing else. Product brochures talk about tripods' usefulness for still, movie, and TV cameras. Fortunately these camera tripods will also adapt to scopes.

What should you look for in a tripod? Steadiness is most important—the least vibration from wind or an accidental touch blurs your view. The tripod you get should be designed to support whatever weight your scope or camera-plus-lens has. But remember that the more weight it's designed to support, the heavier the tripod will be. Lugging a seven-pound tripod in addition to your gear gets tiring fast.

Height is an important factor, too. If you plan to sit on a deck, or remain inconspicuous in a field by lying down, you won't need a tripod more than 12 inches high. On the other hand, nothing is guaranteed to place cricks in your neck faster than a spotting scope that can't quite be raised high enough. Be sure, by the way, that the legs of the tripod you buy lock firmly in place. The author recalls focusing on his first Peregrine Falcon only to have his scope sink towards the ground. Repeated efforts could not get the legs to lock. At last, trying to hold the 20X scope by hand, he shook so much that his view seemed more that from a biplane gone out of control than from a wooded patch of ground.

A tripod's legs usually have retractable rubber caps. The rubber is for use on a smooth surface. When retracted, the rubber gives way to pointed tips that stick in the ground. You can even buy pads to keep the tripod from sinking into snow.

The platform on which you mount your camera, camera lens, or scope is called the tripod's head. This head tilts at least 90° up and

down, as well as rotates (or "pans") 360°. This double maneuverability is important for keeping a flying bird in your field of view.

While most of the products that follow are tripods, we've included a few monopods and one car window mount so that you can see what they look like. The monopod comes in handy when working in crowds, or when light weight is crucial. If you tend towards hypertension, a monopod won't do—it's only as steady as your hand.

Tripods

Gitzo

TELE-STUDEX

Extended height: 72 inches. Carrying height: 24 inches. Weight: 9½ pounds. tubular legs: yes. Radial braces: no. Special features: panning head sold separately. Built-in leveler.

E 1170. Karl Heitz, Inc.

PRO-STUDEX

Extended height: 62 inches. Carrying height: 21 inches. Weight: 7½ pounds. Tubular legs: yes. Radial braces: no. Special features: panning head sold separately. Built-in leveler.

E 1171. Karl Heitz, Inc.

TOTAL-LUXE

Extended height: 58 inches. Carrying height: 14 inches. Weight: 3 pounds. Tubular legs: yes. Radial braces: no. Special features: panning head sold separately. Interchangeable spiked, and rubber tipped, end sections.

E 1172. Karl Heitz, Inc.

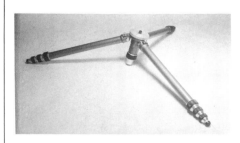

WEEKEND-COMPACT

Extended height: 64 inches. Carrying height: 14 inches. Weight: 2 pounds. Tubular legs: yes. Radial braces: no. Special features: panning head sold separately. Interchangeable spiked, and rubber tipped, end sections.

E 1173. Karl Heitz, Inc.

REPORTER-MODE

Extended height: 56 inches. Carrying height: 16 inches. Weight: 3¾ pounds. Tubular legs: yes. Radial braces: no. Special features: panning head sold separately. Interchangeable spiked, and rubber-tipped, end sections.

E 1174. Karl Heitz, Inc.

Bushnell

CAR WINDOW MOUNT

Height: 4½ inches. Weight: 1.2 pounds. Special feature: Head tilts for vertical use.

E 1175. Bushnell Optical Co.

ALL PURPOSE

Extended height (non adjustable): 64 inches. Weight: 6 pounds. Tubular legs: yes. Radial braces: yes. Special features: three-section legs. Retractable rubber tips reveal spikes.

E 1176. Bushnell Optical Co.

COMPACT

Extended height: 13 inches. Carrying height: 9½ inches. Weight: 1 pound.

E 1177. Bushnell Optical Co.

TABLE TOP

Extended height (non adjustable): 7½ inches. Weight: 0.7 pounds. Special features: ball-socket head. Rubber tipped legs.

E 1178. Bushnell Optical Co.

Slik

SYSTEM S205

Extended height: 63 inches. Carrying height: 19.5 inches. Weight: 4.2 pounds. Tubular legs: yes. Radial braces: no. Special features: head tilts 90° up, 55° down; pans 360°. Retractable rubber leg tips reveal spikes.

E 1179. Berkey Marketing Companies.

FEATHERWEIGHT MONOPOD

Extended height: 60 inches. Carrying height: 19 inches. Weight: 0.5 pounds. Special features: four-section leg. Rubber leg tip. Easy-grip leg lock.

E 1180. Berkey Marketing Companies.

LIGHTWEIGHT 800G

Extended height: 56 inches. Carrying height: 18 inches. Weight: 1.7 pounds. Tubular legs: yes. Radial braces: yes. Special features: Easy-grip leg locks.

E 1181. Berkey Marketing Companies.

COMPAC

Extended height: 67 inches. Carrying height: 31 inches. Weight: 6 pounds. Tubular legs: no. Radial braces: yes. Special features: head tilts 90° up and down, pans 360°. Extension accessory allows instrument (camera, scope, binoculars, lens) to be positioned as low as 1 inch from ground.

E 1182. Davis & Sanford Co., Inc.

RTM MINI

Extended height: 51 inches. Carrying height: 20 inches. Weight: 1.7 pounds. Tubular legs: yes. Radial braces: no. Special features: Handle can be stored in central column. Permanent leg locks. Aluminum parts only.

E 1183. Davis & Sanford Co., Inc.

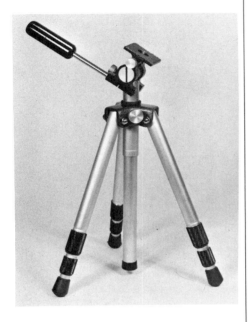

Velbon

PROFESSIONAL

Extended height: 71½ inches. Carrying height: 29½ inches. Weight: 6.4 pounds. Tubular legs: no. Radial braces: yes. Special features: head tilts 115° up and down, pans 360°. Rubber tips threaded on steel spikes. Quick-lever leg locks. Center column is geared.

E 1184. Velbon International Corp.

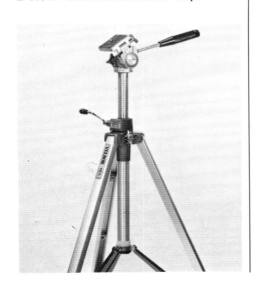

VGB-3

Extended height: 60 inches. Carrying height: 23 inches. Weight: 4.8 pounds. Tubular legs: no. Radial braces: yes. Special features: head tilts 115° up and down, pans 360°. Rubber tips threaded on steel spikes. Quick-lever leg locks. Center column is geared.

E 1185. Velbon International Corp.

STEREO

Extended height: 61 inches. Carrying height: 25 inches. Weight: 4.6 pounds. Tubular legs: no. Radial braces: no. Special features: head tilts 115° up and down, pans 360°. Rubber tips threaded on steel spikes. Quick-lever leg locks. Center column is not only geared but can be used at any angle between the vertical and horizontal. Two instruments (cameras, scopes, lenses, binoculars) can be mounted at the same time.

E 1186. Velbon International Corp.

VE-3

Extended height: 58 inches. Carrying height: 22 inches. Weight: 4.2 pounds. Tubular legs: no. Radial braces: no. Special features: head tilts 115° up and down, pans 360°. Rubber tips threaded on steel spikes. Quick-lever leg locks. Three-section legs.

E 1187. Velbon International Corp.

GROUNDER

Extended height: 60½ inches. Carrying height: 24 inches. Weight: 5.8 pounds. Tubular legs: no. Radial braces: yes. Special features: head tilts 115° up and down, pans 360°. Rubber tips threaded on steel spikes. Quick-lever leg locks. Spreads out to only 10 inches off ground. Leg length independently adjustable.

E 1188. Velbon International Corp.

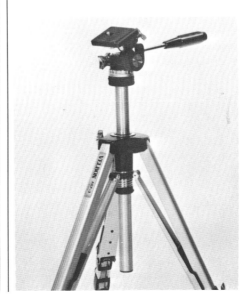

PX-701

Extended height: 72 inches. Carrying height: 28 inches. Weight: 8½ pounds. Tubular legs: no. Radial braces: yes. Special features: head tilts 115° up and down, pans 360°. Rubber ball joint foot pad grips any terrain except snow. Quick-lever leg locks.

E 1189. Velbon International Corp.

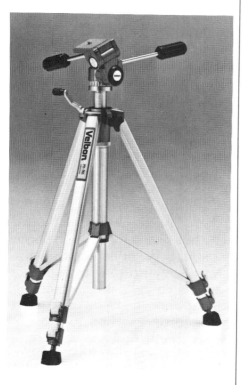

VG-3

Extended height: 59 inches. Carrying height: 23 inches. Weight: 4.4 pounds. Tubular legs: no. Radial braces: no. Special features: head tilts 115° up and down, pans 360°. Rubber tips threaded on steel spikes. Quick-lever leg locks.

E 1190. Velbon International Corp.

UP-3C MONOPOD

Extended height: 60 inches. Carrying height: 25 inches. Weight: 0.9 pounds. Special features: three-section leg. Rubber tip threaded on steel spike.

E 1192. Velbon International Corp.

UP-3D MONOPOD

Extended height: 57½ inches. Carrying height: 24 inches. Weight: 0.84 pounds. Special features: ball-and-socket head. Three-section leg. Rubber tip threaded on steel spike.

E 1191. Velbon International Corp.

Recorder Buying Guide

Bird watchers by definition concentrate on the visual—what does the whole of that Black-tailed Gnatcatcher look like, where can you see him, what besides gnatting can you watch him doing? In 1929, however, when a 41-year-old manufacturer named Albert Brand decided to chuck the world of business for the world of bird sounds, the specialty called bioacoustics was born. Fifty years later, bioacoustics remains a frontier (you won't find the word in most dictionaries.) But, because of its potential for helping us learn more about birds, and because of the excitement any frontier offers, we've decided to give the commercially available instruments of bioacoustics—tape recorders and microphones—their due.

We hope you agree this first-time-ever effort is worthwhile. Fortunately, tape recorders alone add pleasure to birding in several ways. That's why we talk about them before talking about microphones. First:

Why Do Birds Make Sounds Anyway?

Some birds don't. Storks don't, nor do pelicans outside their breeding grounds, nor do the six species of New World vultures (except to hiss). The rest do—more than half of these, of the order Passeriformes, not only squawk, wail, croak, or hoot, but they make up songs as well. Why?

The multiplicity of reasons could fill a book. Briefly, they are these: 1) to tempt a mate 2) to tell unknown birds of the same species to keep their distance 3) To get the young to eat 4) To drive away enemies 5) To keep a flock together 6) to identify oneself to one's friends. Even the most feet-on-the-ground ornithologists admit that birds may also sing for the sheer joy of it. Only male birds, in general, sing. Females sing—but they also make all those other sounds grouped by ornithologists under the term "calls."

Why Record Bird Sounds?

The first reason is to help you identify the birds. A Ruby-crowned Kinglet (Regulus calendula) and a Hutton's Vireo (Vireo huttoni), although in different families, look alike. Their songs, however, are night and day: The Kinglet's song hinges on ascending triplets, the Vireo's is a two-note phrase. By seeing the bird, recording its voice, and playing that recording over and again, you'll learn that bird's identity far sooner than by only having it in your mind's eye. Or you may not see the bird at all. Engineer-turned-naturalist Frank Farran claims that you never see 80% of the land birds heard. That means that 80% of the time, on land, binoculars and scopes become white elephants (albatrosses if you will), dead weight to drag along.

Perhaps the most exciting aspect of recording bird sounds, is the push you can give our knowledge of birds. In 1968, John Dennis, an amateur, using a tape recorder costing less than $50.00, caught the "hant, hant" call of an unseen Ivory-billed Woodpecker, thus giving the lie to the belief that the bird was extinct. W. John Smith has recorded the Eastern Kingbird to show how emotional stress affects its calls. In England researchers found that unborn chicks exposed to the sounds of tape recorders will go to those tape recorders rather than to their own parents once they hatch. So relatively untapped is this field of bioacoustics that over half of the world's 8,600+ bird species have never been recorded. Bird-sound laboratories like those at Occidental College in Southern California, the University of Florida, even the best-known, the Laboratory of Ornithology at Cornell, are eager to hear from you if you want to record a rare bird's call, or explore a hypothesis about bird sound.

Two more-subtle reasons exist for recording the sounds of birds. Having that tape to play back is like having a movie you made—both revive memories of a pleasant outing. Making a tape does more. Acousticians say that the more energy you put into listening to one sort of music, the more attuned your ear becomes to all sorts. In a nutshell: if you get to know the song of the Hermit Thrush, you can grow to love something as complicated as Stravinsky's Firebird Suite.

A Recorder's Many Faces

Preserving bird sounds is one of the reasons to look into buying a tape recorder. Electronic "chumming" is another. If you play a recorded song in the field, often you can bring a bird of the same species closer. Or, by playing an owl's hoot, you can bring several species into view (song birds and hawks attack owls in the daytime—they know he can't see).

You have two ways to chum. Several outfits—Dover Books, Houghton Mifflin, the Federation of Ontario (Canada) Naturalists—produce phonograph records of bird calls. You can transcribe the songs you want into your tape recorder, (perfectly legal if you don't sell the transcriptions), and take the loaded recorder into the field. Or you can take a blank recorder into the field, record a song live, and play the song back to entice the bird closer. Close birds mean better photos, easier visual identification, and better sound recordings. To keep your chumming effective, don't play back the same song in the same territory more than twice a month. If you do, either the bird will overreact or start paying no attention.

Beware: It is unethical ever to play a tape near nesting birds. Thinking you're a bird invader, both parents may get upset enough to leave eggs or babies forever. It is also unethical to play a tape near an endangered species such as a Whooping Crane, a Pribilov Wren, a Clapper Rail.

Even if you don't want to chum, having a tape recorder loaded with known bird songs helps you identify birds in the field. You need not play the songs loudly, only enough to tell which corresponds with the song you hear live.

A portable tape recorder lets you take field notes in far less time than if you use a pad and pencil. Field notes in far less time than if you use a pad and pencil. Field notes enrich your birding experiences. They allow you to describe, and remember, the bird himself, where you saw him, what he was doing. If you move from being a mere onlooker to an amateur ornithologist, you'll want to become accustomed to the discipline of taking field notes.

A reason that's just fun exists for considering a portable tape recorder with a built-in radio. Suppose it rains or suppose, heaven save us, you tire of playing bird songs. Then, how pleasant to be able to switch on music of our own species. Alas: the more expensive the portable recorder, the more electronic gadgets it contains and the less room it has for a radio.

Portable Recorders in General
No commercial machine is designed just to record wild animal sounds. That's a shame. Because these sounds are faint when compared with background noise—a jet, a trail bike, wind, the roar of a river—recording them creates problems not found in recording music or a nearby human voice.

It's also a shame that the type of machine best adapted to recording and editing animal sounds—the 'open reel' portable recorder, as opposed to the 'cassette'—is so scarce and so high priced. You'll find that while we talk about the open reel recorder, only a couple of models appear in the product rundown. Why? Who but the rich can afford $4,000 to $5,000 for a Stellavox or Nagra, exclusive of microphone? To our knowledge only Sony and Uher make portable open reels for under $1,000, and only Uher would send us photos and specifications.

Whether 'cassette' or 'open reel', recorders are only part of the equipment necessary to isolate and preserve bird sounds. You need an external microphone, you may need a parabolic reflector or a pre-amplifier (never mind yet what pre-amplifier means), you may want a pair of earphones. Because so much needs saying about recorders, however, and because recorders can be used in several ways, we've saved talk about the other items for the next section.

One piece of advice fits all situations. If you have never used a recorder for birding, buy an inexpensive one first. This probably means a cassette-type, perhaps incorporating a radio. You can use it for identification, electronic chumming, and field notes, get used to its anatomy, begin to know what you like, what you don't. Where do you wish the dials were placed, is it too heavy for the birding you do, what gadgets do you wish it had that it doesn't? When you can answer these questions, you're ready for a more expensive buy.

It's true that portable cassette recorders are more common than open reel recorders. For either, however, make sure you have a weatherproof carrying case or bag with a strong shoulder strap (unless, of course, it's of the miniature variety that you can carry in your pocket). One hand you'll want free to flick switches and twist dials—the other to hold your Peterson or Robbins' field guild, or a microphone. Make sure, too, if you're chumming, that your machine's speaker has a diameter of at least 3½ inches. Else that Elf Owl's cackle you so carefully transcribed at home may not even be loud enough to

scare you. Many manufacturers, sad to say, do not include speaker size in their descriptive literature.

Cassette and open reel recorders come in the 'mono' variety (one speaker, one input for an external microphone), and in the 'stereo' variety (two speakers, two microphone inputs). You can use either but will chum or record in the mono mode only.

The Cassette Portable Recorder
This is the type of machine the businessman uses to dictate letters and pink memos while jetting between Los Angeles and New York. It's smaller than the open reel type machine, a big advantage to birders. But, the tape itself, ⅛″ wide, is sealed in a plastic case, a disadvantage if you hope to edit what you record by the snip-and-splice method. (It is possible, however, to edit without breaking open the cassette case. How? Buy a second machine. You simply transcribe onto it only the recorded sounds you wish to save.) Analyzing bird sounds by slowing them down is impossible with a cassette machine—the

tape runs at just one speed, 1⅞ inches per second. It can't be further slowed. Higher-priced cassette machines will record bird sounds faithfully enough to suit all but the most finicky.

The Open Reel Portable Recorder
Also called reel-to-reel, the term open-reel fits better—it means that the 5″ or 7″ spool is not sealed in plastic. To edit, the tape can be easily snipped and spliced. Because an open-reel tape is wider (¼″), an open-reel machine has more room on the tape to record a sound accurately. Open-reel tape may be slowed from 7½ inches per second to 1⅞ inches—even 15/16 inches per second. When you know that the song of a Hermit Thrush (*Hylocichla muslelina*) contains 40 notes per second (80 notes for each two-second song), you understand why you must slow the tape down to analyze it.

A Great Many Terms
Tape recorders are described by a dizzying number of terms. In order to do comparison shopping, most of these terms are important for you to understand. We're going to try to make

the job easy.

Speaker Diameter—If you are chumming, the speaker should have at least a 3½ inch diameter (the larger the diameter, the louder and truer the sound). If you are recording bird calls or field notes, or listening to recorded sounds for field identification, speaker size is unimportant.

Recording Level Control—Most cassette machines have a gadget that controls the strength of the sound that gets recorded on tape automatically. For recording bird song you don't want that. You want to control the strength manually, else the sound may get distorted or background noise may overpower it.

Power Source—You want to know the versatility your machine has. Can it be plugged into a wall socket (for loading, listening, or editing at home)? On what sort of batteries does it run? Can you run or recharge it off your car battery?

Tape Type—Tapes come in two varieties, Standard (employing iron oxide, Fe_2O_3 granules) and Chrome (employing chromium dioxide, C_1O_2, granules). Buy Chrome if your machine gives you the option, even though it's more expensive. Chrome tape will give you higher frequency response (that term's coming up next), and with it you'll have to clean your recorder less often.

Frequency Response—Sound is transmitted in waves. The higher the sound, the more frequent the waves. Their frequency, which used to be measured in cycles per second, is now measured in a unit called a Hertz—honoring Heinrich Rudolf Hertz, a 19th century German physicist. Hertz is usually abbreviated Hz. The term Frequency Response tells the range of Hertz's to which the recorder can respond.

A Sage Grouse (*Centrocercus urophasianus*) makes bubbling sounds in the range of 500 to 600 Hz. We talk and sing in the range of 85 to 1100 Hz. The Nashville Warbler (*Vermivora ruficapilla*) trills in the range of 4,000 to 10,000 Hz. If you plan to record or play bird songs, it's important to buy a machine with a range from 100 Hz to at least 10,000 Hz. In order to capture the harmonics, or overtones, of high-pitched birds like warblers, your Frequency Response should go to 15,000 Hz.

Signal-to-noise Ratio—'Signal' is your voice or the bird's voice. Noise is internal noise made by the machine. The higher the Signal-to-noise Ratio

(expressed as a number), the more clearly the signal will record. The abbreviation dB by the way, stands for decibel, the unit that expresses the ratio.

Wow and Flutter—Wow (more like wowww) is the sound the machine makes when the tape speed wavers slowly. Flutter is the quivering sound it makes when the tape speed wavers rapidly. You want neither. Wow and Flutter are expressed as a single percentage, such as 0.25%. The lower this percentage, the better.

External Jacks—If you are going to record bird sounds, you want an external jack for plugging in a microphone, and perhaps another for a set of headphones (also called earphones).

Tape Counter—A window through which, or digits by which, you can see where on the tape you are. It lets you know when you are about to run out of tape but more important, it lets you note down which songs are recorded where. Tape counters are useful for listening, chumming and editing.

Pause Control—Suppose you hear a trail bike roaring up behind you. Or suppose someone starts screaming for help. You don't want to record that. But if you turn your machine all the way off, you'll get the WOW sound (see definition 7) before the tape comes up to speed again. A pause button or switch eliminates WOW.

We've talked about buying a second machine, and transcribing from the first onto the second only those portions of tape you want to save. For this method of editing (it makes editing cassette tapes easy), you need a Pause Control.

Microphone Impedance Rating—The rating on your machine, expressed in ohms, should match the rating on your microphone. We'll talk more about impedance and ohms (honoring Georg Simon Ohm, another 19th century German physicist) in the microphone section.

That does it for terms. Unfortunately, many of the companies whose products follow do not reveal important terms—we hope this book spurs them to do so. Most missed are data on Recording Level Controls, Pause Controls, Microphone Impedance Ratings, and Speaker Sizes. Keep in mind, too, as you study the products pictured, that manufacturers are making improvements all the time. That's why it's important to write them for the latest product literature before you decide what to buy.

Tape Recorders

Pearlcorder

SR 501 CASSETTE MONO

Speaker Diameter: 2¼ inches. Recording level Control: automatic. Power Sources: 4 penlight batteries, optional AC adaptor, optional car battery adaptor. Frequency Response: 300 to 9,000 Hz. Signal-to-noise Ratio: not given. Wow and Flutter: not given. External Jacks: 1 microphone, 1 earphone. Tape Counter: yes. Pause Control: yes. Microphone Impedance Rating: not given. Radio: AM/FM. Dimensions: 6¼ x 3¾ x 1 inches. Weight: 1 pound. Special Features: micro-cassette tape package smaller than standard cassette yet records 1 hour of sound. Automatic shut-off at end of tape. Battery power indicator.

E 1193. Olympus Corp. of America.

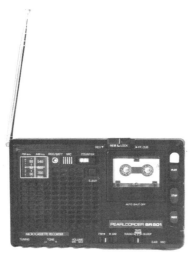

SD CASSETTE MONO

Speaker Diameter: 2 inches. Recording Level Control: automatic. Power Sources: 2 penlight batteries, optional rechargeable battery pack, optional AC adaptor, optional car battery adaptor. Frequency Response: 300 to 7,000 Hz. Signal-to-noise Ratio: not given. Wow and Flutter: not given. External Jacks: 1 microphone, 1 earphone. Tape Counter: no. Pause Control: yes. Microphone Impedance Rating: not given. Radio: optional FM or AM tuner attachments. (FM tuner shown). Dimensions: 5½ x 2½ x 1 inches. Weight: ¾ pound. Special Features: micro-cassette tape package smaller than standard cassette yet records 1 hour of sound. Automatic shut-off at end of tape. Battery power indicator. Soft carrying case.

E 1194. Olympus Corp. of America.

S 301 CASSETTE MONO

Speaker Diameter: 2 inches. Recording Level Control: automatic: Power Sources: 2 penlight batteries, optional AC adaptor, optional car battery adaptor. Frequency Response: 300 to 7,000 Hz. Signal-to-noise Ratio: not given. Wow and Flutter: not given. External Jacks: 1 microphone, 1 earphone. Tape Counter: no. Pause Control: yes. Microphone Impedance Rating: not given. Radio: no. Dimensions: 5½ x 2½ x 1 inches. Weight: ¾ pound. Special Features: micro-cassette tape package smaller than standard cassette yet records up to 2 hours of sound. Black aluminum shell. Battery power indicator.

E 1195. Olympus Corp. of America.

General Electric

3-5311 CASSETTE MONO

Speaker Diameter: not given. Recording Level Control: automatic. Power Sources: 4 penlight batteries, optional AC or car battery converter. Frequency Response: not given. Signal-to-noise Ratio: not given. Wow and Flutter: not given. External Jack: 1 earphone. Tape Counter: no. Pause Control: yes. Microphone Impedance Rating: not given. Radio: no. Dimensions: 1¾ x 5¾ x 4½ inches. Weight: 1¾ pounds. Special Features: automatic end-of-tape shut-off.

E 1196. General Electric Co.

3-5105 CASSETTE MONO

Speaker Diameter: 3½ inches. Recording Level Control: automatic. Power Sources: AC, 5 flashlight batteries, optional car battery adaptor. Frequency Response: not given. Signal-to-noise Ratio: not given. Wow and Flutter: not given. External Jacks: 1 microphone, 1 earphone. Tape Counter: no. Pause Control: yes. Microphone Impedance Rating: not given. Radio: no. Dimensions: 5½ x 3 x 10½ inches. Weight: 4 pounds. Special Features: automatic end-of-tape shut-off.

E 1197. General Electric Co.

3-5003 CASSETTE MONO

Speaker Diameter: not given. Recording Level Control: automatic. Power Sources: 4 flashlight batteries, optional AC or car battery converter. Frequency Response: not given. Signal-to-noise Ratio: not given. Wow and Flutter: not given. External Jacks: 1 microphone, 1 earphone. Tape Counter: no. Pause Control: no. Microphone Impedance Rating: not given. Radio: no. Dimensions: 7 x 3½ x 10¼ inches. Weight: 2¼ pounds. Special Features: automatic end-of-tape shut-off.

E 1198. General Electric Co.

Craig

COMPACT CASSETTE MONO

Speaker Diameter: 2 inches. Recording Level Control: automatic. Power Sources: AC, 4 penlight batteries, optional rechargeable battery pack. Frequency Response: 100 to 7,000 Hz. Signal-to-noise Ratio: 35 dB. Wow and Flutter: 0.35%. External Jacks: 1 microphone, 1 earphone. Tape Counter: yes. Pause Control: yes. Microphone Impedance Rating: 10,000 ohms. Radio: AM/FM. Dimensions: 9 x 4¾ x 2¼ inches. Weight: 2 pounds. Special Features: AC adaptor included.

E 1200. Craig Corp.

2629 HAND-HELD CASSETTE MONO

Speaker Diameter: 2 inches. Recording Level Control: automatic. Power Sources: AC, 4 penlight batteries, optional rechargeable battery pack. Frequency Response: 50 to 7,000 Hz. Signal-to-noise Ratio: 50 dB.

Wow and Flutter: 0.30%. External Jacks: 1 microphone, 1 earphone. Tape Counter: yes. Pause Control: yes. Microphone Impedance Rating: 10,000 ohms. Radio: no. Dimensions: 6¾ x 4½ x 2 inches. Weight: 1 pound. Special Features: carrying case. Automatic shut-off at end-of-tape. Battery-condition light.

E 1201. Craig Corp.

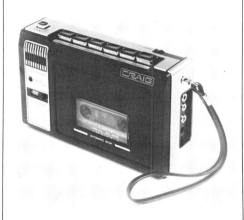

2625 ELECTRONIC NOTEBOOK CASSETTE MONO

Speaker Diameter: 1½ inches. Recording Level Control: not given. Power Sources: AC, rechargable battery pack. Frequency Response: 150 to 5,000 Hz. Signal-to-noise Ratio: 45 dB. Wow and Flutter: 0.4%. External Jacks: 1 microphone, 1 earphone. Tape Counter: yes. Pause Control: yes. Microphone Impedance Rating: 10,000 ohms. Radio: no. Dimensions: 3¼ x 5 x 1¼ inches. Weight: 1 pound. Special Features: micro-cassette tape package smaller than standard cassette yet records 1¼ hours of sound. Battery condition indicator.

E 1202. Craig Corp.

Sony

CF-302 CASSETTE MONO

Speaker Diameter: 4 inches. Recording Level Control: automatic. Power Sources: AC, 4 flashlight batteries. Frequency

Response: 80 to 8,000 Hz. Signal-to-noise Ratio: 40 dB. Wow and Flutter: 0.3%. External Jacks: 1 microphone, 1 earphone. Tape Counter: no. Pause Control: no. Microphone Impedance Rating: not given. Radio: AM/FM. Dimensions: 8 x 11½ x 4 inches. Weight: 6½ pounds. Special Features: battery power indicator. Automatic shut-off at end-of-tape.

E 1203. Sony Corp. of America.

CF-370 CASSETTE MONO

Speaker Size: 4¾ inches. Recording Level Control: automatic. Power Sources: AC, 4 flashlight batteries. Frequency Response: 80 to 8,000 Hz. Signal-to-noise Ratio: 40 dB. Wow and Flutter: 0.3%. External Jacks: 1 microphone, 1 earphone. Tape Counter: yes. Pause Control: yes. Microphone Impedance Rating: not given. Radio: AM/FM. Dimensions: 8½ x 13¼ x 4 inches. Weight: 6½ pounds. Special Features: battery power indicator. Automatic shut-off at end-of-tape.

E 1204. Sony Corp. of America.

CF-440 CASSETTE MONO

Speaker Diameter: 4 inches. Recording Level Control: automatic. Power Sources: AC, 4 flashlight batteries, optional rechargeable battery pack, optional car battery adaptor. Frequency Response: 50 to 10,000 Hz. Signal-to-noise Ratio: 42 dB. Wow and

Flutter: 0.28%. External Jacks: 1 microphone, 1 earphone. Tape Counter: yes. Pause Control: yes. Microphone Impedance Rating: not given. Radio: AM/FM. Dimensions: 9¾ x 12¾ x 4 inches. Weight: 9 pounds. Special Features: battery power indicator. Automatic shut-off at end-of-tape.

E 1205. Sony Corp. of America.

TC-520 CS CASSETTE STEREO

Speaker Diameter: 4 inches. Recording Level Control: automatic. Power Sources: AC, 4 flashlight batteries, optional rechargeable battery pack, optional car battery adaptor. Frequency Response: 50 to 10,000 Hz. Signal-to-noise Ratio: 45 dB. Wos and Flutter: 0.26%. External Jacks: 2 microphones, 1 headphone. Tape Counter: yes. Pause Control: yes. Microphone Impedance Rating: not given. Radio: no. Dimensions: 3½ x 11 x 10 inches. Weight: 7½ pounds. Special Features: carrying case. External microphone. Battery power indicator. Automatic shut-off at end-of-tape.

E 1206. Sony Corp. of America.

TC-62 CASSETTE MONO

Speaker Diameter: 3 inches. Recording Level Control: automatic. Power Sources: AC, 4 flashlight batteries. Frequency Response: 80 to 8,000 Hz. Signal-to-noise Ratio: 40 dB. Wow and Flutter: 0.3%. External Jacks: 1 microphone, 1 earphone. Tape Counter: yes. Pause Control: no. Microphone Impedance Rating: not given. Radio: no. Dimensions: 3¼ x 6½ x 10½ inches. Weight: 3¾ pounds. Special Features: battery power indicator. Automatic shut-off at end-of-tape.

E 1207. Sony Corp. of America.

TC-65 CASSETTE MONO

Speaker Diameter: 4 inches. Recording Level Control: automatic. Power Sources: AC, 4 flashlight batteries. Frequency Response: 80 to 8,000 Hz. Signal-to-noise Ratio: 40 dB. Wow and Flutter: 0.3%. External Jacks: 1 microphone, 1 earphone. Tape Counter: no. Pause Control: no. Microphone Impedance Rating: not given. Radio: no. Dimensions: 7 x 10½ x 3 inches. Weight: 4½ pounds. Special Features: battery power indicator. Automatic shut-off at end-of-tape.

E 1208. Sony Corp. of America.

TC-207 CASSETTE MONO

Speaker Diameter: 3¾ inches. Recording Level Control: automatic. Power Sources: AC, 4 flashlight batteries, optional rechargeable battery pack. Frequency Response: 70 to 8,000 Hz. Signal-to-noise Ratio: 45 dB. Wow and Flutter: 0.28%. External Jacks: 1 microphone, 1 earphone. Tape Counter: yes. Pause Control: no. Microphone Impedance Rating: not given. Radio: no. Dimensions: 3 x 6¾ x 10½ inches. Weight: 4½ pounds. Special Features: carrying case. Battery power meter. Automatic shut-off at

E 1210. Sony Corp. of America.

TC-215 CASSETTE MONO

Speaker Diameter: 3½ inches. Recording Level Control: automatic. Power Sources: AC, 4 flashlight batteries, optional rechargeable battery pack. Frequency Response: 80 to 8,000 Hz. Signal-to-noise Ratio: 45 dB. Wow and Flutter: 0.28%. External Jacks: 1 microphone, 1 earphone. Tape Counter: yes. Pause Control: yes. Microphone Impedance Rating: not given. Radio: no. Dimensions: 3 x 6½ x 10 inches. Weight: 4¼ pounds. Special Features: battery power indicator. Automatic shut-off at end-of-tape.

E. 1209. Sony Corp. of America.

TC-92 CASSETTE MONO

Speaker Diameter: 3¼ inches. Recording Level Control: automatic. Power Sources: Ac, 4 flashlight batteries, optional rechargeable battery pack, optional car battery adaptor. Frequency Response: 50 to 10,000 Hz. Signal-to-noise Ratio: 45 dB. Wow and Flutter: 0.28%. External Jacks: 1 microphone, 1 earphone. Tape Counter: yes. Pause Control: no. Microphone Impedance Rating: not given. Radio: no. Dimensions: 2¾ x 7 x 9¾ inches. Weight: 5 pounds. Special Features: carrying case. External microphone. Battery power meter. Automatic shut-off at end-of-tape.

E 1211. Sony Corp. of America.

TC-110B CASSETTE MONO

Speaker Diameter: 3½ inches. Recording Level Control: automatic. Power Sources: AC, 4 flashlight batteries, optional rechargeable battery pack, optional car battery adaptor. Frequency Response: 50 to 10,000 Hz. Signal-to-noise Ratio: 46 dB. Wow and Flutter: 0.28%. External Jacks: 1 microphone, 1 earphone. Tape Counter: yes. Pause Control: no. Microphone Impedance

Rating: not given. Radio: no. Dimensions: 2½ x 5¾ x 9½ inches. Weight: 3¾ pounds. Special Features: carrying case. External microphone. Automatic shut-off at end-of-tape. Battery power meter.

E 1213. Sony Corp. of America.

TC-142 CASSETTE MONO

Speaker Diameter: 3 inches. Recording Level Control: both automatic and manual. Power Sources: AC, 4 flashlight betteries, optional rechargeable battery pack, optional car battery adaptor. Frequency Response: 70 to 12,000 Hz. Signal-to-noise Ratio: 45 dB. Wow and Flutter: 0.26%. External Jacks: 1 microphone, 1 earphone. Tape Counter: yes. Pause Control: yes. Microphone Impedance Rating: not given. Radio: no. Dimensions: 3 x 10 x 7½ inches. Weight: 5¾ pounds. Special Features: carrying case. Battery power meter.

E 1214. Sony Corp. of America.

TC-48 CASSETTE MONO

Speaker Diameter: 2¾ inches. Recording Level Control: not given. Power Sources: AC, 4 penlight batteries, optional rechargeable battery pack, optional car battery adaptor. Frequency Response: 70 to 8,000 Hz. Signal-to-noise Ratio: 45 dB. Wow and Flutter: 0.38%. External Jacks: 1 microphone, 1 earphone. Tape Counter: yes. Pause Control: no. Microphone Impedance Rating: not given. Radio: no. Dimensions: 7 x 2 x 4¼ inches. Weight: 2 pounds. Special Features: battery power indicator. Automatic shut-off at end-of-tape.

E 1215. Sony Corp. of America.

TC-150A CASSETTE MONO

Speaker Diameter: 2 inches. Recording Level Control: not given. Power Sources: AC, 4 penlight batteries, optional rechargeable battery pack, optional car battery adaptor. Frequency Response: 90 to 10,000 Hz. Signal-to-noise Ratio: 44 dB. Wow and Flutter: 0.22%. External Jacks: 1 microphone, 1 earphone. Tape Counter: yes. Pause Control: yes. Microphone Impedance Rating: not given. Radio: no. Dimensions: 1¼ x 7 x 4½ inches. Weight: 1¾ pounds. Special Features: carrying case. Battery power meter.

E 1216. Sony Corp. of America.

M-102 MICRO-CASSETTE MONO

Speaker Diameter: 1¾ inches. Recording Level Control: not given. Power Sources: AC, 2 penlight batteries, optional rechargeable battery pack, optional car battery adaptor. Frequency Response: 200 to 7,000 Hz. Signal-to-noise Ratio: 45dB. Wow and Flutter: 0.36%. External Jacks: 1 microphone, 1 earphone. Tape Counter: yes. Pause Control: yes. Microphone Impedance Rating: not given. Radio: no. Dimensions: 5¾ x 2½ x 1 inches. Weight: ¾ pound. Special Features: micro-cassette tape package smaller than standard cassette yet records 1¼ hours of sound. Battery check indicator.

E 1217. Sony Corp. of America.

TCM-600 CASSETTE MONO

Speaker Diameter: 1¾". Recording Level Control: not given. Power Sources: AC, 2 penlight batteries, optional rechargeable battery pack, optional car battery adaptor. Frequency Response: 90 to 10,000 Hz. Signal-to-noise Ratio: 45 dB. Wow and Flutter: 0.35%. External Jacks: 1 microphone, 1 earphone. Tape Counter: yes. Pause Control: yes. Microphone Impedance Rating: not given. Radio: no. Dimensions: 5¼ x 1¼ x 3 inches. Weight: 1 pound. Special Features: automatic shut-off. Battery power indicator.

E. 1218. Sony Corp. of America.

JVC

RC-828 CASSETTE STEREO

Speaker Diameter: 6½ inches. Recording Level Control: both automatic and manual. Power Sources: AC, 8 flashlight batteries, car battery. Frequency Response: not given. Signal-to-noise Ratio: not given. Wow and Flutter: 0.09%. External Jacks: 2 microphones, 1 headphone. Tape Counter: yes. Pause Control: yes. Microphone Impedance Rating: not given. Radio: AM/FM. Dimensions: 18½ x 10¾ x 5 inches. Weight: 14 pounds. Special Features: battery power meter. Automatic tape-end stop.

E 1219. JVC America Co.

RC-323 CASSETTE MONO

Speaker Diameter: 6½ inches. Recording Level Control: automatic. Power Sources: AC, 6 flashlight batteries. Frequency Response: not given. Signal-to-noise Ratio: not given. Wow and Flutter: not given. External Jacks: not given. Tape Counter: yes. Pause Control: yes. Microphone Impedance Rating: not given. Radio: AM/FM. Dimensions: 13½ x 9½ x 4 inches. Weight: 7½ pounds. Special Features: battery power meter. Automatic stop-at-end of tape.

E 1220. JVC America Co.

RC-525 JW CASSETTE MONO

Speaker Diameter: not given. Recording Level Control: automatic. Power Sources: AC, 6 flashlight batteries, car battery. Frequency Response: not given. Signal-to-noise Ratio: not given. External Jacks: 1 microphone. Tape Counter: yes. Pause Control: yes. Microphone Impedance Rating: not given. Radio: AM/FM. Dimensions: 9½ x 16 x 4½ inches. Weight: 9¾ pounds. Special Features: detachable microphone. Battery Meter. Automatic stop-at-end of tape.

E 1221. JVC America Co.

RC-717 CASSETTE STEREO

Speaker Diameter: 5 inches. Recording Level Control: automatic. Power Sources: AC, 4 flashlight batteries. Frequency Response: not given. Signal-to-noise Ratio: not given. Wow and Flutter: not given. External Jacks: 2 microphones, 1 headphone. Tape Counter: yes. Pause Control: yes. Microphone Impedance Rating: not given. Radio: AM/FM. Dimensions: 16¼ x 9

x 4½ inches. Weight: 10¼ pounds. Special Features: battery power meter.

E 1222. JVC America Co.

KD-1636 II CASSETTE STEREO

Speaker Diameter: not given. Recording Level Control: not given. Power Sources: AC, 6 flashlight batteries, car battery. Frequency Response: 30 to 16,000 Hz. Signal-to-noise Ratio: 57 dB. Wow and Flutter: 0.08%. External Jacks: 2 microphones, 1 headphone. Tape Counter: yes. Pause Control: not given. Microphone Impedance Rating: not given. Radio: no. Dimensions: 14½ x 4 x 9¾ inches. Weight: 10¼ pounds. Special Features: automatic stop at end-of-tape. Battery life indicator.

E 1223. JVC America Co.

KD-2 CASSETTE STEREO

Speaker Diameter: not given. Recording Level Control: manual. Power Sources: AC, 4 flashlight batteries. Frequency Response: 30 to 16,000 Hz. Signal-to-noise Ratio: 62 dB. Wow and Flutter: 0.09%. External Jacks: 1 headphone. Tape Counter: not given. Pause Control: not given. Microphone Impedance Rating: not applicable. Radio: no. Dimensions: 11 x 11½ x 3¾ inches. Weight: 8 pounds. Special Features: battery check light.

E 1224. JVC America Co.

Pioneer

RK-888 CASSETTE MONO

Speaker Diameter: 6½ inches. Recording Level Control: both automatic and manual. Power Sources: AC, 8 flashlight batteries, car battery. Frequency Response: 50 to 12,000 Hz. Signal-to-noise Ratio: 45 dB. Wow and Flutter: 0.2%. External Jacks: 1 headphone. Tape Counter: yes. Pause Control: yes. Microphone Impedance Rating: not applicable. Radio: AM/FM. Dimensions: 9½ x 14¾ x 4¼ inches. Weight: 10¼ pounds. Special Features: meter shows recording level and battery life. Automatic shut-off at end-of-tape.

E 1225. Pioneer Electronics of America.

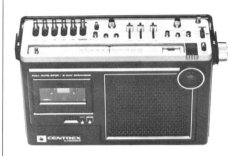

RK-114 CASSETTE MONO

Speaker Diameter: 4¾ inches. Recording Level Control: both automatic and manual. Power Sources: AC, 4 flashlight batteries, car battery. Frequency Response: 80 to 10,000 Hz. Signal-to-noise Ratio: 46 dB. Wow and Flutter: 0.2%. External Jacks: 1 microphone, 1 headphone. Tape Counter: yes. Pause Control: yes. Microphone Impedance Rating: not given. Radio: AM/FM. Dimensions: 8 x 12¾ x 3¾ inches. Weight: 7 pounds. Special Features: automatice shut-off at end-of-tape.

E 1226. Pioneer Electronics of America.

RK-113 CASSETTE MONO

Speaker Diameter: 4¾ inches. Recording Level Control: automatic. Power Source: AC, 4 flashlight batteries, car battery. Frequency Response: 80 to 10,000 Hz. Signal-to-noise Ratio: 46 dB. Wow and Flutter: 0.2%. External Jacks: 1 microphone. Tape Counter: no. Pause Control: yes. Microphone Impedance Rating: not given. Radio: AM/FM. Dimensions: 12¼ x 8 x 3¾ inches. Weight; 6½ pounds. Special Features: meter showing battery condition. Automatic stop at end-of-tape.

E 1227. Pioneer Electronics of America.

Uher

CR 210 CASSETTE STEREO

Speaker Diameter: not given. Recording Level Control: both automatic and manual. Power Sources: AC, 6 flashlight batteries, rechargeable battery pack, or car battery. Frequency Response: 30 to 17,000 Hz. Signal-to-noise Ratio: not given. Wow and Flutter: 0.2%. External Jacks: 2 microphones, 1 headphone. Tape Counter: yes. Pause Control: not given. Microphone Impedance Rating: under 350 ohms. Radio: no. Dimensions: 7½ x 2¼ x 7 inches. Weight: 4½ pounds. Special Features: optional leather carrying case.

E 1230. Uher Corp.

CR 240 CASSETTE STEREO

Speaker Size: not given. Recording Level Control: manual. Power Sources: AC, 6 flashlight batteries, rechargeable battery pack, or car battery. Frequency Response: 30 to 16,000 Hz. Signal-to-noise Ratio: 66 dB. Wow and Flutter: 0.2%. External Jacks: 2 microphones, 1 headphone. Tape Counter: yes. Pause Control: yes. Microphone Impedance Rating: 500 ohms. Radio: no. Dimensions: 9¼ x 2½ x 7¼ inches. Weight: 6 pounds. Special Features: built-in pre-amplifier. Optional leather carrying case. Automatic end-of-tape shut-off. Battery check meter.

E 1231. Uher Corp.

4400 IC OPEN REEL STEREO

Speaker Diameter: not given. Recording Level Control: manual. Power Sources: AC, 4 flashlight batteries, rechargeable battery pack, car battery. Frequence Response: 35 to 20,000 Hz. Signal-to-noise Ratio: 62 dB. Wow and Flutter: 0.2%. External Jacks: 2 microphones, 1 headphone. Tape Counter: yes. Pause Control: yes. Microphone Impedance Rating: 200 ohms. Radio: no. Dimensions: 11 x 3¾ x 8¾ inches. Weight: 8¼ pounds. Special Features: optional leather carrying case.

E 1232. Uher Corp.

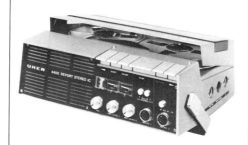

Nakamichi

500 CASSETTE STEREO

Speaker Diameter: does not contain a speaker—for recording and headphones only. Recording Level Control: not given. Power Sources: AC, 8 flashlight batteries, car battery. Frequency Response: 40 to 17,000 Hz. Signal-to-noise Ratio: 65 dB. Wow and Flutter: 0.08%. External Jacks: 2 microphones, 1 headphone. Tape Counter: yes. Pause Control: yes. Microphone Impedance Rating: 600 ohms. Radio: no. Dimensions: 12¼ x 3½ x 13¾ inches. Weight: 11¼ pounds. Special Features: automatic shut-off if tape breakes or ends. Even if battery voltage varies from 7 to 14 volts, device assures constant output of 12 volts.

E 1234. Nakamichi Research (U.S.A.) Inc.

350 CASSETTE STEREO

Speaker Diameter: does not contain a speaker—for recording and headphones only. Recording Level Control: not given. Power Sources: AC, car battery, rechargeable 12 volt battery built into optional carrying case. Frequency Response: 40 to 15,000 Hz. Signal-to-noise Ratio: 58 dB. Wow and Flutter: 0.13%. External Jacks: 2 microphones, 1 headphone. Tape Counter: yes. Pause Control: yes. Microphone Impedance Rating: 10,000 ohms. Radio: no. Dimensions: 7½ x 3½ x 9½ inches. Weight: 6½ pounds. Special Features: automatic shut-off if tape breaks or ends.

E 1239. Nakamichi Research (U.S.A.) Inc.

Superscope

C-106 CASSETTE MONO

Speaker Diameter: not given. Recording Level Control: automatic. Power Sources: 4 penlight batteries, optional AC and car battery adaptor, optional rechargeable battery pack. Frequency Response (Standard tape only): 120 to 8,000 Hz. Signal-to-noise Ratio: 46 dB. Wow and Flutter: 0.25%. External Jacks: 1 microphone, 1 headphone. Tape Counter: no. Pause Control: yes. Microphone Impedance Rating: less than 350 ohms. Radio: no. Dimensions: 1½ x 6 x 4 inches. Weight: 1¾ pounds. Special Features: battery strength indicator. Automatic shut-off when tape breaks or ends. Optional vinyl carrying case.

E 1238. Superscope Inc.

Microphone Buying Guide

When you enter the world of microphones, headphones, and pre-amplifiers, you enter an electronic thicket. Yet the reason for this book is to entice you into the open with the Buffleheads and meadowlarks, not to create a migraine as you hack through jargon. If you are serious about recording bird sound live, however, you need to know what's involved. So this, the last of the technical sections and potentially the most arcane, constitutes a compromise. It's an overview of the field in layman's language, with a smattering of terms and product photos.

Don't rush out to buy a microphone on the strength of what you read now. Through your local Audubon chapter or independent bird club, get to know the folks who already are recording birds live. Go with them on field trips; discover the practical problems involved. Write manufacturers for literature (even though that literature is slanted toward recording human rather than animal sounds). That way, when finally you decide to make your purchase, chances are the decision will be wise.

The whole point of using an external microphone, rather than the small one built into your tape recorder, is to increase the possibility of picking up a specific, distant sound. Most birds won't hop close when they see you laden with electronic gear—in fact, they'll do the opposite. Nor will other sounds cease—the buzzing fly, the purling stream, the jet overhead, a sudden rush of wind, all those wrens, mockingbirds, jays and sparrows whose calls obscure the hoarse squawk of that Great Blue Heron you thought you heard. Not only must you isolate and pick the sound up, but pick it up loud enough so you can identify it over the inherent noise of your machine.

Two Types

For field work, you have two types of microphones from which to choose. The first is the condenser. This works by the action of two closely-placed metalized plates, one of which vibrates with sound. The two-plate device requires a battery to generate the necessary current. It also requires a pre-amplifier because

that current is so weak. What the pre-amplifier does is make the current stronger before it reaches the tape recorder. Although an additional, external pre-amplifier is sometimes necessary, the condenser pre-amplifier and battery are often located right in the condenser microphone's handle—always the case with so-called Electret condenser mikes.

Condenser microphones give somewhat better sound fidelity than the type to be described next. But their fidelity is more susceptible to temperature changes. And condenser microphones won't hold up to rough handling in the field.

The second type of microphone suitable for field work is the dynamic (sometimes called moving coil). Here the current is produced by sound moving a coil of wire past a permanent magnet. The dynamic microphone needs no battery, nor does it require a built-in pre-amplifier. More rugged, it requires less maintenance than a condenser mike. It also, in general, costs less to buy.

Both condenser and dynamic type microphones will work with both cassette and open-reel tape recorders. There is no point, however, in buying a $400 mike for a $100 recorder, or visa versa—the sound fidelity of both should match, else the less expensive component will dictate the sound you get.

Microphone Pick-up Patterns

Some microphones, called omni-directional (condenser or dynamic), pick up sound from all directions. This is fine if you are recording Beethoven's Ninth, but not so good for trying to isolate the peep of a White-rumped Sandpiper. Fortunately, when you place an omni-directional mike in the center of a parabolic reflector, and aim the reflector toward the sound, you not only screen off other noises but, in effect, amplify the sound you want. One manufacturer, R.D. Systems of Canada, sells a pre-assembled parabolic unit called the Dan Gibson Electronic Mike. The drawback to a reflector is its weight.

Other microphone pick-up patterns can be

lumped under the term uni-directional (condenser or dynamic). Mikes with these patterns discard sound behind their backs, and concentrate on sound coming from the direction you point them. The most precise, and the most expensive, are called shotgun-pattern (sometimes rifle-pattern) mikes. Others, which also catch some sounds at the sides, are called cardioid, super cardioid, and hyper cardioid.

Uni-directional mikes need no parabolic reflector. They do, however, need a pre-amplifier, to boost the sound level. Without a microphone pre-amplifier, you have to turn your tape recorder on so high that its internal noise gets in the way of the bird sound. Condenser-type uni-directional mikes carry their own pre-amplifier; you may not need another. With dynamic-type uni-directional mikes, however, you'll have to buy an external pre-amplifier (the pros call it a 'pre-amp'). In some cases you can use your tape recorder battery to make the pre-amp work.

Accessories and Where to Buy

Two accessories can prove useful for recording in the field. Microphone manufacturers make wind screens, usually out of polyurethane foam, that fit over the microphone's head. This screen minimizes the "puff" sounds that even the slightest breeze will transmit to tape.

Headphones (some, like those used by telephone operators, are lightweight indeed) let you know exactly what you are recording. It may be that by the direction of the microphone, you'll get a stronger, cleaner signal. Or it may be that the brook gurgling to your right is obscuring the American Widgeon's call. Headphones will tell you. Headphone detractors claim that the device represents one more item to wrestle with, one more outlay in expense—that, in time, you learn what headphones have to say without putting them on.

Much of the problem with sound recording is finding electronic pros who'll talk. Clerks at the electronic stores, we've discovered, sometimes find it hard to be polite. You have one little-known source, however. Look in the Yellow Pages under "Police Equipment". The outfits listed specialize in selling cloak and dagger stuff—surveillance equipment including tape recorders, microphones, headphones, pre-amps and parabolic reflectors. They'll also sell to you. If you say why

you're calling, chances are you'll find someone who will be happy, and able, to answer your technical questions.

Other sources of accessories include tape recorder and microphone manufacturers themselves. The addresses of those whose products are pictured in this book are listed in an appendix.

Terms

Among the hundreds of technical terms relating to microphones, three need explaining. The first two you've met before, in the tape recorder section.

Frequency Response. This tells the range of sound frequency, expressed in Hertz (Hz), to which your microphone can respond. This range should correspond to the range of your tape recorder.

Impedance Rating. Impedance, or resistance to alternating current, is expressed in ohms. Whether it's high or low is not so important as its matching the microphone impedance rating of your tape recorder. Sometimes you can buy a transformer to help match low-impedance mikes to high-impedance recorders. But remember that every accessory increases the weight you must lug over hillsides and across creeks.

Output Level. This figure tells how strong a signal your microphone can impart to your tape recorder. It is expressed in negative decibels, or -dB. Sometimes the negative decibels are given in terms of watts, sometimes in terms of volts. The closer to zero (0) the negative decibel figure is, the more powerful your mike. A microphone rated at -50 dB is more powerful than one rated at -60 dB.

The mikes you see pictured appear on stands or booms. These are for presentation purposes only—for field work you affix the microphone to a parabolic reflector (omni-directional mikes only), or hold it in your hand.

Microphones

R.D. Systems

DAN GIBSON EPM 650

Type: Dynamic. Pick-up pattern: Omni-directional. Frequency response: 180 to 18,000 Hz. Impedance rating: 150 to 160 ohms. Output level: -42 dB. Dimensions: parabolic reflector is 18¾ inches in diameter. Weight: 1¾ pounds (with reflector, without earphones). Special features: Headphones. Parabolic reflector. Pre-amplifier built into pistol grip for extra amplification. Vinyl carrying case.

E 1241. R.D. Systems of Canada (U.S.A. distributor: A.V. Explorations, Inc.)

Audio-Technica

AT 811

Type: Electret Condenser. Pick-up pattern: Uni-directional (cardioid). Frequency response: 50 to 20,000 Hz. Impedance rating: matches tape recorders rated from 150 to 1,000 ohms. Output level: -54 dB. Dimensions: 8 x 1¼ inches. Weight: 6 oz. Special features: protective carrying case. Optional transformer. Optional foam wind screen.

E 1242. Audio-Technica U.S., Inc.

At 801

Type: Electret Condenser. Pick-up pattern: Omni-directional. Frequency response: 40 to 18,000 Hz. Impedance rating: matches tape recorders rated from 150 to 1,000 ohms. Output level: -48 dB. Dimensions: 7½ x 1½ inches. Weight: 5½ oz. Special features: protective carrying case. Optional transformer. Optional foam wind screen.

E 1243. Audio-Technica U.S., Inc.

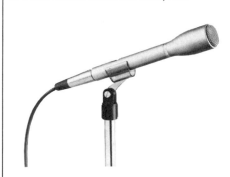

AT 813

Type: Electret Condenser. Pick-up pattern: Uni-directional (cardioid). Frequency response: 20 to 20,000 Hz. Impedance rating: matches tape recorders rated from 150 to 1,000 ohms. Output level: -58 dB. Dimensions: 8 x 2 inches. Weight: 6½ oz. Special features: protective carrying case. Optional transformer.

E 1244. Audio-Technica U.S., Inc.

AT 812

Type: Dynamic. Pick-up pattern: Uni-directional (cardioid). Frequency response: 50 to 18,000 Hz. Impedance rating: matches tape recorders rated from 150 to 1,000 ohms. Output level: -60 dB. Dimensions: 7¾ x 1½ inches. Weight: 7½ oz. Special features: protective carrying case. Optional transformer. Optional foam wind screen.

E 1245. Audio-Technica U.S., Inc.

AT 802

Type: Dynamic. Pick-up pattern: Omni-directional. Frequency response: 50 to 16,000 Hz. Impedance rating: matches tape recorders rated from 150 to 1,000 ohms. Output level: -54 dB. Dimensions: 7 x 1½ inches. Weight: 5 oz. Special features: protective carrying case. Optional transformer.

E 1246. Audio-Technica U.S., Inc.

Electro-Voice

635 A

Type: Dynamic. Pick-up pattern: Omni-directional. Frequency response: 80 to 13,000 Hz. Impedance rating: 150 ohms. Output level: -55 dB. Dimensions: 6 x 1½ inches. Weight: 9¼ oz. Special features: steel-cased. Optional wind screen.

E 1247. Electro-Voice, Inc.

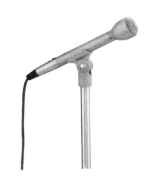

DS 35

Type: Dynamic. Pick-up pattern: Uni-directional (cardioid). Frequency response: 60 to 17,000 Hz. Impedance rating: 150 ohms. Output level: -60 dB. Dimensions: 7¼ x 2 inches. Weight: 9¼ oz. Special features: foam-lined metal case.

E 1248. Electro-Voice, Inc.

CO 15P

Type: Electret Condenser. Pick-up pattern: Omni-directional. Frequency response: 20 to 20,000 Hz. Impedance rating: 150 ohms. Output level: -45 dB. Dimensions: 6¾ x 1 inches. Weight: not given. Special features: wind screen. Foam-lined case.

E 1249. Electro-Voice, Inc.

CS 15P

Type: Electret Condenser. Pick-up pattern: Uni-directional (cardioid). Frequency response: 40 to 80,000 Hz. Impedance rating: 150 ohms. Output level: -45 dB. Dimensions: 7 x 1 inches. Weight: not given. Special features: wind screen. Gray steel case.

E 1250. Electro-Voice, Inc.

Nakamichi

DM-500

Type: Dynamic. Pick-up pattern: Uni-directional (cardioid). Frequency response: 50 to 15,000 Hz. Impedance rating: 250

ohms. Output level: -73 dB. Dimensions: not given. Weight: 6 oz. Special features: built-in wind screen.

E 1251. Nakamichi Research (U.S.A.), Inc.

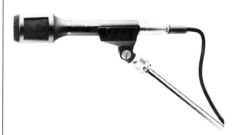

CM-100

Type: Electret Condenser. Pick-up pattern: Uni-directional (cardioid). Frequency response: 30 to 18,000 Hz. Impedance rating: 200 ohms. Output level: -76 dB. Dimensions: not given. Weight: 6 oz. Special features: optional omni-directional or uni-directional (shotgun) head. Enclosed battery and pre-amplifier.

E 1252. Nakamichi Research (U.S.A.), Inc.

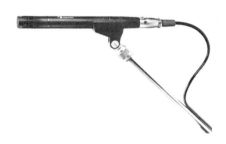

CM-700

Type: Electret Condenser. Pick-up pattern: Omni-directional head or Uni-directional (cardioid) head. Frequency response: 20 to 20,000 Hz. Impedance rating: 600 ohms. Output level: -65 dB. Dimensions: not given. Weight: 5 oz. Special features: optional Uni-directional (shotgun) head. Built-in pre-amplifier. Wind Screen. Powered by 6 Volt silver oxide battery.

E 1253. Nakamichi Research (U.S.A.), Inc.

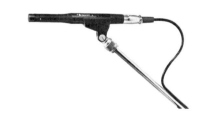

Sennheiser

ELECTRET CONDENSER SYSTEM

Type: Electret condenser. Pick-up pattern: Omni-directional (ME 20 head), or Uni-

directinal (ME 40 super cardioid head, ME 80 shotgun head). Frequency response: 50 to 15,000 Hz. Impedance rating: 200 ohms. Output level: -94 dB. Length of unit with Omni-directional head: 10 inches. Weight: not given. Special features: heads are available separately. Powering module contains built-in pre-amplifier. Optional windscreen and headphones.

E 1254. Sennheiser Electronic Corp.

Shure

SM 57

Type: Dynamic. Pick-up pattern: Uni-directinal (cardioid). Frequency response: 40 to 15,000 Hz. Impedance rating: can handle tape recorders rated at 19 to 300 ohms. Output level: from -82 to -56 dB. Dimensions: 6¼ x 1¼ inches. Weight: 10 oz. Special features: optional windscreen. Dark gray aluminum carrying case.

E 1255. Shure Brothers Inc.

SM 82

Type: Condenser. Pick-up pattern: Uni-directional (cardioid). Frequency response: 40 to 15,000 Hz. Impedance rating: for use with tape recorders rated at 600 ohms or more. Output level: from -19 to 0 dB. Dimensions: 11¾ x 1¾ inches. Weight: 14½ oz. Special features: bronze vinyl enamel carrying case. Will operate in temperatures from 10° to 135°F.

E 1256. Shure Brothers Inc.

SM 61

Type: Dynamic. Pick-up pattern: Omni-directional. Frequency response: 50 to 14,000 Hz. Impedance rating: can handle tape recorders rated at 19 to 300 ohms. Output level: from -82 to -60 dB. Dimensions: 17 x 1½ inches. Weight: 5½ oz. Special features: stainless steel and aluminum carrying case. Windscreen.

E 1257. Shure Brothers Inc.

SM 59 CM

Type: Dynamic. Pick-up pattern: Uni-directional (cardioid). Frequency response: 50 to 15,000 Hz. Impedance rating: can handle tape recorders rated at 19 to 300 ohms. Output level: from -83 to -61 dB. Dimensions: 7¾ x 1½ inches. Weight: 7½ oz. Special features: windscreen. Champagne-colored aluminum carrying case.

E 1258. Shure Brothers Inc.

Sony

ECM-260 F

Type: Electret condenser. Pick-up pattern: Uni-directional (cardioid). Frequency response: 50 to 14,000 Hz. Impedance rating: 200 ohms. Output level: -57 dB. Dimensions: 1½ x 7 inches. Weight: 5 oz. Special features: Detachable windscreen. Carrying Case. Operates 7,000 hours on enclosed battery.

E 1259. Sony Corp. of America.

F 540

Type: Dynamic. Pick-up pattern: Uni-directional (cardioid). Frequency response: 80 to 13,000 Hz. Impedance rating: 300 ohms. Output level: -58 dB. Dimensions: 1½ x 7 inches. Weight: 13 oz. Special features: built-in windscreen.

E 1260. Sony Corp. of America.

ECM-170 A

Type: Electret condenser. Pick-up pattern: Omni-directional. Frequency response: 20 to 16,000 Hz. Impedance rating: 200 ohms. Output level: -56 dB. Dimensions: 1 x 6 inches. Weight: 5½ oz. Special features: Detachable windscreen. Carrying case.

E 1261. Sony Corp. of America.

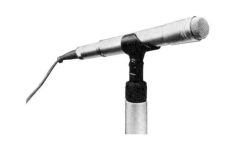

ECM-23 F

Type: Electret condenser. Pick-up pattern: Uni-directional (cardioid). Frequency response: 20 to 20,000 Hz. Impedance rating: 250 ohms. Output level: -56 dB. Dimensions: 1 x 7½ inches. Weight: 6½ oz. Special features: Operates for 6,500 hours with one enclosed battery. Switch prevents overloading in presence of excessively high level sound sources. Carrying case.

E 1262. Sony Corp. of America.

A NOTICE TO THE READER

The prices of all items listed in this book have been omitted primarily because they are subject to frequent change. This would make the book outdated before the next edition could be printed. The publisher does, however, maintain a printed list of current prices. This may be obtained by sending two (2) first class stamps along with your name and address to: The Great Outdoors Trading Company, 24759 Shoreline Highway, Marshall, California 94940

Publications

Perhaps the nicest feature about bird books is that they rarely go out of date. Birds' feeding, flying, and courtship habits, their appearance, their eggs, their songs stay the same for hundreds, if not thousands of years. It's for this reason that ornithologist Olin Sewall Pettingill, Jr. calls A.C. Bent's *Life Histories of North American Birds* "indispensable" to any ornithological library,* even though Bent started his 23-volume series sixty years ago. The only characteristics that can change in a lifetime are how many birds there are left to be seen (their 'abundance') and the places you can see them (their 'range'). Man, and shifts in weather patterns, affect abundance and range.

Many bird books, like any wise investment, increase in value over the years. As late as June, 1977, the world auction record for a bird book was broken by John James Audubon's *The Birds of America.* That year a rare book dealer from

New Orleans paid $352,000 for the four-volume, 1827-1838 classic.

Dr. Laurence C. Binford, Chairman of the Department of Sciences, estimates that a new book about birds is published at least once a week in this country, not counting reprints. True it is that Bowker's annual directory of American publishing, *Books in Print,* lists over 1,000 bird titles under headings that range from "Birds, Folk Lore of" to "Birds as Pets". Book stores, by the way, keep a copy of the three-volume, orange-covered *Books in Print* by the cash register; libraries keep it by the reference desk. It's the bible for discovering if the book you want can be purchased new.

The books that follow represent title for which the publisher had review copies to send. Here's the way the books are arranged: (1) How to Watch. (2) Recordings. (3) Field Guides. (4) Directories & Checklists. (5) Birds by Location—State, Region, North America, Beyond North America. (6) Birds by Type. (7) Biology & Behavior. (8) Bird Care.

*"**Choosing a Basic Ornithological Library,**" *American Birds,* October, 1976.

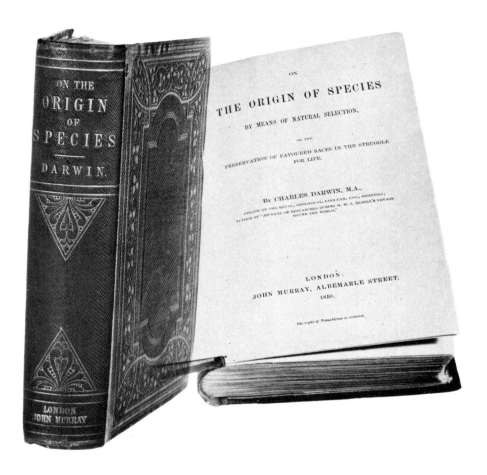

(9) Preservation. (10) History, Poetry, Narrative, Essays. (11) Especially for Children. (12) Misc.

For days of inclement weather, days when you're sick, or days when you just don't feel like mingling with our feathered friends, the books shown—many lavish with color photos and paintings—will offer hours of pleasure and provocation.

Book stores rarely carry more than a few of the books described here, and a number of the periodicals we list are not available on news-stands. In most cases the books or periodicals must be ordered from the publishers, special ordered by your local book store or they may be ordered through The Great Outdoors Trading Company, 24759 Shoreline Hwy., Marshall, CA 94940.

Subscribing to one or more periodicals is the best way for beginning and advanced bird watchers to stay current on behavior (what the birds themselves are doing, and what people are doing to birds), on the advance of scientific know-ledge, and on the equipment and activities that make up a birder's world.

The inventory that follows represents those publishers who answered our queries. All the periodicals listed are national in scope; many come free with membership in the sponsoring organization.

Nine of the periodicals deal strictly with birds, the others deal with all forms of wildlife. *Birding* devotes itself solely to the sport of bird watching. *American Birds* talks both to bird watchers and to naturalists with scientific leanings. *The Auk, The Condor,* and *The Wilson Bulletin* are ornithological journals using ornithological language. *Ducks Unlimited* and the *Game Bird Breeders, Aviculturists, Zoologists and Convervationists' Gazette* deal with those birds whose lives often get snuffed out by men—we include these period-icals because of the scientific knowledge they contain.

For publications of regional interest, the reader is referred to the "Clubs and Organizations" section of this book. Many local clubs and organi-zations publish newsletters or magazines to which non-members may subscribe.

Periodicals

Birds Only

AMERICAN BIRDS

A bimonthly devoted to changing distribution, population, migration, and rare occurrence of birds in North America, Mexico, and the West Indies. Last two-thirds of issue devoted to sightings, with black and white photos. Some color photos, paintings. Site guide to particular birding location is a regular feature. Scholarly but simply-written articles.

E 4001. 6 issues. 6½″ x 9½″. Approximately 150 pages. Published by the National Audubon Society. Established 1946.

AMERICAN CAGE-BIRD MAGAZINE

This magazine features parrots, budgies, canaries, finches, cockatiels. Publishes results of bird shows around the country. Black and white photos, mostly by amateurs. Issue shown includes features on Cuba, the Pekin Nightingale, how humidity affects cage birds. Directory of cage-bird societies printed each month.

E 4002. 12 issues. 7″ x 10″. Approximately 50 pages. Published by American Cage-Bird Magazine. Established 1928.

THE AUK

A quarterly of ornithological research that contains black and white photographs, lots of graphs and statistics. Sample features are "Gull Nest Site Selection", "Radiotelemetry of Gull Heart Rates", "Timing of Egg Laying by Geese." Membership in The American Ornithologists' Union includes subscription.

E 4003. 4 issues. 7″ x 10″. Approximately 225 pages. Published by the American Ornithologists' Union. Established 1883.

BIRDING

A bimonthly on foreign and domestic bird finding, identification techniques, equipment, trip experiences, and other topics of birding interest. Special inserts on best birding sites include directions, lodgings and probable species. Membership in American Birding Association includes subscription.

E 4005. 6 issues. 6″ x 9″. Approximately 40 pages. Published by American Birding Association. Established 1969.

BOOKS ABOUT BIRDS

A newsletter published 10 times yearly. Regular columns include book reviews, news about bird books and bookstores, catalogues of special interest to birders, and coming auctions. Classified advertising from collectors, bookstores and other with books and prints for sale.

E 4006. 10 issues. 8½″ x 11″. Approximately 5 pages. Published by Books About Birds. Established 1975.

THE CONDOR

This quarterly emphasizes ornithological research findings west of the Rocky Mountains, but becoming national in scope. Contains some drawings and black and white photos. Membership in the Cooper Ornithological Society includes year subscription.

E 4007. 4 issues. 7½″ x 10½″. Approximately 150 pages. Published by the Cooper Ornithological Society. Established 1898.

DUCKS UNLIMITED

A bimonthly devoted to conservation and propagation of North America's waterfowl. Directed at the sportsperson, articles include site and species descriptions, a look at sports paraphernalia, and what the various chapters of Ducks Unlimited are doing. Black and white, and color photographs.

E 4008. 6 issues. 8½″ x 11″. Approximately 50 pages. Published by Ducks Unlimited. Established 1937.

GAME BIRD BREEDERS, AVICULTURISTS, ZOOLOGISTS AND CONSERVATIONISTS GAZETTE

This monthly (except October) includes amateur black and white photographs of breeders, and of the birds they breed (swans, pheasants, guineafowl, turkeys, quail, pigeons, etc). Articles on bird feed and medicaments, how to raise particular species, show and convention news. Buy/sell/trade section in back.

E 4009. 11 issues. 7″ x 9″. Approximately

40 pages. Published by the Game Bird Breeders, Aviculturists, Zoologists and Conservationists Gazette. Established 1951.

THE WILSON BULLETIN

This quarterly of ornithological research contains some color photos, some black and white, lots of graphs and statistics. Sample features are "Growth and Survival of Florida Scrub Jays", "Breeding Behavior of Louisiana Heron", reviews of scientific texts. Membership in Wilson Ornithological Society includes year subscription.

E 4010. 4 issues. 6" x 9". Approximately 160 pages. Published by the Wilson Ornithological Society. Established 1888.

All Wildlife

ANIMAL KINGDOM

This bimonthly includes half- and full-page color photos. Sample features on birds: Galapagos Islands' Flightless Cormorants, Torishima Island's Steller's Albatross, what to do about oil-slicked birds. Membership in zoological societies in Boston, Chicago, Florida, Fort Wayne, Houston, Jacksonville, Minnesota, New York, Philadelphia, St. Louis, San Francisco, or Toronto includes subscription.

E 4011. 6 issues. 8½" x 11". Approximately 35 pages. Published by New York Zoological Society. Established 1898.

AUDUBON

This bimonthly uses breathtaking color to punctuate importance of preserving environment and its denizens. Articles, often first-person narratives written with humor, describe encounters with birds and animals. Wheatstock section in back deals with environmental goofs. Membership in the National Audubon Society includes year subscription.

E 4012. 6 issues. 8½" x 11". Approximately 150 pages. Published by the National Audubon Society. Established 1898 (under title *Bird Lore*).

AWARENESS

Quarterly edited by a park naturalist, for children and their teachers. Each issue contains a nature quiz, several black and white photographs. Written in rambling style, articles concern themselves with birds, animals, insects, wilderness.

E 4013. 4 issues. 5½" x 8½". Approximately 20 pages. Published by Awareness Nature Publications. Established 1971.

DEFENDERS

A bimonthly dedicated to the preservation of wildlife. Sample features are on eagles, Ospreys, bears, and whales. Regular columns on threatened species as well as book reviews and updates on conservation legislation. Special *Defenders* poster enclosed periodically. Subscription

included with membership in Defenders of Wildlife.

E 4014. 6 issues. 8½" x 11". Approximately 55 pages. Published by Defenders of Wildlife. Established 1924.

INTERNATIONAL WILDLIFE

A bimonthly dedicated to wise use of earth's recources. Half and full page color photographs throughout. Sample features on Bengal tiger, Lappet-Faced Vulture, Fairy Tern, octopus, snow monkeys, rare Australian flowers. Subscription included as World associate member or International associate member of National Wildlife Federation.

E 4015. 6 issues. 8½" x 11". Approximately 45 pages. Published by the Natinal Wildlife Federation. Established 1970.

THE LIVING WILDERNESS

This quarterly includes half and full page color photographs. Devoted to fostering wilderness preservation. Color photographic portfolio is a standard feature. Sample articles are on Alaska's falcons and a tribute to Ernest Oberholtzer. Membership in the Wilderness Society includes subscription.

E 4016. 4 issues. 8½" x 11". Approximately 50 pages. Published by the Wilderness Society. Established 1937.

NATIONAL GEOGRAPHIC

Each issue of this monthly contains at least one lengthy article about wildlife, often about birds. Other articles concern themselves with science, geography, adventure. Two-thirds of the editorial matter consists of color photographs.

E 4017. 12 issues. 7" x 10". Approximately 175 pages. Published by the National Geographic Society. Established 1890.

NATIONAL WILDLIFE

A bimonthly dedicated to preserving quality of environment. Regular features include conservation legislation, anecdotes and cartoons, wildlife sketchbook, environmental quality index, and accounts of outdoor survival. Color photographs capture America's world of nature. Subscription through membership in National Wildlife Federation.

E 4018. 6 issues. 8½" x 11". Approximately 45 pages. Published by the National Wildlife Federation. Established 1962.

NATURAL HISTORY

This monthly (summer bimonthly) runs both color and black and white photographs. Articles treat all aspects of natural science: biology, geology, astronomy, weather, anthropology. Membership in the American Museum of Natural History includes year subscription.

E 4019. 10 issues. 8½" x 11". Approximately 125 pages. Published by the American Museum of Natural History. Established 1891.

THE NATURE CONSERVANCY NEWS

A quarterly devoted to land and species conservation through private action. "New Projects" section describes, by state, parcels of land acquired by the Conservancy to be preserved. Illustrations include black and white and color photographs,

and drawings. Membership in The Nature Conservancy includes subscription.

E 4020. 4 issues. 7" x 10". Approximately 30 pages. Published by The Nature Conservancy. Established 1950.

PURPLE MARTIN NEWS

This monthly dedicates itself to enriching the natural history of homesteads nationwide, particularly those whose owners favor birds. Simple articles include "Did We Have Another Bad Bluebird Winter?", "Martins and Bees Thrive in Florida", "More About Fringillids," "Birding Adds Dimension to Travel."

E 4021. 12 issues. 12" x 15". Approximately 32 pages. Published by The Nature Society. Established 1963.

RANGER RICK

A monthly aimed at children, to foster their interest in nature and conservation. Non-fiction and fiction. Sample features include pieces on hummingbirds, food for birds, the secret of the sand dollar, nature club news. Mostly color photographs. Membership in National Wildlife Federation's "Ranger Rick Nature Club" includes year subscription.

E 4022. 12 issues. 8" x 10". Approximately 50 pages. Published by the National Wildlife Federation. Established 1966.

THE SIERRA CLUB BULLETIN

This monthly (except August and December) reflects Sierra Club's purpose: "To restore the quality of the natural environment and maintain the integrity of ecosystems in the U.S. and other countries." Wildlife, including birds, and conservation stressed. Color and black and white photographs. Membership in the Sierra Club includes year subscription.

E 4023. 10 issues. *½" x 11". Approximately 75 pages. Published by the Sierra Club. Established 1895.

Books

Recordings

BIRD SONG AND BIRD BEHAVIOR

Phonograph record and accompanying 32 pages of text show how to differentiate among woodpecker drummings, songs and calls of various birds, and noise problems encountered when recording birds (what to do when a truck rolls by). One section features dual singing. Sounds of 74 species. Written by Donald J. Borror.

E 3161. Dover Publications, Inc. 1972.

A FIELD GUIDE TO WESTERN BIRD SONGS

Songs and calls of more than 500 species of land and water birds in Western North America and Hawaii, recorded in the field. Arranged to accompany Roger Tory Peterson's *A Field Guide to Western Birds,* 2nd Edition. Matching Kodachrome slides available from Cornell Laboratory of Ornithology. Booklet gives scientific names, where and when sounds were recorded. Supervised by Peter Paul Kellogg, Arthur A. Allen, Roger Tory Peterson.

E 3162. Houghton Mifflin Company. 1975.

A FIELD GUIDE TO BIRD SONGS

Songs and calls of more than 300 species of land and water birds in Eastern and Central North America, recorded in the field. Arranged to accompany Roger Tory Peterson's *A Field Guide to the Birds.* Matching Kodachrome slides available from Cornell Laboratory of Ornithology. Booklet gives scientific names and breeding grounds. Supervised by Peter Paul Kellogg, Arthur A. Allen, Roger Tory Peterson.

E 3163. Houghton Mifflin Company. 1975.

How To Watch

THE BIRD WATCHER'S HANDBOOK

Topics discussed include mechanics of bird flight, 18 pages on equipment and accessories (including clothing and footwear), where and when best to see birds, how to identify them, how to track and record them, various bird watching activities. 42 photos and drawings. Written by Mark Clifford Brunner.

E 3003. Softcover. 5½" x 7½". 80 pages. Ideals Publishing Corp. 1977.

THE BIRD WATCHER'S BIBLE

Eighteen pages devoted to why and hows of watching, 30 pages to bird-watching sites in the United States. Other sections include equipment for watching and listening, how to attract birds, verbal descriptions of common birds, a Life List format. 205 photos, 32 in color. Written by George Laycock.

E 3001. Softcover. 7½" x 10". 208 pages. Doubleday & Co., Inc. 1976.

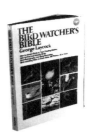

A GUIDE TO BIRD WATCHING

Written in 1943, this classic remains apropos. Author inspires readers to watch migrations, make counts, band, and just observe (taking notes), in order to further scientific knowledge. How to Begin Bird Study, and An Introduction to Bird Tracks included. Long list of books published before 1943. Written by Joseph J. Hickey.

E 3002. Softcover. 5½" x 8½". 252 pages. Dover Publications, Inc. 1975.

PROJECTS WITH BIRDS

80 suggested bird watching activities to add useful information to the findings of professional ornithologists. Projects arranged by category: nests, song, feeding habits, behavior, counting birds. Drawings, black and white photographs. First chapter deals with how to keep a notebook. Written in Britain by Peter Goodfellow.

E 3004. Hardcover. 5½" x 8½". 136 pages. David & Charles Publishers. 1973.

BEGINNER'S GUIDE TO BIRD WATCHING

This book shows how the English do it, especially useful if you plan spending time in Great Britain. Chapters on The British Bird List, equipment, bird recognition (accompanied by sketches), bird song (including unique list of up-at-dawn bird calls). 16 black and white photos. Written by Reg Harrison.

E 3005. Hardcover. 5½% x 8½". 176 pages. Transatlantic Arts, Inc. 1974.

Field Guides

HOW TO KNOW THE BIRDS

Slanted towards the area east of the Rockies, meant for the reader who has never had a bird book in his hand. In highly readable fashion, this book describes 13 habitats and over 200 birds. Illustrated with silhouettes, 400 drawings, and 72 color plates. Lots of bird lore. Written by Roger Tory Peterson.

E 3010. Pocketbook. 4" x 7". 168 pages. New American Library. Established 1957.

A FIELD GUIDE TO THE BIRDS

Second edition, for all 702 species found east of the Rocky Mountains. 1000 illustrations, 500 in color. Original version, publish-

ed in 1934, won the Brewster Medal from American Ornithologists' Union. Characteristic marks, sound of voice, where found, and illustration given for 440 species. Written by Roger Tory Peterson.

E 3006. Pocketbook. 4½" x 7". 230 pages. Houghton Mifflin Co. 1947.

A FIELD GUIDE TO WESTERN BIRDS

This second edition contains a new section on Hawaiian birds, plus 1242 illustrations, 658 in color. Characteristic marks, sound of voice, where found, and picture given for 583 species. Sponsored by the National Audubon Society. Written by Roger Tory Peterson.

E 3007. Pocketbook. 4½" x 7". 309 pages. Houghton Mifflin Co. 1961.

BIRDS OF NORTH AMERICA

Field guide to nearly 700 species found north of Mexico, all pictured in color. Range maps show summer, winter, all-year residences. Both verbal and Sonogram (oscilloscope-like) descriptions of sounds. Silhouettes, male and female, immatures included. Behavior and close comparisons. Written by Chandler S. Robbins, Bertel Bruun, and Herbert S. Zim.

E. 3008. Pocketbook. 4½" x 7½". 340 pages. Golden Press. 1966.

THE AUDUBON SOCIETY FIELD GUIDE TO NORTH AMERICAN BIRDS—WESTERN REGION

Newest of the field guides, this contains

627 full color photographs for identification. Songbirds grouped by color, others by shape. Photos fill front half of book; text (organized by habitat) back half. Description, voice, habitat, range, nesting data, and miscellaneous remarks about each bird given. Written by Miklos D.F. Udvardy.

E 3009. Pocketbook. 4" x 7½". 855 pages. Alfred A. Knopf. 1977.

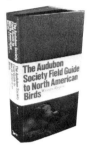

BIRDS OF THE OCEAN

Second edition handbook identifies all species of sea-birds, with notes on range and habits. 115 black and white photographs, 12 full pages of drawings by the author. Systematic list of ocean birds plus notes on the origin of English bird names. Fully indexed. Written by W.B. Alexander.

E 3011. Hardcover. 4½" x 7". 306 pages. G.P. Putnam's Sons 1963.

WATER BIRDS

Over 225 species in the U.S. and Canada are keyed and pictured for identification. Keys based on male spring plumage with additional notes on females. Maps of the U.S. show range for each species. Two chapters on bird watching equipment. Illustrated glossary. Illustrations by Harry J. Baerg and William Long. Written by H.E. Jacques and Roy Ollivier.

E 3012. Softcover. 5" x 8½". 159 pages. Wm. C. Brown Company. 1960.

LAND BIRDS

Pictured-keys for determining all land birds

of the U.S. and Southern Canada, with maps showing geographic distribution. Characteristics most apparent in the field are used in the keys. List of state birds, index and illustrated glossary. Drawings by Martha W. Cutkomp. Written by H.E. Jaques.

E 3013. Softcover. 5" x 8½". 196 pages. WM. C. Brown Company. 1947.

BIRDS OF THE EAST

This North American field guide, companion to *Birds of the West,* uses unusual system for identifying bird. Opposite statements are made in pairs (the bird has white, the bird has no white). By eliminating one, and going to next statement pair, user finally reaches only one bird. 48 color plates, appendices on photography, and eggs. Written by Dr. Ernest S. Booth.

E 3014. Hardcover. 5½" x 8½". 335 pages. Outdoor Pictures, 1962.

A FIELD GUIDE TO THE BIRDS OF MEXICO

Author has led trips to Mexico since 1946. Bilingual descriptions of birds, over 400 shown in color paintings. Habitat and vocal sounds given. Brief notes on Central American birds. Written by Ernest P. Edwards.

E 3015. Softcover. 5½" x 9". 300 pages. Ernest P. Edwards. 1972.

BIRD GUIDE—LAND BIRDS EAST OF THE ROCKIES

This 1951 enlarged edition of the 1906 field guide contains more than 300 full-color reproductions of the author's paintings. 222 species of birds described, with notes on song, nest, and range. Identification key organized by most prominent color, and body size. Written by Chester A. Reed.

E 3016. Hardcover. 3½" x 5½". 238 pages. Doubleday & Company, Inc.. 1951.

Directories

1978-79 NATURE GUIDE

National and international listing of local naturalist volunteer guides with addresses and phone numbers. Canadian and U.S. listings for nature centers, national forests, wildlife refuges and parks, and Audubon wildlife sanctuaries. Includes choice birding spots, bird-finding books, and phone numbers for local rare bird alerts. Edited by Ilene Marckx.

E 3017. Softcover. 6" x 8½". 76 pages. Tacoma Audubon Society. 1978.

DIRECTORY OF NATURE CENTERS

Visiting nature centers and arboretums is a good way to see and learn about local birds. This directory lists 558 locations (giving addresses, phones, number of acres) in the U.S., 41 in Canada. Those catering to children are stressed. Does not say which have bird lists available.

E 3018. Softcover. 8½" x 10½". 124 pages. National Audubon Society. 1975.

BIRDWATCHER'S GUIDE TO WILDLIFE SANCTUARIES

Includes 295 major and smaller sanctuaries, arboretums, and refuges open to the public in the U.S. and Canada. Location, facilities, kinds of birds, bird checklists available, geographical descriptions. Indexed by location and by bird. Written by Jessie Kitching.

E 3019. Softcover. 5½" x 8". 233 pages. Arco Publishing Co., Inc. 1976.

THE BIRD WATCHER'S AMERICA

Forty-four leading naturalists write in the first person about 44 of the best birding areas in the United States and Canada. Includes avian specialties like High Rocky Rosy Finches and Trumpeter Swans. Indexed geographically and by bird variety. Edited by Olin Sewall Pettingill, Jr., Director of Cornell's Laboratory of Ornithology.

E 3020. Softcover. 5" x 7½". 442 pages. Thomas Y. Crowell Co. 1974.

WHERE TO WATCH BIRDS IN EUROPE

Tells where to go in 27 countries, with birds that can be seen in each of four seasons. Abbreviated history and description of each spot. Twenty-seven maps, 25 black and white bird photos. Indexed by places; needs index by species. Addresses of each country's ornithological organizations included. Written by John Gooders.

E 3021. Hardcover. 5½" x 8". 299 pages. Taplinger Publishing Co., Inc. 1974.

FINDING BIRDS IN MEXICO

2nd edition includes 1976 paperbound supplement. 80 localities from all regions of Mexico, including Yucatan. Detailed descriptions of how to get to particular spots, down to dirt roads, canyons, parks. Six maps, 15 pages of illustrations, 970 species listed by region. Written by Ernest P. Edwards.

E 3022. Hardcover. 6" x 9". 417 pages. Ernest P. Edwards. 1968.

CONSERVATION DIRECTORY

23rd edition lists organizations, agencies, and officials concerned with natural resource use and management. Each listing contains address, phone number, description, membership figures, date established and officers. Among listings are bird clubs and wildlife organizations, U.S. federal departments, state and territorial agencies, Canadian government agencies. Edited by Fran Mitchell.

E 3023. Softcover. 8½" x 11". 264 pages. National Wildlife Federation. 1978.

A GUIDE TO NORTH AMERICAN BIRD CLUBS

Over 835 clubs in the 50 states, Canada, Mexico, and Panama, including club locator maps, meeting times and places, membership and newsletter subscription information. Special sections: list of local birding contacts with phones, local bird finding guides. Compiled by Jon E. Rickert.

E 3024. Hardcover. 5½" x 8½". 575 pages. Avian Publications, Inc. 1978.

BIRDS OF THE WORLD: A CHECK LIST

Second edition contains nearly 9000 known species of birds arranged in taxonomic sequence with space for site recording. Listings cover scientific and common names, cross references, world wide range, and status as endangered species. 15 recently discovered species included. No illustrations. Written by James F. Clements.

E 3026. Hardcover. 6½" x 9½". 532 pages. The Two Continents Publishing Group. 1978.

ABA CHECKLIST

Up-to-date list of 794 bird species recorded in continental U.S. and Canada: natives, regular visitors, established introduced species. Common names precede Latin names. Reference list of species recorded less than 10 times in the ABA area during 20th century. Fully indexed.

E 3027. Softcover. 6" x 9½". 64 pages. American Birding Association, 1975.

Location By State

SUPPLEMENT TO BIRDING

Addresses and phone numbers of American Birding Association members in the U.S. and Canada. Divided into two sections: one lists by state and province, the second by members' last names. The two sections are cross referenced. Publications dealing with local areas listed. Brief history of A.B.A.

given. Edited by James A. Tucker.

E 3029. Softcover. 5" x 8". 192 pages. American Briding Association, Inc.. 1976.

ALABAMA BIRDS

Life histories and identification of 378 bird species that range in Alabama. The 662 illustrations include 365 birds in color, 201 black and white photos, and 88 maps. Glossary, history of Alabama ornithology, how to watch and to attract birds, 13-page bibliography, index by Latin and common names. Written by Thomas A. Imhof.

E 3028. Hardcover. 7½" x 10". 541 pages. University of Alabama Press. 1976.

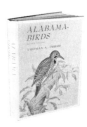

A BIRDER'S GUIDE TO SOUTHEASTERN ARIZONA

Not a field guide—meant for the dedicated, fast-moving birder who wants to know when and where to see as many species as he can. Precise directions with occasional maps and photos. Fully indexed. Companion volumes include The Texas Coast, Eastern Colorado, Texas' Rio Grande Valley, Southern California. Written by James A. Lane.

E 3029. Softcover. 5½" x 8½". 110 pages. L&P Press. 1977.

THE BIRDS OF ARIZONA

Descriptions of more than 400 species, records of sightings, 126 distribution maps. 51 color photographs by Eliot Porter, 12 full-page field sketches in color by George

Miksch Sutton. Eight black and white photos accompany History of Habitats. Written by Allan Phillips, Joe Marshall, and Gale Monson.

E 3030. Hardcover. 9" x 12". 247 pages. University of Arizona Press. 1964.

BIRDS OF NORTHWESTERN CALIFORNIA

Black and white photographs and maps of habitats followed by records of sightings for each species. Not a field guide (no visual or aural descriptions). Indexed both by common and Latin names. Written for the serious birder by Charles F. Yocom and Stanley W. Harris.

E 3031. Softcover. 8½" x 10½". 74 pages. Humboldt State University. 1975.

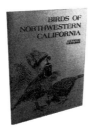

THE BIRDS OF CALIFORNIA

Excellent introduction to bird study, followed by annotated list of 518 species (seasonal status, habitat, range). Last half of book deals with where to see certain birds, arranged by habitat. Over 100 black and white photos taken by author, president of the American Birding Association. Taxonomic checklist, index. Written by Arnold Small.

E 3032. Softcover. 6" x 9". 310 pages. Macmillian Publishing Co. 1974.

GEORGIA BIRDS

General distribution, status in Georgia, and habits and recognition given for the 460 species nesting, wintering, or in transit in the state. Accompanied by 35 full-color paintings by George M. Sutton, 13 black and white photos, 12 distribution maps, and a history of Georgia ornithology. Written by Thomas D. Burleigh.

E 3033. Hardcover. 7½" x 10". 747 pages. University of Oklahoma Press. 1958.

BIRDS OF HAWAII

Revised from the original 1944 edition, this book gives descriptions and habits of all Hawaii's birds, along with alternative names. Rather muddy black and white photographs, full-color plates, by Y. Oda. English and Latin index. Written by George C. Munro.

E 3034. Hardcover. 6" x 9". 192 pages. Charles E. Tuttle Co.. Inc. 1976.

HAWAIIAN BIRDLIFE

Comprehensive survey of all the birds of all the Hawaiian Islands, including the Leeward Islands. Author traces history of native birds and those introduced. Habitat, feeding, and breeding behavior given for all species. Appendices cover migrants and stragglers, escapees. 126 black and white photos, 59 color plates. Written by Andrew J. Berger.

E 3035. Hardcover. 9" x 11". 270 pages. University of Hawaii Press. 1972.

BIRDS OF IDAHO

Few states have a more diversified habitat than Idaho, yet this is the first book to collect details of its birdlife. Sitings given by county, habits listed for each species. 12 color plates, 21 black and white photos. Extensive bibliography. Written by Thomas D. Burleigh, who spent 11 years compiling book.

E 3036. Hardcover. 7" x 10". 467 pages. The Caxton Printers, Ltd. 1972.

KENTUCKY BIRDS

This model book describes every bird in the state (321 species), lists when and where it can be found. There are 239 color photographs of birds. Then 47 birding localities are described, some with maps, all in readable terms, including 9 color photographs. Latin and English index. Written by R.W. Barbour, C.T. Peterson, D. Rust, H.E. Shadowen, A.L. Whitt, Jr.

E 3037. Hardcover. 5½" x 8½". 306 pages. The University Press of Kentucky. 1973.

LOUISIANA BIRDS

Louisiana contains over half the birds (411 species) occurring in the U.S. This 3rd edition describes them, including 99 black and white photos, 147 drawings, 14 full-color plates. First 100 pages introduces ornithology and bird watching. Special summary of seasonal occurrences. Written by George H. Lowery, Jr.

E 3038. Hardcover. 6" x 8½". 651 pages. Louisiana State University Press. 1974.

ENJOYING BIRDS IN MICHIGAN

100 common Michigan birds described and drawn in pen-and-ink. Full color frontispiece of rare Kirtland Warblers by Rober Tory Peterson. Chapters include checklist, special Michigan birds, where to find all birds, how to study and attract them. Detailed maps of 7 Audubon Sanctuaries. 3rd edition edited by William L. Thompson.

E 3039. Softcover. 6″ x 8½″. 80 pages. Michigan Audubon Society. 1973.

MINNESOTA BIRDS—WHERE, WHEN, AND HOW MANY

Migration maps and dates, summer and winter residences given for 374 species. Introduction describes Minnesota's geography and ecology. 20 black and white photographs. Bibliography. Indexed by common name. Written by Janet Green and Robert Janssen.

E 3040. Hardcover. 6″ x 9″. 217 pages. University of Minnesota Press. 1975.

A BIRDER'S BUIDE TO MINNESOTA

This guide to over 150 birding areas contains detailed directions and maps, including official highway map bound into back of book—plus short descriptions of probable birds. Names and phones of enthusiastic Minnesota bird watchers. Indexed by bird, and by location. 6 black and white photos. Written by K.R. Eckert.

E 3041. Softcover. 5½″ x 8½″. 114 pages. Minnesota Ornithologists Union. 1974.

BIRDS OF NEW JERSEY

Well-organized book by the state ornithologist starts with best-bet birding sites (a chapter for each of 8 sites), including birds probably encountered. Bird seasonality, and Christmas bird count, comprise final chapters. Annotated checklist and accidental birds included. 39 black and white photo-

graphs. No index. Written by Charles Leck.

E 3042. Hardcover. 5½″ x 8½″. 190 pages. Rutgers University Press. 1975.

FIFTY COMMON BIRDS OF OKLAHOMA

Includes the Southern Great Plains. Fifty color paintings by author. Text, written for general reader, describes birds' habits, songs and calls, personal observations and anecdotes. Complete list of Oklahoma species in back. Written by George Miksch Sutton, curator of birds at Stovall Museum, University of Oklahoma.

E 3043. Hardcover. 5″ x 8½″. 113 pages. University of Oklahoma Press. 1977.

SOUTH CAROLINA BIRD LIFE

Revised edition surveys over 600 species and subspecies. Gives ranges, probable occurrence, sighting dates, history and status. Cross-referenced supplement contains all ornithological records since 1949. 34 original paintings in color by Francis Lee Jacques, Roger Tory Peterson, Edward S. Dingle and John Henry Dick. Written by Alexander Sprunt, Jr. and E. Burnham Chamberlain.

E 3044. Hardcover. 7½″ x 10″. 669 pages. University of South Carolina Press. 1970.

THE BIRD LIFE OF TEXAS

Massive boxed 2-volume set, with 34 full-page color paintings by Louis Agassiz

Fuertes, 36 black and white reproductions by same artist. Exhaustive descriptions of everything one could want to know about each species. 49-page introduction (with 34 photos), "Ecology of Texas Birds", plus maps. Bibliography and index. Written by Harry C. Oberholser.

E 3045. Hardcover. 9½″ x 12″. 1069 pages. University of Texas Press. 1974.

THE BIRD LIFE OF GREAT SALT LAKE

Describes the life history, ecology, and population trends of the California Gull. (Utah's state bird), White Pelican, Double-crested Cormorant, and Great Blue Heron, together with history of the Bear River Migratory Bird Refuge. Charts, 26 black and white photos. Written by Dr. William H. Behle.

E 3046. Hardcover. 6″ x 9″. 203 pages. University of Utah Press. 1958.

WASHINGTON BIRDS

Where to find and how to identify them. Illustrated with pen-and-ink drawings, 8 color plates. Includes average breeding dates, and factors affecting changes in bird ranges. Written by Earl J. Larrison and Klaus G. Sonnenberg.

E 3047. Softcover. 6″ x 9″. 258 pages. The Seattle Audubon Society, Wash. 1968.

BIRDS OF WISCONSIN

105 full-color, full-page plates of the 328

species known in the state today, and the recent past. Opposite each plate is a silhouette of each bird named in English and Latin, with a map showing its territory, and months it can be seen. Back of book contains 16 habitat paintings. Written and illustrated by Owen J. Gromme.

E 3048. Hardcover. 9½" x 12". 220 pages. University of Wisconsin Press. 1964.

Location By Region

WINTER BIRDS OF THE CAROLINAS AND NEARBY STATES

Strengths of this book are the 104 color photographs taken by author over a period of six years. Each of 86 species described by field marks, length, voice, range, habitat, habits, and author's personal experiences. Equipment used, and location for each photograph given. Written by Michael A. Godfrey.

E 3049. Hardcover. 8½" x 9½". 137 pages. John F. Blair. 1977.

BIRDS OF MINNESOTA AND NEIGHBORING STATES

This identification manual, primarily for use in the home but also in the field, is sparsely illustrated with pen-and-ink drawings, including close-ups of bills and feet. Seasonal plumages, downy and juvenal stages, tip-to-tail measurements described. Written by Thomas S. Roberts, M.D.

E 3050. Softcover. 6" x 9". 298 pages. University of Minnesota Press. 1955.

Photo not available.

FAMILIAR BIRDS OF THE PACIFIC SOUTHWEST

Originally published in 1935, this book is in its 6th printing. Size and color keys lead to full behavior, habitat, and appearance descriptions. 132 species. The 102 old color photographs have grown muddy. Written by Florence Van Vechten Dickey.

E 3051. Hardcover. 5" x 7". 241 pages. Stanford University Press. 1958.

BIRDS OF THE WEST COAST

52 species of birds frequenting North America's Pacific Coast, each represented in full color with accompanying text by the painter. Four fold-out double pages. 46 pages of sketches. Indexed by common and Latin name. Written by J. Fenwick Landsdowne.

E 3052. Hardcover. 10½" x 14". 176 pages. Houghton Mifflin Company. 1976.

BIRDS OF THE WEST

Organized by habitat, the more-than 200 species that range the 13 western states are briefly described, and shown in color photographs taken by the authors. Each bird likened in size to sparrow, robin, or crow. 13 introductory pages on behavior and classification. Latin and common name index. Written by Herbert Clarke and Arnold Small.

E 3053. Hardcover. 9½" x 12½". 192 pages. A.S. Barnes and Co., Inc. 1976.

BIRDS OF WESTERN NORTH AMERICA

Fifty full-page, full-color portraits of non-passeriformes (non-perching or non-singing) birds by Kenneth L. Carlson, including Trumpeter Swan, Prairie Falcon, Elegant Tern. Each accompanied by mood-setting text with description of habits. Seven page introduction gives concise whys and hows of bird watching. Written by Laurence C. Binford.

E 3054. Hardcover. 9½" x 12½". 223 pages. Macmillan Publishing Co., Inc. 1974.

A NATURALIST'S GUIDE TO ONTARIO

Along with maps and descriptions of the flora, fauna, and geology of Ontario, Canada, this book contains over forty guides to particular spots, with details of how to get there. Indexed both geographically and by species. Illustrated with maps and full-page drawings. Edited by W.W. Judd and J. Murray Speirs.

E 3055. Softcover. 6" x 9". 210 pages. University of Toronto Press. 1965.

BIRDS OF ONTARIO AND QUEBEC

Survey of birding, locales, probable species, clubs to join, and a checklist. Generalized information about birds, plus the various bird groups. Over 100 black and white photos, and 25 color photos, highlight book. Index simplifies complicated layout. Written by David Hancock and James Woodford.

E 3056. Hardcover. 7" x 10". 68 pages. General Publishing Co., Ltd. 1973

BIRDS OF ALBERTA, SASKATCHEWAN AND MANITOBA

First three-fourths of book same as *Birds of Ontario & Quebec* (generalized information on classification, flight, nests; how to go about bird watching and bird recording; the main groups of birds—all accompanied by color and black and white photos.) Last part of book devoted to local birding sites. Written by David Hancock and Jim Woodford.

E 3057. Hardcover. 7″ x 10″. 68 pages. General Publishing Co., Ltd. 1973.

BIRDS OF THE EASTERN FOREST

Birds stretching from the Great Lakes to the Gulf of St. Lawrence—18 waterfowl and shore birds, 10 birds of prey, 5 woodpeckers, 19 others. Unique format gives artist J. Fenwick Lansdowne's sketches from life, then a page of text, faced by full-color painting rendered from sketch. Written by John A. Livingston.

E 3058. Hardcover. 10″ x 13″. 232 pages. Houghton Mifflin Company. 1968.

BIRDS OF THE NORTHERN FOREST

56 species of birds seen mostly in Canada (not the arctic portions) and the northern United States. Unique format gives artist J. Fenwick Landsdown's sketches from life, then a page of text, faced by full-color painting rendered from sketch. Bibliography, index. Written by John A. Livingston.

E 3059. Hardcover. 10″ x 13″. 247 pages. Houghton Mifflin Company. 1966.

A GUIDE TO BIRD FINDING EAST OF THE MISSISSIPPI

An expansion of the classic 1st edition (1951), with drawings by George Miksch Sutton. Bird lists and geographical descriptions for each of the sites near 148 cities in 26 states, with explicit highway directions. Special chapter on New York City. Indexed by site and species. Written by Olin Sewall Pettingill, Jr.

E 3060. Hardcover. 5½″ x 8½″. 689 pages. Oxford University Press. 1977.

AUDUBON LAND BIRD GUIDE

Covers birds of eastern and central North America from southern Texas to central Greenland. 275 species described, including habits, voice, nest, location, eggs, and range. 400 full color illustrations show males, females, immatures, and juveniles. Sponsored by National Audubon Society. Written by Richard H. Pough.

E 3061. Hardcover. 5″ x 7½″. 312 pages. Doubleday & Company, Inc. 1949.

North America

WILD BIRDS OF THE AMERICAS

Sixty-seven color portraits (mostly close-ups of heads and feet), 110 black and white sketches, drawn from 47 years experience as a field ornithologist. Easy-readin text taken mostly from personal observations. Glossary, index to illustrations. Written by Terence Michael Shortt.

E 3062. Hardcover. 7½″ x 9½″. 272 pages. Houghton Mifflin Company. 1977.

BIRDS

129 of the most familiar American birds in color. Range maps show summer, winter, all-year residences. Charts give data on migration, eggs, nests, food. Supplements include museums, zoos, refuges, bird classification, bird watching, banding. Written by Ira N. Gabrielson, former director, U.S. Fish and Wildlife Service.

E 3063. Pocketbook. 4″ x 6″. 160 pages. Golden Press. 1956.

BIRD PORTRAITS IN COLOR

295 North American species by 561 figures in 92 full-color watercolor plates. Artists include George Miksch Sutton and Louis Agassiz Fuertes. Opposite each plate occur description of birds' habitat, appearance, and song. Common and Latin name index. Written by Thomas S. Roberts, M.D.

E 3064. Hardcover. 8½″ x 11″. 107 pages. University of Minnesota Press. 1968.

BIRDS OF NORTH AMERICA

First-hand account of the 600+ species of regular-occurring birds in the United States and Canada. Illustrated with 119 photographs, 66 in color. Bird behavior stressed, including courtship, mating, migration, feeding habits, flight, and present status. Written by Dr. Austin L. Rand of Chicago Field Museum.

E 3065. Hardcover. 6″ x 9″. 256 pages. Doubleday & Company, Inc. No publication date given.

BIRDS OF AMERICA

This reprint of the 1917 classic includes chapters on migration and how to stalk birds. Treats every North American species by other names, general description, color, nest and eggs, distribution. 100's of black and white photos, 111 full color plates by Louis Agassiz Fuertes. Edited by T. Gilbert Pearson, 1st president of National Audubon Society.

E 3066. Hardcover. 8″ x 11″. 1021 pages. Doubleday & Company, Inc. 1936.

AMERICAN BIRDS

120 species photographed in full color, with brief descriptions. Organized according to family. Introductory material includes guidelines to bird watching, North American life zones, bird names and groupings, adaptations, where to go. Index by common name only. Written by Roland C. Clement, vice president, National Audubon Society.

E 3067. Pocketbook. 4″ x 7″. 159 pages. Bantam Books. 1973.

BIRDS

Personal experiences with 44 species of birds often encountered in the U.S. and Canada, one chapter/species, each accompanied by at least one black and white photograph (83 photos in all). Birds include Whooping Crane, Northern Oriole, Horned Grebe, Turkey Vulture, Canada Goose, Killdeer. Index. Written by R.D. Lawrence.

E 3068. Softcover. 5″ x 8″. 256 pages. Chilton Book Co. 1974.

LAMBERT'S BIRDS OF GARDEN AND WOODLAND

Fifty-nine birds of Britain—wren, blackbird, robin, the thrushes; kestril, pigeons and doves, owls, woodpeckers, warblers, tits, finches, flycatchers; starling, hedge and house sparrows; rook, magpie, jay and jackdaw—are described and illustrated. Information on habitat, range, voice and nesting habits. Paintings by Terrance Lambert. Written by Alan Mitchell.

E 3069. Hardcover. 7½″ x 11″. 128 pages. Charles Scribner's Sons. 1976.

BIRDS OF TOWN AND VILLAGE

A record, in word and picture, of 56 British birds. Basil Ede's 36 paintings, specially commissioned, show the birds in typical surroundings. Haunts, appearance, voice, and nesting habits described. Foreword by H.R.H. Prince Philip, Duke of Edinburgh. Written by W.D. Campbell.

E 3070. Hardcover. 9″ x 11½″. 155 pages. Country Life Books, Hamlyn Publishing Group Limited. 1977.

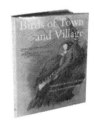

PORTRAITS OF MEXICAN BIRDS

Fifty full-color paintings done from life by the author, each accompanied by a page of text telling, in first-hand narrative, how the author found the bird. Paintings span 35 years. Foliage is prominent. Written by George Miksch Sutton, curator of birds at University of Oklahoma.

E 3071. Hardcover. 11½″ x 14″. 106 pages. University of Oklahoma Press. 1975.

BIRDS OF THE WORLD IN FIELD AND GARDEN

Fifty full-color photographs of a smattering of birds, mostly common. Each photo accompanied by a 250-word description of the bird, where it is found, and its call. Both common and scientific names given. Written by Klaus Paysan.

E 3072. Hardcover. 9½″ x 8½″. 108 pages. Lerner Publications Company. 1974.

THE DELL ENCYCLOPEDIA OF BIRDS

More than 641 entries with 395 color illustrations of birds. Extensive write-ups on anatomy, behavior, breeding, and migration, plus biographical notes on 63 ornithologists of the past. 400 bird species described. Written by Bertel Bruun.

E 3073. Pocketbook. 4½″ x 7″. 240 pages. Dell Publishing Co. 1974.

FAMILIES OF BIRDS

Thumbnail sketches of the 208 bird families (172 living, 36 fossil) into which scientists group 9,600 known species (8,700 living, 900 fossil). Designed for those who wish to know more about bird relationships. Full color paintings, with feet and bill close-ups. Distribution, characteristics, habits. Written by Oliver L. Austin, Jr.

E 3074. Pocketbook. 4″ x 6″. 200 pages. Golden Press. 1971.

THE AUDUBON SOCIETY BOOK OF WILD BIRDS

Sea, shore, pond, meadow, tropical forest, tundra, wader, reed upland birds, and birds of prey are organized by habitat and life styles. 203 color photographs of 174 species captured in detail by 67 outstanding bird photographers. Detailed descriptive text accompanies each chapter. Written by Les Line, Editor of Audubon magazine, and Franklin Russell.

E 3079. Hardcover. 9½" x 12". 292 pages. Harry N. Abrams, Inc. 1976.

LIVING BIRDS OF THE WORLD

Combination coffee-table book and naturalist's guide, with 400 illustrations, 217 in color. Migration and homing activities, hibernation, the effects of radiation, the use of tools, bizarre methods of hunting are all covered. Written by E. Thomas Gilliard, former Associate Curator of Birds, American Museum of Natural History.

E 3076. Hardcover. 8½" x 11". 400 pages. Doubleday & Co., Inc. 1967.

Birds By Type

BIRDS OF PREY

A study of the Order of Falconiformes, their relationship with their habitats and the animals or carrion upon which they feed. Chapters on conservation and ecology of predation. 48 full-color and 50 black and white photographs. 24 black and white line drawings by Ian Willis. Indexed. Written by Leslie Brown.

E 3077. Hardcover. 7" x 9½". 256 pages. A & W Publishers, Inc. 1977.

THE MAGNIFICENT BIRDS OF PREY

Covers owls, ospreys, buteos, kites, eagles, falcons—discusses their flight, ranges, display behavior, courtship, nesting, and territories. Chapter devoted to reviving sport of falconry. 34 drawings and black and white photos. Written by Dr. Philip S. Callahan.

E 3078. Hardcover. 6" x 9". 190 pages. Holiday House. 1974.

BIRDS OF PREY

Covers every genus of the Order of Falconiformes. Outlines perilous position of birds of prey today; considers possible solutions. 130 full color photographs, 2 maps, 3 line drawings. Full list of species, giving both scientific and common names. Fully indexed. Foreword by Peter Conder, Director of the Royal Society for the Protection of Birds. Written by Michael Everett.

E 3079. Hardcover. 9" x 12". 128 pages. G.P. Putnam's Sons. No publication date given.

A GUIDE TO EASTERN HAWK WATCHING

Book divided into sections on hawk identification (each species described and photographed), the mechanics of hawk flight (with drawings), and detailed descriptions of where to go in 22 states and eastern Canada to see hawks. Good condensed stuff on field

equipment and migration seasons. Written by Donald S. Heintzelman.

E 3080. Softcover. 5" x 8½". 99 pages. Pennsylvania State University Press. 1976.

AUTUMN HAWK FLIGHTS (IN EASTERN NORTH AMERICA)

Chapters on how to study and identify hawks are followed by description of sightings at 123 locations, including states as far west as Texas, and down into Mexico and Central America. Anatomy, migration routes, daily rhythms, and evolution also covered. 88 black and white photos, 48 maps. Written by Donald S. Heintzelman.

E 3081. Hardcover. 6½" x 9½". 399 pages. Rutgers University Press. 1975.

EAGLES OF THE WORLD

Surveys the four main groups of eagles: fishing, serpent, buteonine and booted eagles. Appendix summarizes data given throughout the book, with specialized coverage of the African Fish Eagle. Cross indexed. 38 black and white photographs, and 15 line drawings and charts. Written by Leslie Brown.

E 3082. Hardcover. 7" x 9". 224 pages. Universe Books. 1976.

OWLS OF NORTH AMERICA

All the species and subspecies of owls north of Mexico. Described by features, flight pattern, legs, feet, talons, eyes and ears, plumage, voice, sex differences, longevity, markings, habits, habitat, enemies, courtship, food gathering, nesting habits, eggs,

family life. 59 full page color plates, lots of drawings. Written by Allan W. Eckert.

E 3083. Hardcover. 9½" x 12½". 336 pages. Doubleday & Company, Inc. 1974.

GAMEBIRDS

With 266 illustrations in color, local names, weights, flight speeds and migration habits given for each species of North American game bird. Nesting habits, visual descriptions included. Introductory sections on classification, migration, banding, and National Refuge Systems. Written by Alexander Sprunt IV and Herbert S. Zim.

E 3084. Pocketbook. 4" x 6". 160 pages. Golden Press. 1961.

NORTH AMERICAN GAME BIRDS

33 species of non-waterfowl game birds described and shown in pen-and-ink drawings, black and white and color photographs. Field marks, age and sex criteria, habitat and foods, social behavior, reproductive biology, and range (including maps) given for each species. Written by Paul A. Johnsgard.

E. 3085. Softcover. 5½" x 8½". 183 pages. University of Nebraska Press. 1975.

GROUSE AND QUAILS OF NORTH AMERICA

25 species treated, partridges included. Ranges, identification in the hand and in the field, summaries of ecology and breeding biology (including mating rituals) given.

140 color plates, black and white photos, sonagrams of calls. Index, extensive bibliography. Written by Paul A. Johnsgard.

E 3086. Hardcover. 8" x 10". 553 pages. University of Nebraska Press. 1973.

TRAVELS AND TRADITIONS OF WATERFOWL

Waterfowl refers to North American ducks, geese, and swans. Both migration, and movement in a limited area are discussed. Book recommended by American Association for Advancement of Science. 7-page index, 24-page bibliography. Drawings and maps. Written by H. Albert Hochbaum, director of Manitoba's Waterfowl Research Station.

E 3087. Softcover. 7" x 10". 301 pages. University of Minnesota Press. 1955.

WATERFOWL: THEIR BIOLOGY AND NATURAL HISTORY

With 148 photographs, 59 in color, and 16 pages of figures, author pictures all species of world's waterfowl, including extinct forms. Non-technical but authoritative text, plus key to identification. Section on endangered species. Written by Paul A. Johnsgard.

E 3088. Hardcover. 7½" x 10". 138 pages. University of Nebraska Press. 1968.

THE SWANS

Each of the eight swan species pictured and described. Subsequent chapters treat swan distribution, feeding habits, reproduction, art and mythology, exploitation, and conservation. Eight appendices include life expectancy and egg weight. 48 pages of black and white photographs, over 100 drawings. Edited by Peter Scott.

E 3089. Hardcover. 8½" x 10". 242 pages. Houghton Mifflin Company. 1972.

BIRDS OF SEA, SHORE & STREAM

Mainly a book of color photographs of penguins, pelicans, loons, albatrosses and other forms around the world. Excerpts from Thoreau's *Walden*, Coleridge's *Ancient Mariner*, Lorenz' *King Solomon's Ring*, Audubon's *Canada Goose*. Index of common names only. Written by Will Bradbury.

E 3090. Hardcover. 9½" x 10½". 128 pages. Time-Life Films. 1976.

WATER BIRDS OF CALIFORNIA

Pen-and-ink drawings and 12 color plates help describe 165 species, all identified by visual description, habits, voice, and range. Introductory chapters treat feeding, flocking, migration, nesting, habitat use, conservation, techniques in observation and record keeping. Written by Howard L. Cogswell.

E 3091. Softcover. 4½" x 8". 399 pages. University of California Press. 1977.

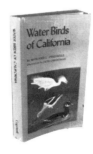

BIRDS OF FIELD & FOREST

Magnificent color photographs of peacocks, pheasants, eagles, falcons, owls, hummingbirds, parrots, pigeons, woodpeckers, cranes. Text is secondary. Literary selections by Ben Franklin, John J. Audubon, James Thurber. Index by common names only. Written by Peter Wood.

E 3092. Hardcover. 9½" x 10½". 128 pages. Time-Life Films. 1977.

GUIDE TO THE PIGEONS OF THE WORLD

Illustrated history of man's use of pigeons is followed by chapters on anatomy, breeding and rearing, showing, flying and racing, designs for pigeon houses. Rest of book describes 55 breeds—more than 175 varieties—each illustrated in full color. History emphasized throughout. Bibliography, index. Written by Andrew McNeillie.

E 3093. Softcover. 4½" x 7½". 160 pages. Distributed by Two Continents Publishing. 1976.

CROWS, JAYS, RAVENS AND THEIR RELATIVES

Members of the crow family (Corvidae) are the most intelligent of birds, yet have been little written about. This world-survey rectifies that. Distribution and habits featured. Maps, black and white photos, and drawings accompany text. Indexed by behavior and by name. Written by Sylvia Bruce Wilmore.

E 3094. Hardcover. 5½" x 8½". 208 pages. Paul S. Eriksson. 1977.

THE LIFE OF THE ROBIN

Authoritative study of Britain's most popular bird, told in readable style, garnished with 22 drawings and quotations from literature. Contents of 4th edition include song, fighting, courtship, nesting, migration, age, feeding, territory. Includes how to tame a robin and a digression upon instinct. Fully

indexed. Written by David Lack.

E 3095. Hardcover. 5½" x 8½". 240 pages. Distributed in U.S. by Beekman Publishers, Inc. 1976.

THE AMERICAN ROBIN

Subtitled "A Backyard Institution", this readable book, based on six years' study, describes the Robin's success as a species, its distribution and its habits—migration, mating, nesting and feeding. Scattered pen-and-ink drawings, 9 full-color photographs. Written by Leonard A. Eiserer, a psychologist.

E 3096. Hardcover. 8½" x 8½". 175 pages. Nelson-Hall. 1976.

THE LARKS

Professional poet's prose narrative about his experience with two horned larks (Eremophila alpestris), including observations of nesting habits and rearing of young. Large print, pen-and-ink drawings. Written by George Abbe.

E 3097. Softcover. 5" x 8". 144 pages. William L. Bauhan. 1974.

Biology

FUNDAMENTALS OF ORNITHOLOGY

This updated 2nd edition of the 1959 text contains over 500 black and white photos and drawings. Subjects include origins, behavior, voice, flight and flightlessness, feeding, distribution, and courtship. Each of the 168 bird families gets its page. Written by Josselyn Van Tyne and Andrew J. Berger, editors of The Wilson Bulletin.

E 3098. Hardcover. 6" x 9½". 808 pages. John Wiley & Sons. 1976.

THE LIFE OF BIRDS

Twin aims of this 2nd edition are to present the basic facts of bird biology, and to arouse enthusiasm in reader for the amazing things birds do. Author claims he surveyed 14,000 articles and books to compile this well-illustrated textbook. 44-page bibliography, 33-page index. Written by Joel Carl Welty.

E 3099. Hardcover. 8" x 10½". 623 pages. W.B. Saunders Co. 1975.

BIRD LIFE

Scientific study of the activities of birds; evolution and spead, courtship and display, nest building, self defence, flight and migration. 144 color plates. Fully indexed. 10 page introduction by Noble Prize winner Konrad Lorenz analyzes bird behavior. Written by Jurgen Nicolai.

E 3100. Hardcover. 9½" x 12". 224 pages. G.P. Putnam's Sons. 1977.

BIRDS THEIR LIFE THEIR WAYS THEIR WORLD

Discusses all aspects of avian biology, including evolution, anatomy, feeding, habitats, social behavior, breeding and migration. Birds depicted are common European and American species, as well as African, Australian, South American and Asian. 29 full page color illustrations, plus hundreds of others, by Ad Cameron. Written by Dr. Christopher Perrins.

E 3101. Hardcover. 9½" x 12". 160 pages. Harry N. Abrams, Inc. 1976.

BIRD BEHAVIOR

This easily-read treatise on the psychology of birds has a goal in mind: to induce more people to study them. Laced with personal anecdotes, topics include territory, defense, reproduction, bird song, nesting, and how to have fun with birds. 73 black and white photos and drawings. Written by Philip S. Callahan.

E 3102. Hardcover. 6½" x 9". 188 pages. Four Winds Press. 1975.

LIFE HISTORIES OF NORTH AMERICAN BIRDS OF PREY IN TWO VOLUMES

Originally Bulletin 170 of the Smithsonian Institution, 1937. An encyclopedic collection of information on more than 100 different subspecies of hawks, eagles, falcons, buzzards, condors and owls. Supplemented by 197 full-page plates containing 400 black and white photographs. Indexed for each volume. Extensive bibliographies. Written by Arthur Cleveland Bent.

E 3103. Softcover. 5" x 8½". 907 pages. Dover Publications. 1961.

AVIAN BIOLOGY

This collection of scientific papers by world-famous ornithologists summarizes what's now known, and defines research problems for the years ahead in these areas: flight mechanics, migration, daily and yearly rhythms, vocal behavior, incubation, zoogeography. Thorough index. Edited by

Donald S. Farner and James R. King.

E 3104. Hardcover. 6½" x 9". 523 pages. Academic Press. 1975.

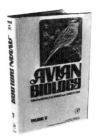

GROWING WINGS

Written with a flair for drama, book gives different birds' struggles to get through a bird year. Subjects include spring and fall migrations, territory, courtship, nest building, fertilization, hatching, independence, flocking, wintering. Pen and ink drawings. Written by Sarita Van Vleck.

E 3105. Softcover. 6" x 9". 141 pages. William L. Bauhan. 1977.

PARENT BIRDS AND THEIR YOUNG

Organized by subject rather than by bird type, this world-wide survey of family life and reproductive behavior starts at the formation of pairs, ends at the attainment of independence. How chicks escape the shell, how they interrelate given special treatment. 119 black and white photos, 21 page bibliography. Written by Alexander F. Skutch.

E 3106. Hardcover. 9" x 11". 503 pages. University of Texas Press. 1975.

BREEDING BIOLOGY OF BIRDS

Proceedings of a symposium on breeding behavior and reproductive physiology. Topics discussed are nutrition, role of the environment, reproductive endocrinology. Changes in the breeding bird fauna of North Europe, and disparate sex rations in water-

fowl also discussed. Graphs and diagrams. Edited by Donald S. Farner.

E 3107. Softcover. 6" x 9". 515 pages. National Academy of Sciences. 1973.

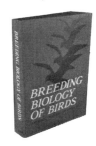

BORN TO SING

This interpretation and world survey of bird song covers the "whys" of animal music in general, compares bird song to human music, describes bird songs and calls, and talks about the monotony threshold. Both well-equipped and less-well-equipped singers individually discussed. Glossary and index. Written by Charles Hartshorne.

E 3108. Hardcover. 6½" x 9½". 304 pages. Indiana University Press. 1973.

HOW BIRDS FLY

An account of bird flight in all its aspects; flapping, soaring, gliding, dynamic soaring, hovering, and underwater flight. Chapters on the development, height, speed and unusual maneuvers of bird flight. Tables give wingspans, weights, and body lengths. 14 line drawings. Nine page bibliography. Fully indexed. Written by John K. Terres.

E 3109. Softcover. 6" x 9". 177 pages. Hawthorn Books, Inc. 1968.

Bird Care

THE HUNGRY BIRD BOOK

Adapted from the British *Bird-Table Book*, uses American birds, insects, flowers. Easy-going information on how to feed, water, house, and protect birds. Appendices include how to treat casualties. Pen-and-ink drawings. Written by Robert Arbib (editor, *American Birds*) and Tony Soper.

E 3110. Hardcover. 5½" x 8½". 126 pages. Taplinger Publishing Co. 1971.

HOW TO ATTRACT, HOUSE AND FEED BIRDS

50 descriptions of plants that attract birds, 17 feeder plans, 30 house plans, plus directions on how to mix your own food. Ways of providing water, tips for bird watching, caring for sick birds also included. Black and white photos are muddy, but drawings and plans are clear. Written by Walter E. Schutz.

E 3111. Softcover. 7" x 10". 196 pages. Macmillan Publishing Co., Inc. 1974.

SONG BIRDS IN YOUR GARDEN

Third edition details the methods used to attract birds for hand feeding. Includes information on bird food, regional plant listings, nesting records for city and rural birds of U.S. and Canada, descriptions of nests. Appendix gives life spans of 60 birds. Introduction by Edwin Way Teale. Illustrated by Matthew Kalmenoff. Written by John K. Terres.

E 3112. Softcover. 6" x 9". 301 pages. Hawthorn Books, Inc. 1977.

THE COMPLETE BOOK OF BIRDHOUSES AND FEEDERS

Plans for six houses and two feeders given.

Rest of book devoted to 15 birds and what they eat. Hand-lettered text somewhat difficult to read. Large, cross-hatched pen-and-ink drawings. Written by Monica Russo and Robert Dewire.

E 3113. Softcover. 8" x 11". 128 pages. Drake Publishers, Inc. 1976.

102 BIRD HOUSES, FEEDERS YOU CAN MAKE

House designs for 26 species (several designs per species), including woodpeckers, owls, swallows, bluebird, Robin, hawks, and Wood Duck. Dozens of feeders. Simple, full-page plans. 11 black and white photos. Written by Hi Sibley.

E 3114. Softcover. 8½" x 11". 96 pages. Goodheart-Wilcox Co., Inc. 1976.

BIRD FEEDERS AND SHELTERS

Describes and illustrates bird feeders, shelters and boxes. Gives bird house dimensions and instructions for accommodating bluebirds, wrens, chickadees, swallows, Screech Owls and Crested Flycatchers. Chapters on how to provide water, food, and cover for backyard bird sanctuaries. 47 pages of black and white drawings by Leon A. Hausman. Written by Ted S. Pettit.

E 3115. Hardcover. 7" x 9". 80 pages. G.P. Putnam's Sons. 1970.

HOW TO ATTRACT BIRDS

Describes various bird foods, tells what to feed birds in fall, winter, and spring. Tells

what bushes and trees to plant to attract birds to the garden. Easy-to-make feeders and houses shown in line drawings. Section devoted to baths and fountains. Color key for easy bird identification. Written by Leon Hausman.

E 3116. Softcover. 5" x 8". 127 pages. Cornerstone Library. 1976.

KNOW YOUR WILD BIRDS

Simplified text covers subjects of bird watching, feeding, birdhouses, nest materials, hummingbirds, pedators, bird pests, raising young birds, and making pets of wild birds. Illustrated with 40 color photographs. Edited by Earl Schneider.

E 3117. Softcover. 5½" x 8". 64 pages. The Pet Library Ltd. No publication date given.

BIRDS IN YOUR BACKYARD

Not copiously illustrated, this book contains so much data you don't miss pictures. Subjects in this 4th edition include hummingbirds, attracting birds with sound, regional lists of favored plantings, how to build a bluebird trail, food you can make, care of young birds. Written by Clarence Waverly Darragh.

E 3117½. Softcover. 7" x 10". 286 pages. Julian Press. 1976.

Photo not available.

Preservation

FEATHER FASHIONS AND BIRD PRESERVATION

Story of the world's first widespread conservation movement, to protect birds against the millinery trade. Covers 19th and early 20th centuries. Includes short biographies of well-known naturalists, histories of bird-protection societies. 12 photographs of ladies' hats and anti-millinery cartoons. Written by Robin W. Doughty.

E 3118. Hardcover. 6" x 9½". 184 pages. University of California Press.

THEY SAVED OUR BIRDS

This history of bird-killing in the United States deals with the women who bought dead birds for their hats, ornithologists who shot birds to study or paint them, birds used as food, and birds kept as pets. The book's second half is devoted to birds we are trying to save now. Six photographs. Written by Helen Ossa.

E 3119. Hardcover. 5½" x 8½". 287 pages. Hippocrene Books. 1973.

BIRDS IN PERIL

Half a million species of birds have come and gone since *Archeopteryx* 140 million years ago, leaving a mere 8,600 species alive today. Author devotes a chapter each to 20 of these, giving history, life cycle, cause for decline, and the probable future. Black and white and color illustrations by Terence

Shortt. Written by John P.S. Mackenzie.

E 3120. Hardcover. 6½" x 9½". 191 pages. Houghton Mifflin Company. 1977.

TO SAVE A BIRD IN PERIL

Author writes of 10 North American species and subspecies whose number fell below 50 birds, and what was—and is being—done about it. Birds include the Osprey, the Whooping Crane, the Cahow, the Nene Goose, the Peregrine Falcon, Kirtland's Warbler. Each accompanied by drawing, and map of breeding area. Index. Written by David R. Zimmerman.

E 3121. Hardcover. 6" x 9". 286 pages. Coward, McCann & Geoghegan. 1975.

EXTINCT AND VANISHING BIRDS OF THE WORLD

Since disappearance of the Dodo 280 years ago, 130 species and subspecies have gone or are going. This book describes all of them, with details about where they lived. 36 steel engravings accompany text. 46 page bibliography. Appendix gives museums where extinct birds can be seen. Written by James C. Greenway, Jr.

E 3122. Softcover. 5" x 8". 520 pages. Dover Publications, Inc. 1967.

Literature

ORNITHOLOGY FROM ARISTOTLE TO THE PRESENT

Anecdotes, quotes, and free-flowing narrative keep lively this account of man's attempt to classify birds. One chapter devoted to effect of evolution, another to the French scholar and charlatan, Francois Levaillant (he glued feathers on birds to claim new species). Epilogue on American ornithology. No illustrations. Written by Erwin Stresemann, translated by Ernst Mayr.

E 3123. Hardcover. 6½" x 9½". 432 pages. Harvard University Press. 1975.

MOMENTS OF DISCOVERY: ADVENTURES WITH AMERICAN BIRDS

Excellent but too-brief history of American ornithology from 18th century to present, followed by 72 breath-taking color photographs by Eliot Porter. Quotations by well-known naturalists of the past accompany photographs. Index. Written by Michael Harwood.

E 3124. Hardcover. 15" x 10½". 120 pages. E.P. Dutton. 1977.

THE WORLD OF ROGER TORY PETERSON

The first biography of the grand old man of bird watchers, from the beginnings through his third marriage. Fast-moving narrative illustrated by Peterson's drawings, 16 full-color paintings, 30 photos of people in his life. Fully indexed. Written by John C. Devlin and Grace Naismith.

E 3125. Hardcover. 6½" x 9½". 300 pages. New York Times Books. 1977.

AUDUBON IN FLORIDA

Contains the research and illustrations done by John J. Audubon in Florida during 1831 and 1832. Included is a biography tracing his travels, with excerpts from letters and journals. 21 black and white photographs. 61 black and white renditions of Audubon paintings. Fully indexed.

Introduced and organized by Kathryn Hall Proby.

E 3126. Hardcover. 6½" x 9½". 384 pages. University of Miami Press. 1974.

THE BIRDS OF JOHN BURROUGHS

Eleven essays collected from naturalist Burroughs' 84-year life. Forty-one birds mentioned—helpful list gives modern equivalents to the 19th century bird names. 30-page introduction to Burroughs' philosophy and life. Nine black and white drawings by Louis Agassiz Fuertes. Bibliography. Editing and introduction by Jack Kligerman.

E 3127. Softcover. 5½" x 8". 240 pages. Hawthorn Books, Inc. 1976.

BIRDS IN LEGEND, FABLE AND FOLKLORE

Chapter subjects include a primitive view of the Origin of Species, birds in Christian tradition, the folklore of migration, birds as national emblems. Lots of American Indian legends. 5-page bibliography. Indexed by type of bird. No illustrations. Written by Ernest Ingersoll.

E 3128. Hardcover. 5½" x 8". 292 pages. Singing Tree Press. 1923 reprint.

THE POETRY OF BIRDS

Forty four poems, mostly complete, by well-known authors (W.B. Yeats' "The Wild Swans at Coole", Shelley's "To a Skylark", etc.), each illustrated by full-page, quality reproduction of work by well-known artist

(Audubon, Durer, Tiepolo, etc.). Four color plates. Edited by Samuel Carr.

E 3129. Hardcover. 5½" x 8½". 88 pages. Taplinger Publishing Co., Inc. 1976.

THE THIRD BIRD-WATCHER'S BOOK

This anthology includes the following pieces: The Changing Image of the British Ornithologists' Union, Feeding Niches of Seabirds, Wild Geese on Farmland, The Flyway Concept, African Inland Bird Observatory, Titmice in the Garden. Black and white photographs. Edited by John Gooders.

E 3130. Hardcover. 5½" x 8½". 160 pages. David & Charles Publishers. 1976.

THE COUNTRYMAN BIRD BOOK

Gleanings from Britain's *Countryman Magazine*, short essays and poems about birds, organized by bird name in alphabetical order. Illustrated with black and white photographs, and drawings. Selections include No Honor Among Crows, Rare Birds in Texas, Lincolnshire Swifts, Speed Among Swans. Edited by Bruce and Margaret Campbell.

E 3131. Hardcover. 5½" x 8½". 194 pages. David & Charles Publishers. 1974.

A TREASURY OF BIRDLORE

This anthology contains writings by well-known American ornithologists and naturalists, past and present, from the 18th

century's Mark Catesby writing about the Bald Eagle to our own century's George Mitsch Sutton writing about Roadrunners. 85 selections, plus 32 pages of black and white photos and prints. Edited by Joseph Wood Krutch and Paul S. Eriksson.

E 3132. Softcover. 6" x 9". 390 pages. Paul S. Eriksson. 1977.

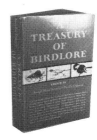

BIRD TALK

Personal observations of birds seen near Shreveport, Louisiana, by a long-time watcher, written in folksy tone but crammed with facts and illustrated by ink drawings. Originally were monthly articles in the *Shreveport Times*. Written by Caroline Dormon.

E 3133. Hardcover. 5½" x 8½". 122 pages. Claitor's Publishing Division. 1969.

WINGSPREAD—A WORLD OF BIRDS

Written in first person narrative, with 69 crisp black and white photos, this book deals with 16 unusual North American birds, including the albatross, the loon, the trumpeter swan, the osprey, the wild turkey, the condor, the Peregrine Falcon, the Arctic Tern, the Prairie Chicken. No index. Written by George Laycock.

E 3134. Hardcover. 6½" x 9½". 125 pages. Four Winds Press. 1972.

THE ADVENTURE OF BIRDS

Personal, but well-researched, inquiry into

what makes birds so appealing to so many people. The major subjects—migration, anatomy, classification, habits—tucked painlessly into narrative rhythms. 14 drawings by Matthew Kalmenoff. Bibliography, index. Written by Charlton Ogburn.

E 3135. Hardcover. 6½" x 9½". 381 pages. William Morrow and Company, Inc. 1976.

WINGS UPON THE HEAVENS

Discursive text records a naturalist's personal observations, with religious overtones. Book's impact comes from 31 full-page, full-color bird paintings (not related to text) by Richard Sloan. 200-word captions describe each bird's habits, often adding historical anecdotes. Written by Mark Clifford Brunner.

E 3136. Hardcover. 8½" x 11½". 78 pages. Ideals Publishing Corp. 1976.

THE VIEW FROM GREAT GULL

Carefully written account, posing as a diary, of six months spent at the ornithological research station on Great Gull Island, in Long Island Sound. Intensity, loneliness, and concern for both avians and homo sapiens recall Loren Eisley's books. Delicate pen-and-ink drawings. Written by historian Michael Harwood.

E 3137. Hardcover. 5½" x 8½". 139 pages. E.P. Dutton & Co., Inc. 1976.

THE VIEW FROM HAWK MOUNTAIN

Narrative of one man's discovery of bird watching. Focuses on Hawk Mountain Bird Sanctuary, the only place in the Northeast where the migration of birds of prey has been observed on a daily basis throughout the fall for 40 years. Its history, birds (broadwings, redtails, sharpskins, roughlegs) and present status are thoroughly discussed.

E 3138. Softcover. 5½" x 8". 191 pages. Charles Scribner's Sons. 1973.

ICELAND SUMMER—ADVENTURES OF A BIRD PAINTER

Engaging story of summer spent with the Olin Pettingills, recording birds with pen and brush. Black and white drawings, five color plates, eight black and white photos. Author was knighted by Iceland upon publication. Written by George Miksch Sutton.

E 3139. Hardcover. 6" x 9". 254 pages. University of Oklahoma Press. 1974.

AT A BEND IN A MEXICAN RIVER

Easy-going but scientifically accurate tale of camping-trip adventures in Mexico. Text and illustrations (including 12 full-page, full-color plates) by one of America's leading ornithologists, black and white photos by another—Olin Pettingill, Jr. 147 species of birds described. Written by George Miksch Sutton.

E 3140. Hardcover. 8½" x 11". 184 pages. Paul S. Eriksson, Inc. 1972.

HIGH ARCTIC

Narrative by one of great American bird artists about his journey to the Canadian north, above Baffin Bay. Sixteen black and white photos of people, animals, birds, plus small wash drawings. Eleven full-page and two-page full-color watercolors (also available separately in portfolio form). Written by Dr. George Miksch Sutton.

E 3141. Hardcover. 8½" x 11". 119 pages. Paul S. Eriksson, Inc. 1971.

BIRDLAND

This is the story of England's 5-acre private bird sanctuary. Visited by 700,000 people annually, it houses 1,200 birds, mostly penguins. The owner also bought two Falkland Islands to preserve breeding grounds. Laced with color and black and white photographs. Written by Len Hill and Emma Wood.

E 3142. Hardcover. 7" x 9". 148 pages. Taplinger Publishing Co. 1976.

A SEASON OF BIRDS

Written in the spirit of Anne Morrow Lindberb's *A Gift From the Sea*, this slender book with its full-page black and white drawings treats the year by seasons. Each season gets its several essays, based on particular birds. Written by Dion Henderson, Chief of Associated Press' Milwaukee Bureau.

E 3143. Hardcover. 6" x 9". 87 pages. Tamarack Press. 1977.

CONVERSATIONS WITH A BARRED OWL

Illustrated poems and personal observations by Canadian author who sees parallels between bird watching and the joys of a Christian life. Keen observations of the minutiae of birds' habits. Written by Margaret Clarkson.

E 3144. Hardcover. 5½" x 8". 115 pages. Zondervan Publishing House. 1974.

For Children

ALBUM OF NORTH AMERICAN BIRDS

Life stories of 52 species, described in non-technical language with special appeal to children. Includes the Bald Eagle, Great Blue Heron, Bobolink, Baltimore Oriole, and the Arctic Tern (whose migration route stretches 11,000 miles). Drawings plus 26 full-color illustrations. Written by Vera Dugdale.

E 3145. Hardcover. 9" x 11½". 112 pages. Rand McNally & Company. 1967.

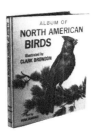

PENGUINS

Part of children's series, "Animals of the World". Describes physical characteristics and habits of penguins, focusing on the Adelie Penguin, the most common type on the Antarctic continent. Future of penguins discussed. 40 color photographs. Includes index, glossary and list for further reading. Written by Ralph Whitlock.

E 3146. Softcover. 6" x 9". 63 pages. Raintree Publishers Limited. 1977.

THE SCIENCE-HOBBY BOOK OF BIRD WATCHING

This young people's guide includes sections on natural history, how to recognize, feeding and bird houses, binocular selection, color map of 6 principal migratory flyways, photography, and scattered bibliographies. Color and black and white illustrations. Written by Robert Wells.

E 3147. 7" x 10". 47 pages. Lerner Publications Co. 1971.

BIRDS

Directed towards a juvenile audience. Covers basic facts of bird life. All bird habitats—polar, forest, tropical, grassland, river, lake, ocean and coast—are discussed. Chapters on endangered species, and on birds and their relationship with man. Fully indexed. Illustrated throughout with color photographs and drawings. Edited by Jane Olliver and Valerie Pitt. Written by Neil Ardley.

E 3148. Hardcover. 8½" x 11". 48 pages. Warwick Press. 1974.

A CLOSER LOOK AT BIRDS

Part of "Closer Look" series for children. Describes how birds evolved, ways of flying, birds that can't fly, bird variety, beaks, eyes, ears, and feet, camouflage, courtship and display, nest building, eggs, and hatching, caring for the brood and migration. 28 pages of full color and black and white illustrations. Written by J.L. Hicks.

E 3149. Hardcover. 7½" x 10½". 30 pages. Franklin Watts. 1976.

BIRDS IN FLIGHT

Each family of birds develops its own kind of flight. Writing to young readers, author describes bird anatomy and basic aerodynamics. Gliding, soaring, flapping, hovering —the four basic types of flight—described in detail. Over 75 diagrams and drawings. Written and illustrated by John Kaufmann.

E 3150. Hardcover. 6½" x 8½". 96 pages. William Morrow and Company. 1970.

Miscellaneous

AN EYE FOR A BIRD

With a foreword by the Duke of Edinburgh, this autobiography (helped by ghostwriter Frank Lane) of one of the world's foremost wildlife photographers contains 16 color photos, and 149 black and white photos, including one of Roger Tory Peterson. Lively anecdotes, full index. Written by Eric Hosking.

E 3151. Softcover. 6" x 9". 382 pages. Paul S. Eriksson. 1972.

ALL ABOUT PHOTOGRAPHING ANIMALS AND BIRDS

While most of book deals with cats, dogs, and zoos, good chapter on photographing wildlife, another on choosing the right camera and lens. 72 crisp black and white photographs. Extended glossary, list of wildlife parks around the world. Written by British professional David Hodgson.

E 3152. Hardcover. 7" x 9". 190 pages. Transatlantic Arts, Inc. 1974.

BIRDS OF NORTH AMERICA AND HOW TO PHOTOGRAPH THEM

145 color photos rendered from transparencies of 102 species of birds. Introduction gives alternates in equipment and methods of bird photography. Each bird pictured includes a range map, summer habitat, nesting habits, photo equipment used, and how bird was photographed. Written by Perry D. Slocum.

E 3153. Softcover. 8½" x 11". 226 pages. Perry D. Slocum. 1971.

THE BIRD FINDER'S 3-YEAR NOTEBOOK

Plastic spiral binding lets this diary lie open. One-third page each year for recording bird description and habits, where you saw it, with whom, weather. Quotes from famous naturalists at bottom of each page. Life List Index of more than 700 species of North American birds. Written by Paul S. Eriksson.

E 3154. Softcover. 6½" x 9". 381 pages. Paul S. Eriksson, Inc. 1976.

NATURALIST'S COLOR GUIDE

This 2-part package contains a red vinyl looseleaf binder in which 86 names for colors are identified by appropriate color swatches (made of non-fading lacquer). Supplement gives details of the color chosen. Aids in correct identifications and description of plumage. Written by Frank B. Smithe.

E 3155. Softcover. 5½" x 8½". 241 pages. American Museum of Natural History. 1974.

DICTIONARY OF AMERICAN BIRD NAMES

Bridde, brid, or bryd was how "bird" was spelled in Chaucer's time. This book gives origins and sidelights to all common, and scientific names, for all 8,600+ species of birds in the world. Thumbnail biographies of ornithologists, English/Latin glossary included. No illustrations. Written by Ernest A. Choate.

E 3156. Hardcover. 5" x 7½". 261 pages. Gambit Press. 1973.

PEOPLE ARE FOR THE BIRDS

Adventures with America's first municipal park naturalist at Lake Merritt, Oakland, California—America's oldest waterfowl refuge. Trials of establishing a nature center and interpretive program there. 30 black and white photographs, three area maps, 25 line drawings by Nancy Clement. Fully indexed. Written by Paul F. Covel.

E 3157. Softcover. 6" x 9". 229 pages. Western Interpretive Press. 1978.

WILD BIRDWATCHERS I HAVE KNOWN

Larded with jokes, anecdotes, some poetry, this book may appeal more to those already into birding than those just starting. Some of most amusing material deals with types of lists (birds seen in your dreams, birds seen on TV), and caricatures of bird watcher varieties. No illustrations. Written by Gerry Bennett.

E 3158. Softcover. 4½" x 7". 102 pages. Gerry Bennett. 1977.

AMERICAN BIRD ENGRAVINGS

All 103 plates from *American Ornithology* by Alexander Wilson, "Father of American Ornithology". First published in nine volumes between 1808 and 1814. 95 black and white drawings and eight color plates. Bibliographical notes on the history of *American Ornithology*. New introduction by Dean Amadon.

E 3159. Softcover. 9½" x 12". 103 pages. Dover Publications, Inc. 1975.

MAN & BIRDS

The book deals with the economic aspects of man's interrelationships with birds. Although referring to problems that exist in England, the survey has wide applications. Birds on the farm, in horticulture, in town, in relation to fishermen, comprise book's brunt. 70 black and white photos, bibliography, index. Written by R.K. Murton.

E 3160. Hardcover. 6" x 9". 364 pages. Taplinger Publishing Co. 1972.

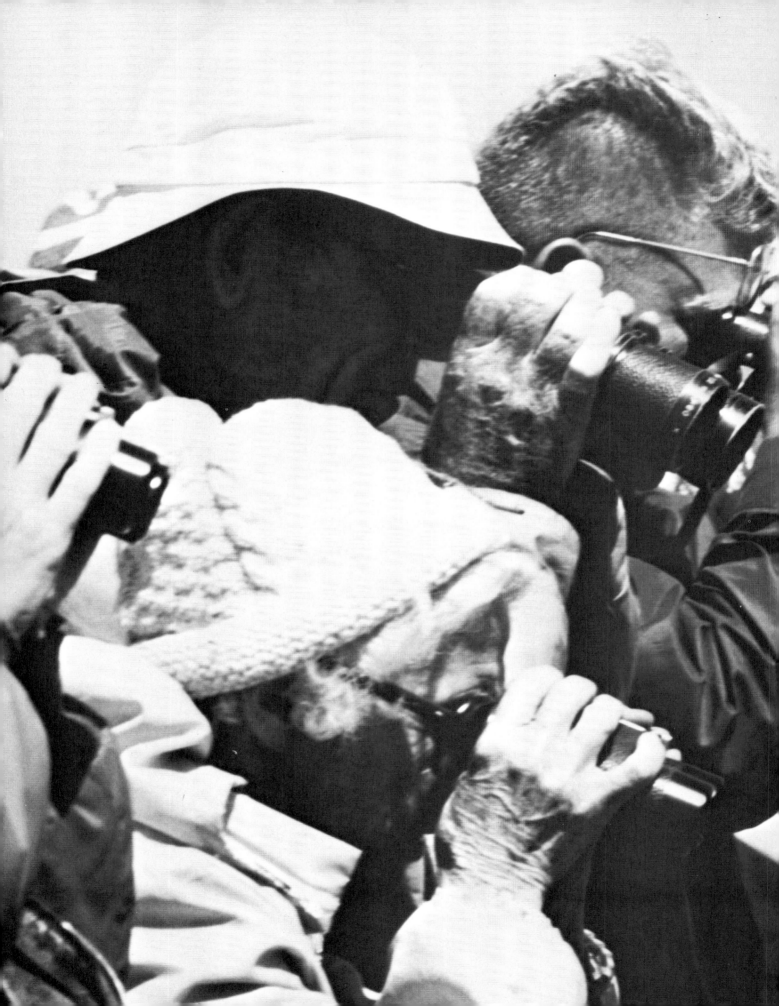

Clubs and Organizations

In the Introduction to this book we asked, Why bother with birds? That answered to the satisfaction of most, we trust, the time has come to ask the companion question, Why bother with people? That's what joining a club, after all, means.

One of the National Audubon Society's first presidents, T. Gilbert Pearson, said, "The expert who sees all the birds has taken lessons from the fox—he hunts alone." Perhaps, although experienced birders will tell you that three pairs of eyes often can spot more birds than one.

Pearson may have liked to bird alone, but he knew that in other ways strength lies in numbers. At the turn of the century had the Massachusetts Audubon Society not had 1,300 angry members to spearhead the protest against de-pluming herons and terns, our first national bird protection law, the Lacey Act, would never have gotten passed. Making a common dream come true is a major reason to form, or join, a club. Another is that often you can coax an expert on recording bird sounds, on identifying the 50 species of wood warblers, on describing the courtship of the Western Grebe, on whatever, to travel far to speak to a group, when he would not travel far to speak to you alone. The third reason for joining a club is both powerful and simple: good fellowship. You will find that conservationists and well-wishers to wildlife are some of the friendliest folks around.

In this preface to the information blocks we'll trace the history of the club movement in America, introduce you to the variety of organizations you can join today, delve into their activities a bit, then show how you can get the most from the blocks themselves—there's more meat there (and not there) than may at first meet your eye.

The Organization Movement in North America

Thomas Nuttall, the Harvard ornithologist and botanist who died from heart strain ripping open a case of rhododendrons, founded America's first club devoted to birds in 1873. Thirteen years later the Nuttall Ornithological Club published its first scientific paper, "Bird Migration," by William Brewster. Headquartered at Harvard, the club is still going strong; its latest announced publication, by Angela Kay Kepler is the 206-page *Comparative Study of Todies* [green-and-red kingfisher-like birds] *with Emphasis on the Puerto Rican Tody*. Nuttall membership remains mostly local, although persons as famous as Roger Tory Peterson belong. The club does not publish a journal.

Three early Nuttall members, including Brewster and Dr. Elliott Coues, wanted more than local membership. They invited the U.S. and Canada's 48 best-known ornithologists to meet on September 26, 1883, at New York's American Museum of Natural History. Twenty-one of them showed up; they formed the core of what today is the largest (4,000 members) and most prestigious group devoted to bird study in the world, the A.O.U. For $18.00 anyone can join. In return you get the 1,000 pages a year its quarterly journal, *The Auk*, (named for the great Auk, extinct since 1844) comprises. You can also go to the annual meeting in August, for movies, field trips, hearing scientific papers read, and a wrap-up banquet. According to *Auk* editor Dr. Kendall Corbin, this meeting "has become a clearing house for the exchange of ideas, a forceful stimulus to further study, and a tradition of memorable fellowship."

It's the *Check List of North American Birds* for which the A.O.U. is most famous—and, by some, most feared. Now in its fifth edition (1957), with a sixth underway, the A.O.U. *Check List* is the reference book for those who hope they've discovered a new species. Life listers, too, use it to check off the birds they've seen—unless they prefer the American Birding Association's rival work (this taxonomic business gets pretty complicated).

What data the American Ornithologists' Union assembled on bird distribution and migration was soon turned over to the U.S. Department of Agriculture. This is how, in 1885, the U.S. Fish and Wildlife Service (now a branch of the U.S. Department of Interior) got its start. Thanks to the work of the A.O.U., along with help by state Audubon societies and Canada's Ottawa Field Naturalists Club (founded in 1879), the U.S. Fish and Wildlife Service at last was able, in 1916, to sign with Canada a treaty protecting migratory waterfowl from being gunned down.

In addition to the A.O.U., two other national, birds-only organizations sprang up in the last part of the 19th century. The Wilson Ornithological Club, centered at the University of Michigan's Zoology Museum, honors America's first ornithologist, Alexander Wilson (1766-1813). From a membership of seven in 1888, the Wilson roster has grown to 2,100, scattered throughout North America. Its quarterly journal is *The Wilson Bulletin;* from 1939 until 1948 Josselyn Van Tyne, the eminent writer of ornithology texts, was its editor. Out west a group of bird lovers, now 2,500 strong, founded the Cooper Ornithological Society in 1893. Although its namesake remains obscure, Cooper's guiding light was the University of California's Dr. Joseph Grinnell, editor of the quarterly *Condor* from 1902 until his death in 1939. Both the Wilson and the Cooper groups hold meetings monthly, feature field trips and a banquet once a year.

As influential as these groups have been in keeping North American birds from being butchered, and in furthering our knowledge about them, it's to the National Audubon Society we must mainly give thanks. Incorporating in 1905 as an amalgam of 35 state clubs, first with the purpose of saving plume birds (egrets, herons, terns, and gulls) from being plucked for ladies' hats, then with the purpose of saving all wildlife from slaughter, to some the National Audubon Society has become as great a national treasure as the gold at Fort Knox. Even those birders who started the American Birding Association in 1969 because National Audubon, they felt, was devoting too little time to bird watching as a sport, acknowledge the debt they owe.

Audubon has been, and continues to be, this country's grass roots college of wildlife appreciation and conservation. Its 400,000 members distribute themselves in 402 local chapters, writing letters to congressmen, firing themselves up at monthly meetings (often not in the summertime), concocting schemes to save this marsh from a townhouse development, that spit from summer homes. As testimony to a true Auduboner's determination to get the job done no matter what is the notice posted by the Marin, California, chapter's field trip chairwoman, Ruth Scott: "Bring lunch, field guide, binoculars. Dress warmly. RAIN OR SHINE."

National Audubon Society's 100-page bimonthly, *Audubon,* is a collector's item of full-color photos. It comes free with the $15.00 individual, $18.00 family, annual dues. National Audubon's specialized bimonthly, *American Birds,* costs $10.00 extra a year.

Allied with National Audubon in its distaste for hunting is the Sierra Club, founded in 1892 by walker/naturalist John Muir. The Sierra Club's 180,000 members spend as much energy as National Audubon on preserving the land, but more on backpacking across it, less on watching birds. To find out more about Sierra Club local chapter activities across the nation, contact the Sierra Club, 530 Bush Street, San Francisco, CA 94108—phone 415/981-8634.

It may be that the National Wildlife Federation, founded in 1936, has more clout today in conservation matters than any other organization in the country including Audubon. With three tightly edited, pictorial magazines—*Ranger Rick* for children, *National Wildlife,* and *International Wildlife*—the National Wildlife Federation boasts 3.5 million members.

"Most of our support," states a National Wildlife Federation pamphlet, "comes from people who have one thing in common: concern for wildlife, even though their methods of appreciating birds, mammals, and fish may differ." What this means is that the National Wildlife Federation supports both fishing and hunting for sport. National Audubon president Elvis Stahr has said, "We accept sport hunting as a legitimate use of wildlife providing it is legally pursued and conducted under biologically sound regulations;" many members of the National Audubon Society also belong to the National Wildlife Federation. But you will find on a grass roots level that, although they may fish, those Auduboners who watch birds don't pack guns.

The National Wildlife Federation's address is 1412 - 16th Street N.W., Washington D.C. 20036. Its phone is 202/797-6800.

Two additional national groups, both with about 50,000 members and headquartered at the same address, drum up funds to preserve lands for wildlife, including birds. One is the Isaak Walton League of America, named for the 17th century English author of *The Compleat Angler.* Formed in 1936, it publishes the monthly *Outdoor America.* The other is the Nature Conservancy, formed in 1951. It publishes a quarterly, *The Nature Conservancy News.* The address for both is 1800 N. Kent St., Arlington, VA 22209. Isaak's phone is 703/528-1818, Nature's is 703/841-5300.

In 1969 a group of 100 led by Ph.D. psychologist Jim Tucker started the American Birding Association. These enthusiasts got frustrated because the National Audubon Society was turning its attention more and more to wildlife preservation—no group was promoting the sport of simply finding and naming birds. The ABA's first president, G. Stuart Keith of New York's American Museum of Natural History, holds the official world record in species of birds seen (5,340+). Joe Taylor, retired treasurer of the

Bausch & Lomb Optical Company, is treasurer of the ABA. Taylor holds the official record in species of North American birds seen (704+).

The American Birding Association has no local chapters yet, but it does have a magazine, the bimonthly *Birding,* and 4,000 members in 20 countries who read it. You can get involved with the ABA by contacting Jim Tucker or his wife, Priscilla, at the American Birding Association, Box 4335, Austin, TX 78765—phone 512/474-4804.

Kinds of Organizations to Join

Even if mixing with people is what you like to do best, the number of groups that deal with birds in whole or part is so vast that the whole idea may send you into hiding. For $3.00 you can get the National Wildlife Federation's annual 264-page *Conservation Directory;* it has 621 listings of governmental and private organizations. Fifteen dollars sent to Avian Publications, Box 310, Elizabethtown, KY 42701 gets you the hardcover *Guide to North American Bird Clubs,* with 835 listings. Neither of these tomes includes the hundreds of zoos, museums, and nature centers that solicit memberships, hold meetings, and feature birds. Nor has anyone before now attempted to publish more than bare-bones data about clubs outside North America. (This information has value to birders who travel and to those who wish to learn more about an area's birds by joining a club faraway. If you belong to a bird club outside North America, please, send us news about yourselves so that we can incorporate it in this book's second edition.)

To help you decide what sort of group you'd like to join, here are the three major categories:

General Bird Study—These groups include friends of museums, zoos, sanctuaries, arboretums, nature centers, observatories—bird banders, too. The group may be as august as Washington D.C.'s National Museum of Natural History (part of the Smithsonian Institution), or as little known as the Santa Cruz Bird Club (even we didn't know about this one until the time had passed to send out a questionnaire). The United States has at least three Bird Banding Associations—the Northeastern, the Inland, and the Western.

General bird study groups include ornithological societies. If you see 'ornithologist' or 'ornithological' in the club's name, you know it has a scientific bent and probably meets at a nearby university.

Particular Bird Study—Such groups often are worldwide in scope—the International Bird Rescue Center, the Society for the Preservation of Birds of Prey (T.S.F.T.P.O.B.O.P), the International Crane Foundation. Others concentrate on particular species in particular places, like the

Society of Tympanuchus Cupido Pinnatus (it's purchased 10,000 acres so far in order to save the Prairie Chicken). What these groups need most is your money.

Wildlife and Land Conservation—The two go hand in hand. Organizations such as the National Audubon Society, Sierra Club, National Wildlife Federation, Isaak Walton League, and Nature Conservancy belong in this category. With all five you can merely send money or participate at the grass roots level. National Audubon and the Sierra Club are the most active locally.

What's In It For Me

That's the important question. Yet even if a group is not now doing what you want to do, you'll find its members usually are open to innovation. Joe Allen, for instance, of Tennessee's Warioto Audubon Society (a National Audubon chapter) includes a "Bible Thought" in each issue of the society's newsletter. Birding zealots Mike Brady, Hand Weston, Jr., and Bob Yutzy of National Audubon Chapter 0515 have come up with a bird check list for California's Santa Clara County that ought to be copied. Its eight pages not only organize the local birds into families, but show what seasons they're most likely to be seen, and in what sorts of habitats.

Independents as well as chapters of national groups get involved in far more activities than you might imagine. Some sponsor tours, in this country and abroad (see the Tours section of this book for details). Most publish newsletters, some publish books (the Audubon Society of Western Pennsylvania's *Where to Find Birds in Western Pennsylvania*, the Tahoma Audubon Society's *Nature Guide*, are reviewed in the Publications section of this book). This means reporting, writing, and production assignments for you if you want them. Many organizations start special groups for youngsters, such as the Delaware-Otsego Audubon Chapter's Junior Woodchucks, led by Lillian Buck. Field trips to coax you into the fresh air, speakers to refresh your brain, are group staples. So is raising money. 'Counts,' those mass forays into the wild to discover where and how many poppies are blooming or beavers damming or orioles nesting, gain in vogue—best of all, scientists can use the data the counters garner.

But there's no denying that fellowship (personship if you like) is the main reason most of us pay our fees and dues, fellowship with folks close by and fellowship-by-pen with folks too far away to visit except during trips.

How To Use The Listings

Remember that because volunteers run most of the groups, officers and addresses change fast. What we give you is the name, address, and phone of someone who, even though not officer when you make contact, can tell you what you need to know. Remember, too, that most groups get—or have the capacity for getting—involved in far more activities than the main ones listed.

Those groups serving primarily a local area often have members around the country; those serving North America sometimes serve the world. We list them according to the area in which their energy gets concentrated.

Local Audubon societies, unless stated otherwise, are chapters of the National Audubon Society. In order to maintain control, National Audubon no longer releases the addresses of its chapters and affiliates. In one sense that's too bad. It means that, unless you find the information here or in your phone book, you'll have to wait six to seven weeks after sending New York headquarters your $15.00 individual, $18.00 family membership fee before hearing from the local group. To speed a reply, try contacting the Audubon Regional Office nearest you—there are 10 of them. Audubon national and regional addresses follow, preceding the regular listings.

National Audubon Society National Headquarters
950 Third Avenue
New York, NY 10022
(212) 832-3200
Linda Petito, Chapter Services Supervisor

National Audubon Society Regional Offices
Alaska Audubon
2 Marine Way, Room 11
Juneau, Alaska 99801
(907) 586-1167
David Cline, Regional Representative

Western Audubon (California, Hawaii, Nevada, Oregon, Washington)
555 Audubon Place
Sacramento, CA 95825
(916) 481-5332
Richard Martyr, Regional Representative

Rocky Mountain Audubon (Arizona, Colorado, Idaho, Montana, Utah, Wyoming)
Box 3232
Boulder, CO 80307
(303) 499-0219
Robert Turner, Regional Representative

Southwest Audubon (Louisiana, Mexico, New Mexico, Texas)
Box 416 Brownwood, TX 76801
(915) 752-7331
Dede Armentrout, Regional Representative

West Central Audubon (Arkansas, Kansas, Missouri, Nebraska, Oklahoma)
813 Juniper Drive
Manhattan, KS 66502
(913) 537-4385
Ronald Klataske, Regional Representative

North Midwest Audubon (Iowa, Michigan, Minnesota, North & South Dakota, Wisconsin)
Box 1591
Jamestown, ND 58401
(701) 252-8376
Richard Madson, Regional Representative

Central Midwest Audubon (Illinois, Indiana, Kentucky, Ohio, Tennessee)
Elizabethtown Mall, Suite 15
Elizabethtown, KY 42701
(502) 765-6734
Marshal Case, Regional Representative

Northeast Audubon (Connecticut, Maine, Massachusetts, New Hampshire, New York, Rhode Island, Vermont)
Box 151
Stephentown, NY 12168
(518) 733-5690
Richard Rhindress, Regional Representative

Mid-Atlantic Audubon (Delaware, Maryland, New Jersey, Pennsylvania, Virginia, Washington D.C., West Virginia)
Box 4181
Harrisburg, PA 17111
(717) 939-9844
Frank Dunstan, Regional Representative

Southeast Audubon (Alabama, Florida, Georgia, Mississippi, North & South Carolina)
Box 1268
Charleston, SC 29402
(803) 723-3336
W. Carlyle Blakeney, Jr., Regional Representative

United States Clubs

Alabama

Alabama Ornithological Society. 2708-43rd Avenue East. Tuscaloosa, AL 35401. Serving: Alabama and NW Florida. Established 1950. Purpose and Activities: Knowledge and conservation of birds and other wildlife. Active members: 160. Meetings: Spring and Fall. Dues: $5.00 per year. Publication: *Alabama Birdlife*, twice a year. Advertising: No. Subscription: Free to members. For information write: Alabama Ornithological Society.

Mobile Bay Audubon Society. P.O. Box U 581, Mobile, AL 36688. Serving: Southwestern Alabama. Established: not given Purpose: Conservation of natural resources. Activities: Field trips, meetings. Active members: 400. Meetings: Monthly. Dues: $18.00 per family per year. Publication: monthly newsletters. Advertising: No. Subscription: $1.50 per year. For information call: John Winn, Board Member, (205) 666-1317.

Alaska

Anchorage Audubon Society. P.O. Box 1161, Anchorage, AK 99510. Serving: Alaska except S.E. Established: 1973. Purpose: Conservation through education and action. Activities: Birding & wildflower field trips; spring and Christmas bird counts; natural history classes. Active members: 1,240. Meetings: 3rd Thursday monthly, September through May. Dues: $15.00 per year (includes National Audubon). Publication: *Okiotak*, 10 times a year. Advertising: No. Subscription: Free to members, $3.50 per year non-members. For information call: Gordn Tans, President, (907) 276-5846.

Arizona

Western Bird Banding Association. c/o Mrs. Shirley Spitler, Treasurer, 3301 E. Linden, Tucson, AZ 85716. Serving: Western states. Established: 1925. Purpose: Publish information relevant to bird-banding activities and studies. Activities: Publication of journal. Active members: 550. Meetings: Annually. Dues: $6.00 per year. Publication: *North American Bird Bander*, quarterly. Advertising: Yes. Subscription: Free to members; $6.00 non-members. For information call: Mrs. Shirley Spitler, Treasurer, (602) 327-7503.

Arkansas

Arknsas Audubon Society. 2600 Riviera Circle, Fort Smith, AR 72903. Serving: Arkansas. Established: 1955. Purpose: Study and support birds and conservation issues. Activities: Meetings: Active members: 900. Meetings: Spring and Fall. Dues: $1.00 to $10.00 per year. Publication: *Arkansas Audubon Newsletter,* quarterly. Advertising: No. Subscription: $2.00 per year. For information call: Carol Wooten, President, (501) 452-3059.

California

International Bird Rescue Center. Aquatic Park, Berkeley, CA 94710. Serving: Bay Area — in emerencies and for training, nationwide. Established: 1971. Purpose: To rehabilitate waterbirds that have been injured or oiled. Activities: Training seminars. Active members: 700. Meetings: Annually (March). Dues: None. Publication: *IBRC Newsletter*, irregular publication dates. Advertising: No. Subscription: $10.00 per year to non-members. For information call: Alice Berkner, Executive Director, (415) 841-9086.

Los Angeles Audubon Society. 7377 Santa Monica Blvd., Los Angeles, CA 90046. Serving: Los Angeles city and county. Established: 1910. Purpose: Conservation, birding, wildlife education. Activities: Weekly field trips, sponsor pelagic (ocean) trips, library and bookstore. Active members: 3500. Meetings: 2nd Tuesday, September to June. Dues: None. Publication: *Western Tanager*, ten times a year. Advertising: No. Subscription: $4.00 per year. For information call: Carol Niles, Office Manager, (213) 876-0202.

Marin Audubon Society. Box 441, Tiburon, California 94920. Serving: Marin County. Established: 1956. Purpose: Educational, scientific, literary, historical and charitable pursuits. Activities: Field trips and wildlife programs. Active members: 3700. Meetings: First Friday of every month except June through September. Dues: $18.00 family membership per year. Publication: *Redwood Log*, monthly. Advertising: No. Subscription: Free to membership; $3.00 per year to non-members. For information call: Thomas S. Price, President, (415) 435-1121.

Pacific Seabird Group. Wildlife Department, Humboldt State University, Arcta, CA 95521. Serving: Pacific Coast. Purpose: Seabird research and conservation. Activities: Sponsor annual meeting, working committees, publish bulletin. Active members: 250. Meetings: Annually. Dues: $5.00 per year. Publication: *Pacific Seabird*, two times per year. Advertising: No. Subscription: Free to members; $5.00 non-members. For information call: S.W. Harris, Secretary (707) 826-3450.

Sacramento Valley Audubon Society. 3615 Auburn Blvd., Sacramento, CA 95821. Serving: Sacramento and vicinity. Established: 1950. Purpose: Apreciation of nature. Activities: Field trips, educational activities. Active members: 2200. Meetings: Monthly, 3rd Thursday, except summer. Dues: $18.00 per family per year. Publication: *The Observer*, monthly. Advertising: No. Subscriptions: $5.00 per year. For information call: Dorothy Harvey, Membership Chairman, (916) 362-2557.

Santa Barbara Audubon Society. P.O. Box 2067, Santa Barbara, CA 93102. Serving: Santa Barbara and parts of Ventura Counties. Established: 1963. Purpose: Environmental and wildlife education and conservation. Activities: Field trips, special programs for schools, bird walks, Rare Bird Alert, (805) 964-8240. Active members: 1200. Meetings: 4th Friday monthly except June, July, August. Dues: Same as National Audubon Society. Publication: *El Tecolote*, 8-9 times per year. Advertising: No. Subscription: Free to members, $2.00 per year non-members. For information cal Joy Parkinson, President, (805) 967-9371.

Santa Clara Valley Audubon Society, Inc., 1176 Emerson Street, Palo Alto, CA 94301. Serving: Santa Clara County. Established: 1954. Purpose: Wildlife and natural environment conservation. Activities: Field trips for bird-watching, ocean birding trips, weekenders and local weekday trips. Active members: 2700. Meetings: 3rd Wednesday of month, October-May. Dues: $15.00 individual per year. Publication: *Avocet*, 10 months of year. Advertising: No. Subscription: Free to members, $3.00 per year non-members. For information call: Nance Holmes, President, (415) 948-1854.

Western Field Ornithologists, 376 Greenwood Beach Road, Tiburon, CA 94920. Serving: Rocky Mountain states westward. Established: 1969. Purpose: Education & Scientific field studies. Activities: Sponsor numerous pelagic field trips for ocean bird studies; publish journal. Active members: 1,000. Meetings: Annual.

Dues: $7.50 per year. Publication: *Western Birds*, approx. quarterly. Advertising: Yes. Subscription: Free to members, $7.50 non members. For information call: Phil Schaeffer, Treasurer, (415) 388-2524.

Colorado

Denver Audubon Society. 1325 Delaware Street, Denver, CO 80210. Serving: Metropolitan Denver. Established: 1968. Purpose: Wildlife conservation. Activities: Field trips, classes, bird talks, meetings. Active members: 1900. Meetings: 2nd Tuesday monthly. Advertising: Informal. Subscription: Free to members, $3.00 per year non-members. For information call: B. Downing, Office Administrator. (303) 893-5883.

Fort Collins Audubon Society. c/o Dept. of Fishery & Wildlife Biology, Colorado State University, Ft. Collins, CO 80523. Serving: Ft. Collins and north central Colorado. Established: 1962. Purpose: Study of birds and wildlife. Activities: Field trips, annual Christmas bird count, Fall and Spring counts. Active members: 400+. Meetings: 3rd Tuesday of every month. Dues: Vary according to category. Publication: *The Ptarmigan*, monthly. Advertising: No. Subscription: Free to members; $2.00 non-members. For information call: Dr. Ronald A. Ryder, Dept. Fishery and Wildlife Biology.

Connecticut

Connecticut Audubon Society. 2325 Burr Street, Fairfield, CT 06430. Serving: State of Connecticut. Established: 1898. Purpose: State-wide non-profit, conservation and nature education organization dedicated to the wise use of our natural resources. Activities: Field trips, classes, lectures, special events. Active members: over 3,000. Meetings: Annual in May. Dues: $10.00 individual, $15.00 family per year. Publication: *Connecticut Audubon Bulletin*, bimonthly. Advertising: No. Subscription: Free to members. For information call: Mr. Le Corey, Executive Director, (203) 259-6305.

Greenwich Audubon Society. 238 Greenwich Ave., Greenwich, CT 06830. Serving: Greenwich. Established: 1960. Purpose: Conservation and education. Activities: Tours, sanctuary development, wildlife films. Active members: 1300. Meetings: Every six weeks. Dues: $15.00 individual, $18.00 family per year. Publication: Newsletter, bimonthly. Advertising: No. Subscription: Free to members. For information call: Joseph Zeranski, Vice President, (203) 661-9607.

Housatonic Audubon Society. RR 1 Box 280, Lakeville, CT 06039. Serving: Litchfield County, CT, Eastern New York. Establish-

ed: 1956. Purpose: conservation, birding, environmental involvement. Activities: Field trips, programs, festival. Active members: 830. Meetings: Monthly, 3rd Friday. Dues: $15.00 individual, $18.00 family. Publication: *HAS Newsletter*, monthly. Advertising: No. Subscription: Free to members. For information call: Vicki Oppenheimer, President, (203) 435-9267.

Saugatuck Valley Audubon Society. P.O. Box 684, Westport, CT 06880. Serving: Fairfield County. Purpose: Natural history education. Activities: Meetings, lectures, field trips. Active members: 450. Meetings: Monthly. Dues: $15.00 per year. Publication: *The Night Heron*, monthly, September-May. Advertising: No. Subscription: Free to members. For information call: Alan McKissock, President, (203) 838-0455.

Delaware

Delmarva Ornithological Society. P.O. Box 4237, Greenville, DE 19807. Serving: Delaware. Established: 1963. Purpose: Study of birds to advance ornithological knowledge. Activities: Field trips, bird counts. Active members: 285. Meetings: Monthly, 3rd Wednesday, September-June. Dues: $10.00 per year. Publication: *Delmarva Ornithologist*, biannually. Advertising: No. Subscription: $4.00 per year. For information write: Delmarva Ornithological Society.

Florida

Azalea Audubon Society of Palatka. 422 North First St., Palatka, FL 32077. Serving: Palatka and area. Established: 1967. Purpose: To preserve endangered species and the environment. Activities: field trips and communtiy relations. Active members: 40. Meetings: monthly. Dues: $15.00 individual, $18.00 family. Publication: *The Wind*, monthly. Advertising: No. Subscription: Free to members. For information write: Azalea Audubon Society of Palatka.

Florida Audubon Society (not affiliated with National Audubon Socity). 921 Lake Sybelia Drive, Maitland, FL 32751. Serving: Florida. Established: 1900. Purpose: Environmental protection for all living things. Active members: 35,000. Meetings: bi-annually. Publication: *Florida Naturalist*, bimonthly. Advertising: Yes. Subscription: Free to members: $1.25 per copy through FAS office. For information call: Janet Roth, Vice President-Development, (305) 647-2615.

Lake Region Audubon Society. P.O. Box 2471, Lakeland, FL 33803. Serving: Lakeland and Winterhaven area. Established: not given. Purpose: Provide Audubon and conservation activities. Activities: Field trips, educational programs, conservation

activities. Active members: 750. Meetings: Board meetings, monthly, 2nd Wednesday, October-May. Dues: $15.00 individual, $18.00 family, per year. Publication: *Lake Region Naturalist*, annually, plus newsletters as needed. Advertising: No. Subscription: $1.00 per year. For information call: Dr. Paul Fellers, Board member, (813) 293-0486.

Orange Audubon Society. P.O. Box 1142, Maitland, FL 32751. Serving: Orange County & South Seminole County. Established: 1951. Purpose: National Audubon membership, wildlife conservation. Activities: Field trips monthly. Active members: 200. Meetings: monthly. Dues: $15.00 per year. Publication: *Oasis* (newsletter), monthly, September-May. Subscription: Free to members. For information call: Fred Harden, President (305) 293-8480.

Pelican Island Audubon Society. P.O. Box 1833, Vero Beach, FL 32960. Serving: Indian River County. Purpose: Environmental education. Activities: Field trips, conservation programs, meetings. Active members: 700. Meetings, 3rd Monday monthly. Dues: $15.00 individual, $18.00 family per year. Publication: *Peligram*, 9 or 10 months per year. Advertising: No. Subscription: Free to members, $3.00 per year non-members. For information call: Dr. Herb Kale, First VP, (305) 567-3520.

Ridge Audubon Society. c/o Audubon Center, P.O. Box, Babson Park, FL 33827. Serving: Southern Polk County. Florida. Established: 1960. Purpose: Increase nature appreciation and need for natural resource conservation. Activities: Audubon wildlife film series, field trips, study classes. Activ-members: 415. Meetings: third Monday every month November-April. Dues: $15.00 individually; $18.00 family per year. Publication: *R.A.S. Bulletin*, monthly November-April. Advertising: No. Subscription: Free to members, $2.50 per year non-members. For information call: Mildred Kaucher, President, (813) 676-5950.

Sanibel-Captiva Audubon Society. 1332 Tahiti Drive, Sanibel Island, FL 33957. Serving: Sanibel Island-Captiva Island in Lee County, Florida. Purpose: To promote birding, ecology and an appreciation of nature. Activities: Weekly programs during winter season, off-island trips to birding areas, instructional classes in bird recognition. Meetings: Every week-December 1 to April 30. Dues: $15.00 per year. No Publication. For information call: Borwell C. Ryckman, President, (813) 472-2089.

Tropical Audubon Society. 5530 Sunset Dr., S. Miami, FL 33143. Serving: Dade County. Established: 1947. Purpose: Conservation action and education. Activities: Meetings, field trips, conservtion activities. Active members: 3000. Meetings: Monthly. Dues: $18.00 per year. Publication: *Tropical Audubon Bulletin*, monthly.

Venice Area Audubon Society. P.O. Box 1181, Venice, FL 33595. Serving: Venice, Englewood and area. Establihes: 1966. Purpose: Promoting an interest in wildlife and conservation. Activities: Field trips monthly. Active members: 400. Meetings: monthly. Dues: $15.00. per year. Publication: *Wings & Things*, 3 times per year. Advertising: No. Subscription: Free to members. For information call: Stanley Stedman, President, (813) 485-2168.

Georgia

Floyd County Audubon Society (not affiliated with National Audubon Society). Serving: Floyd County. Established: 1950. Purpose: Conservation of wildlife and habitat. Activities: Field trips, etc. Active members: 50. Meetings: 5 times a year. Dues: $3.00 per family per year. Publication: *The Bird Watcher*, at least 12 issues per year. Advertising: No. Subscription: Free to members. For information call: Philip Ham, President, (404) 232-6359.

Georgia Ornithological Society. 755 Ellsworth Dr., Atlanta, GA 30318. Serving: Georgia. Established: 1936. Purpose: Gather information, promote an interest, and insure conservation of bird life. Activities: Lecturs, films, field trips. Active members: 380. Meetings: Fall and Spring. Dues: $8.00 per year. Publication: *The Oriole*, quarterly. Advertising: No. Subscription: Free to members. For information call: McRae Williams, Business Manager, (404) 355-4335.

Hawaii

Hawaii Audubon Society. P.O. Box 22832, Honolulu, Hawaii 96822. Serving: Hawaii and Pacific region. Established: 1939. Purpose: Protection and preservation of Hawaii's native wildlife. Activities: Monthly field trips, publications and materials, legislative testimony, etc. Active members: 1000. Meetings: 3rd Monday evening each month. Dues: $15.00 per year joint membership in Hawaii and National Audubon Societies; $3.00 per year Hawaii Audubon only. Publications: *'Elepaio*, monthly; *Hawaii's Birds*, one time 96-page color-illustrated book. Advertising: No. Subscription: *'Elepaio*, $3.00 per year non-members; free to members. For information write: Hawaii Audubon Society.

Illinois

Chicago Audubon Society, 120 South LaSalle, Chicago, IL 60603. Serving: Chicago and suburbs. Established: 1972. Purpose: Environmental action, education, habitat preservation, scientific research. Activities: Research projects, education, field trips, Rare Bird Alert. Active members: 4500. Meetings: Monthly. Dues: Membership included in National Audubon Society dues. Publication: *Chicago Audubon Compass*, monthly. Advertising: Yes.Subscription: Free to members; $5.00 per year non-members. For information call: Chicago Audubon Rare Bird Alert, (312) 283-2144.

Vermilion County Audubon Society. Box 229, Danville, IL 61832. Serving: Vermilion County and adjacent Indiana counties. Established: 1950. Purpose: Natural areas preservation, conservation education, bird record keeping. Activities: Prairie restoration, bluebird trail, public education. Active members: 150. Meetings: 3rd Thursday monthly. Dues: $15.00 annually. Publication: *Audubonite*, monthly. Advertising: No. Subscription: non-members $2.00 per year. For information call: Dave Watson, President, (217) 267-2992.

Indiana

Amos W. Butler Audubon Society. 3650 Cold Spring Rd., Indianapolis, IN 46222. Serving: Indianapolis and area. Established: 1920. Purpose: Environmental education. Activities: Lectures, films, field trips. Active members: 1200. Meetings: Monthly. Dues: $15.00 per year. Publication: *Audubon News*, monthly. Advertising: No. Subscription: Free to members. For information call: Michael Eoff, Board member, (317) 926-9456.

Indiana Audubon Society. Rt. Box 165, Connersville, IN 47331. Serving: Indiana. Established: 1898. Purpose: Birding, conservation and education. Activities: Summer Bird Fest. Active members: 600. Meetings: Semi-annual. Dues: $15.00 family, $10.00 individual, per year. Publication: *Indiana Audubon*, quarterly, *Cardinal*, bi-monthly. Advertising: No. Subscription: $10.00 per year. For information call: Denzel Barenklow, Sanctuary Manager, (317) 925-9788.

Indiana Sassafras Audubon Society. 1608 East Second Street, Bloomington, IN 47401. Serving: 5 counties in southern Indiana. Established: 1971. Purpose: Support National Audubon Society policies, environmental protection, nature study. Activities: Bird counts & naturalist hikes, environmental forums. Active members: 750. Meetings: varied program. Dues: $15.00 annually. Publication: *The Leaflet*, bi-monthly. Advertising: No. Subscription: Free to members. For information call: Mr. John A. Eyed, President, (812) 988-2359.

Iowa

Iowa Ornithologist's Union. 235 McClellan Blvd., Davenport, IA 52803. Serving: State of Iowa. Established: 1923. Purpose: Study and protection of birds. Activities: Publishes annotated list and field a separate check list of Iowa birds, has quarterly publication, etc. Active members: 600. Meetings: May and September. Dues: $6.00 per year. Publication: *Iowa Birdlife*, quarterly. Advertising: No. Subscription: Free to members, $6.00 per year non-members. For for information call Peter C. Petersen, Editor, (319) 324-1933.

Kansas

Northern Flint Hills Audubon Society. 1816 Elaine Drive, Manhattan, KS 66502. Serving: Riley, Pottowatomie & Geary Counties. Established: 1970. Purpose: Audubon membership and principles, promote understanding & appreciation of natural world. Activities: Field trips to Nebraska, Oklahoma, Missouri, as well as Cheyenne Bottoms & Konza Prairie Reserch Areas of Kansas. Various conservation projects, programs, Arbor Day Tree Planting. Active members: 170. Meetings: 3rd Thursday monthly. Dues: $15.00 annually. Publication: *NFHAS Newsletter*, *The Prairie Falcon*, monthly, September-May. Advertising: No. Subscription: Free to all. For information call: Ms. Dru Clarke, (913) 539-1842.

Kentucky

Henderson Audubon Society. P.O. Box 821, Henderson KY 42420. Serving: Henderson County. Established: 1896. Purpose: Conservation and study of natural resources. ctivities: Field trips, bird counts, natural history studies. Active members: 120. Meetings: Monthly, 2nd Tuesday. Dues: $18.00 per year. Publication: *Audubon Newsletter*, monthly. Advertising: No. Subscription: Free to members. For information call: Con Jodton, President, (502) 826-8810.

Maine

Maine Audubon Society (not affiliated with National Audubon Society). Established: 1843. Purpose: Natural history, energy and environmental education, public policy. Activities: Field trips, 13 nature centers, scientific research, teacher training, lobbying, television programing, etc. Active members: 7000. Meetings: Daily activities throughout year. Dues: $15.00 regular, $20.00 family, $5.00 student. Publication: *Maine Audubon Quarterly*; *Maine Audubon News*, monthly. Advertising: No. Subscription: Free to members. For information call: William Ginn, Executive Director, (207) 781-2330.

Western Maine Audubon Society. Box 232, Farmington, Maine 04938. Serving: Western Maine. Established: 1972. Purpose: Environmental education and action. Activities: Audubon wildlife film series, natural history and conservation education, field trtips, study of birds, flowers, geology, mammals, etc. Active members: 160. Meetings: Monthly. Dues: $15.00 (same as National Audubon). Publication: *Western Maine Audubon Newsletter*, monthly. Advertising: No. Subscription: Free to members, $5.00 per year non-members. For information call: Beverly Dunst, President, (207) 364-7711.

Maryland

Audubon Naturalist Society of the Central Atlantic States, Inc., 8940 Jones Mill Road, Chevy Chase, MD 20015. Serving: Central Atlantic Region. Established: 1897. Purpose: Conservation, natural history education: Activities: Field ecology studies for children and adults, field trips, bird sightings recorded message (301) 652-1088. Active members: 3000. Meetings: Monthly-Mondays. Dues: $15.00 individual; $20.00 family, per year. Publication: *Audubon Naturalist News*, monthly. Advertising: Yes. Subscription: Free to members. For information call: Charles Williams, Executive Director, (301) 652-9188.

Maryland Ornithological Society. Cylburn Mansion, 4915 Greenspring Ave., Baltimore, MD 21209. Serving: Maryland. Established: 1945. Purpose: Promote the study and enjoyment of wildlife, protection of natural resources. Activities: Bird counts, sanctuary program, scholarships, publishing, plus field trips and seminars at local chapters. Active members: 2007. Meetings: 14 local chapters hold regular meetings. Dues: $5.00 per year. Publication: *Maryland Birdlife*, quarterly. Advertising: Yes. Subscription: Free to members. For information call: Helen Ford, Executive Secretary, (301) 267-8417.

Prince George's Audubon Society. P.O. Box 693, Bowie, MD 20715. Serving: Northern Prince George's County, MD. Established: 1972. Purpose: Environmental awareness; conservation of wildlife and natural resources. Activities: Field trips, Eastern Bluebird restoration project, local environmental participation, Christmas bird count. Active members: 500. Meetings: Monthly. Dues: No. Publication: *P.G.A.S. Newsletter*, monthly except July and August. Advertising: No. Subscription: Free to members only. For information call: Bruce Newman, President, (301) 422-7442.

Massachusetts

Essex County Ornithology Club. Peabody Museum of Salem, East India

Square, Salem, MA 01970. Serving: Essex County. Established: 1916. Purpose: Study of birds. Activities: Meetings and bird walks. Active members: 56. Meetings: Monthly, September-May. Dues: $3.00 per year. Publication: No. Subscription: No. For information call: Sarah Ingalls, Peabody Museum of Salem, (617) 745-1876.

Massachusetts Audubon Society (not affiliated with National Audubon Society). South Great Road, Lincoln, MA 01773. Serving: State of Massachusetts. Established: 1896. Purpose: Preservation and conservation of wildlife and its habitat. Activities: 16 staffed sanctuaries, wetlands project, public education, solar energy study. Active members: 26,719. Meetings: In conjunction with various activities. Dues: $12.00 per year. Publication:*Massachusetts Audubon Newsletter*, 10 times a year. Advertising: No. Subscription: Free to members. For information write: Masschusetts Audubon Society.

Manomet Bird Observatory, Manomet, MA 02345. Serving: Northest, Canada, etc.

Established: 1969. Purpose: Baseline studies of bird populations and other ecological research. Activities: Shorebird studies, seabird surveys in NW Atlantic, studies of heronries, migrant passerines, fire ecology in pine barrens, etc. Active members: 1500. Dues: $10.00 individual per year. Publications: *The Manomet Observer*, 2-3 times per year; *Annual Report*. Advertising: No. Subscription: Free to members; on request by non-members with stamped envelope. For information call: Kathleen S. Anderson, Executive Director, (617) 224-3359.

Northeastern Bird Banding Association. 631 Main St., Concord, MA 01742. Serving: International. Established: 1929. Purpose: Publication of scientific ornithological information. Activities: same as foregoing. Active members: 1500. Meetings: Annually. Dues: $6.00 per year. Publication: *Bird Banding*, quarterly. Advertising: No. Subscription: Free to members. For information write: Robert Shaw, Treasurer, Northeastern Bird Banding Association.

Nuttall Ornithological Club. c/o Museum of Comparative Zoology, Harvard University, Cambridge, MA 02138. Serving: Local area; international through publications. Established: 1873. Purpose: Promote scientific ornithology. Activities: Meetings and publications. Active members: 125. Meetings: Once a month. Dues: $10.00 per year. Publications: *Publications of the Nuttall Ornithological Club,* irregular basis. Advertising: No. Subscription: Prices vary with publication. For information call: Dr. Raymond A. Paynter, Jr., Editor, (617) 495-2471.

Michigan Audubon Society, 7000 N. Westnedge, Kalamazoo, MI 49007. Serving: Michigan and surrounding areas. Established: 1904. Purpose: All aspects of birding, field trips, protection of habitat. Activities: 3 campouts per year in different parts of state, bimonthly board meetings, state convention in Spring: Active members: 12,000. Meetings: 4 times year. Dues: $15.00 per year. Publications: *Jack Pine Warbler,* quarterly; *Newsletter,* bimonthly. Advertising: No. Subscription: Free to members, $10.00 per year non-members. For information call: Patricia Adams, Office Manager, (616) 381-1575.

Minnesota

Albert Lea Audubon Society, c/o Mrs. Edna Aakre, 915 Stanley Ave., Albert Lea, NM 56007. Serving: Albert Lea, Freeborn County. Established: 1948. Purpose: Wildlife and natural resource conservation. Activities: co-sponsor Audubon wildlife film series, field trips, monitor community conservation activities, present special programs. Active members: 65. Meetings: 1st Tuesday, September to May. Dues: No local dues. Publication: *Albert Lea Chickadee,* monthly September-May. Advertising: No. Subscription: Free to members, $3.00 per year non-members. For information call: Mrs. Edna Aakre, (507) 373-4071.

Audubon Chapter of Minneapolis. Box 566, Minneapolis, MN 55440. Serving: Minneapolis. Purpose: Wildlife conservation. Activities: Maintain telephone hotline (933-6682), monitor legislation, Minneapolis library educational programs, school talks, birding. Active members: 2935. Meetings: 1st & 3rd Tuesday monthly. Dues: $15.00 annually. Publication: *Kingfisher,* monthly. Advertising: No. Subscription: Free to members. For information call: Keith Sherck, President, (612) 588-7087.

Austin Audubon Society. P.O. Box 8, Austin, MN 55912. Serving: Austin area. Established: 1971. Purpose: Nature, environmental protection. Activities: Field trips, programs, lobbying for environmental issues. Active members: 100. Meetins: 3rd Monday monthly. Dues: $18.00 family membership

per year. Publication: *Austin Jay,* monthly. Advertising: No. Subscription: Free. For information call: Richard Smaby, President, (507) 433-7867.

Duluth Audubon Society, Biology Department, University of Minnesota. Duluth, MN 55812. Serving: Duluth-Superior metro area. Purpose: Wildlife and environmental conservation and education. Activities: Management of Duluth's Hawk Ridge Nature Reserve, field trips, special programs, etc. Active members: 200+. Meetings: 2nd Thursday, monthly. Dues: $15.00 per year. Publication: *The Gull,* monthly. Advertising: No. Subscription: Free to members and non-members. For information call: K.R. Eckert, President (218) 525-5654.

Minnesota Ornithologists' Union. James Ford Bell Museum of Natural History, 10 Church Street S.E., University of Minnesota, Minneaspolis, MN 55455. Serving: Minnesota. Established: 1938. Purpose: Protection of and interest in birds and their environment, good fellowship. Activities: 3 field trips a year plus December convention. Active members: 1200. Meetings: quarterly. Dues: $6.00 per year. Publication: *The Loon,* published quarterly. Advertising: Yes. Subscription: Free to members; $6.00 per year to non-members. For information call: Robert B. Janssen, (612) 938-7464 or Henry C. Kyllingstad, (507) 537-7213.

Nebraska

Inland Bird Banding Association, R. 2, Box 26, Wisner, NE 68791. Serving: Central U.S. and Canadian Provinces of Saskatchewan & Manitoba. Established: 1922. Purpose: Promote state, federal and local cooperation in bird banding & other scientific pursuits; public education. Activities: Field trips, workshops, annual meetings for paper presentations, social. Active members: 1000. Meetings: Annual in fall. Dues: $5.00 per year. Publication: *Inland Bird Banding News,* bi-monthly. Advertising: Yes. Subscription: Free to members, $6.00 per year non-members. For information call: Mrs. John Lueshen, (402) 529-6679.

Nebraska Ornithologists' Union, Inc. University of Nebraska State Museum, Lincoln, NE 68508. Serving: State of nebraska. Established: 1899. Purpose: Promote study of ornithology and natural history in Nebraska. Activities: Published summaries of nesting, spring and fall migration; workshops; annual meeting and field days in May — different area of state each year. Active members: 190. Meetings: mid-May annually. Dues: $5.00 per year, individual, $7.00 family, $3.00 student, sustaining & family $9.00. Publications: *Nebraska Bird Review,* quarterly; *Newsletter,* bimonthly. Advertising: No. Subscription: *Nebraska Bird Review* Free to members, $5.0 non-members per year. For inormation call Neva

L. Pruess, Librarian (402) 464-6939.

New Jersey

Highlands Audubon Society. Oak Ridge NJ 07438. Serving: Sussex, Morris & Passaic Counties. Established: 1970. Purpose: Wildlife and natural resources conservation. Activities: Hawk Watch, field trips, Christmas count, wildflower restoration project. Active members: 200. Meetings: 4th Monday monthly. Dues: $15.00 annually. Publication: *H.A.S. News Letter,* monthly. Advertising: No. Subscription: Free to members; $2.50 per year non-members. For information call: Adam Martin, 1st VP, (201) 838-0735.

Morris Highlands Audubon Society. Box 935, Denville, NJ 07834. Serving: Morris County (Central NJ). Established: 1972. Purpose: Environmental and ecological education & recreation. Activities: "hands-on studies", Christmas count, field trips, programs & lectures. Active members: 500. Dues: $15.00 per year individual; $18.00 per family. Publication: *Lenapeland Log,* monthly September to May. Advertising: No. Subscription: Free to members; $4.50 per year non-members. For information call: Glenn Mahler, President, (201) 335-1657.

New Jersey Audubon Society (not affiliated with National Audubon Society). 790 Ewing Avenue, Franklin Lakes, NJ 07417. Serving: New Jersey, Philadelphia and NYC metropolitan area. Established: 1897. Purpose: Conservation, education and research. Activities: 5 nature centers, field programs, education, research, 11 natural areas. Active members: 14,000. Meetings: In 5 separate facilities around the state (Bernardsville, Mt. Holly, Cape May, Holmdel, Franklin Lakes) with weekly field trips, programs, etc. Dues: $10.00 per year. Publication: *New Jersey Audubon,* published ten times a year. Advertising: Yes. Subscription: $10.00 to members only. For information call: Karen Nolan, Director of Public Affairs, (201) 891-1211.

Raccoon Ridge Bird Observatory, Box 81, Layton, NJ 07851. Serving: Northern New Jersey. Established: 1974. Purpose: Biological research and education. Activities: Bird banding station, botonical surveys, raptor research, high school work study program, college internship program. Active members: 60. Meetings: Annual in September. Dues: $10.00 per person; $25.00 for banding instruction or bird rehabilitation. Publication: *The Ridge,* yearly. Advertising: No. Subscription: Free to members, $3.00 per year non-members. For information call: Mrs. Dorothy Hughes, Director, (201) 948-6102.

New Mexico

New Mexico Ornithological Society. 223 Morningside Drive, N.E., Albuquerque, NM

87108. Serving: New Mexico. Estblished: 1962. Purpose: Scientific study of state birds. Activities: Breeding records program, census-taking, publications. Active members: 200+. Meetings: Annual. Dues: $5.00 per year ($2.50 students). Publications: *New Mexico Ornithological Society Bulletin*, 3-4 times per year; *Nex Mexico ornithological Society Field Notes*, 2-times a year. Advertising: No. Subscription: Free to members, $5.00 ($2.50 students) per year non-members. For information call: John P. Hubbard, Editor, N.M.O.S. Bulletin, (505) 988-5918.

Southwestern New Mexico Audubon Society, P.O. Box 1473, Silver City, NM 88061. Serving: Grant, Luna, Hidalgo and Southern half of Catron Counties. Established: 1968. Purpose: Conservation of wildlife and natural environment. Activities: Monthly field trips, educational programs, special project support. Active members: 94. Meetings: 1st Friday monthly. Dues: same as National Audubon Society. Publication: *The Ravens*, monthly. Advertising: No. Subscription: Free to members, $2.00 non-members per year. For information call: May O'Byrne, Editor, (505) 538-9672.

Delaware-Otsego Audubon Society. P.O. Box 544, Oneonta, NY 13820. Serving: Northern Delaware County and Otsego County, NY. Established: 1968. Purpose: Conservation of wildlife & habitat, protection of natural resources, public education. Activities: Educational & travel programs, field trips, censuses and counts,brohures & checklist, etc. Active members: 242. Meetings: 3rd Friday monthly, September through May. Dues: $15.00 individual, $18.00 family, $8.50 student per year. Publication: *Kingfisher*, monthly, September through June. Advertising: No. Subscription: Free to members, $2.00 per year non-members. For information call: Mrs. Jean T. Miller, President, (607) 432-5767.

Federation of New York State Bird Clubs. c/o Cornell Laboratory of Ornithology, Ithaca, NY 1853. Serving: New York State. Established: 1950. Purpose: Bird study and protection of habitat. Activities: Pelagic trips, field trips, annual meetings. Active members: 1000+. Dues: $8.00 per year. Publication: *The Kingbird*, quarterly. Advertising: No. Subscription: Free to members, $8.00 per year non-members. For information call: Emanuel Levine, Co-Editor, (516) 486-5854.

Hudson Valley Audubon Society. P.O. Box 204, Dobbs Ferry, New York 10522. Serving: Westchester County. Established: 1970. Purpose: Wildlife study and conservation. Activities: Lectures, field trips, environmental action. Active members: 350. Meetings: September-June. Dues: $15.00 per year. Publication: *HVAS Newsletter*, bimonthly. Advertising: No. Subscription: Free to members. For information call: Berna Weisman, Director, (914) 693-4573.

Huntington Audubon Society. Box 735, Huntington, NY 11743. Serving: Huntington, NY. Purpose: Wildlife and environmental conservation and education. Activities: Wednesday and weekend field trips for birding (open to non-members); monthly programs. Active members: 1000+. Meetings: 2nd Wednesday each month, September to June. Dues: $15.00 individual, $18.00 family. Publication: *Killdeer*, bimonthly. Advertising: Yes. Subscription: Free to members, available by special request to non-members. For information call: Mr. Dale Alexander, President, (516) 261-7237.

New York Zoological Society, New York Zoological Park, Bronx, NY 10460. Serving: Metropolitan New York, national. Established: 1895. Purpose: Conservation, education & research of wildlife at Bronx Zoo, New York Aquarium, & worldwide conservation programs, special events at Bronx Zoo and New York Aquarium. Active members:

9000. Meetings: Annual business, annual general, garden parties, other activities as appropriate. Dues: $15.00 individual, $35.00 family per year, on up. Publication: *Animal Kingdom*, bimonthly. Subcription: Free to members, $6.00 per year non-members. For information call Eugene J. Walter, Jr.,

North Fork Audubon Society. Box 973, Mattituck, Long Island, NY 11952. Serving: North Folrk of Long Island. Established: 1970. Purpose: To enjoy and preserve the natural environment. Activities: Educaional programs, field trips, ecological activities. Active members: 370. Meetings: Monthly, September-May. Dues: $15.00 per family per year. Publication: *The Bulletin*, bimonthly. Advertising: No. Subscription: Free to members. For information call: Terry Harnan, Editor, (516) 765-2740.

Orange County Audubon Society. Box 836, Middletown NY 10940. Serving: Orange County. Established: 1971.

Purpose: National Audubon Society membership. Activities: Field trips for bird sightings all months but February, July and August. Meetings: 1st Wednesday of month except July-August. Dues: $15.00 annually. Publication: *Orange Owl,* bimonthly. Advertising: No. Subscription: Free. For information call: Ann Wanser, President, (914) 361-1921.

Saw Mill River Audubon Society, c/o Frank Gillette, 53 Greenmeadow Street, Pleasantville, NY 10570. Serving: Westchester Co., Mt. Pleasant, New Castle, Ossining, Croton, Pleasantville. Established: 1953. Purpose: Preservation and understanding, through education, of natural resources. Activities: Maintain 9 sanctuaries, field trip series, one full-time paid naturalist working in schools. Active members: 800+. Meetings: 3rd Friday monthly, September to June. Dues: $15.00 individual per year on up. Publication: *Saw Mill River Audubon Bulletin,* bimonthly. Advertising: No. Subscription: Free to

members, $3.00 per year non-members. For information call: Katherine Anderson, Naturalist, (914) 769-7430.

North Carolina

Carolina Bird Club, Inc. P.O. Box 1220, Tryon, NC 28782. Serving: North Carolina and South Carolina. Established: 1937. Purpose: Promote bird study and conservation of wildlife and wildlife habitat. Activities: Field trips and bird counts. Active members: 1100. Meetings: fall, midwinter and spring. Dues: $5.00 per year. Publication: *The Chat,* quarterly. Advertising: No. Subscription: Free to members. For information call: Eloise Potter, Editor, (919) 269-8508.

Ohio

Black Swamp Audubon Society. Rt. 5, Defiance, OH 43512. Serving: Putman,

Paulding, Williams, Henry and Defiance Counties, Established: 183. Purpose: Preserve and protect wildlife and the environment. Activities: Meetings, field trips. Active members: 183. Meetings: Monthly, 3rd Monday. Dues: $18.00 per family per year. Publication: *Audubon Views,* lmonthly. Advertising: No. Subscription: Free to members. For information call: Mel Chapman, President, (419) 393-2266.

Oklahoma

Oklahoma Ornithological Society. Rt. 2, Box 130, Durant, OK 74701. Serving: Oklahoma. Established: 1952. Purpose: Observation, study and conservation of birds in Oklahoma. Activities: Field trips, meetings, publish quarterly newsletter and scientific bulletin. Active members: 450. Meetings: fall and spring. Dues: $5.00 per year. Publications: *Scissortail,* quarterly. Advertising: No. Subscription: Free to members; $5.00 non-members. For information call: Jack Tyler, Editor of Bulletin, (405) 248-2200.

Oregon

Audubon Society of Corvallis. P.O. Box 148, Corvallis, OR 97330. Serving: Linn & Benton Counties. Purpose: Bird outings, natural resources conservation. Activities: Field trips, Bluebird Trail (provides nests for birds), birding classes. Active members: 620. Meetings: 3rd Wednesday every Month. Dues: $15.00 per year. Publication: *The Chat,* monthly. Advertising: No. Subscription: Free to members; $4.00 per year non-members. For information write: Audubon Society of Corvallis.

Oakridge Audubon Society. 77095 Westridge Avenue, Westfir, OR 97492. Serving: Lane County. Established: 1970. Purpose: To teach man his ecological place, and the conservation of natural resources and wildlife. Activities: Programs, field trips, community projects, education. Active members: 650. Meetings: 4th Thursday of each month except August. Dues: $15.00 per year. Publication: *Quail Quips and Quotes,* bimonthly except August. Advertising: No. Subscription: Free to members, $2.00 per year to non-members. For information call: Joanne Ralston, Chairman, (503) 782-2609 or (503) 686-5006.

Portland Audubon Society. 5151 N.W. Cornell Road, Portland, OR 97210. Serving: Portland and points south. Established: 1909. Purpose: Preservation of wildlife in its environment. Activities: Field trips, educational classes, meetings. Active members: 2400. Meetings: Every other Friday. Dues: $15.00 individual; $18.00 family. Publication:

Audubon Warbler, published monthly. Advertising: No. Subscription: Free to members; $3.50 per year to non-members. For information call: Mike Uhtoff, Director, (503) 292-6855.

Pennsylvania

Bucks County Audubon Society. Box Doylestown, PA 18901. Serving: Bucks County. Established: 1969. Purpose: Education. Activities: Field trips, Audubon movie series, speakers' bureau. Active members: 1600. Meetings: First Tuesday each month except July and August. Dues: $15.00 per year. Publication: *Newsletter*, eight times a year. Advertising: "No one has ever offered". Subscription: $4.00 per year for non-members; free to membership. For information call: John Mertz, Editor, (215) 794-8990.

Hawk Mountain Sanctuary Association, Rt. 2, Kampton, Pa 19529. Serving: Berks Co., PA; Eastern and New England states. Established: 1934. Purpose: Privately maintained wildlife refuge for birds of prey and their conservation. Activities: Trail hikes, naturalist activities, museum, bookshop, fall hawk migrations, elementary, secondary and college courses & programs, workshops. Active members: 6000. Meetings: None. Dues: $5.00 individual, $10.00 contributing or family, on up per year. Publications: *Hawk Mountain News*, yearly in February; *Annual Report to Members*, yearly in August. Advertising: No. Subscription: Free to members only. For information call: Hawk Mountain Sanctuary, (215) 756-6961.

Audubon Society of Western Pennsylvania. 614 Dorseyville Road, Pittsburgh, PA 15238. Serving: 11 counties of Southwestern Pennsylvania. Established: 1916. Purpose: Study, conservation and protection of birds and all natural resources. Activities: Two wildlife sanctuaries, a wildlife film series, nature education, and field outings. Active members: 2500. Meetings: 4th Wednesday monthly. Dues: $15.00 per year individual membership. Publication: Monthly Bulletin. Advertising: No. Subscription: Free to members, $5.0 per year to non-members. For information call: Joseph A. Grom, President, (412) 935-4283.

Tiadaghton Audubon Society. P.O. Box 402, Mansfield, PA 16933. Serving: Potter and Tioga Counties. Established: 1952. Purpose: Conservation and natural resources. Activities: Bird counts, public information programs. Active members: 120. Meetings: Monthly, 3rd Wednesday, September-May. Dues: $15.00 per year. Publication: *Tiadaghton Raven*, bimonthly. Advertising: No. Subscription: Free to members. For information call: Patrick Kennedy, President, (814) 258-7202.

Rhode Island

Audubon Society of Rhode Island. 40 Bowen St., Providence, RI 02903. Serving: Rhode Island. Established: 1897. Purpose: Conservation and education about natural resources. Activities: Field trips, educational programs, environmental action. Active members: 2500. Meetings: Annual. Dues: $10.00 per year. Publication: *Rhode Island Audubon Report,* 10 times per year. Advertising: Yes. Subscription: $3.00 per year. For information call: Alfred Hawks, Executive Director, (401) 521-1670.

South Carolina

Columbia Audubon Society. P.O. Box 5923, Columbia, SC 29250. Serving: Richland, kershaw, Newberry, Saluda, Fairfield, Lexington, Calhoun and Sumter Counties. Established: 1972. Purpose: Education, conservation and enjoyment of nature. Activities: Field trips, meetings, programs. Active members: 100. Meetings: Monthly, 2nd Tuesday. Dues: $15.00 per year. Publication: Newsletter., monthly. Advertising: No. Subscription: Free to members. For information call: Kay Sisson, Board Member, (803) 256-2655.

Hilton Head Audubon Society. P.O. Box 6185, Hilton Head Island, SC 29928. Serving: Hilton Head Island and environs. Established: 1960. Purpose: Engage in educational, scientific & charitable activities in behalf of and for public benefit within guidelines of National Audubon Society. Activities: Elementary school educational programs & natural history films, bird & plant walks, field trips. Active members: approx 460. Meetings: January, May and September. Dues: $15.00 per year. Publication: *Ecobon*, bimonthly. Advertising: No. Subscription: Free to members, available to non-members on an exchange basis. For information write: President, Hilton Head Audubon Society.

Tennessee

Warioto Audubon Society. Dept. of Biology, Austin Peay State University, Clarksville, TN 37040. Serving: Clarksville and Montgomery Counties and surrounding areas. Established: 1970. Purpose: Conservation of natural resources, education. Activities: Field trips, environmental action. Active members: 75. Meetings: Monthly, 1st Thursday, except July and August. Dues: $15.00 per year. Publication: *Newsletter of the Warioto Audubon Society*, monthly. Advertising: No. Subscription: $2.50 per year. For information call: Dr. Floyd Ford, President, (615) 648-7781.

Texas

Trinity Valley Audubon Society. P.O. Box 423, Gradpeland, TX 75844. Serving: Houston, Leon, Madison and Trinity Counties. Established: 1971. Purpose: Teaching appreciation and preservation of the natural environment. Activities: Lectures, field trips, bird study groups. Active members: 64. Meetings: Monthly, 1st. Thursday, January-June. Dues: $15.00 per year. Publication: *Chit-Chat News*, bimonthly. Advertising: No. Subscription: $5.00. For information call: Nance Butcher, President, (713) 687-2666.

Vermont

Central Vermont Audubon Society. Box 1122, Montpelier, VT 05602. Serving: Central Vermont. Established: 1968. Purpose: Conservation and enjoyment of natural resources. Activities: Meetings, field trips. Active members: 230. Meetings: Monthly, 4th Friday. Dues: $18.00 per year. Publication: *The Osprey*, monthly. Advertising: No. Subscription: $2.00 per year. For information call: Virginia Cole, Editor, (803) 223-7556.

Green Mountain Audubon Society, P.O. Box 33, Burlington, VT 05402. Serving: Chittenden County. Established: 1962. Purpose: Wildlife and natural environment conservation, education. Activities: Field trips, nature center, teacher's workshops, ecology day camps, a maple sugaring program, ten different ecosystems for students. Audubon film series, bird counts, special publications, etc. Active members: 653. Meetings: Monthly except June, July, August & December. Dues: National Audubon membership categories. Publication: *Hermit Thrush*, bimonthly. Subscription: Free to members, $1.50 per year non-members. For information call: Caryn D. Gronvold, President, (802) 985-3917.

Northeast Kingdom Audubon Society. c/o Fairbanks Museum, St. Johnsbury, VT 05819. Serving: Orleans, Essex and Caledonia Counties. Established: 1969. Purpose: Education, support Fairbanks Museum. Activities: Field trips, bird counts. Active members: 130. Meetings: Bimonthly. Dues: Not given. Publication: Newsletter, quarterly. Advertising: No. Subscription: Free to members. For information call: Frank Braman, (802) 748-9639.

Otter Creek Audubon Society. Box 482, Middlebury, VT 05753. Serving: Addison County. Established: 1970. Purpose: Conservation and wildlife education. Activities: Meetings, field trips. Active members: 180. Meetings: Monthly, 3rd Thursday. Dues: $15.00. Publication: Newsletter, bimonthly. Advertising: No. Subscription: Free to members. For information write:

Otter Creek Audubon Society.

Virginia

Northern Neck of Virginia Audubon Society. Box 991, Kilmarnock, VA 22482. Serving: Lancaster, Northcumberland, Westmoreland and Richmond Counties. Established: 1970. Purpose: Conservation and wildlife. Activities: Meetings, field trips. Active members: 250. Meetings: Monthly. Dues: $15.00. Publication: *Northern Neck Audubon Newsletter*; quarterly. Advertising: No. Subscription: Free to members. For information write: Evelyn Thurston, Historian, Northern Neck Audubon Society.

Virgina Society of Ornithology. 2636 Marcey Rd., Arlington, VA 22207. Serving: Virginia. Established: 1929. Purpose: Promote study of bird life and conservation. Activities: Annual convention, field trips. Active members: 650. Meetings: Annual in spring. Dues: $5.00 per year. Publication: *The Raven*, quarterly. Advertising: No. Subscription: $6.00 per year. For information call: F.R. Scott, Editor, (804) 282-2666.

Washington

Blue Mountain Audubon Society. P.O. Box 1106, Walla Walla, WA 99362. Serving: Walla Walla area. Established: 1971. Purpose: Education on conservation, bird life. Activities: Meetings, field trips, public hearings. Active members: 120. Meetings: Monthly, September-May. Dues: $15.00. Publication: *Magpiper*, monthly. Advertising: No. Subscription: $2.50 per year. For information call: Shirley Muse, Editor, (509) 529-2540.

Pacific Northwest Bird and Mammal Society. Puget Sound Museum, University of Puget Sound, Tacoma, WAA 98416. Serving: Pacific Northwest, British Columbia. Established: 1920. Purpose: Encourage student research, publish new observations, promote common interest in northwest birds & mammals. Activities: Field trips, regional meetings. Active members: 328. Meetings: 6 per year regionally, fall through spring. Dues: $4.00 per year (increasing in 1979). Publication: *Murrelet*, tri-annual. Advertising: No. Subscription: Free to members. For information call: Ellen Kritzman, Secretary, (202) 756-3189.

Seattle Audubon Society. 714 Joshua Green Building, Seattle, WA 98101. Serving: King County. Established: 1916. Purpose and activities: Conservation education. Active members: 5000. Meetings: Monthly. Dues: $15.00 per year. Publication: Seattle Audubon *Notes* published monthly. Advertising: No.

Subscription: $3.0 per year to non-members, free to members. For information call: hazel A. Wolf, Secretary, (206) 322-3041.

Spokane Audubon Society. N. 15418 Little Spokane Dr., Spokane, WA 99208. Serving: Eastern Washington. Established: 1965. Purpose: Conservation of natural resources. Activities: Field trips. Active members: 500. Meetings: Monthly, September-June. Dues: $15.00. Publication: *Pygmy Owl*, monthly. Advertising: No. Subscription: $2.50 per year. For information call: Margaret Haggin, President, (509) 487-5554.

Tahoma Audubon Society, 3320 N. Puget Sound Ave., Tacoma, WA 98407. Serving: Pierce County and portion of King County. Established: 1969. Purpose: Wildlife and habitat conservation and preservation. Activities: Wildlife films, workshops, *Nature Guide*, special tours and field trips. Active members: 1400. Meetings: 2nd Friday of winter months. Dues: $18.00 to $20.00 and up per year. Publication: *Towhee*, 10-times a year. Advertising: No. Subscription: Free to members, $2.50 per year non-members. For information call: Ms Nancy Kroening, President, (206) 752-8246.

Yakima Valley Audubon Society. P.O. Box 9701, yakima, WA 98909. Serving: Kittitas and Yakima Counties. Established: 1970. Purpose: Conserve and enhance the environment. Activities: Field trips. Active members: 225. Meetings: Monthly, 4th Friday. Dues: $13.00 to $75.00 per year. Publication: *Calliope Carier*, monthly. Advertising: No. Subscription: $2.00 per year. For information call: Don Jameson, President, (509) 453-1448.

West Virginia

Brooks Bird Club, 707 Warwood Avenue, Wheeling, WV 26003. Serving: West Virginia, Ohio, Pennsylvania, Maryland & Virginia. Established: 1932. Purpose: Independent, educational nonprofit organization to encourage study of birds & other divisions of natural history. Activities: annual two-week camp (Foray), annual sortie (3-day weekend, usually Memorial Day), maintain club library, backyard sanctuaries, various publications, studies, check lists, record keeping, field trips, etc. Active members: Approx. 1000. Meetings: or fields: Monthly. Dues: $10.00 individual, $12.00 family, $3.00 student, on up. Publications: *The Redstart*, quarterly; *The Mail Bag*, bimonthly. Advertising: No. Subscription: Free to members; $10.00 per year non-members. For information call: A.R. Buckelew, Editor, (304) 829-7641.

George Miksh Sutton Audubon Society, P.O. Box J. Bethany, W.V. 26032. Serving: Northern panhandle of W.

VA., S.W. Pennsylvania, E.C. Ohio. Established: 1969. Purpose: Study of natural conservation of natural resources. Activities: Annual Audubon Weekend at Bethany College, field trips, camp scholarships, speakers. Active members: 150. Meetings: Monthly. Dues: $15.00 individual, $18.00 family per year. Publication: *Sutton Screech*, bimonthly. Advertising: No. Subscription: Free to members. For information call: A.R. Buckelew, Jr., Editor, (304) 829-7641.

Wisconsin

Burnett County Audubon Society. Grantsburg, WI 54840. Serving: Burnett County. Established: 1954. Purpose: National Audubon Society Membership, ornithology. Activities: Field trips, tours, sponsorship of local conservation activities and education. Active members: 51. Meetings: Last Friday monthly. Dues: $15.00 annually. Publication: *Newsletter*, quarterly. Advertising: No. Subscription: Free to all. For information call: Norman R. Stone, President, (715) 463-2299.

Wisconsin Society for Ornithology. c/o Secretary, 6855 No. Hwy. 83, Hartland, WI 53029. Serving: Wisconsin. Established: 1937. Purpose: Preservation and study of Wisconsin birds and habitat, public education, protection of natural resources. Activities: Disseminating conservation education materials statewide, maintain birding supply department, campouts and field trips, providing program material, various books, publications and checklists. Active members: 1000+. Meetings: Annual. Dues: From $6.00 individual to $500.00 per year. Publications: *Passenger Pigeon*, quarterly. Advertising: Yes. Subscription: Free to members; $6.00 per year non-members. For information contact: Secretary, Wisconsin Society for Ornithology.

Wyoming

Bighorn Audubon Society, Box 535, Sheridan, Wyoming 82801. Serving: Northern Wyoming. Established: 1970. Purpose: To engage in educational, scientific, investigative, literary, historical, philanthropic and charitable pursuits for the benefit of birds and birding. Activities: Field trips, environmental activism, meetings. Active members: 180. Meetings: 3rd Monday monthly, September through June. Dues: $18.00 family (National Audubon membership). Publication: *Bighorn Audubon Notes*, monthly, September-June. Subscription: Free to members, $2.00 per year non-members. For information call: Jean Daly, President, (307) 674-9728.

Canadian Clubs

Alberta

The Calgary Field Naturalists' Society. Box 981, Calgary, Alberta, Canada T2P 2K4. Serving: Calgary and environs. Established: 1970. Purpose: Wildlife and natural resources conservation; preservation of natural habitat; educational and statistical record-keeping. Activities: Field trips, study groups in botany, mammals & ornithology, Natural Areas Study Program, special publications, Audubon-sponsored nature films, observation and check list programs. Active members: 300. Meetings: Every 3rd Wednesday monthly. Dues: $5.00 individual, $8.00 family, $10.00 supporting-sustaining per year. Publication: *Calgary Field Naturalist*, monthly. Advertising: Seldom. Subscription: Free to members. For information call President, The Calgary Field Naturalists' Society. (403) 252-4364.

B.C.

British Columbia Waterfowl Society. 5191 Robertson Rd., Delta, British Columbia, Canada V4K 3N2. Serving: British Columbia. Established: 1961. Purpose: Operates the George C. Reifel Migratory Bird Sanctuary, a self-supporting facility. Activities: Outings, photography. Active members: 1200. Meetings: Monthly directors meetings. Dues: $7.00 per year. Publications: *Marshnote*, quarterly. Advertising: No. Subscription: Free to members. For information call: Donald Davies, Refuge Manager, (604) 946-6980.

Victoria Natural History Society. P.O. Box 1747, Victoria, B.C., Canada V8W 2Y1. Serving: Southern Vancouver Island. Established: 1944. Purpose: Stimulate interest in natural history; study & protect flora, fauna and their habitat. Activities: Films & lectures in natural history, co-sponsor Audubon wildlife films, field trips in botany, ornithology, marine biology, geology; sponsor junior naturalist group. Active members: 500. Meetings: 2nd Tuesday monthly, September to May. Dues: $7.00 single, $9.00 per year family, $2.50 junior. Publication: *The Victoria Naturalist*, bi-monthly. Advertising: No. Subscription: Free to members, $6.50 to institutions. For information call: Mrs. J. Rimmington, Seretary, (606) 592-6037.

Manitoba

Manitoba Naturalists Society. 214-190 Rupert Avenue, Winnipeg, Manitoba, Canada R3B 0N2. Serving: Manitoba with scattered membership throughout Canada, USA, England, Australia and Africa. Established: 1920. Purpose: To foster the appreciation and preservation of our natural environment and history through research and education. Activities: Field trips, lectures and workshops. Active members: 1800. Meetings: Mondays — bi-monthly — October to April. Dues: $12.00 single — $18.00 family per year. Publication: *Bulletin*, monthly, free to membership; *Manitoba Nature*, quarterly. Advertising: Yes. Subscription: *Manitoba Nature*: $3.00 per year in Canada; $3.50 per year foreign. For information call: Jean Pollock, Office Co-ordinator, (204) 943-9029.

Manitoba Wildlife Federation. 1770 Notre Dame Ave., Winnipeg, Manitoba, Canada R3E 3E6. Serving: Western Canada. Established: 1944. Purpose: Conservation of wildlife & environment. Activities: Wild turkey introduction, pollution action, habitat retention, junior rifle training. Active members: 16,560. Meetings: 142 affiliates — over 6,000 meetings annually. Dues: $6.00 per year. Publication: *Wildlife Crusader*, 7-times annually. Advertising: Yes. Subscription: $3.00 per year to members. For information call: Paul Murphy, Managing Editor, (204) 633-5967.

Newfoundland

Natural History Society of Newfoundland. P.O. Box 1013, St. John's, Newfoundland, Canada A1C 5M3. Serving: Newfoundland. Purpose: To promote interest in natural history. Activities: Field trips, monthly meetings. Active members: 75. Meetings: 3rd Thursday monthly. Dues: $8.00 individual, $6.00 student & corresponding members per year. Publication: *The Osprey*. Advertising: No. Subscription: Free to members. For information write: D.J. Larson, Secretary at Natural History Society of Newfoundland.

Nova Scotia

Nova Scotia Bird Society. 1747 Summer Street, Halifax, Nova Scotia, Canada. Serving: Primarily Nova Scotia, national and international. Established: 1955. Purpose: Study and enjoyment of birds. Activities: Christmas counts, birding hikes & field trips, purchase of land for bird conservation, meetings. Active members: 493. Monthly except May, June, July, August. Dues: $6.00 individual, $8.00 family, $4.00 student per year. Publication: *Nova Scotia Bird Society Newsletter*, 3 times yearly. Advertising: No. Subscription: Free to members. For information call: Miss Margaret Clark, President, (902) 443-3993

Ontario

Federation of Ontario Naturalists. #76, 1262 Don Mills Road, Don Mills, Ontario, Canada M3B 2W7. Serving: Ontario province. Established: 1931. Purpose: Conservation and education for future generations. Activities: Small weekend outings, larger nature vacation tours, bookshop, magazine, environmental activism. Active members: 10,000. Meetings: Annual. Dues: $12.00 individual, $14.00 family, $6.00 student per year. Publication: *Onatario Naturalist*, 5 times a year. Advertising: yes. Subscription: Free to members, $12.00 per year non-members. For information call: Carolyn Turnbull, membership services, (416) 444-8419.

Kingston Field Naturalists. P.O. Box 831, Kingston Ontario, Canada K7L 4X6. Serving: Kingston & environs. Established: 1949. Purpose: Acquire, record, and disseminate knowledge of natural history; stimulate public interest in wild life conservation. Activities: Manage Prince Edward Point Observatory (bird banding), 300-acre KFN-owned woodland tract, Audubon Christmas count, breeding bird surveys, mid-winter waterfowl census, field trips, special counts and round-ups. Active members: 220. Meetings: 3rd Thursday monthly except June, July, August. Dues: $6.00 regular, $8.00 family, $1.00 junior per year. Publication: *The Blue Bill*, quarterly. Advertising: No. Subscription: Free to members and non-members. For information call: Mrs. Helen R. Quilliam, Honary President, (613) 542-6211.

Long Point Bird Observatory. P.O. Box 160, Port Rowan, Ontario, Canada NOE 1M0. Serving; Ontario and Great Lakes states. Established: 1960. Purpose: Ornithological and environmental research, education and conservation; voluntary participation in natural history data gathering. Activities: Daily bird-banding, census-taking and migration monitoring. Special breeding studies, educational programs and several province-wide natural history surveys. Active members: 500. Meetings: 1 annual meeting plus varying daily programs. Dues: $10.00 per year individual; $12.00 family, $5.00 senior and students. Publications:

LPBO Newsletter published 3 times a year; *LPBO Annual Report.* Advertising: No. subscription: Free to membership. For information call: Dr. David J.T. Mussell, Executive Director, (519) 586-2909.

McIlwraith Field Naturalists. 834 Dufferin Ave., London, Ontario, Canada N5W 3K1. Serving: London and area. Established: 1890. Purpose: Study of wildlife and environmental action. Activities: Speakers, field trips and publications. Active members: 225. Meetings: 3rd Friday of each month. Dues: $7.00 per year. Publications: *Cardinal,* quarterly. Advertising: No. Subscription: Free to members. For information call: Mrs. W.G. Wake, treasurer, (519) 455-4903.

The Ottawa Field Naturalists Club. Box 3264, Postal Station 'C', Ottawa, Canada K1Y 4J5. Serving: Local and national. Established: 1879. Purpose: To foster appreciation, preservation, conservation of Canada's natural heritage; investigation, publication and dissemination of natural history research; environmental preservation. Activities: Frequent field trips, conservation, education, junior naturalists' club, meetings, etc. Active members: 660 local, 1160 total. Meetings: 2nd Tuesday monthly except July & August. Dues: $10.00 individual, $12.00 family per year. Publications: *The Canadian Field-Naturalist,* quarterly, free to members, $10.00 individual or $20.00 institutional per year; *Trail & Landscape,* 5 times a year, free to local members and out of town members by request, $10.00 institutional subscription; *Shrike,* bimonthly newsletter, available by $3.00 subscription only. Advertising: No. For information call: Mrs. E. Dickson, (613) 722-3050.

South Peel Naturalists Club. P.O. Box 91, Port Credit, Ontario, Canada L5G 4L5. Serving: Halton, Peel. Established: 1952. Purpose: Promote conservation and field study of natural history. Activities: Lectures, field trips. Active members: 200. Meetings: Third Monday of each month. Dues: $5.00 individual, $7.00 family. Publications: newsletter, monthly. Advertising: No. Subscription: Free to members. For information call: Barry Ranford, President, (416) 277-9364.

Thunder Bay Field Naturalists. Box 1073, Thunder Bay, Ontario, Canada P7C 4X8. Serving: Northwest Ontario, Thunder Bay & environs. Established: 1933. Purpose: Study and recording of natural history of area; environmental protection. Activities: Field trips, environmental studies, bird censuses, submission of briefs to governmental bodies, wildlife study. Active members: 249. Meetings: 4th Monday monthly, September to May. Dues: $8.00 individual, $10.00 family, $4.00 students & senior citizens per year. Publication: *Newsletter,* quarterly. Advertising: No. Subscription: Free to members, available to institutions for $4.00 per year. For

information write: Mr. J. Crowe, Secretary, Thunder Bay Field Naturalists.

Toronto Field Naturalists Club. 65 Havenbrook Blvd., TH 1, Scarborough, Ontario, Canada M2J 1A7. Serving: Toronto. Established: 1923. Purpose: To acquire and disseminate knowledge of natural history and to encourage concern for natural heritage. Activities: Lectures, outings, study groups, publications. Active members: 1800. Meetings: Monthly, September to May. Dues: $10.00 individual, $14.00 family, $6.00 student. Publications: *The Ontario Field Biologist,* biannually, plus a club newsletter, 8 times per year. Advertising: No. Subscription: $3.00 for biannual journal, newsletters free to members. For information call: Carole Parsons, Secretary, (416) 494-8487.

Willow Beach Field Naturalists Club. c/o President, 578 Lakeshore Road, Cobourg, Ontario, Canada. Serving: Port Hope — Cobourg. Established: 1954. Purpose: Promote interest in wildlife and conservation. Activities: Outings, speakers, films. Active members: 75. Meetings: Last Friday every month, September to May. Dues: $3.00 individual; $5.00 family; $1.00 student. Publication: *Curlew,* monthly, September to June. Advertising: No. Subscription: Free to members. For information call: Mrs. Susan Smith, Treasurer, (416) 372-6119.

Quebec

Le Club Des Orinthologues Du Quebec. 8191 Ave. du Zoo, Charlesbourg, Quebec, Canada G1G 4G4. Serving: Province of Quebec. Established: 1955. Purpose: Promote knowledge and appreciation of birds. Activities: Field trips, seminars, bird counts, publications. Active

members: 600. Meetings: Annually in November. Dues: $10.00 per year., $6.00 for students. Publications: *Bulletin Ornithologique* (bird observations and articles), quarterly, *Feuille de Contact* (newsletter), bimonthly, *Cahiers D' Ornithologie Victor Gaboriault* (monographs), biannaully. Advertising: No. Subscription: All publications free to members. For information call: Jean Piuze, Vice President, (418) 849-2154.

The Province of Quebec Society for the Protection of Birds. 9 Springfield Avenue, Westmount, Quebec, Canada H3Y 2K9. Serving: Montreal, and all Quebec. Established: 1917. Purpose: To interest public in birds and conservation by education and recreation. Activities: Annual nature film, field trips, wine & cheese party, lectures. Active members: 800. Meetings: 2nd Monday monthly, October to May. Dues: $8.00 individual per year. Publications: *Tchebec,* yearly; *Tchebec Newsletter,* monthly. Advertising: No. Subscription: Free to members. For information call: Brooke Wright, Secretary, (514) 931-7869.

Saskatchewan

Saskatchewan Natural History Society. Box 1784, Saskatoon, Saskatchewan, Canada S7K 3S1. Serving: Saskatchewan and adjacent regions, central and western Canada. Established: 1949. Purpose: Study and preservation of natural environment. Activities: Blue Jay Bookshop, maintain special sanctuaries, Prairie Nest Records Scheme, special publications, etc. Active members: 2400. Meetings: June and October. Dues: $5.00 per year on up. Publication: *The Blue Jay,* quarterly. Advertising: On occasion. Subscription: Available free to members. For information call: Mrs. Betty Mundy, Treasurer, (306) 664-2946

Other N. American Clubs

North America

American Birding Assn., Inc. P.O. Box 4335, Austin, TX 78765. Serving: International. Established: 1969. Purpose: To promote birding. Activities: Field trips, tours, publications. Active members: 4000. Meetings: Convention every 2 years. Dues: $10.00 per year. Publication: *Birding*, bimonthly. Advertising: Yes. Subscription: $12.50 per year. For information call: Priscilla Tucker, Adminstrative Assistant, (512) 474-4804

American Ornithologists' Union. National Museum of Natural History, Smithsonian Institution, Washington, D.C. 20560. Serving: International with U.S. emphasis. Established: 1888. Purpose: The advancement of ornithological science. Activities: Annual scientific meeting, seminars, educational activities, the AOU Monographs. Active members: over 4000. Meetings: yearly. Dues: $18.00 individual, $14.00 student ($2.00 discount for prompt payment on both categories). Publication: *The Auk*, published quarterly. Subscription: $18.00 per year to members; $20.00 to non-members. Advertising: Yes. for information call: Dr. Kendall W. Corbin, Secretary, (612) 373-5643.

Bird Friends Society. Essex, CT 06426. Serving: United States and Canada. Established: 1972. Purpose: Encourage preservation of North America's wild birds. Activities: Free birding books to libraries, materials for garden clubs and schools, backyard sanctuary program. Active members: 4500. Meetings: Annually in June. Dues: $2.00 per year. Publication: *Wild Bird Guide*, semiannually. Advertising: No. Subscription: Free to members. For information call: Robert Sampson, (203) 767-0668.

Canadian Nature Federation. Suite 203, 75 Albert Street, Ottawa, Ontario K1P 6G1. Serving: All Canada. Established: 1971 (formerly: Canadian Audubon Society). Purpose: Protection and conservation of wildlife and natural resources, act as spokesman in national environmental and conservation issues, support environmental education. Activities: Maintains Canada's largest Nature Bookshop, The Nature Canada Bookshop; sponsors annual Canadian Conference for Nature; tours, field trips, nature art and field programs & symposia; numerous briefs and publications, including Canadian Conservation Directory. Active members: 19,000. Dues: $12.00 per year. Publications: *Nature Canada*, quarterly. Advertising: Yes. Sub-

scription: Free to members, $12.00 per year non-members. For information call: Peggy Heppes, Administrator, (613) 238-6154.

The Canvasback Society. P.O. Box 101, Gates Mills, OH 44040. Serving: United States and Canada. Established: 1976. Purpose: To conserve and promote the increase of Canvasback species of duck in North America. Activities: A variety of projects related to purpose. Active members: 500. Meetings: Annually. Dues: $10.00 per year. Publication: *Canvasbacker*, quarterly. Advertising: No. Subscription: Free to members. For information call: Keith Russel, (216) 623-2040.

Cooper Ornithological Society. Dept of Biology, University of California, Los Angeles, CA 90024. Serving: International. Established: 1893. Purpose: To promote the science of Ornithology. Activities: Publication of ornithological papers and periodicals. Active members: 2481. Meetings: Annually. Dues: $15.00 per year. Publications: *The Condor*, quarterly, *Studies in Avian Biology*, irregularly. Advertising: Yes. Subscription: $20.00 per year. For information Call: J.G. Miller, Asst. Treasurer, (213) 825-1282.

Cornell University Laboratory of Ornithology, 159 Sapsucker Woods Road, Ithaca, NY 14853. Serving: North America. Established: 1956. Purpose: World center for the study and appreciation of birds. Activities: The Sapsucker Woods Sanctuary, The Library of natural Sounds (Cornell University Bird records), photography, special scientific, educational and cultural activities, Nest Record Card Program, Colonial Bird Register, captive breeding program, post-doctoral fellowships to conduct research on behavior & ecology of birds, etc. Active members: 3000. Meetings: Monday evenings, September-May. Dues: $15.00 per year individual, $25.00 family, on up. Publications: *The Living Bird,* annual; *Newsletter, quarterly. Advertising: No. Subscription: Both free to members, Living Bird* $12.00 to non-members. For information call: Dr. Charles R. Smith, Assistant Director, (607) 256-5056.

Ducks Unlimited, Inc., P.O. Box 663000, Chicago, IL 60666. Serving: U.S., Canada, Mexico. Established: 1937. Purpose and activities: Raise money for developing, preserving, restoring & maintaining waterfowl habitat on the North American Continent. Active members: 250,000. Dues: $10.00 per year. Publication: *Ducks Unlimited Magazine*, bi-monthly. Advertising: Yes. Sub-

scription: Free to members. For information call: Catherine Kasha, Advertising Manager, (312) 299-3334.

Eagle Valley Environmentalists, Box 155, Apple River, IL 61001. Serving: 50 states. Established: 1972. Purpose: preservation of Bald Eagle lands and natural habitat. Activities: Bald Eagle Days, Leadership Training and Environmental Workshops, monthly Wildflower weekends, bird counts. Active members: 700. Meetings: annual 1st Saturday in December. Dues: $10.00 individual, $15.00 family, $5.00 student, and up. Publication: *Eagle Valley News*, quarterly. Advertising: Yes. Subscription: Free to members, $3.00 per year non-members.

Eastern Bird Banding Assn. RD #1 Box 212, Monticello, NY 12701. Serving: East of the Mississippi. Established: Not given. Purpose: To encourage investigations into the biology and migration of birds by the use of banding under license and permission of the Department of Interior and to encourage its members in other ornithological studies. Activities: Individual members carry on these studies by banding projects in their own area. Active members: 634. Meetings: Annually in the spring. Dues: $8.00 per year. Publication: *North American Bird Bander*, quarterly. Advertising: Yes. Subscription: Free to members. For information write: Eastern Bird Banding Assn.

International Crane Foundation. City View Road, Baraboo, WI 53913. Serving: International. Established: 1973. Purpose: Dedicated to preservation of cranes and their habitats. Activities: Research, habitat preservation, captive breeding, restocking and education. Active members: 1200+. Meetings: Annual. Dues: $10.00 per year minimum. Publication: *Brolga Bugle*, quarterly. Advertising: No. Subscription: Free to members. For information call: John Wiessinger, Education Coordinator, (608) 356-3553

International Wild Waterfowl Association. Box 1075, Jamestown, North Dakota 58401. Serving: International membership. Established: 1958. Purpose: Preservation and conservation of waterfowl. Activities: Authoring and sponsoring books on propagation of wild waterfowl. Active members: about 500. Meetings: Annually in October. Dues: $6.00 per year. Publication: No. For information write: Director.

National Wild Turkey Federation, Inc. Wild Turkey Building, Edgefield, SC 29824. Serving: National plus some foreign. Established: 1973. Purpose: Wise management and conservation of the American

Wild Turkey and other wildlife as valuable natural resources. Supports sport hunting. Activities: Public education seminars, research grants to Wild Turkey biologists, turkey calling demonstrations and contests, chapter functions. Active members: 35,000. Meetings: Set by state and local chapters. Dues: $10.00 per year, graduating membership categories. Publication: *Turkey Call.* bimonthly. Advertising: Yes. Subscription: $10.00 per year regular; $6.00 introductory to new members only. For information call: Tom Rodgers, Executive Vice President, (803) 637-3106.

Nature Society. Purple Martin Junction, Griggsville, IL 62340. Serving: North America. Established: 1965. Purpose: Promote interest in natural history, especially birds. Activities: Publication, sponsorship of Purple Martin Time events; wildlife. Dues: $5.00 per year; $6.00 Canada and elsewhere. Publication: *Purple Martin News*, monthly. Advertising: No. Subscription: $5.00 per year for non-members. For information call: J.L. Wade, Sponsor, (217) 833-2323.

Northeastern Bird-banding Association, Inc. c/o Mr. Robert Shaw, 639 Main Street, Concord, MA 01742. Serving: U.S.A. and foreign. Established: 1923. Purpose: To promote the study of birds. Activities: Publish quarterly journal of ornithological research. Import mist nets for licensed banders. Active members: 1200. Meetings: Every year. Dues: $6.00 per year. Publication: *Bird Banding*, published quarterly. Subscription: free to members;

$8.00 per year to non-members. Advertising: No. For information call: James O. Seamans, President, (602) 945-3372.

Save the Tallgrass Prairie. 4101 W. 54th Terrace, Shawnee Mission, KS 66205. Serving: National. Established: 1973. Purpose: Promote legislation toward creation of a Tallgrass Prairie National Park & National Preserve. Activities: Workshops, conferences, field trips, speakers bureau, lobbying, many publications. Active members: 600+. Meetings: Quarterly Board of Directors, Annual Fall Conference. Dues: $5.00 regular. Advertising not accepted in any publications. For information call: Elaine Shea, Executive Secretary, (913) 384-3197.

Society for the Preservation of Birds of Prey. P.O. Box 891, Pacific Palisades, CA 90272. Serving: International in scope. Established: 1966. Purposes: Protection and preservation of birds of prey and their habitat. Meetings: None. Dues: $8.00 for two years. Publication: *The Raptor Report*, tri-annually. Advertising: No. Subscription: Free to members. For information contact the Society.

Trumpeter Swan Society. P.O. Box 296, Maple Plain, MN 55359. Serving: North America. Established: 1968. Purpose: Full phase scientific and educational organization promoting the protection and management of the Trumpeter Swan. Activities: Fund-raising and related activities. Active members: 150. Meetings: Directors - semi-annually; general membership - biennially.

Dues: $5.00 per fiscal year. Publication: *The Trumpeter Swan Society Newsletter*, twice a year. Advertising: No. Subscription: free to members. For information call: David K. Weaver, Secretary-Treasurer, (612) 473-4693.

U.S. Section, International Council for Bird Preservation. c/o National Audubon Society, 950 Third Avenue, New York, NY 10022. Serving: U.S.A. (I.C.B.P. has national sections in more than 60 countries). Established: 1922. Purposes: Bird conservation. Activities: Habitat preservation, scientific publications, research grants for rare and endangered species, statements on conservation issues. Active members: 12 member organizations (including National Audubon Society); approximately 100 individual contributing members. Meetings: Annually. Dues: $15.00 minimum per year; Other categories in advanced amounts. Publications: *President's Letter*, three times a year; *Bulletin*, issued after each international conference at 4-year intervals. Subscription: *President's Letter* free to members only; *Bulletin* may be ordered by non-members at per issue cost. Advertising: No. For information call: Richard L. Plunkett, Secretary U.S. Section, (212) 832-3200.

Wetlands for Wildlife, Inc. P.O. Box 147, Mayville, Wisconsin 53050. Serving: National membership. Established: 1960. Purpose: Protection and promotion of wetlands and wildlife thereon. Activities: Directly related to above. Active members: 300. Meetings: Quarterly. Dues: $10.00 per year. Publication: *Wetlands for Wildlife News*, published quarterly for membership only. Advertising: Yes. For information call: Richard Goff, President, (414) 276-9362 or (414) 281-8936.

Wilson Ornithological Society. c/o Josselyn Van Tyne Memorial Library, Museum of Zoology, University of Michigan, Ann Arbor, MI 48104. Serving: North America. Established: 1888. Purpose: Advance science of ornithology. Activities: Scientific papers, sessions and field trips. Active members: 2100. Meetings: Annually. Dues: $10.00 per year. Publication: *The Wilson Bulletin*, quarterly. Advertising: No. Subscription: Free to members; $15.00 per year non-members. For information contact: Museum of Zoology, University of Michigan, (313) 764-0457.

Whooping Crane Conservation Association. 3000 Meadowlark Drive, Sierra Vista, AZ 85635. Serving: North America. Established: 1961. Purpose: Scientific and educational. Activities: Collecting and disseminating information about the Whooping Crane. Active members: 400. Meetings: Annual. Dues: $5.00 per year (or $100.00 for life). Publication: *Grus americana*, quarterly. Advertising: No. Subscription: Free to members. For information call: Jerome J. Pratt, Secretary-Treasurer, (602) 458-0971.

Outside North America

Australia

The Avicultural & Wildlife Assn. 165 Planet St., Carlisle 6101, Western Australia. Serving: Western Australia. Established: 1968. Purpose: Promote the appreciation of birds, wildlife and conservation. Activities: Field trips, meetings, conservation programs. Active members: 1000. Meetings: Monthly, 1st Sunday. Dues: $2.00 Aust. per year. Publication: *Aviary Bird & Wildlife*, monthly. Advertising: Yes. Subscription: Free to members. For information call: Jan Sheahan, Secretary, Perth 361-9730 or 458-1104.

Bird Observers Club. Box 2167T, G.P.O., Melbourne, Victoria 3001, Australia. Serving: Australia. Established: 1905. Purpose: The study and protection of Australian native birds. Activities:Conservation, education, surveys, outings. Active members: 2700. Meetings: Monthly, 3rd Tuesday. Dues: Not given. Publication: *The Bird Observer*, monthly, *The Australian Bird Watcher*, quarterly. Advertising: No. Subscription: $5.00 per year. For information call: Ellen McCulloch, Secretary, (03) 877-5342.

South Australian Ornithological Association. c/o S.A. Museum, North Terrace, Adelaide, South Australia 5000. Serving: State of South Australia. Established: 1899. Purpose: Increased Ornithological understanding. Activities: Meetings, lectures, field trips. Active members: 500. Meetings: Monthly, last Friday. Dues: $8.00 per year. Publication: *The South Australian Ornithologist*, biannually. Advertising: No. Subscription: $6.00 per year. For information write: South Australian Ornithological Association.

Belgium

Ornithologische Vererijing De Wielewaal. Graatakker 11, 2300 Turnhout, Belgium. Serving: Northern Belgium. Established: 1933. Purpose: Bird study and protection. Activities: Meetings, bird banding, sanctuaries, field trips. Active members: 7000. Meetings: Annually. Dues: $10.00 per year. Publication: *De Wielewaal*, 10 times per year. Advertising: No. Subscription: $10.00 per year. For information call: R. Franckx, President 014-412252.

Reaerves naturelles Et Ornithologiques De Belgique. 31, rue Vautier, 1040 Bruxelles, Belgium. Serving: Belgium. Established: 1951. Purpose: Nature conser-

vation. Activities: Management of 50 bird sanctuaries in Belgium, excursions, workcamps. Active members: 10,000. Meetings: Almost every weekend. Dues: $10.00 per year. Publication: *Feuille de Contact*, quarterly, *Bulletin*, annually. Advertising: No. Subscription: $10.00 per year. For information call: Edgar Kesteloot, President, 02/6483746.

Brazil

Sociedade Ornithologica Mineira. Rua da Bahia, 1148 — Conjnto 631, Belo Horizonte, Brasil. Serving: Brasil. Established: 1967. Purpose: Protestion of Brasil's flora and fauna. Activities: Meetings, publishing. Active members: 1030. Meetings: Not given. Dues: Not given. Publication: *Revista "SOM".*, quarterly. Advertising: Yes. Subscription: $20.00 per year. For information call: Sociedade Ornithologica Mineira, (031) 226-6302.

Denmark

Dansk Ornithologisk Forening. Vesterbrogade 140, 1620 Kobenhaven, DK-Denmark. Serving: Denmark and Greenland. Established: 1906. Purpose: Development of knowledge of birds and conservation. Activities: Meetings, excursions, research. Active members: 6000 Meetings: Every 2nd Wednesday. Dues: D kr 120 per year. Publications: *Dansk Ornithologisk Forenings Tidsskrift*, quarterly, *Feltornithologen*, quarterly, *Fuglevaern*, annually. Advertising: Yes. Subscription: D kr 135 per year. For information call: N.E. Franzmann, Vice President, 01 318105.

England

British Ornithologists Club. c/o British Ornithologists Union, Zoological Society of London, Regent's Park, London NW1 4RY, England. Serving: United Kingdom. Established: 1892. Purpose: Promote scientific discussion and publication of information connected with ornothology. Activities: Meetings, lectures, publications. Active members: 300. Meetings: Every 2 months. Dues: $7.50 per year. Publication: *Bulletin of the British Ornithologists' Club*, quarterly. Advertising: No. Subscription: $11.00 per year. For information write: British Ornithologists Club.

Bristish Ornithologists Union. c/o Zoological Society of London, Regent's Park,

London NW1 4RY, England. Serving: International. Purpose: The advancement of the science of ornithology. Activities: Thise for a scientific society. Active members: 1800. Meetings: Annually. Dues: $19.00 per year. Publication: *The ibis*, quarterly. Subscription: $43.50 per year. For information call: Assistant Secretary, 01-586 4443.

British Trust for Ornithology. Beech Grove, Tring, hertfordshire HP23 5NR, England. Serving: Great Britian. Established: 1933. Purpose: Understanding the balance between bird opulations and their environment. Activities: Fieldwork, nest recording, censusing, ringing. Active members: 7000. Meetings: Annually. Dues: 15 Pounds per year. Publication: *Bird Study*, quarterly. Advertising: Yes. Subscription: 5 pounds per year. For information call: Mrs. G. Bonham, Membership Secretary, Tring (044 282) 3461.

Ray Society. c/o The British Museum (Natural History), Cromwell Rd., London SW7 5BD, England. Serving: British Isles. Established: 1844. Purpose: To publish original works on natural history. Activities: Publication of books and maps. Active members: 355. Meetings: Annually. Dues: $7.50 per year. Publications: Various titles, one book per year. Advertising: No. Subscription: No. For information call: G.A. Boxshall., Director, 01-589-6323.

The Royal Society for the Protection of Birds. The Lodge, Sandy, Bedsforshire, England. Serving: Great Britain and Northern Ireland. Established: 1889. Purpose: To encourage study and conservation of birds. Activities: Manages 68 reserves, research, education, publishing. Active members: 250,000. Meetings: Held by 130 local groups. Dues: 5 Pounds per year. Publication: *Birds*, quarterly. Advertising: Yes. For information call: Ian Prestt, Director, Sandy (0767) 80551.

Wildfowl Trust. Slimbridge, Gloucestershire, GL2 7BT, England. Serving: England and Scotland. Established: 1946. Purpose: Research, conservation, education. Activities: Courses, lectures, tours, operates refuges. Active members: 10,000. Meetings: Not given. Dues: 3.50 Pounds per year. Publication: *Wildfowl*, annually, *Wildfowl News*, biannaully. Advertising: Yes, *Wildfowl News*. Subscription: Free to members. For information call: S.A. Rolfe Smith, Administrative Officer, Cambridge 333 Ext. 29.

Young Ornithologists Club. The Lodge, Sandy, Bedfordshire, SG14 2DL, England. Serving: England and Ireland. Established:

1965. Purpose: To encourage a greater interest in birds and their place in nature in young people up to 15 years of age. Activities: Competitions, projects, holiday courses, field trips. Active members: 75,000. Meetings: Not given. Dues: 2 Pounds per year. Publication: *Bird Life*, bimonthly. Advertising: Yes. Subscription: Free to members. For information call: Peter Holden, National Organizer, 0767 80551.

Finland

Societas Pro Fauna Et Flora Fennica. Snellmansgatan 9-11, SF-00170 Helsngfors 17, Finland. Serving: Finland. Established: 1821. Purpose: Study of natural environment. Activities: Meetings, excursions, seminars, exchange of scientific publications. Active members: 640. Meetings: Monthly, except summertime. Dues: None. Publications: *Acta Botanica Fennica*, quarterly, *Acta Zoologici Fennici*, quarterly, *Annales Botanici Fennici*, quarterly, *Annales Zoologici Fennici*, quarterly, *Memoranda Societatis pro Fauna et Flora Fennica*, biannually. Advertising: Yes. Subscription: $12.00 per year for Annales, $8.00 per year for Memoranda. For information call: Bjorn Federley M.Sc., Finland 90-647003 or 90-533636.

France

Ligue Pour la Protection Des Oiseaux. 57 rue Cuvier, 75005 Paris, France. Serving: France. Established: 1912. Purpose: Protection, observation and study of bird. Activities: Lectures, conservation campaigns, publishing, guided tours. Active members: 3000. Meetings: Annually in May. Dues: $6.00 per year. Publication: *Le Courrier de la Nature*, bimonthly. Advertising: No. Subscription: 50 F. per year. For information call: M. Metais, 99-59-97.

Societe D Etudes Ornithologiques. Ecole Normale Superieure, Zaboratoire de Zoologie, 46, rue d' Ulm, 75230 Paris CEDEX 05, France. Serving: International. Established: 1929. Purpose: Study of birds. Activities: Publications, meetings, colaborative inquires. Active members: 850. Meetings: Monthly. Dues: 80,00 F. per year. Publication: *Alauda*, quarterly. Advertising: No. Subscription: 110,00 F. per year. For information write: Prof. Heim de Balsac, President, Societe d Etudes Ornithologiques.

Ireland

Irish Wildbird Conservancy. c/o Royal Irish Academy, 19 Dawson St., Dublin 2, Ireland. Serving: Republic of Ireland. Established: 1968. Purpose: To promote conservation, education and appreciation of wild-life in Ireland. Activities: Conferences, training courses, lectures, field outings. Active members: 2000. Meetings: Monthly. Dues: Not given. Publication: *Irish Birds*, annually, newsletter, quarterly. Advertising: Yes. Subscription: $3.64 per year. For information call: Vincent Sheridan, Education Officer, 977193.

Japan

Ornithological Society of Japan. c/o National Science Museum, Hyakunin-cho 3-23-1, Shijuku-ku, Tokyo 160, Japan. Serving: Japan. Established: 1912. Purpose: The advancement of ornithology in general. Active members: 500. Meetings: Quarterly. Dues: 3000 yen per year. Publication: *Tori*, quarterly. Advertising: No. Subscription: 4,000 yen per year. For information write: Dr. N. Morioka, Secretary, Ornithological Society of Japan.

Luxembourg

Lique Luxembourgeoise Pour L'Etude Et La Protection Des Oiseaux. 32 rue de la Foret, Luxembourg-Cessange, G.D. Luxembourg. Serving: Luxembourg. Established: 1920. Purpose: Study of bird life. Activities: Field work, research, education, publishing. Active members: 2500. Meetings: Annually. Dues: 10 Frlux per year. Publication: *Regulus*, quarterly. Advertising: Yes. Subscription: 100 Frlux per year. For information call: Henri Rinnen, President, 48 61 37.

Middle East

Ornithological Society of the Middle East. c/o R.S.P.B., The Lodge, Sandy, Beds., England. Serving: The Middle East. Established: 1967. Purpose: To study and report on the birds of the area. Activities: Publishing reports and bulletins. Active members: 100. Meetings: Annually. Dues: 2 Pounds per year. Publication: The *Sandgrouse*, annually. Advertising: No. Subscription: Free to members. For information call: Donald Parr, Secretary, Ashtead 73031.

Netherlands

Nederlandse Ornithologische Unie. c/o Dr. G.C. Boere, Voorstraat 7, 4153 A H Beesd, Holland. Serving: Netherlands. Established: 1901. Purpose: Promotion of the study of ornithology. Activities: Meetings, excursions. Active members: 1000. Meetings: Quarterly. Dues: $25.00 per year. Publication: *Ardea*, biannually, *Limosa*, biannaully. Advertising: Yes. Subscription: $25.00 per year. For informa-tion write: Nederlandse Ornithologische Unie.

Vereniging Tot Behoud Van Natuurmonumenten In Nederland. Noordereinde Go 's-Graveland, Netherlands. Serving: Netherlands. Established: 1905. Purpose: Nature conservation. Activities: Meetings, field trips. Active members: 251,000. Meetings: 25 times a year at various locations throughout the country. Dues: DF1 25 per year. Publication: *Natuurbehoad*, quarterly. Advertising: No. Subscription: Free to members. For information write: Vereniging Tot Behoud Van Natuurmonumenten in Nederland.

New Zealand

Ornithological Society of New Zealand. P.O. Box 3011, Dunedin, New Zealand. Serving: New Zealand. Established: 1939 Purpose: Study of Ornithology. Activities: Sutdy courses, bird counts, banding programs. Active members: 1325. Meetings: Each region has its own meetings. Dues: $8.00 per year. Publication: *Notornis*, quarterly. Advertising: No. Subscription: Free to members. For information call: H.W.M. Hogg, Dunedin 47139.

North Ireland

Royal Society for the Protection of Birds. Belvoir Park Forest, Belfast BT8 4QT Northern Ireland. Serving: Northern Ireland. Established: 1968. Purpose: Study of birds. Activities: Field trips, meetings, films. Active members: 2000. Meetings: Meetings held by groups in various centers. Dues: £ 5 per year. Publication: *Birds*, quarterly. Advertising: Yes. Subscription: Free to members. For information call: Dinah Browne, Regional Officer, Belfast 692547.

Norway

Norsk Ornithologisk Forening. Zoologisk Institutt, Rosenborg, 7000 Trondheim, Norway. Serving: Norway. Established: 1958. Purpose: To stimulate the investigation and interest in bird life in Norway. Activities: Research projects, excursions. Active members: 3000. Meetings: Annually in April. Dues: Nkr. 40 per year. Publication: *Var Fuglefauna*, quarterly. Advertising: Yes. Subscription: Not given. For information write: Norsk Ornithologisk Forening.

Rhodesia

Rhodesian Ornithological Society. Box 8382, Causeway, Salisbury, Rhodesia. Serving: Rhodesia. Established: 1950.

Purpose: To encourage an interest in the bird life of the country. Activities: Lectures, field trips. Active members: 500. Meetings: Monthly, 3rd Thursday. Dues: $3.00 per year. Publication: *Honeyguide*, quarterly. Advertising: Yes. Subscription: $3.00 per year. For information write: Rhodesian Ornithological Society.

Scotland

Scottish Ornithologists Club. 21 Regent Terrace, Edinburgh EH7 5BT, Scotland. Serving: Scotland. Established: 1936. Purpose: Encourage the study and promote an interest in birds and conservation. Activities: Meetings, field trips. Active members: 3000. Meetings: Monthly in 12 branches. Dues: 5 Pounds per year. Publication: *Scottish Birds*, quarterly. Advertising: Yes. Subscription: 6 Pounds per year. For information call: Major A.D. Peirse, Duncombe Secretary, 031-556-6042.

South Africa

Southern Africa Ornithological Society. P.O. Box 97234, Houghton, Johannesburg 2041, South Africa. Serving: Southern Africa. Established: 1929. Purpose: Promotion of interest in ornithology and protection of bird life. Activities: Lectures, field trips. Active members: 3000. Meetings: Monthly. Dues: $10.00 per year. Publications: *The Ostrich*, quarterly, *Bokmakierie*, quarterly. Advertising: Yes in *Bokmakierie*. Subscription: Free to members. For information call: Secretary, Johannesburg 643-4528.

Spain

Sociedad Espanola De Ornithologia. 3er Pabellon, Planta 9, Facultad de Biologia, U. Complutense, Madrid 3, Spain. Serving: Spain. Established: 1954. Purpose: Conservation and scientific study of wild birds in the Spanish Territory. Activities: Bird counts, meetings, publishing. Active members: 1100. Meetings: Biannually. Dues: 800 pts. per year. Publication: *Ardeola*, annually. Advertising: No. Subscription: $20.00 per year. For information call: Dr. Manuel Fernandez-Cruz, Secretary, 91-9991318.

Sweden

Seriges Ornithologiska Fornening. Runebergsgatan 8, S-11429 Stockholm, Sweden. Established: 1942. Purpose: Protection, research and education about birds. Activities: Bird counts, research, lectures, excursions, conservation programs. Active members: 6500. Meetings: Monthly. Dues: $10.00 per year.

Publication: *Var Fagelvarld*, quarterly. Advertising: Yes. Subscription: $12.00 per year. For information call: Peter Ohman. Intendent, 08/210508.

Switzerland

Ala Schweizerische Gesllschaft Fur Vogelkunoe Und Vogelschutz. Kernstrasse 27, CH-8406 Winterthur, Switzerland. Serving: Switzerland. Established: Not given. Purpose: Scientific bird study. Activities: Publishing, bird conservation. Active members: 1250. Meetings: Biannually. Dues: $15.00 per year. Publication: *Der Ornithologische Beobachter*, bimonthly. Advertising: Yes. Subscription: $20.00 per year. For information call: Dr. B. Bruderer, 041 99 13 59.

Yugoslavia

Ornitholoski Zavod Zagreb. Istrazivacki Center JAZU, Jedinica Ornithologija, 4100 Zagreb, Ilirski trg /11, Yugoslavia. Serving: Yugoslavia. Established: Not given. Purpose: Scientific orthinological investigation. Activities: Bird banding, publishing, meetings. Active members: 40 volunteers. Meetings: Not given. Dues: None. Publication: *Larus*, annually. Advertising: No. Subscription: 150.00 Din. per year. For information call: Dr. Ljubica Stromar, (041) 35-798.

Zambia

Zambian Ornithological Society. P.O. Box 3944, Lusaka, Zambia. Serving: Zambia. Established: 1968. Purpose: Study and conservation of birds. Activities: Field trips, meetings, bird counts. Active members: 150. Meetings: Monthly. Dues: K 8.00 per year. Publication: *Z.O.S. Bulletin*, biannually. Advertising: No. Subscription: K 10.00 per year. For information write: Miss I.L. Johansson, Secretary, Zambian Ornithological Society.

Best Bet
Birding Sites

The incredible fact about the sport of bird watching is that, provided there's daylight, you can start anywhere, right now. Don't move a muscle except to look out the window. In time you'll see a bird.

It's true that some sites provide more to look at than others. Roadside rests, particularly in the prairie or dessert, are great. So are zoos. Says Jane Church, Director of California's Point Reyes Bird Observatory, "I have done some excellent birding on zoo grounds. The [uncaged] birds are attracted to food fed to the captive animals."

Three categories of best-bet birding sites exist. One is where two biotic communities meet: woods and marsh, seashore and forest, field and chaparral. In Palm Springs, California, you can move from the desert to an alpine environment in fifteen minutes by means of an airborn tram. The second category is the oasis, of which zoos and roadside rests are examples. So are arboretums and city parks—local chambers of commerce are a good way to find out about these.

The third category is the flyway, an established air route of migrating birds. In North America the four north/south flyways for waterfowl are the Pacific Coast Flyway, the Central or Rocky Mountain Flyway, the Mississippi Flyway, and the Atlantic Coast Flyway. During the migration months of April-May and mid September-mid November, many song birds (order Passeriformes) have their own, more localized flyways. In the spring they move to higher altitudes, and come down in the fall.

National and State Parks make excellent bird watching sites. So do National and State Wildlife Refuges, and the sanctuaries run by the National Audubon Society and local Audubon chapters. Most furnish on request a list of birds you're likely to see. Of course a lot depends on the time (dawn and dusk are best) and the weather—birds hate to expose themselves in wind or fog. You'll find that the first day following a storm gives excellent birding.

We couldn't begin to cover all the special birding sites in North America. Four other books devote 2,041 pages to nothing but: Kitching's *Birdwatcher's Guide to Wildlife Sanctuaries* (Arco 1976), Pettingill's *A Guide to Bird Finding East of the Mississippi* (Oxford 1977) and its soon-to-be-updated companion *Bird Finding West of the Mississippi,* and Pettingill's *The Bird Watcher's America* (Crowell 1974). This year the

Tahoma Audubon Society (34915 - 4th Ave. South, Federal Way, WA 98003) published a *Nature Guide.* In it the addresses and phones of 963 people who will show you birding sites in their localities are listed. In 1976 the American Birding Associaiton (Box 4335, Austin, TX 78765) did a similar guide.

Still, in addition to the sites we do list (National Parks and Monuments, National Wildlife Refuges, National Audubon Society Wildlife Sanctuaries), there are a few others we'd like to mention. First is the 180-acre Sapsucker Woods Sanctuary, run by Cornell's Laboratory of Ornithology three miles north of Ithaca. The Laboratory of Ornithology (159 Sapsucker Road, Ithaca, NY 14850—phone 607, 256-5056) is Mecca for students of birds; its sanctuary boasts four miles of boardwalks and trails. There you will find spotting scopes for the public's use and the world's largest collection of tape-recorded bird sounds.

To our knowledge, no one has heretofore listed bird observatories in Canada and the U.S. Although these primarily are research stations, the staffs are always willing to suggest local birding spots. By writing ahead, you may even be invited to watch serious ornithologists in action. In alphabetical order eight of these observatories are: 1) Ashby Bird Observatory, RFD Box 30, Ashby, MA 01431; 2) Cape May Bird Observatory, c/o New Jersey Audubon Society, 790 Ewing Ave., Franklin Lakes, NJ 07417; 3) Long Point Bird Observatory, Box 160, Port Rowan, Ontario, Canada NOE 1M0; 4) Manomet Bird Observatory, Manomet, MASS 02345; 5) Point Reyes Bird Observatory, 4990 Shoreline Highway, Stinson Beach, CA 94970; 6) Prince Edward Point Bird Observatory, c/o Kingston Field Naturalists, Box 831, Kingston, Ontario, Canada K7L L1X6; 7) Raccoon Ridge Bird Observatory, Box 81, Layton, NJ 07851; 8) Southern Illinois Bird Observatory, Box 2471, Carbondale, IL 62901.

More and more of our 154 National Forests are catering to bird watchers. In each you'll find naturalists happy to answer questions, and a labyrinthine web of trails. Nineteen National Forests now have full-fledged Visitor Centers. For details and maps write Forest Service, U.S. Department of Agriculture, Washington, D.C. 20250.

You may find our last tip stinks but here it is:

one of the best birding sites a town has is its garbage dump. Even if you prefer to stay in your car with the windows up, give it a try. The species you discover there may surprise you.

Why do we single out National Parks and Monuments, National Wildlife Refuges, and the National Audubon Society's Wildlife Sanctuaries for listing in this book? Because they offer the best variety of habitats we could discover. All the National Parks and Monuments welcome visitors. So do the Refuges and Sanctuaries you find here, but for some you'll have to write ahead for an appointment. That's to your advantage; a private look, with the Refuge manager or Sanctuary warden to answer your questions, is an experience you'll not forget. Be sure to ask for a complete list of probable birds, so that you can study up beforehand.

The National Park System got its start in 1872 when Congress established Yellowstone's 2,219,823 acres as "a public park or pleasuring ground for the benefit and enjoyment of the people". The Park System now comprises 31 million acres (including historical areas not listed here). Its purpose is to conserve scenery and wildlife for enjoyment now and later. You can get brochures on any of the Parks by writing them or National Park Service, U.S. Department of the Interior, Washington, D.C. 20250.

President Teddy Roosevelt started the National Wildlife Refuge System in 1903 by preserving a colony of pelicans, Royal Terns, and herons off Florida's east coast. Today 400 Refuges exist on 34 million acres (those you can't visit aren't listed). Their importance is threefold: to protect endangered species, to protect migrating waterfowl, and to draw birds off private farmland so they won't eat the crops. For information write the individual Refuges or National Wildlife Refuge System, Fish and Wildlife Service, U.S. Department of the Interior, Washington, D.C. 20240.

You'll find out more about the National Audubon Society in the Organizations section. It is enough to say here that between Teddy Roosevelt and two of National Audubon's early presidents, Bill Dutcher and T. Gilbert Pearson, wildlife in this country got a fighting chance to live. The 367-acre Little Duck Island off the coast of Maine, a nesting spot for Black Guillemots and pelagic (open-sea) birds was the first Audubon Sanctuary, set up in 1900. It remains off-limits to

visitors. The purpose of National Audubon Society Sanctuaries is to preserve all endangered wildlife, not only birds. For information of likely birds, days open, and possible admission fees, contact the 45 Sanctuaries listed or National Audubon Society Sanctuary Director, Miles Wildlife Sanctuary, West Cornwall Road, Sharon, CT 06069—phone 203, 364-0048.

Wherever you bird, the attitude you bring along is crucial. Both journals of American bird watching, *American Birds* and *Birding,* call attention to the importance of ethics. The following eyewitness account by birder Dale Zimmerman points up the problem:

"The arrival of birding tour groups is anticipated with something less than enthusiasm in parts of Arizona . . . Full-sized chartered buses down in little Guadalupe Canyon disgorged birders in all directions. Few saw any but the most common species because all the shy resident birds were driven to cover. The late morning visit was ill-timed for bird-finding. Alarmed birds probably left their nests, leaving exposed eggs or young to be cooked by the fierce Arizona sun."[1]

Concerned bird watcher Richard L. Glinski proposes these rules of etiquette:

1. Avoid the use of tape-recorded territorial calls of rare birds that are actively breeding.
2. Observe nests from a distance great enough so that parent birds and their activities are not disturbed.
3. Photography should never include the removal of nestlings nor of foliage close to the nest.
4. Respect the property and wishes of the landowner.
5. Do not associate with large groups that are bussed *en masse* to critical habitats and then turned loose without responsible guides.[2]

To all this we'd like to add our own statement about litter. When you visit the sites that follow, we urge you to leave nothing on the ground but your footprints.

[1]*Birding,* Volume 10, Number 1, Jan.-Feb. 1978. Reprinted by permission of the American Birding Association.
[2]*American Birds,* V olume 30, Number 3, June 1976, page 657. Reprinted by permission of the National Audubon Society.

Birding Sites

Alabama

Choctaw National Wildlife Refuge. Size: 4,218 acres. Established: 1964. Terrain: river bottom land, water. Attractions: Tombigbee River. Watch for: ducks, Canada Goose, Bobwhite. Information: Box 325, Jackson, AL 36545. Phone: (205) 246-3583.

Wheeler National Wildlife Refuge. Size: 34,120 acres. Established: 1938. Terrain: farmland, pastures, river and reservoir banks. Attractions: Tennessee River, Wheeler Lake (reservoir); fishing, hunting. Watch for: Canada Goose, Black Duck, Bobwhite, Peregrine Falcon, Wood Ibis. Information: Box 1643, Decatur, AL 35601. Phone: (205) 353-7243.

Alaska

Aleutian Islands National Wildlife Refuge. Size: 2,720,225 acres. Established: 1913. Terrain: heather-covered hillsides, sea cliffs, no trees. Attractions: two Aleut villages, fishing. Watch for: Ptarmigan, Fulmar, Emperor Goose, cormorants, Laysan Albatross, Smew. Information: box 5251, Adak, AK 98791. Phone: (907) 579-8418.

Glacier Bay National Monument. Size: 2,805,071 acres. Proclaimed: 1925. Terrain: tidewater glaciers, estuary, brushlands. Attractions: rare species of wildlife. Watch for: Bald Eagle, Northern Phalarope, Mew Gull, Marbles Murrelet, Orange-crowned Warbler. Information: P.O. Box 1089, Juneau, AK 99802.

Izembek National Wildlife Range. Size: 320,802 acres. Established: 1960. Terrain: glaciated uplands, grass meadows, volcanic pinnacles. Watch for: Emperor Goose, Pintail, Oldsquaw, Rock Sandpiper, Steller's Eider, Yellow Warbler. Information: Pouch #2, Cold Bay, AK 99571. Phone: (907) 532-2445.

Katmai National Monument. Size: 2,792,137 acres. Proclaimed: 1918. Terrain: lakes, forests, mountains, marshlands. Attractions: Valley of Ten Thousand Smokes. Watch for: ducks, grebes, Whistling Swan, hawks, falcons, Ptarmigan. Information: P.O. Box 7, King Salmon, AK 99613.

Kodiak National Wildlife Refuge. Size: 1,815,000 acres. Established: 1941. Terrain: islands, tundra and treed areas, many wildflowers. Attractions: two modern hotels; fishing by chartered boat. Watch for: Harlequin Duck, Lapland Longspur, Belted Kingfisher, Common Loon, Mew Gull, Tufted Puffin. Information: Box 825, Kodiak, AK 99615. Phone: (907) 486-3325.

Mount McKinley Natinal Park. Size: 1,939,492 acres. Established: 1917. Terrain: Alaska Range. Attractions: camping, lodge, naturalist programs, bus tours, hiking. Watch for: Short-eared Owl, Ptarmigan, Marsh Hawk, Golden Eagle, Townsend's Solitaire. Information: P.O. Box 9, McKinley Park, AK 99755. Phone: (907) 683-2294.

Arizona

Cabeza Prieta National Wildlife Refuge. Size: 860,000 acres. Established: 1939. Terrain: desert. Watch for: Gila Woodpecker, Verdin, Black-tailed Gnatcatcher, Black-throated Sparrow, Lawrence's Goldfinch, Golden Eagle. Information: Ajo, AZ 85321. Phone: (602) 387-6483.

Chiricahua National Monument. Size: 10,634 acres. Proclaimed: 1924. Terrain: strange rock forms, canyons, glens with trees and shrubs. Attractions: visitor center, camp grounds, hiking and horseback trails. Watch for: White-necked Raven, Bridled Titmouse, White-throated Swift, Olivaceous Flycatcher, Black-chinned Hummingbird. Information: Dos Cabezas Star Route, Willcox, AZ 85643.

Grand Canyon National Park. Size: 673,575 acres. Established: 1919. Terrain: forested, arid area; Colorado river, with adjacent uplands. Attractions: visitor center, museum, Ranger-naturalist trips, lodges. Watch for: Pinyon Jay, Mountain Bluebird, hawk, Violet-green Swallow, Western Tanger, Dipper. Information: P.O. Box 129, Grand Canyon, AZ 86023. Phone: (602) 638-2411.

Imperial National Wildlife Refuge. Size: 25,765 acres. Established: 1941. Terrain: desert-mountain; lakes, ponds, sloughs, waters of Imperial Dam. Watch for: Clapper Rail, Red-tailed Hawk, Roadrunner, Verdin, Great Blue Heron, Hooded Merganser. Information: P.O. Box 2217, Martinez Lake, AZ 85364. Phone: (602) 783-3400.

Organ Pipe Cactus National Monument. Size: 329,064 acres. Proclaimed: 1937. Terrain: Sonoran Desert. Attractions: the majestic organ cactus. Watch for: White-winged Dove, Lesser Nighthawk, Costa's Hummingbird, Vermilion Flycatcher, Sage Sparrow, Gambel's Quail. Information: P.O. Box 38, Ajo, AZ 85321.

Petrified Forest National Park. Size: 94,189. Established: 1962. Attractions: fossilized forest, Triassic rock formations, Indian petroglyphs. Watch for: Golden Eagle, Cooper's Hawk, Roadrunner, Pinyon Jay, Rock Wren. Information: Petrified Forest National Park, AZ 86025. Phone: (602) 524-6228.

Saguaro National Monument. Size: 78,169 acres. Proclaimed: 1933. Terrain: Sonora Desert. Attractions: giant saguaro cactus; camping, hiking trails. Watch for: Curved-billed Thrasher, Phainopepla, Loggerhead Shrike, Roadrunner, Gilded Flicker, Gila Woodpecker. Information: P.O. Box 17210, Tucson, AZ 85731.

Arkansas

Big Lake National Wildlife Refuge. Size: 11,038 acres. Established: 1915. Terrain: woods, farmland, open water, river bottom. Attractions: fishing, boating, swimming, picnicking. Watch for: Blue-winged Teal, Cardinal, Eastern Meadowlark, Bald Eagle, Dickcissel. Information: P.O. Box 67, Manila, AR 72442. Phone: (501) 564-2429.

Holla Bend National Wildlife Refuge. Size: 4,083 acres. Established: 1957. Terrain: open water bordered with grain fields and forest. Attractions: Arkansas River; fishing, hunting. Watch for: ducks, geese, Bobwhite, Cardinal, Turkey Vulture. Information: P.O. Box 1043, Russellville, AR 72801. Phone: (501) 968-2800.

Hot Springs National Park. Size: 3,345 acres. Established: 1921. Terrain: woodland. Attractions: 47 mineral hot springs; 18 miles of hiking trails; campgrounds, visitor center. Watch for: Tufted Titmouse, Carolina Wren, Caroline Chickadee, warblers. Information: P.O. Box 1219, Hot Springs National Park, AR 71901. Phone: (501) 624-3383.

Wapanocca National Wildlife Refuge. Size: 5,484 acres. Established: 1961. Terrain: farmlands, swamp, lake. Attractions: nature boat trail, observation tower. Watch for: Killdeer, Screech Owl, Belted Kingfisher, woodpeckers, Wood Duck, Turkey. Information: P.O. Box 257, Turrell, AR 72384. Phone: (501) 343-2595.

White River National Wildlife Refuge. Size: 112,399 acres. Established: 1935. Terrain: lakes, bayous, bottomlands along lower White River. Watch for: Sprague's

Pipit, warblers, bitterns, gallinules, Cardinal, American Coot. Information: P.O. Box 308, DeWitt, AR 72042. Phone: (501) 946-1468.

California

Bobelaine Audubon Sanctuary. Size: 430 acres. Established: 1975. Terrain: wooded floodplain. Attractions: Feather River. Watch for: raptors, songbirds, wild ducks. Information: c/o National Audubon, 555 Audubon Place, Sacramento, CA 95825. Phone: (916) 481-5333. Appointment necessary.

Channel Islands National Monument. Size: 18,384 acres (land area: 1,120 acres); includes Santa Barbara and Anacapa Islands. Proclaimed: 1938. Attractions: rookery of sea lions, nesting sea birds; unique plants. Watch for: Sooty Shearwater, Wilson's Warbler, American Kestrel, Brown Pelican, Peregrine Falcon. Information: 1699 Anchors Way Dr., Ventura, CA 93003.

Death Valley National Monument. Size: 2,048,850 acres. Established: 1933. Terrain: salt beds, sand dunes, borax formations, desert shrub land, cliffs, canyons. Attractions: contains lowest point in Western Hemisphere; Furnace Creek Ranch; Scotty's Castle. Watch for: Costa's Hummingbird, Verdin, Rough-winged Swallow, Sage Thrasher, Roadrunner. Information: Death Valley, CA 92328.

Havasu National Wildlife Refuge. Size: 41,500 acres. Established: 1941. Terrain: marsh, lake, canyons, uplands. Attractions: canoe and float trips (Colorado River), fishing, boat ramps, camping. Watch for: Avocets, Black-necked Stilt, Northern Phalarope, California Gull, willet, Violet-green Swallow. Information: P.O. Box A, Needles, CA 92363. Phone: (714) 326-3853.

Hopper Mountain National Wildlife Refuge. Size: 1,871 acres. Established: 1974. Terrain: rugged mountain area. Attractions: California Condor recovery area. Watch for: variety of raptorial birds. Information: P.O. Box 219, Delano, CA 93215. Visitation by special arrangement only.

Humboldt Bay National Wildlife Refuge. Size: 130 acres. Established: 1971. Terrain: tidal flats, salt marshes. Attractions: fishing, clamming, nature study. Watch for: Pacific Black Brant, other migratory waterfowl. Information: P.O. Box 1386, Eureka, CA 95501. Phone: (707) 445-1352.

Joshua Tree National Monument. Size: 531,781 acres. Proclaimed: 1936. Terrain: desert. Attractions: variety of desert plants and animals; camping and self-guiding nature trails. Watch for: Costa's Humming-bird, Bullock's Oriole, Say's Phoebe, Ladder-backed Woodpecker, Elf Owl. Information: 74485 Palm Vista Dr., Twentynine Palms, CA 92277.

Kern-Pixley National Wildlife Refuge. Size: 14,800 approx. Established: 1958-60. Terrain: semi-desert. Attractions: developed for migrating and wintering waterfowl. Watch for: Green-winged Teal, Avocet, Burrowing Owl, Long-billed Marsh Wren, Fulvous Tree Duck, Cassin's Kingbird. Information: P.O. Box 219, Delano, CA 93215. Phone: (805) 725-2767.

Kings Canyon National Park. Size: 459,956 acres. Established: 1940. Terrain: Sierra Nevada Mountains. Attractions: wilderness area; General Grant Grove (park section with giant sequoias). Information: Three Rivers, CA 93271. Phone: (209) 565-3341.

Klamath Basin National Wildlife Refuges. (Tule Lake, Lower Klamath, Clear Lake, Klamath Forest, Upper Klamath.) Size: 121,158 acres. Terrain: forests, juniper, sagebrush, farmlands, rough lava, marshes, meadows, open lakes. Attractions: auto trails and tour routes. Watch for: Cackling, White-fronted and Snow Goose; Sandhill Crane, Gadwall and Cinnamon Teal, White Pelican. Information: Route 1, Box 74, Tulelake, CA 96134. Phone: (916) 667-2231.

Lassen Volcanic National Park. Size: 105,797 acres. Established: 1916. Terrain: pine forests, lakes. Attractions: hot springs, volcanic cones; camping fishing, boating, guided walks. Watch for: Evening Grosbeak, Green-tailed Towhee, White Pelican, Townsend's Solitaire. Information: Mineral, CA 96063. Phone: (916) 595-4444.

Merced National Wildlife Refuge. Size: 2,562 acres. Established: 1951. Terrain: San Joaquin Valley land. Attractions: feeding area for waterfowl. Watch for: Sandhill Crane, ducks, geese. Information: P.O. Box 2176, Los Banos, CA 93625. Phone: (209) 826-3508.

Modoc National Wildlife Refuge. Size: 8,016 acres. Established: 1960. Terrain: rolling hills, ponds. Attractions: fishing, picnicking, wildlife observation. Watch for: "Western" Canada Goose, Mallard, Cinnamon Teal, Ring-necked Pheasant, Ross' Goose, Osprey. Information: P.O. Box 1610, Alturas, CA 96101. Phone: (916) 233-3572.

Muir Woods National Monument. Size: 492 acres. Proclaimed: 1908. Terrain: Pacific coast redwoods stand at foot of Mount Tamalpais. Attractions: hiking; Braille trail for blind. Watch for: Chestnut-backed Chickadee, Winter Wren, Hermit Thrush, Brown Creeper, Spotted Owl. Information: Mill Valley, CA 94941.

Pinnacles National Monument. Size: 14,177 acres. Proclaimed: 1908. Terrain: variety of volcanic features (located on San Andreas Fault). Attractions: hiking trails to view spirelike rock formations 500 to 1,200 feet high. Watch for: Hutton's Vireo, Lawrence's Goldfinch, Peregrine Falcon, Phainopepla. Information: Paicines, CA 95043.

Redwood National Park. Size: 27,953 acres. Established: 1968. Attractions: coastal redwood forests, virgin groves of ancient trees, including the world's tallest; 40 miles of Pacific coastline. Information: Drawer N, Crescent City, CA 95531. Phone: (707) 464-6101.

Richardson Bay Wildlife Audubon Sanctuary. Size: 911 acres. Established: 1961. Terrain: shallow bay, some uplands. Attractions: wintering area for birds; harbor seals in winter; Whittell Education Center. Watch for: sandpipers, Sanderling, Dunlin, Western Grebe. Information: 376 Greenwood Beach Road, Tiburon, CA 94920. Phone: (415) 388-2524.

Sacramento National Wildlife Refuge. Size: 10,783 acres. Established: 1937. Terrain: Sacramento Valley. Attractions: wintering area for waterfowl of Pacific Flyway. Watch for: ducks, geese, Whistling Swan, White-tailed Kite. Information: Rt. 1, Box 311, Willows, CA 95988. Phone: (916) 934-4090.

Salton Sea National Wildlife Refuge. Size: 2,500 acres. Established: 1930. Terrain: croplands and desert. Attractions: guided tours. Watch for: Fulvous Tree Duck, Gambel's Quail, Verdin, Canada Goose, Roadrunner, Brown Pelican. Information: P.O. Box 247, Calipatria, CA 92233. Phone: (714) 348-2323.

San Francisco Bay National Wildlife Refuge. Size: 23,000 acres. Established: 1974. Terrain: baylands, slough. Watch for: California Least Tern, Brown Pelican, Peregrine Falcon, California Clapper Rail, Forster's Tern. Information: 3849 Peralta Blvd., Suite D, Fremont, CA 94536. Phone: (415) 792-0222.

Seal Beach National Wildlife Refuge. Size: 977 acres. Established: 1974. Terrain: salt marsh, tidal wetlands. Watch for: Light-footed Clapper Rail, California Tern, Brown Pelican, shore and wading birds. Information: P.O. Box 219, Delano, CA 93215. Visitation by special arrangement only. Phone: (805) 725-2767.

Squoia National Park. Size: 386,471 acres. Established: 1890. Terrain: Sierra Nevada Mountains. Attractions: camping, fishing, naturalist-guided trips; Mount Whitney. Watch for: Mountain Quail, Gray-crowned Rosy Finch, Blue Grouse, Pileated Woodpecker, Canyon Wren, Western Tanager. Information: Three Rivers, CA 93271. Phone: (209) 565-3341.

Starr Ranch Audubon Sanctuary. Size: approx. 4000 acres. Established: 1973.

Terrain: Santa Ana foothills; grasslands, woodlands, canyons. Attractions: resident mamals include deer, coyotes, mountain lions. Watch for: warblers, flycatchers, hummingbirds, woodpeckers, eagles. Information: P.O. Box 435, Trabuco Canyon, CA 92678. Phone: (714) 586-6190. Appointment necessary.

Yosemite National Park. Size: 759,206 acres. Established: 1890. Terrain: Sierra Nevada Mountains. Attractions: granite peaks and domes, mountain lakes, waterfalls, groves of giant sequoias; fishing, field seminars in ornithology, ski in winter. Watch for: Goshawk, Hammond's Flycatcher, Band-tailed Pigeon, Western Bluebird, Calliope Hummingbird, Black-backed Three-toed Woodpecker. Information: P.O. Box 577, Yosemite National Park, CA 95389. Phone: (209) 372-4461.

Colorado

Alamosa National Wildlife Refuge. Size: 9,186 acres. Established: 1963. Watch for: ducks, "Western" Canada Goose, Ring-necked Pheasant. Information: P.O. Box 511, Monte Vista, CO 81144. Phone: (303) 589-4910.

Arapaho National Wildlife Refuge. Size: 8,019 acres. Established: 1967. Terrain: Illinois River area. Attractions: waterfowl nesting grounds. Information: Box 457, Walden, CO 80480. Phone: (303) 723-4717.

Black Canyon of the Gunnison National Monument. Size: 13,323 acres. Established: 1933. Attractions: deep canyon, see ancient rocks of obscure origin. Informatoin: P.O. Box 1648, Montrose, CO 81401.

Browns Park National Wildlife Refuge. Size: 12,215 acres. Established: 1965. Terrain: Green River land. Attractions: waterfowl nesting area. Watch for: ducks, "Western" Canada Goose, Peregrin Falcon. Information: Box 398, Vernal, Utah 84078. Phone: Colorado (303) 365-3695.

Colorado National Monument. Size: 17,655 acres. Proclaimed: 1911. Attractions: sheer-walled canyons, monoliths, unusual rock formations. Information: P.O. Box 438, Fruita, CO 81152.

Dinosaur National Monument. Size: 199,550 acres. Proclaimed: 1914. Terrain: hills, narrow valleys, mountain streams. Attractions: river trips, camping along Yampa and Green Rivers; excellent birding. Watch for: Lazuli Bunting, Mountain Chickadee, Rosy Finch, Great Blue Heron, Common Nighthawk, Turkey Vulture, Brewer's Blackbird. Information: P.O. Box 210, Dinosaur, CO 81610.

Eagle Rock Audubon Sanctuary. Size: 14,360 acres. Established: 1973. Terrain: short-grass prairie. Attractions: nesting raptors. Watch for: Golden Eagle, Prairie Falcon, Ferruginous Hawk. Information:

P.O. Box 3232, Boulder, CO 80303. Phone: (303) 323-4011.

Monte Vista National Wildlife Refuge. Size: 13,548 acres. Established: 1952. Terrain: brushland, water. Attractions: touring roads, picnicking. Watch for: Snowy Egret, Yellowthroat, Black-crowned Night Heron, Black Tern, Marsh Hawk, Short-eared Owl, Hooded Merganser. Information: P.O. Box 511, Monte Vista, CO 81144. Phone: (303) 852-2435.

Rocky Mountain National Park. Size: 261,196 acres. Established: 1915. Terrain: mountain peaks up to 14,000 feet, upland meadows, forests. Attractions: naturalist program, mountaineering, fishing camping, winter sports. Watch for: Bald Eagle, Williamson's Sapsucker, Goshawk. Information: Estes Park, CO 80517. Phone: (303) 586-2371.

Connecticut

Audubon Center of Greenwich. Size: 477 acres. Established: 1941. Terrain: woodland. Attractions: Fairchild Wildflower Garden. Watch for: owls, hawks, woodpeckers, nuthatches, Eastern Meadowlark. Information: 613 Riversville Rd., Greenwich, CT 06830. Phone: (203) 869-5272.

Miles Wildlife Audubon Sanctuary. Size: 751 acres. Established: 1963. Terrain: Berkshire Hills (streams, swamps, beaver ponds). Attractions: four miles of nature trails—guided field trips by appointment. Watch for: geese, ducks, Hooded Merganser, woodpeckers, flickers, owls, Kestrel. Information: West Cornwall Rd., Sharon, CT 06069. Phone: (203) 364-5302. Appointment necessary.

Salt Meadow National Wildlife Refuge. Size: 183 acres. Established: 1971. Terrain: salt marsh. Watch for: Black Duck, geese,

mallards, Blue-winged Teal. Information: 191 Sudbury Rd., Concord, Massachusetts 01742. Phone: (617) 369-5518.

Sharon Audubon Center. Size: 526 acres. Established: 1961. Terrain: woodland, ponds, streams. Attractions: Sharon Interpretive Center. Watch for: ducks, Canada Goose, various nesting waterfowl. Information: Route 4, Sharon, CT 06069. Phone: (203) 364-5826.

Delaware

Bombay Hook National Wildlife Refuge. Size: 15,135 acres. Established: 1937. Terrain: uplands, wooded areas, rivers, freshwater pools, marsh. Attractions: picnic area, observation towers, boardwalk across marsh. Watch for: Willet, plovers, dowitchers, Snow Goose, Wilson's Phalarope, Osprey. Information: Box 147, Smyrna, DE 19977. Phone: (302) 653-9345.

Florida

Big Cypress National Preserve. Size: (not available). Established: 1974. Terrain: (adjoins Everglades National Park). Attractions: subtropical plant and animal life. Information: c/o Everglades National Park, P.O. Box 279, Homestead, FL 3303. Phone: (305) 247-6211.

Big Pine Key Audubon Sanctuary. Size: 747 acres. Established: 1963. Terrain: island. Attractions: refuge for the endangered key deer. Watch for: Peregrin Falcon, Great White Heron, White-crowned Pigeon, Laughing Gull, Frigatebird. Information: Key Deer National Wildlife Refuge, Box 510, Big Pine Key, FL 33043. Phone: (305) 872-2239.

Biscayne National Monument. Size:

94,367 acres. Established: 1968. Terrain: island chain, bordered by Biscayne Bay on west and Atlantic Ocean on east. Information: P.O. Box 1369, Homestead, FL 33030.

Chassahowitzka National Wildlife Refuge. Size: 30,143 acres. Established: 1943. Terrain: marshes, estuaries, salt bays, swamps, coastal sandhills. Attractions: most of this refuge is seen only by boat. Watch for: Black Rail, Connecticut Warbler, Osprey, White Ibis, Limpkin, Hooded Merganser. Information: Rt. 2, Box 44, Homosassa, FL 32646. Phone: (904) 795-2201.

Corkscrew Swamp Audubon Sanctuary. Size: approx. 11,000 acres. Established: 1954. Terrain: bald cypress swamp. Attractions: mile-long hike on boardwalk through swamp. Watch for: Wood Stork, Roseat Spoonbill, Bachman's Sparrow, White Ibis, herons, Sandhill Crane. Information: Box 1875, Rte. 2, Sanctuary Road, Naples, FL 33940. Phone: (813) 657-3771.

Cowpens Key Audubon Sanctuary. Size: 10 acres. Terrain: island formed of deposits of calcium carbonate. Attractions: island teems with seasonal nesting activity. Watch for: White Ibis, Louisiana Heron, Great, Reddish, and Snowy Egret, Osprey, West Indian Yellow Warbler. Information: 115 Indian Mound Trail, Tavernier, FL 33070. Appointment necessary.

J.N. "Ding" Darling National Wildlife Refuge. Size: 4,786 acres. Established: 1945. Terrain: coastal island. Attractions: observation towers, canoe trail through mangrove swamps; shelling on adjacent island. Watch for: herons, Roseate Spoonbill, Bald Eagle, Gray Kingbird, Swallow-tailed Kite, Mangrove Cuckoo, Black Vulture. Information: P.O. Drawer B, Sanibel, FL 33957. Phone: (813) 472-1100.

Everglades National Park. Size: 1,385,723 acres. Established: 1934. Terrian: fresh and saltwater areas, open Everglades prairies, mangrove forests. Attractions: interpretive centers, boardwalks, guided boat caravans, lodge, campgrounds, fishing. Watch for: pelicans, egrets, herons, Roseate Spoonbill, Anhinga, Boat-tailed Grackle, Fish Crow. Information: P.O. Box 279, Homestead, FL 33030. Phone: (305) 247-6211.

Great White Heron National Wildlife Refuge. Size: 4,122 acres. Established: 1938. Terrain: scattered islands, only accessible by boat. Watch for: Roseate Spoonbill, Brown Pelican, White-crowned Pigeon, Bald Eagle, Peregrin Falcon. Information: Box 510, Big Pine, FL 33040. Phone: (305) 372-2239.

Kissimmee Prairie Audubon Region. Size: 60,000 acres. Terrain: wet grasslands, marshes. Attractions: breeding area for birds. Watch for: Sandhill Cranes, egrets,

ibises, Caracara, Burrowing Owl. Information: Lake Okeechobee Warden, 505 SW 10th St., Okeechobee, FL 33472. Phone: (813) 763-3946. Appointment necessary.

Kitchen Creek Wildlife Audubon Sanctuary. Size: 42 acres. Terrain: woodland of bald cypresses and pines. Attractions: located along Loxahatchee River; contiguous to Jonathan Dickinson State Park. Information: c/o Tom Tomlinson, 4906 N. Dixie Hwy., W. Palm Beach, FL 33407. Appointment necessary.

Lake Okeechobee Audubon Sanctuary. Size: 28,250 acres. Established: 1938. Terrain: shallow water, marsh. Attractions: prime bird feeding and breeding areas. Watch for: endangered Everglade Kite, Sandhill Crane, egrets, ibises, Caracara. Information: 505 SW 10th St., Okeechobee, FL 33472. Phone: (813) 763-3946. Appointment necessary.

Lake Woodruff National Wildlife Refuge. Size: 18,400 acres. Established: 1963. Terrain: open water, swamps, pinelands (access by boat only). Watch for: Great Crested Flycatcher, White-eyed Vireo, Pine Warbler, King Rail, Sandhill Crane, Bald Eagle. Information: P.O. Box 488, Deleon Springs, FL 32028. Phone: (904) 985-4673.

Lake Worth Islands Audubon Sanctuary. Size: 100 acres. Established: 1943. Terrain: keys located in town of Palm Beach. Attractions: bird rookeries. Watch for: ibises, egrets, herons, Information: c/o Tom Tomlinson, 4906 N. Dixie Hwy. W. Palm Beach, FL 33407. Appointment necessary.

Loxahatchee National Wildlife Refuge. Size: 145,636 acres. Established: 1951. Terrain: prairie and marshland. Attractions: nature trails, fishing, boating. Watch for: Cardinal, Chuckwill's-Widow, Limpkin, Peregrin Falcon, Pileated Woodpecker. Information: Rt. 1, Box 278, Boynton Beach, FL 33437. Phone: (305) 732-3684.

Merritt Island National Wildlife Refuge. Size: 134,143 acres. Established: 1963. Terrain: lagoons, marshlands, mangroves, sand dunes. Attractions: bounded by Kennedy Space Center. Watch for: Wood Stork, Cardinal, Red-tailed Hawk, Royal Tern, Black Skimmer, Brown Pelican. Information: P.O. Box 6504, Titusville, FL 32780. Phone: (305) 867-4820.

Rookery Bay Audubon Sanctuary. Size: approx. 3,050 acres. Established: 1960. Terrain: estuary. Attractions: birding, fishing, boating. Watch for: Brown Pelican, Louisiana Heron, egrets. Information: P.O. Box 997, Naples, FL 33940. Appointment necessary.

St. Marks National Wildlife Refuge. Size: 65,000 acres. Established: 1931. Terrain: marsh, ponds, pine flatwoods, bay waters. Watch for: Canada Goose, Turkey,

rails, Oystercatcher, Yellow-billed Cuckoo, Orchard Oriole, Limpkin, Anhinga. Information: Box 68, St. Marks, FL 32355. Phone: (904) 925-6280.

St. Vincent National Wildlife Refuge. Size: 12,490 acres. Established: 1968. Attractions: fishing, shelling. Watch for: waterfowl, Bald Eagle, Turkey. Information: Box 447, Apalachicola, FL 32320. Phone: (904) 653-8808.

Tampa Bay Audubon Sanctuary. Size: 200 acres. Established: 1933. Terrain: estuary. Attractions: aquatic bird rookeries. Watch for: herons, egrets, ibises, terns, Brown Pelican. Information: Route 1, Box 205-U, Ruskin, FL 33570. Phone: (813) 645-9484. Appointment necessary.

Georgia

Blackbeard Island National Wildlife Refuge. Size: 5,168 acres. Established: 1924. Terrain: hardwood timber, marshland. Attractions: fishing. Watch for: Bald Eagle, herons, waterfowl, shore birds. Information: Savannah National Wildlife Refuge, Box 8487, Savannah, GA 31402. Phone: (912) 232-4321, X415.

Harris Neck National Wildlife Refuge. Size: 2,687 acres. Established: 1962. Terrain: coastal. Watch for: Canada Goose, Wood Duck, Turkey. Information: Savannah National Wildlife Refuge, Box 8487, Savannah, GA 31402. Phone: (912) 232-4321, X415.

Okefenokee National Wildlife Refuge. Size: 377,528 acres. Established: 1937. Terrain: floating peat beds in cypress swamp. Attractions: visitor center, Suwanee Canal Recreation Area; swamp tours, observation tower; picnicking. Watch for: Barred Owl, vultures, Parula Warbler, Brown Thrasher, Sandhill Crane, Glossy Ibis. Information: P.O. Box 117, Waycross, GA 31501. Phone: (912) 283-2580.

Piedmont National Wildlife Refuge. Size: 34,738 acres. Established: 1939. Terrain: forested hills. Attractions: trails, fishing. Watch for: Turkey, Bobwhite, Pileated Woodpecker, Great Horned Owl, Brown-headed Nuthatch, Bachman's Sparrow. Information: Round Oak, GA 31080. Phone: (912) 986-3651.

Wassaw National Wildlife Refuge. Size: 10,242 acres. Established: 1969. Terrain: tidal marsh, timbered dunes. Attractions: hiking trails, fishing, shelling, picnicking. Watch for: waterfowl, wading and shore birds. Information: Savannah National Wildlife Refuge, Box 8487, Savannah, GA 31402. Phone: (912) 232-4321, X415.

Hawaii

Haleakala National Park. Size: 20,929

acres. Established: 1972. Terrain: volcano crater. Attractions: Seven Pools, Kipahulu Valley; native and migratory birdlife. Information: P.O. Box 537, Makawao, Maui, HI 96768. Phone: (808) 572-7749.

Hawaii Volcanoes National Park. Size: 217,029 acres. Established: 1916. Attractions: active volcanism; lower elevations have luxuriant and rare vegetation; variety of wildlife. Watch for: Cardinal, House Finch, Apapane. Information: Hawaii Volcanoes National Park, HI, 96718. Phone: (808) 967-7311.

Hawaiian Islands National Wildlife Refuge. Size: 1,907 acres (approx.). Established: 1909. Terrain: chain of eight volcanic and coral islands; little vegetation. Watch for: Bonin Island Petrel, Nihoa Finch, Laysan Teal, Nihoa Millerbird, albatrosses. Information: 300 Ala Moana Blvd., Honolulu, HI 96850. Phone: (808) 546-7507. Permit necessary to land on islands.

Idaho

Bear Lake National Wildlife Refuge. Size: 16,033 acres. Established: 1968. Terrain: marsh, water. Attractions: nesting, resting and feeding area for waterfowl. Watch for: Greater Sandhill Crane, "Western" Canada Goose, swans, ducks, shore birds. Information: Box 837, Soda Spring, ID 83276 or Box 9, Montpelier, ID 83254. Phone: (208) 847-1757.

Camas National Wildlife Refuge. Size: 10,471 acres. Established: 1937. Terrain: water, marsh, grassland; altitude—4,700 feet. Watch for: Ferruginous Hawk, Golden Eagle, Whistling Swan, Long-billed Curlew, Avocet. Information: Hamer, ID 83425. Phone: (208) 662-5423.

Craters of the Moon National Monument. Size: 53,545 acres. Proclaimed: 1924. Terrain: lava flows, caves, volcanic cones, craters. Attractions: visitor center, seven-mile loop drive, interpretive program. Watch for: Blue Grouse, Saw-whet Owl, Rock Wren, Horned Lark, Golden Eagle, Prairie Falcon. Information: P.O. Box 29, Arco, ID 83213.

Grays Lake National Wildlife Refuge. Size: 16,033 acres. Established: 1965. Terrain: lake bed marsh. Attractions: nesting and migrating waterfowl. Watch for: Whooping Crane, Canada Goose, Sandhill Crane. Information: Box 837, Soda Springs, ID 83276. Phone: (208) 547-4996.

Kootenai National Wildlife Refuge. Size: 2,762 acres. Established: 1964. Terrain: uplands. Attractions: fishing, walking trails. Watch for: geese, ducks. Information: Rt. 1, Box 160, Bonners Ferry, ID 83805. Phone: (208) 267-3888.

Minidoka National Wildlife Refuge. Size: 25,630 acres. Established: 1909. Terrain: Lake Walcott marsh land, grassland, desert vegetation, altitude—4,545 feet. Attractions: Minidoka Dam, Snake River; fishing, swimming, boating, camping. Watch for: California Gull, Canada Goose, Sage Grouse, Willet, White-faced Ibis. Information: Rupert, ID 83350. Phone: (208) 456-3589.

Illinois

Chautauqua National Wildlife Refuge. Size: 5,114 acres. Established: 1936. Terrain: river bottoms, sand dunes. Attractions: observation tower, boat ramp, picnicking. Watch for: Towhee, Black Duck, Sora, Bell's Vireo, Red-headed Woodpecker. Information: R.R. 2, Havana, IL 62644. Phone: (309) 595-2290.

Crab Orchard National Wildlife Refuge. Size: 42,825 acres. Established: 1947. Terrain: marshes, forests, farmland, two lakes. Attractions: nature trails, boat ramps, camping, fishing. Watch for: Bachman's Sparrow, Dickcissel, Snow Goose, Turkey Vulture, Eastern Blue-bird, Parula Warbler. Information: P.O. Box J, Carterville, IL 62918. Phone: (618) 997-3344.

Mark Twain National Wildlfe Refuge. Size: 24,000 acres (takes in land in Iowa and Missouri, also). Established: 1947. Attractions: borders Mississippi River; road and boat access. Watch for: Great Blue Heron, Yellow-billed Cuckoo, woodpeckers, Purple Martin. Information: 311 N. 5th St., #100, Quincy, IL 62301. Phone: (217) 224-8580.

Indiana

Muscatatuck National Wildlife Refuge. Size: 7,724 acres. Established: 1966. Terrain: wetlands, farm land, timber. Attractions: walking trails, fishing, visitor center. Watch for: waterfowl, marsh birds. Information: Box 631, Seymour, IN 47274. Phone: (812) 522-4352.

Iowa

De Soto National Wildlife Refuge. Size: 3,496 acres. Established: 1958. Terrain: flood plains, freshwater marshes, open water, farmland. Attractions: swimming, fishing, boating. Watch for: Yellow Warbler, American Redstart, Piping Plover, Bald Eagle, Bank Swallow. Information: Route 1, Box 114, Missouri Valley, IA 51555. Phone: (712) 642-4121.

Union Slough National Wildlife Refuge. Size: 2,074 acres. Established: 1938. Terrain: marsh, cropland. Attractions: swimming, fishing, picnicking. Watch for: Franklin's Gull, Yellow-shafted Flicker, Tree Swallow, Wilson's Phalarope, Pied-billed Grebe. Information: P.O. Box AF, Titonka, IA 50480. Phone: (515) 928-2523.

Kansas

Kirwin National Wildlife Refuge. Size: 10,778 acres. Established: 1954. Terrain: open water, marsh, grasslands. Attractions: boating, swimming, waterskiing. Watch for: Canada Goose, Green-winged Teal, Golden and Bald Eagle, Whooping Crane, Ferruginous Hawk. Information: Kirwin, KS 67644. Phone: (913) 646-2373.

Quivira National Wildlife Refuge. Size: 1,900 acres. Established: 1955. Terrain: marsh, grassland, canals. Attractions: travel only on township roads (no public facilities). Watch for: Snowy Plover, Avocet, Mississippi Kite, Canada Goose, Peregrin Falcon, Sandhill Crane. Information: P.O. Box G, Stafford, KS 67578. Phone: (316) 486-2393.

Kentucky

Clyde E. Buckley Audubon Sanctuary. Size: 285 acres. Terrain: hill land overlooking Kentucky River. Attractions: Ray Harm House, nature museum. Watch for: Wilson's Phalarope, Golden Eagle, Bald Eagle, owls, grebes, American Bittern. Information: Route 3, Frankfort, KY 40601. Phone: (606) 873-5711.

Jefferson County Forest Audubon Sanctuary. Size: almost 1,800 acres. Established: 1975. Terrain: rugged woodland wilderness. Located within sight of Louisville's skyscrapers. Information: P.O. Box 5248, Louisville, KY 40205. Phone: (502) 451-0331.

Mammoth Cave National Park. Size: 51,303 acres. Established: 1941. Terrain: woodlands, farmlands, Green River. Attractions: cave trips, hiking trails, guided walks, boating, fishing; hotel, campgrounds. Watch for: Eastern Bluebird, Wood Thrush, Prothonotary Warbler, Green Heron. Information: Mammoth Cave, KY 42259. Phone: (502) 758-2251.

Vernon Douglas Audubon Wildlife Sanctuary. Size: 682 acres. Established: 1971. Terrain: hill, mostly forested. Information: Rt. 1, Box 19, Mauckport, IN. Phone: (812) 732-2349. Appointment necessary.

Louisiana

Catahoula National Wildlife Refuge. Size: 5,308 acres. Established: 1958. Attractions: Catahoula Lake, fishing. Watch for: wintering waterfowl. Information: Drawer LL, Jena, LA 70549. Phone: (318) 992-5261.

Delta-Gulf Islands National Wildlife Refuge. Size: 48,799 acres. Established: 1935. Terrain: Mississippi Delta marshland. Attractions: deer, fur-bearing animals, alligators frequently seen. Watch for: Blue Goose, Snow Goose, egrets, shore birds. Information: 1216 Amelia St., Gretna, LA 70053.

Lacassine National Wildlife Refuge. Size: 31,766 acres. Established: 1937. Attractions: 16,000-acre fresh water pool; fishing. Watch for: White-fronted Goose, Fulvous Tree Duck, Roseate Spoonbill, Glossy Ibis. Information: Rt. 1, Box 186, Lake Arthur, LA 70549. Phone: (318) 774-2750.

Rainey Wildlife Audubon Sanctuary. Size: 26,800 acres. Established: 1923. Terrain: bayou, brackish marsh. Attractions: winter feeding ground for geese/ducks; 8 miles frontage on Gulf. Watch for: Virginia Rail, Least Tern, Roseate Spoonbill, egrets, herons, Boat-tailed Grackle, Eastern Kingbird. Information: Rt. 4, Box 92-D, Abbeville, LA 70510. Phone: (318) 893-4703. Appointment necessary.

Sabine National Wildlife Refuge. Size: 142,845 acres. Established: 1937. Terrain: three fresh water impoundments, two large brackish lakes. Attractions: fishing, wildife trail. Watch for: Yellowleg, herons, egrets, vultures, Clapper Rail, Black-necked Stilt, White-faced Ibis. Information: M.R.H. Box 107, Sulphur, LA 70645. Phone: (318) 762-5135.

Maine

Acadia National Park. Size: 36,363 acres. Established: 1929. Terrain: rocky but treed coastal mainland, including number of off-shore islands. Attractions: Abbe Museum of Archaeology, Isleford Historical Museum; nature walks, boat cruises (park facilities only open in summer months). Watch for: Great Blue Heron, Virginia Rail, Ruby-throated Hummingbird, Cliff Swallow, Scarlet Tanager, Bald Eagle. Information: RFD #1, Bar Harbor, ME 04609. Phone: (207) 288-3338.

Moosehorn National Wildlife Refuge. Size: 22,666 acres. Established: 1937. Terrain: upland, ponds, marshes, sphagnum bogs, forests. Attractions: visitor center, self-guided auto tour, hiking trails. Watch for: Ring-necked Duck, Woodcock, Red-necked Grebe, Boreal Chickadee, Parula Warbler. Information: P.O. Box X, Calais, ME 04619. Phone: (207) 454-3521.

Nanjemoy Marsh Sanctuary. Size: 58 acres. Established: 1972. Terrain: tidal wetlands, part of Potomac estuary. Attractions: bird nesting area. Watch for: Black Rail, Least Bittern, Marsh Wren, Bald Eagle, Great Blue Heron. Information: Dr. George B. Wilmot, 401 Amherst Rd., Bryan's Rd., ME 20616. Phone: (301) 748-2552. Appointment necessary.

Pond Island National Wildlife Refuge. Size: 10 acres. Established: 1973. Terrain: treeless island. Watch for: Woodcock, Black Duck, Ring-necked Duck, Leach's Petrel. Information: Northern Blvd., Plum Island, Newburyport, Massachusetts 01950. Phone: (617) 465-5753.

Rachel Carson National Wildlife Refuge. Size: 1,400 acres. Established: 1966. Terrain: coastal marsh. Watch for: Black Duck, marsh birds, Peregrin Falcon. Information: Northern Blvd., Plum Island, Newburyport, Massachusetts 01950. Phone: (617) 465-5753.

P.W. Sprague Memorial Audubon Sanctuary. Size: approx. 30 acres. Established: 1958. Terrain: coastal islands. Attractions: nesting and roosting area for shorebirds. Information: contact Prout's Neck Audubon Society, 11 Brown Court, Cambridge, MA 02138.

Todd Wildlife Audubon Sanctuary. Size: 345 acres. Established: 1936. Terrain: forested island. Attractions: summer session ecology workshops. Watch for: Osprey, Black Guillemot, Wood Warbler, Leach's Petrel, Double-crested Cormorant, Great Horned Owl. Information: Keene Neck Road, Medomak, ME 04551. Phone: (207) 529-5148. Appointment necessary.

Maryland

Blackwater National Wildlife Refuge. Size: 11,802 acres. Established: 1933. Terrain: swamp, marsh, freshwater ponds. Attractions: visitor center, wildlife drive, picnic area. Watch for: Brown-headed Nuthatch, Barn Owl, Osprey, King Rail, Bald Eagle. Information: Rt. 1, Box 121, Cambridge, MD 01613. Phone: (301) 228-2677.

Eastern Neck National Wildlife Refuge. Size: 2,286 acres. Established: 1962. Attractions: wintering and nesting area for birds. Watch for: geese, diving ducks, swans, Bobwhite, eagles. Information: Rt. 2, Box 225, Rock Hall, MD 21661. Phone: (301) 639-7415.

Massachusetts

Great Meadows National Wildlife Refuge. Size: 3,800 acres. Established: 1944. Terrain: open water, marsh, Concord and Sudbury River bottomlands. Attractions: bicycle paths, observation tower, canoeing, boating, fishing. Watch for: Hooded Merganser, Osprey, Goshawk, Herring Gull, sandpipers. Information: 191 Sudbury Rd., Concord, MA 07142. Phone: (617) 369-5518.

Monomoy National Wildlife Refuge. Size: 2,698 acres. Established: 1944. Terrain: two islands dotted with dune grass, brush, pine and oak. Attractions: fishing, shelling, photograph and study nature. Watch for: Red-breasted Merganser, Great Black-backed Gull, Wilson's Phalarope, Cape May Warbler. Information: Morris Island, Chatham, MA 02633.

Parker River National Wildlife Refuge. Size: 4,650 acres. Established: 1942. Terrain: salt marsh, sand dunes, tidal waters, freshwater marsh, glacial upland, ocean beach. Attractions: swimming, picnicking, surf fishing, cranberry picking. Watch for: Semipalmated Sandpiper, Myrtle Warbler, White-throated Sparrow, Hooded Merganser, Hudsonian Godwit. Information: Northern Blvd., Plum Island, Newburyport, MA 01950. Phone: (617) 465-5753.

Michigan

Isle Royale National Park. Size: 539,279 acres. Established: 1931. Terrain: Lake Superior. Forested island. Attractions: refuge for moose and wolves; hiking trails, fishing; lodges, campgrounds. Watch for: Swainson's Thrush, Boreal Chickadee, Gray Jay, Black-backed Three-toed Woodpecker, Osprey. Information: P.O. Box 27, Houghton, MI 49931. Phone: (906) 482-3310.

Seney National Wildlife Refuge. Size: 95,455 acres. Established: 1935. Terrain: marshes, sand ridges, stands of pine. Attractions: Manistique River, visitor center, picnic areas, trails, observation tower, fishing. Watch for: ducks, grouse, Common Merganser, Bobolink, Grosbeak, Sandhill Crane, Le Conte's Sparrow. Information: Seney, MI 49883. Phone: (906) 586-9851.

Shiawassee National Wildlife Refuge. Size: 8,850 acres. Established: 1953. Terrain: freshwater marshes, cropland. Watch for: Whistling Swan, Bald Eagle, Sandhill Crane, Snow Bunting, Red-headed Woodpecker, Snow Goose. Information: 6975 Mower Rd., Route 1, Saginaw, MI 48601. Phone: (517) 777-5930.

Minnesota

Agassiz National Wildlife Refuge. Size: 61,500 acres. Established: 1937. Terrain: woodland, spruce bogs, freshwater marshes. Watch for: Sharp-tailed Grouse, Yellow-headed Blackbird, Canada Goose, swallows, Golden and Bald Eagle, Goshawk. Information: Middle River, MN 56737. Phone: (218) 449-4115.

Big Stone National Wildlife Refuge. Size: 10,794 acres. Established: 1975. Terrain: shallow marshes along Minnesota River. Attractions: auto tour route, interpretive facilities. Watch for: geese, ducks, swans, herons, shore birds. Information: 25 NW 2nd St., Ortonville, MN 56278. Phone: (612) 839-3700.

Northwoods Audubon Center. Size: 535 acres. Established: 1969. Terrain: glacial till plain; woodland, marsh fields, lake and lakeshore. Attractions: education center. Watch for: Bald Eagle, Black-backed Three-toed Woodpecker. Information: Route 1, Sandstone, MN 55072. Phone: (612) 245-2648.

Rice Lake National Wildlife Refuge. Size: 18,000 acres. Established: 1935. Terrain: lakes, bogs, freshwater marshes. Attractions: birding, fishing. Watch for: American Woodcock, Snipe, White Pelican, Whooping Crane, Great Blue Heron, Black Duck. Information: Route 2, McGregor, MN 55760. Phone: (218) 768-2402.

Sherburne National Wildlife Refuge. Size: 30,479 acres. Established: 1965. Terrain: shallow pools created by low-level earthen dikes. Attractions: fishing, environmental and interpretive studies. Watch for: waterfowl, herons, shore birds. Information: Route 2, Zimmerman, MN 55398. Phone: (612) 389-3323.

Tamarac National Wildlife Refuge. Size: 43,000 acres. Established: 1938. Terrain: marshes, lakes, prairies, forest area. Attractions: trails, fishing, picnicking. Watch for: Ruddy Duck, Ruffed Grouse, Goldeneye, Osprey, Pileated Woodpecker, Holboell's Grebe. Information: Rural Route, Rochert, MN 56578. Phone: (218) 847-4355.

Upper Mississippi River National Wildlife Refuge. Size: 33,000 acres. (Additional portions in Wisconsin, Iowa, and Illinois.) Established: 1924. Terrain: open water, sandbars, wooded bottomlands, marshlands. Attractions: birding, by auto, by boat. Watch for: sandpipers, Hooded Merganser, Surf Scoter, Bald Eagle, Merlin, Yellow-throated Vireo, Trumpeter Swan. Information: 122 W. 2nd St., Winona, MN 55987. Phone: (507) 452-4230.

Voyageurs National Park. Size: 31,092 acres. Established: 1971. Attractions: beautiful northern lakes, once route of French-Canadian voyageurs, surrounded by forest. Information: P.O. Drawer 50, International Falls, MN 56649. Phone: (218) 283-4492.

Mississippi

Noxubee National Wildlife Refuge. Size: 46,000 acres. Established: 1940. Terrain: woods, brushy fields, and impounded water (Bluff Lake). Attractions: fishing. Watch for: Dickcissel, Orchard Oriole, warblers, Blue Grosbeak, Turkey, Brown-headed Nuthatch, Red-cockaded Woodpecker. Information: Rt. 1, Box 84, Brooksville, MS 39739. Phone: (601) 323-5548.

Yazoo National Wildlife Refuge. Size: 12,471 acres. Established: 1936. Terrain: cropland, marshes, open water. Attractions: trails to walk and drive. Watch for: Prothonotary Warbler, Upland Plover, Blue-grey Gnatcatcher. Information: Rt. 1, Box 286, Hollandale, MS 38748. Phone: (601) 839-2638.

Missouri

Mingo National Wildlife Refuge. Size: 21,650 acres. Established: 1944. Terrain: forested hills, swamp, cropland, limestone

bluffs. Attractions: self-guided automobile tour. Watch for: Red-headed Woodpecker, Canada Goose, Bald Eagle, Bewick's Wren, Harlan's Hawk. Information: Rt. 1, Box 9A, Puxico, MO 63960. Phone: (314) 222-3589.

Squaw Creek National Wildlife Refuge. Size: 6,809 acres. Established: 1935. Terrain: woodland, pools, freshwater marshes. Attractions: auto, bicycle tour roads, fishing, picnicking; extensive bird-banding program being conducted. Watch for: Tree Swallow, Snow Goose, White Pelican, White-rumped Sandpiper, White Faced Ibis, ducks. Information: Box 101, Mount City, MO 64470. Phone: (816) 442-3570.

Swan Lake National Wildlife Refuge. Size: 10,670 acres. Established: 1937. Terrain: marsh, water. Watch for: Canada Goose, Cardinal, Indigo Bunting, Golden and Bald Eagle. Information: Box 68, Sumner, MO 64681. Phone: (816) 856-3323.

Montana

Benton Lake National Wildlife Refuge. Size: 12,383 acres. Established: 1929. Terrain: uplands, marshes, water. Attractions: on-going experiments with bird behavior, courtship, nesting, rearing of young. Watch for: Peregrine Falcon, ducks, hawks, Horned Lark, McCown's Longspur, Burrowing Owl. Information: Box 450, Black Eagle, MT 59414. Phone (406) 761-5266.

Glacier National Park. Size: 1,012,084 acres. Established: 1932. Terrain: Rocky Mountains. Attractions: glaciers, lakes— boating, fishing, camping, lodges. Watch for: White-tailed Ptarmigan, Clark's Nut-cracker, Dipper, Bald Eagle. Information: West Glacier, MT 59936. Phone: (406) 888-5441.

Medicine Lake National Wildlife Refuge. Size: 31,458 acres. Established: 1935. Terrain: uplands, open water. Attractions: picnicking, boating, swimming, fishing. Watch for: Double-crested Cormorant, Great Blue Heron, Le Conte's Sparrow, Sandhill Crane, Peregrine Falcon, Sprague's Pipit. Information: Medicine Lake, MT 59247. Phone: (406) 789-2305.

Red Rock Lakes National Wildlife Refuge. Size: 40,000 acres. Established: 1935. Terrain: valley marsh, lakes, rolling foothills. Attractions: campgrounds, fishing, wildflowers. Watch for: Barrow's Goldeneye, Trumpeter Swan, Whistling Swan, Sandhill Crane, Great Blue Heron, Willet. Information: Monida Star Route, Lima, MT 59739. Phone: (406) 276-3347.

Charles M. Russell National Wildlife Range. Size: 910,000 acres. Established: 1936. Terrain: high plateau, marsh, open water. Attractions: 21-mile auto tour. Watch for: Sage Grouse, Great Blue Heron,

White Pelican, Sharp-tailed Grouse, Mountain Plover. Information: P.O. Box 110, Airport Rd., Lewistown, MT 59457. Phone: (406) 538-8707.

Nebraska

Agate Fossil Beds National Monument. Size: 2,736 acres. Established: 1965. Terrain: quarries. Attractions: Miocene mammal fossils. Information: P.O. Box 427, Gering, NB 69341.

Lillian Annette Rowe Audubon Sanctuary. Size: 1,074 acres. Established: 1973. Terrain: meadows, Platte River land. Attractions: wintering and migrating birds. Watch for: Sandhill Cranes, Whooping Crane, Bald Eagle, large numbers water-fowl. Information: 2611 S. Cochin St., Grand Island, NB 68801. Phone: (308) 382-3695. Appointment necessary.

Valentine National Wildlife Refuge. Size: 71,516 acres. Established: 1934. Terrain: sandhills—lakes, meadows, marshes, grassy hills. Attractions: fishing. Watch for: Long-billed Curlew, Upland Plover, herons, terns, ducks, shorebirds. Information: Valentine, NB 96201. Phone: (402) 376-3789.

Nevada

Desert National Wildlife Range. Size: 1,588,000 acres. Established: 1936. Terrain: desert, plains, mountains. Precaution: primitive road system. Watch for: Gambel's Quail, Pinyon Jay, Rock Wren, Water Pipit, Mountain Chickadee. Information: 1500 North Decatur Blvd., Las Vegas, NV 89108. Phone: (702) 598-6510.

Pahranagat National Wildlife Refuge. Size: 5,381 acres. Established: 1963. Terrain: desert. Watch for: finches, Black-throated Sparrow, Killdeer, Roadrunner, Crissal Thrasher, Double-crested Cormorant. Information: 1500 North Decatur Blvd., Las Vegas, NV 98108. Phone: (702) 598-6510.

Ruby Lake National Wildlife Refuge. Size: 37,191 acres. Established: 1938. Terrain: grasslands, marsh, ponds, all between to mountain ranges. Attractions: picnicking, fishing. Watch for: ducks, Peregrine Falcon, Sage Grouse, Avocet, Turkey Vulture. Information: Box 649, Elko, NV 89801. Phone: (702) 738-4320.

Stillwater National Wildlife Refuge. Size: 24,203 acres. Established: 1948. Terrain: desert, marsh, saline ponds. Attractions: camping, boating, 24 mile loop tour. Watch for: Whistling Swan, Northern Phalarope, Horned Lark, Snowy Plover, Barn Owl, Golden Eagle. Information: Box 592, Fallon, NV 89406. Phone: (702) 423-5128

Whittell Audubon Center. Size: 630 acres. Established: 1973. Terrain: forest and marsh. Attractions: nature center; Washoe Lake. Information: P.O. Box 2304, Rene, NV. Phone: (702) 323-1933. Appointment necessary.

New Hampshire

Wapack National Wildlife Refuge. Size: 738 acres. Established: 1972. Terrain: mountain, swamp, bog. Attractions: 3-mile nature trail. Watch for: Magnolia Warbler, Swainson's Thrush, hawks, ravens. Information: Parker River National Wildlife Refuge, Northern Blvd., Plum Island, Newburyport, MA 01950. Phone: (617) 465-5753.

New Jersey

Brigantine National Wildlife Refuge. Size: 20,236 acres. Established: 1939. Terrain: tidal bays, marsh, barrier beach, brushland. Attractions: trails, observation towers, 7-mile auto tour route. Watch for: Glossy Ibis, Ruddy Turnstone, Hudsonian Godwit, Wilson's Phalarope, Roseate Tern, Blue Goose. Information: P.O. Box 72, Great Creek Road, Oceanville, NY 08231. Phone: (609) 652-1665.

Great Swamp National Wildlife Refuge. Size: 5,892 acres. Established: 1960. Terrain: swamp, upland, marsh, water. Attractions: foot trails, canoeing, educational center. Watch for: White-eyed Vireo, Blue-winged Warbler, Long-billed Marsh Wren, Glossy Ibis, Goshawk, Bald Eagle. Information: R.D. 1, Box 148, Basking Ridge, NJ 06920. Phone: (201) 647-1222.

New Mexico

Bitter Lake National Wildlife Refuge. Size: 23,310 acres. Established: 1937. Terrain: desert, tamarisk and cottonwood treed valley, small lakes. Attractions: fishing, picnicking. Watch for: American Bittern, Pied-billed Grebe, Scaled Quail, Roadrunner, Snowy Plover, Baird's Sandpiper. Information: P.O. Box 7, Roswell, NM 88201. Phone: (505) 622-6755.

Bosque Del Apache National Wildlife Refuge. Size: 57,191 acres. Established: 1939. Terrain: desert, marsh. Attractions: wintering area for number of bird species. Watch for: Sandhill Crane, Purple Gallinule, Hepatic Tanager, Wilson's Phalarope, White-necked Raven. Information: P.O. Box 1246, Socorro, NM 87801. Phone: (505) 835-1828.

Capulin Mountain National Monument. Size: 680 acres. Proclaimed: 1916. Attractions: geologically recent, extinct volcano. Information: Capulin, NM 88414.

Guadalupe Mountains National Park. Size: 79,972 acres. Established: 1972. Terrain: mountain mesa. Attractions: Permian limestone fossil reef; earth fault, unusual flora and fauna. Information: 3225 National Parks Highway, Carlsbad, NM 88220. Phone: (915) 828-3385.

San Andres National Wildlife Refuge. Size: 57,217 acres. Established: 1941. Terrain: mountainous, semidesert. Watch for: Harlequin Quail, Zone-tailed Hawk, White-necked Raven, Black Phoebe, Cooper's Hawk, Golden Eagle. Information: San Acacia, NM 87831. Phone: (505) 864-4021.

New York

Amagansett National Wildlife Refuge. Size: 36 acres. Established: 1968. Terrain: sand dunes, barrier beach. Attractions: environmental study of beach ecology; fall flights of hawks and shorebirds. Information: Target Rock Road, Lloyd Neck, Huntington, NY 11743. Phone: (516) 271-2409.

Brinton Brook Audubon Sanctuary. Size: 129 acres. Established: 1958. Terrain: woods, meadows, lake. Attractions: hiking trails. Information: Saw Mill River Audubon Society, Pleasantville, NY 10570. Phone: (914) 769-7430. Appointment necessary.

Constitution Island Marsh Audubon Sanctuary. Size: 267 acres. Established: 1970. Terrain: tidal marsh land in Hudson River estuary. Attractions: nursery area for fish; habitat of many resident and migratory birds. Watch for: vireos, warblers, wrens, finches, White-winged Crossbill. Information: RFD #1, Rte. 9D, Garrison, NY. Phone: (914) 265-3119. Appointment necessary.

Graff Audubon Sanctuary. Size: 33 acres. Established: 1975. Terrain: unspoiled, heavily wooded. Attractions: exceptional stand of tulip trees, also white and red oaks, maples. Information: Saw Mill River Audubon Society, Pleasantville, NY 10570. Phone: (914) 769-7430. Appointment necessary.

Iroquois National Wildlife Refuge. Size: 10,818 acres. Established: 1958. Terrain: swamp, marsh, meadowland. Attractions: bird watching, fishing. Watch for: Pied-billed Grebe, Turkey Vulture, Virginia Rail, Sora, Screech Owl, Rose-breasted Grosbeak, Golden-winged Warbler. Information: RFD 1, Basom, NY 14013. Phone: (716) 948-5445.

Montezuma National Wildlife Refuge. Size: 6,334 acres. Established: 1938. Terrain: marsh, water impoundments, woodlands. Attractions: hiking trails, picnic areas, observation towers, self-guided auto tour, fishing. Watch for: Hooded Merganser, Holboell's Grebe, Bald Eagle,

Osprey, Peregrine Falcon, Hudsonian Godwit. Information: RD 1, Box 1411, Seneca Falls, NY 13148. Phone: (315) 568-5987.

Morton National Wildlife Refuge. Size: 187 acres. Established: 1954. Terrain: wooded bluffs, beach area. Attractions: hiking. Watch for: Black-capped Chickadee, Cardinal, Great Black-backed Gull, Wilson's Plover, Roseate Tern, Osprey. Information: Target Rock Rd., Huntington, NY 11743. Phone: (516) 271-2409.

Oyster Bay National Wildlife Refuge. Size: 3,117 acres. Established: 1968. Terrain: marsh, open bay. Attractions: observe protection and management of migratory birds. Information: Target Rock Road, Lloyd Neck, Huntington, NY 11743. Phone: (516) 271-2409.

Palmer Lewis Audubon Sanctuary. Size: 24 acres. Established: 1967. Terrain: woods, small fields. Attractions: hiking trails, spectacular rock formation; bluebird nesting program. Information: Linda I. Shoumatoff, R.D. 2, Rte. 10, Katonah, NY 10536. Phone: (914) 232-8349.

Ruth Walgreen Franklin and Winifred Fels Audubon Sanctuaries. Size: two adjoining tracts totalling 202 acres. Established: 1974/75. Terrain: woodland. Attractions: trails, wildflowers, berry-producing shrubs which attract large numbers of songbirds. Information: Linda I. Shoumatoff, R.D. 2, Rte. 100, Katonah, NY 10536. Phone: (914) 232-8349.

Target Rock National Wildlife Refuge. Size: 80 acres. Established: 1970. Attractions: interpretive trails. Watch for: migratory birds, particularly warblers. Information: Target Rock Road, Lloyd Neck, Huntington, NY 11743. Phone: (516) 271-2409.

Theodore Roosevelt Audubon Sanctuary. Size: 12 acres. Established: 1923. Terrain: heavily wooded. Attractions: songbird and botanical perserve as well as a nature center. Information: P.O. Box 5, Oyster Bay, NY 11771. Phone: (516) 922-3200.

North Carolina

North Carolina National Wildlife Refuge. Size: 50,179 acres. Established: 1934. Terrain: marsh, swampland, Lake Mattamuskeet. Watch for: Whistling Swan, Turkey Vulture, Glossy Ibis, Osprey. Information: New Holland, NC 27885. Phone: (919) 926-4021.

Pea Island National Wildlife Refuge. Size: 5,915 acres. Established: 1938. Terrain: barrier beach. Attractions: salt-water fishing; photography blinds available.

Watch for: Snow Goose, Canada Goose, shore birds, gulls, terns. Information: Box 1026, Manteo, NC 27954. Phone: (919) 987-2394.

Pee Dee National Wildlife Refuge. Size: 8,438 acres. Established: 1964. Watch for: Wood Duck nests; wintering area for geese and ducks. Information: Box 780, Wadesboro, NC 28170. Phone: (704) 694-4424.

Pungo National Wildlife Refuge. Size: 12,350 acres. Established: 1963. Attractions: 2,500 acre Pungo Lake; nature studies, photography, walking trails. Watch for: Canada Goose, Wood Duck, herons, egrets, ibises, Bald Eagle. Information: P.O. Box 267, Plymouth, NC 27962. Phone: (919) 793-2143.

North Dakota

Arrowwood National Wildlife Refuge. Size: 15,934 acres. Established: 1935. Terrain: lakes, marshes, grasslands. Attractions: fishing, picnicking, swimming. Watch for: American Widgeon, Shoveler, White Pelican, Canada Goose, Sharp-tailed Grouse, Peregrine Falcon. Information: Rural Route 1, Pingree, ND 58476. Phone: (701) 285-4100.

Audubon National Wildlife Refuge. Size: 13,498 acres. Established: 1956. Terrain: prairie, marshland. Attractions: Lake Sakakawea. Watch for: Sandhill Crane, Whooping Crane, White Pelican, Double-crested Cormorant, ducks, geese. Information: Rural Route 1, Coleharbor, ND 58531. Phone: (701) 442-5474.

Des Lacs National Wildlife Refuge. Size: 18,841 acres. Established: 1935. Terrain: river valley, marshland, open water. Attractions: camping, fishing, picnicking. Watch for: ducks, geese, Gray Partridge, Ring-necked Pheasant, Sharp-tailed Grouse, Sprague's Pipit, Chestnut-collared Longspur. Information: Box 578, Kenmare, ND 58746. Phone: (701) 385-4468.

Lake Ilo National Wildlife Refuge. Size: 3,963 acres. Established: 1939. Terrain: semi-arid, rolling prairie with 1,250 acres surface water. Attractions: boating, swimming, fishing. Watch for: Double-crested Cormorant, Great Blue Heron, Black-crowned Night Heron, American Bittern, Marbled Godwit, phalaropes. Information: Box 148, Crosby, ND 58730. Phone: (701) 965-6488.

Long Lake National Wildlife Refuge. Size: 22,310 acres. Established: 1932. Terrain: prairie grasslands, fields (cultivated for bird feeding ground). Watch for: Sandhill Crane, Golden Eagle, Cooper's Hawk, Greater Prairie Chicken. Information: Moffit, ND 58560. Phone: (701) 387-4397.

Sullys Hill National Game Preserve/

Wildlife Refuge. Size: 1,674 acres. Established: 1931. Terrain: wooded, glacial hills; grasslands. Attractions: big-game auto tour route, picnic area, nature trail. Watch for: Whistling Swan, Blue and Snow Goose, ducks. Information: Box 159-D, Devils Lake, ND 58301. Phone: (701) 662-2924.

Tewaukon National Wildlife Refuge. Size: 7,869 acres. Established: 1945. Terrain: rolling countryside with marshland and open water. Watch for: Baird's Sandpiper, Hudsonian Godwit, Western Grebe, Double-crested Cormorant, Franklin's Gull, herons, geese, ducks. Information: Cayuga, ND 58013. Phone: (701) 724-3598.

Ohio

Aullwood Audubon Center. Size: 70 acres. Established: 1957. Terrain: forest, marsh, bog, pond, running brook. Attractions: visitor center; naturalist-led trail hikes. Information: 1000 Aullwood Road, Dayton, OH 45415. Phone: (513) 890-7360.

Aullwood Audubon Farm. Size: 122 acres. Established: 1961. Terrian: farmland. Attractions: educational farm with century-old barn, windmill, springhouse, kitchen garden, farm animals; farm abounds with songbirds, hawks, owls, foxes,

raccoons and other wildlife. Information: 9101 Frederick Road, Dayton, OH 45414. Phone: (513) 890-2963.

Ottawa National Wildlife Refuge. Size: 4,800 acres. Established: 1961. Terrain: marshlands, open waters. Attractions: walking trails. Watch for: Blue-winged Teal, Canada Goose, Whistling Swan, Black-crowned Night Heron, Great Egret, Kirtland's Warbler. Information: 14000 West State, Rt. 2, Oak Harbor, OH 43449. Phone: (419) 897-0211.

Oklahoma

Platt National Park. Size: 912 acres. Established: 1906. Terrain: woods, waterfalls in foothills of Arbuckle Mountains. Attractions: freshwater and cold mineral springs, nature center, bison range. Watch for: Red-eyed Vireo, Downy Woodpecker, Red-tailed Hawk, Osprey, Townsend's Solitaire. Information: P.O. Box 201, Sulphur, OK 73086.

Salt Plains National Wildlife Refuge. Size: 32,008 acres. Established: 1930. Terrain: marshland, salt flats, field plantings for wildfowl. Attractions: camping, fishing, observation tower, picnic areas. Watch for: Bald and Golden Eagle, Franklin Gull, Avocet, sandpipers, bodwits, ducks, Snowy Plover. Information: Box 76, Route

1, Jet, OK 73749. Phone: (405) 626-4794.

Sequoyah National Wildlife Refuge. Size: 20,800 acres. Established: 1968. Terrain: Kerr Lock and Dam, some farm land, some wooded with steep ridges and hills. Attractions: fishing, picnicking at junction of Canadian and Arkansas Rivers. Watch for: waterfowl, herons, egrets, shore birds, hawks. Information: Box 398, Sallisaw, OK 74955. Phone: (918) 775-4931.

Tishomingo National Wildlife Refuge. Size: 16,500 acres. Established: 1946. Terrain: lakes, marsh, grassland. Attractions: camping. Watch for: Painted Bunting, Scissor-tailed Flycatcher, Blue Grosbeak, Bald Eagle, Ferruginous Hawk. Information: P.O. Box 248, Tishomingo, OK 73460. Phone: (405) 371-2402.

Wichita Mountains National Wildlife Refuge. Size: 59,020 acres. Established: 1905. Terrain: oak-covered hills, grasslands, lakes. Attractions: hiking trails, camping, fishing, swimming, boating. Watch for: Turkey, Bobwhite, ducks, Mississippi Kite, Dickcissel, Black-capped Vireo. Information: P.O. Box 448, Cache, OK 73527. Phone: (405) 429-3221.

Oregon

Cape Mears National Wildlife Refuge. Size: 139 acres. Established: 1938. Terrain:

museum, trout fishing; campgrounds on adjacent lands. Watch for: Sandhill Crane, shore birds, raptors, Whistling Swan, White-faced Ibis. Information: P.O. Box 113, Burns, OR 97720. Phone: (503) 493-2323.

Oregon Caves National Monument. Size: 465 acres. Proclaimed: 1909. Terrain: Siskiyou Mountains. Attractions: guided tour of caves; campgrounds, hotel, trails. Watch for: Steller's Jay, Red-breasted Nuthatch, Pine Siskin, Townsend's Solitaire. Information: P.O. Box 649, Cave Junction, OR 97523.

Umatilla National Wildlife Refuge. Size: 29,370 acres (portion of this acreage within State of Washington). Established: 1969. Terrain: rolling hills, John Day Lock and Dam Project. Watch for: ducks, geese, marsh and water birds. Attractions: fishing, boating. Information: Box 239, Umatilla, OR 97882. Phone: (503) 922-3232.

William L. Finley National Wildlife Refuge. Size: 4,325 acres. Established: 1964. Attractions: wintering area for Canada Goose. Watch for: "Dusky" Canada Goose, ducks, Band-tailed Pigeon, pheasants. Information: Rt. 2, Box 208, Corvallis, OR 97330. Phone: (503) 753-8056.

Pennsylvania

Crosswicks Audubon Sanctuary. Size: 16 acres. Established: 1956. Attractions: nature center. Information: Wyncote Bird Club, P.O. Box 2, Wyncote, PA 19095.

Erie National Wildlife Refuge. Size: 4,967 acres. Established: 1959. Terrain: valley, creeks, swamp woodland, marsh area. Attractions: trails, picnic area, fishing. Watch for: Whistling Swan, Killdeer, Yellow-throated Vireo, Cooper's Hawk, Hooded Merganser. Information: RD 2, Box 191, Guys Mills, PA 16327. Phone: (814) 789-3585.

Rhode Island

Block Island National Wildlife Refuge. Size: 29 acres. Established: 1973. Terrain: sand dunes. Attractions: superb bird watching during spring and fall migrations. Watch for: waterfowl, shore birds, migrant hawks and land birds. Information: Box 307, Charlestown, RI 02813. Phone: (401) 364-3106.

Ninigret National Wildlife Refuge. Size: 27 acres. Established: 1970. Terrain: barrier beach. Attractions: hiking, fishing. Watch for: waterfowl, shore birds. Information: Box 307, Charlestown, RI 02813. Phone: (401) 364-3106.

South Carolina

coastal headland. Watch for: Common Murre, Tufted Puffin, Pelagic Cormorant, Band-tailed Pigeon. Information: Wm. L. Finley Complex, Rt. 2, Box 208, Corvallis, OR 97330. Phone: (503) 753-8056.

Cold Springs National Wildlife Refuge. Size: 3,117 acres. Established: 1909. Terrain: reservoir. Attractions: resting and feeding area for birds. Watch for: Canada Goose, and ducks. Information: Umatilla National Wildlife Refuge, Box 239, Umatilla, OR 97882. Phone: (503) 922-3232.

Crater Lake National Park. Size: 160,290 acres. Established: 1902. Terrain: wooded. Attractions: deep blue lake lying in the heart of collapsed Mount Mazama; exhibit building, hiking trails, fishing. Lodge,

campgrounds. Watch for: Red Crossbill, Oregon Junco, Steller's Jay, Golden Eagle. Information: P.O. Box 7, Crater Lake, OR 97604. Phone: (503) 594-2211.

Hart Mountain National Antelope Wildlife Refuge. Size: 241,104 acres. Established: 1936. Terrain: rugged mountains (4,500 to 8,065 feet in elevation), steep canyons. Attractions: primitive camping facilities, spectacular wildlife. Information: U.S. Fish & Wildlife Service, P.O. Box 111, Lakeview, OR 97630. Phone: (503) 947-3315.

Malheur National Wildlife Refuge. Size: 180,795 acres. Established: 1908. Terrain: marshes, meadows, shallow lakes, sage-brush and juniper uplands. Attractions: bird watching and wildlife photography;

Cape Romain National Wildlife Refuge. Size: 34,197 acres. Established: 1932. Terrain: beach, marshland, islands, waterways. Attractions: fishing, swimming, boating. Watch for: Wilson's Plover, Willet, Parula Warbler, Brown Pelican, Peregrine Falcon, rails, ducks. Information: Rt. 1, Box 191, Awendaw, SC 29458. Phone: (803) 928-3368.

Carolina Sandhills National Wildlife Refuge. Size: 46,000 acres. Established: 1939. Terrain: rolling hills. Attractions: picnic area, fishing. Watch for: Wood Duck, Black Duck, American Widgeon, Pine Warbler, Turkey, Osprey. Information: Box 447, McBee, SC 29101. Phone: (803) 335-8401.

Francis Beidler Forest Audubon Sanctuary. Size: 3,415 acres. Established: 1974. Terrain: swamp, forest. Attractions: visitor center and boardwalk, naturalist-assistant on hand. Watch for: Night Heron, Pileated Woodpecker, Bachman's Warbler. Information: P.O. Box 47, Dorchester, SC 29437. Phone: (803) 563-4313. Appointment necessary.

Santee National Wildlife Refuge. Size: 74,361 acres. Established: 1941. Terrain: lakes, marsh, upland forest. Attractions: walking trails, observation tower, boating, waterskiing. Watch for: geese, ducks, Bald Eagle, Glossy and White Ibis, Mississippi Kite. Information: P.O. Box 158, Summerton, SC 29148. Phone: (803) 478-2217.

Savannah National Wildlife Refuge. Size: 13,173 (partly in Georgia) acres. Established: 1927. Terrain: Savannah River flat ground. Watch for: herons, egrets, King Rail, Pine Warbler, Brown Pelican, Osprey. Information: Box 8487, Savannah, GA 31402. Phone: (912) 232-4321, X415.

Silver Bluff Plantation Audubon Sanctuary. Size: 3,000 acres. Established: 1975. Terrain: pine plantations, croplands, hardwood forest, swamp. Attractions: monitored environmental program being conducted. Watch for: hawks, owls, Red-Cockaded Woodpecker. Information: Rt. 1, Box 391, Jackson, SC 29831. Phone: (803) 471-2367. Appointment necessary.

South Dakota

Badlands National Monument. Size: 151,369 acres. Established: 1929. Terrain: prairie grasslands, low hills, multi-colored rock formations. Attractions: visitor center, foot trails, campgrounds. Watch for: Mountain Bluebird, Rock Wren, Cliff Swallow, Horned Lark, Golden Eagle. Information: P.O. Box 72, Interior, SD 57750.

Great Smoky Mountains National Park. Size: 514,757 acres. Established: 1934. Terrain: lofty mountain range. Attractions:

diversified bird and plantlife. Information: Gatlinburg, TN 37738. Phone: (615) 436-5615.

Lacreek National Wildlife Refuge. Size: 9,825 acres. Established: 1935. Terrain: river valley, man-made lakes, marsh area. Attractions: self-guiding tours. Watch for: Common Goldeneye, Common Merganser, Double-crested Cormorant, White Pelican, Yellow-headed Blackbird, Western Burrowing Owl. Information: Martin, SD 57551. Phone: (605) 685-6508.

Sand Lake National Wildlife Refuge. Size: 21,451 acres. Established: 1935. Terrain: marsh, uplands, impounded waters. Watch for: ducks, White Pelican, Double-crested Cormorant, Blue Goose, Snow Goose, Golden Eagle, Buff-breasted Sandpiper. Information: Columbia, SD 57433. Phone: (605) 885-6320.

Waubay National Wildlife Refuge. Size: approx. 80,000 acres. Established: 1935. Terrain: prairie. Attractions: picnic area, winter ice fishing. Watch for: Blue-winged Teal, Gadwall, Western Grebe, Willet, Franklin's Gull, Osprey. Information: RR 1, Waubay, SD 57273. Phone: (605) 947-4695.

Wind Cave National Park. Size: 28,060 acres. Established: 1903. Terrain: Black Hills—grasslands, ponderosa pine, river. Attractions: guided tour of limestone cave, Ranger guided nature hikes in summer. Watch for: Cliff Swallow, Rock Wren, Black-billed Magpie, woodpeckers, Peregrine Falcon. Information: Hot Springs, SD 57747. Phone: (605) 727-2301.

Tennessee

Cross Creeks National Wildlife Refuge. Size: 8,861 acres. Established: 1962. Watch for: waterfowl, Turkey, Bobwhite. Information: Route 1, Box 229, Dover, TN 37058. Phone: (615) 232-7477.

Hatchie National Wildlife Refuge. Size: 9,399 acres. Established: 1964. Terrain: Hatchie River bottomland. Attractions: fishing. Watch for: Wood Duck, other water birds, Turkey. Information: P.O. Box 187, Brownsville, TN 38012. Phone: (901) 772-0501.

Reelfoot National Wildlife Refuge. Size: 8,102 acres (partly in Kentucky). Established: 1941. Attractions: Reelfoot Lake—fishing, sightseeing. Watch for: ducks, geese, grebes, other water birds. Information: Box 295, Samburg, TN 38254. Phone: (901) 538-2481.

Tennessee National Wildlife Refuge. Size: 51,000 acres. Established: 1945. Terrain: Tennessee River flat land. Watch for: Great Blue Heron, Black-billed Cuckoo, American Goldfinch, Osprey, Red-shouldered Hawk, Yellow-throated Vireo. Information: Box 849, Paris, TN 38242. Phone: (901) 642-2091.

Texas

Anauac National Wildlife Refuge. Size: 9,837 acres. Established: 1963. Attractions: bird watching and fishing. Watch for: "Lesser" Canada Goose, Snow Goose, Mottled Duck, Yellow Rail, Bald Eagle, Peregrine Falcon. Information: Box 278, Anahuac, TX 77514. Phone: (713) 267-3337.

Aransas National Wildlife Refuge. Size: 90,069 acres. Established: 1937. Terrain: ponds, tidal marsh, meadowland. Attractions: foot trails. Watch for: prairie chickens, Sandhill Crane, orioles, warblers, grosbeaks, buntings. Information: P.O. Box 100, Austwell, TX 77950. Phone: (512) 286-3559.

Big Bend National Park. Size: 707,478 acres. Established: 1944. Terrain: desert, mountains, Rio Grande River. Attractions: camping, fishing, hiking trails. Watch for: Mexican Jay, Cactus Wren, Mockingbird, Audubon's Warbler, House Finch, Spotted Sandpiper, Sprague's Pipit. Information: Big Bend National Park, TX 79834. Phone: (915) 477-2251.

Big Thicket National Preserve. Established: 1974. Attractions: see alligator, Texas red wolf, black bear, ocelot, over 300 bird species. Watch for: possibly extinct Ivory-billed Woodpecker. Information: c/o Southwest Regional Office, P.O. Box 728, Santa Fe, NM 87501.

Buffalo Lake National Wildlife Refuge. Size: 7,664 acres. Established: 1958. Terrain: area surrounding Buffalo Lake. Attractions: fishing, swimming, boating. Watch for: Mississippi Kite, Peregrine Falcon, ducks, Wigeon. Information: P.O. Box 228, Umbarger, TX 79091. Phone: (806) 499-3382.

Hagerman National Wildlife Refuge. Size: 11,320 acres. Established: 1946. Attractions: camping, fishing. Watch for: Great Blue Heron, American Widgeon, Red-tailed Hawk, Roadrunner, Great Horned Owl, Chimney Swift, Tufted Titmouse, Peregrine Falcon. Information: Rt. 3, Box 123, Sherman, TX 75090. Phone: (214) 786-2826.

Laguna Atascosa National Wildlife Refuge. Size: 45,147 acres. Established: 1946. Terrain: lower Rio Grande Valley. Watch for: herons, ibises, gulls, terns, doves, cranes, White-Tailed Hawk, White-Tailed Kite. Information: Box 2683, Harlingen, TX 78550. Phone: (512) 423-8328.

Lydia Ann and Harbor Islands Audubon Sanctuary. Size: approx. 200 acres. Terrain: low flat islands. Attractions: rookeries of fish-eating birds. Watch for: Laughing Gull, Willet, egrets, herons, Sandwich Tern, Oystercatcher. Information: P.O. Box 112, Port Arkansas, TX 78373. Phone:

(512) 854-5283. Appointment necessary.

Matagorda Island Audubon Sanctuary. Size: 5,720 acres. Established: 1960. Terrain: coastal island. Attractions: wintering waterfowl area. Watch for: Whooping Crane. Information: 721 Pine St., Rockport, TX 78382. Phone: (512) 729-5649. Appointment necessary.

Muleshoe National Wildlife Refuge. Size: 5,809 acres. Established: 1935. Terrain: lakes, marshland. Attractions: camping, tour roads. Watch for: Great Horned Owl, Osprey, Western Kingbird, Peregrine Falcon, Pigeon Hawk, Snowy Plover. Information: P.O. Box 549, Muleshoe, TX 79347. Phone: (806) 946-3341.

Santa Ana National Wildlife Refuge. Size: 2,000 acres. Established: 1943. Terrain: subtropical woodland on Rio Grande River. Attractions: auto route, foot trails, lunch areas. Watch for: Black-bellied Tree Duck, Hook-billed Kite, Ruddy Ground Dove, Green Parakeet, Yellow-headed Ani, Tropical Kingbird, Rufous-backed Robin. Information: Rt. 1, Box 202A, Alamo, TX 78516. Phone: (512) 787-3079.

Second Chain of Islands Audubon Sanctuary. Size: 200 acres. Terrain: five small islands. Attractions: popular fishing spot for redfish and trout. Watch for: Black Skimmer, Brown Pelican, herons, Reddish, Common and Snowy Egret, Whooping Crane. Information: 721 Pine St., Rockport, TX 78382. Phone: (512) 729-4649. Appointment necessary.

Sydney Island Audubon Sanctuary. Size: 126 acres. Terrain: island in Sabine River. Watch for: Roseate Spoonbill, White and White-faced Ibis, Olivaceous Cormorant, Louisiana and Black-crowned Night Heron. Information: P.O. Box 11, Bridge City, TX 77611. Phone: (713) 735-4298. Appointment necessary.

Utah

Arches National Park Utah. Size: 65,097 acres. Established: 1971. Terrain: area of erosion-formed arches and pinnacles. Information: Moab, UT 84532. Phone: (801) 259-7165.

Bryce Canyon National Park. Size: 36,007 acres. Established: 1924. Terrain: pinnacles, walls, spires bordering edge of a plateau. Attractions: one of the most colorful and unusual erosional formed areas in the world; visiter center, guided hikes, bus tours, camping. Watch for: Black-headed Grosbeak, Rock Wren, Say's Phoebe, Golden Eagle, Turkey, Flammulated Owl. Information: Bryce Canyon, UT 94717. Phone: (801) 834-5322.

Canyonlands National Park. Size: 330,556 acres. Established: 1964. Terrain: mesas, rocks, spires. Attractions: Indian petroglyphs; unusual geological formations. Information: 446 S. Main St., Moab, UT 84532. Phone: (801) 259-7165.

Capitol Reef National Park. Size: 221,101 acres. Established: 1971. Terrain: high-walled gorges cutting through 60-mile uplift of sandstone cliffs. Attractions: rock formations and archaeological ruins; guided walks, campgrounds. Information: Torrey, UT 84775. Phone: (801) 425-3871.

Cedar Breaks National Monument. Size: 6,154 acres. Proclaimed: 1933. Attractions: natural amphitheater which has eroded into variegated Pink Cliffs. Information: P.O. Box 749, Cedar City, UT 84720.

Fish Springs National Wildlife Refuge. Size: 17,992 acres. Established: 1959. Terrain: marsh area of Great Salt Desert. Watch for: merganser, Greater Sandhill Crane, Lapland Longspur, Ferruginous Hawk, Golden Eagle, Baird's Sandpiper. Information: Dugway, UT 84022. Phone: (801) 744-2488.

Ouray National Wildlife Refuge. Size: 10,466 acres. Established: 1960. Terrain: marsh, open water, fields, wooded areas along Green River. Watch for: Great Horned Owl, Red-tailed Hawk, Flicker, Evening Grosbeak, Whistling Swan, Long-billed Curlew. Information: 447 E. Main St. #4, Vernal, UT 84078. Phone: (801) 789-0351.

Zion National Park. Size: 141,274 acres. Established: 1919. Terrain: canyon and mesa, desert vegetation. Attractions: visitor center, interpretive program, self-guiding nature trails, scenic drive. Watch for: Yellow-breasted Chat, Turkey Vulture, Western Kingbird, Scrub Jay, Golden Eagle, Flammulated Owl. Information: Springdale, UT 84767. Phone: (801) 772-3256.

Vermont

Missisquoi National Wildlife Refuge. Size: 5,651 acres. Established: 1943. Terrain: Lake Champlain bays, woods, freshwater marsh, bog areas. Attractions: walking trails, fishing. Watch for: Pileated Woodpecker, Black-capped Chickadee, Philadelphia Vireo, Pigeon Hawk. Information: RD 2, Swanton, VT 05488. Phone: (802) 868-4781.

Virginia

Back Bay National Wildlife Refuge. Size: 4,589 acres. Established: 1938. Terrain: open water, marshes, dunes. Watch for: Yellow-rumped Warbler, Black Rail, American Bittern, Sooty Shearwater, Glossy Ibis. Information: Pembroke #2 Bldg., Suite 218, 287 Pembroke Office Park, Virginia Beach, VA 23462. Phone: (804) 939-6635.

Chincoteague National Wildlife Refuge. Size: 9,439 acres. Established: 1943. Terrain: beach, sand dunes, marshland. Attractions: swimming, surf fishing, guided walks. Watch for: Laughing Gull, Willet, Yellowlegs, sandpipers, plovers, Bald Eagle, Black Rail. Information: P.O. Box 62, Chincoteague, VA 23336. Phone: (804) 336-6122.

Mackay Island National Wildlife Refuge. Size: 6,995 acres (partly in North Carolina). Established: 1960. Watch for: Hooded Merganser, Black Vulture, Osprey, Barn Swallow, Rufous-sided Towhee, wintering snow geese. Information: 287 Pembroke Office Park #218, Virginia Beach, VA 23462. Phone: (804) 939-6635.

Presquile National Wildlife Refuge. Size: 1,329 acres. Established: 1952. Terrain: uplands, tidal swamp, tidal marsh areas. Watch for: Bank Swallow, Water Pipit, Pied-billed Grebe, Red-headed Woodpecker, Osprey. Information: P.O. Box 620, Hopewell, VA 23860. Phone: (804) 458-7541.

Shenandoah National Park. Size: 190,416 acres. Established: 1935. Terrain: forests, streams, waterfalls, sixty mountain peaks. Attractions: 105-mile-long Skyline Drive along crest; Appalachian Trail, a foot trail follows for 94 miles; camping, visitor centers. Watch for: flycatchers, owls, Yellow-throated Vireo, 34 species of warblers. Information: Luray, VA 22835. Phone: (703) 999-2242.

Virgin Islands

Buck Island Reef National Monument. Size: 850 acres. Established: 1961. Attractions: marine garden; rookery for frigate birds and pelicans, and habitat of green turtles. Information: Box 160, Christiansted, St. Croix, VI 00820.

Virgin Islands National Park. Size: 11,760 acres. Established: 1956. Terrain: St. John Island—coves, blue-green waters, white sandy beaches fringed by green hills. Attractions: early Carib Indian relics; remains of Danish colonial sugar plantations. Information: P.O. Box 806, Charlotte Amalie, St. Thomas, VI 00801. Phone: (809) 775-2050.

Washington

Columbia National Wildlife Refuge. Size: 28,800 acres. Established: 1944. Terrain: lakes, sloughs, meadows, marsh area. Watch for: Black-billed Magpie, Sandhill Crane, Hooded Merganser, waterfowl. Information: Drawer F, Othello, WA 99344. Phone: (509) 488-3831.

McNary National Wildlife Refuge. Size:

3,366 acres. Established: 1955. Terrain: cultivated land and water impoundments. Watch for: Canada Goose, Whistling Swan, Long-billed Curlew, Killdeer, Yellow-headed Blackbird, Wilson's Phalarope. Information: P.O. Box 308, Burbank, WA 99323. Phone: (509) 547-4942.

Mount Rainier National Park. Size: 235,193 acres. Established: 1899. Terrain: dense forests, subalpine meadows. Attractions: four visitor centers, exhibits, guided walks, hiking trails, mountain climbing, fishing, boating. Watch for: Vaux's Swift, Pygmy Owl, Violet-green Swallow, Gray-crowned Rosy Finch. Information: Longmire, WA 98397. Phone: (206) 569-2211.

North Cascades National Park. Size: 503,240 acres. Established: 1968. Terrain: Cascade Mountains, lush forests and meadows. Attractions: Glaciers, icefalls, plant and animal life thrive in valleys. Information: Sedro Woolley, WA 98284. Phone: (206) 855-1331.

Olympic National Park. Size: 893,779 acres. Established: 1938. Terrain: rain forest, ocean shore. Attractions: three visitor centers, nature trails, mountain climbing, Indian villages; campgrounds, lodges. Watch for: mergansers, Mountain Bluebird, kinglets, Gray-crowned Rosy Finch, Western Tanager. Information: 600 East Park Ave., Port Angeles, WA 98362. Phone: (206) 452-9715.

San Juan Islands Wildlife Refuge. Size: approx. 458 acres. Established: 1960. Terrain: 84 islands, islets and reefs in Puget Sound. Attractions: Marine Parks on Matia and Turn Islands. Watch for: Glaucous-winged Gull, cormorants, scoters, murres, Pigeon Guillemot, Oystercatcher. Information: Route 1, Box 376C, Cathlamet, WA 98612. Phone: (206) 795-4915.

Turnbull National Wildlife Refuge. Size: 15,565 acres. Established: 1937. Terrain: grasslands, marsh and lake areas. Attractions: hiking, auto tours, picnicking. Watch for: Trumpeter Swan, Ruffed Grouse, Tree Swallow, Pygmy Nuthatch, Dark-eyed Junco, Red-necked Grebe. Information: Rt. 3, Box 107, Cheney, WA 99004. Phone: (509) 234-4723.

Willapa National Wildlife Refuge. Size: 9,608 acres. Established: 1937. Terrain: tidal marsh area, uplands, Willapa Bay. Attractions: photo blinds. Watch for: Great Blue Heron, Bald Eagle, Sora, Aleutian Canada Goose, Black Brant. Information: Ilwaco, WA 98624. Phone: (206) 484-3492.

Wisconsin

Dory's Bog Audubon Sanctuary. Size: 40 acres. Established: 1963. Terrain: sphagnum bog. Attractions: unusual flora, including several species of orchids. Watch

for: Osprey, Bald Eagle. Information: Hunt Hill Audubon Sanctuary, Sarona, WI 54870. Phone: (715) 635-3379. Appointment necessary.

Horicon National Wildlife Refuge. Size: 21,000 acres. Established: 1941. Terrain: marsh. Attractions: walking trails, formation displays, fishing. Watch for: Canada Goose, ducks, Blue-winged Teal, Wilson's Phalarope, Common Gallinule. Information: Rt. 2, Mayville, WI 53050. Phone: (414) 387-2658.

Hunt Hill Audubon Sanctuary. Size: 342 acres. Established: 1954. Terrain: lakes, bogs, meadows, woodlands. Attractions: Audubon camp located here; summer classes in ecology. Watch for: Western Meadowlark, Yellow-headed Blackbird, White-throated Sparrow, loons, Osprey, Wood Duck. Information: Sarona, WI 54870. Phone: (715) 635-3379. Appointment necessary.

Necedah National Wildlife Refuge. Size: 39,549 acres. Established: 1939. Terrain: ponds and marsh area. Attractions: fishing, boating. Watch for: Snow Goose, Ruffed Grouse, Rose-breasted Grosbeak, Red-headed Woodpecker, Northern Shrike, Hooded Merganser. Information: Star

Route, Necedah, WI 54646. Phone: (608) 565-2551.

Schlitz Audubon Center. Size: 200 acres. Established: 1971. Terrain: wooded ravines, meadows, ponds, Lake Michigan frontage. Attractions: interpretive building. Information: 1111 East Brown Deer Road, Milwaukee, WI 53217. Phone: (414) 352-2880.

Wyoming

Grand Teton National Park. Size: 304,507 acres. Established: 1929. Terrain: part of Teton Range, Snake River. Attractions: lodges, marinas, instruction in mountaineering, float trips, fishing. Watch for: Bald Eagle, Violet-green Swallow, Trumpeter Swan, Blue Grouse. Information: P.O. Box 67, Moose WY 83012. Phone: (307) 733-2880.

Yellowstone National Park. Size: 2,219,736 acres. Established: 1872. Attractions: world's largest collection of geysers and hot springs; Yellowstone Lake, a 'Grand Canyon;' elk, buffalo, bears. Watch for: Great Horned Owl, Gray Jay, Cliff Swallow, Mountain Chickadee, Trumpeter Swan. Information: Yellowstone National Park, WY 82190. Phone: (307) 344-7381.

Tours and Expeditions

What do words like these do for you?

"We hike into Kenya's most remote, mystical and rugged country, with camels carrying our gear . . . Birdlife is plentiful, and we should see huge flocks of vulturine guineafowl and sand grouse . . . We dig for water in the sand; we walk in the cool of the morning. . ."[2]

Or these?

"We have picnic lunch and visit on foot the Linnaean Garden, planted in 1889 and containing 2500 Alpine plants from all parts of the world . . . At the Swiss National Park we bird before breakfast . . . We take a boat trip on Lake Lucerne, and in the evening have a farewell candlelight dinner . . ."[2]

How about these?

"This remote nature reserve, rarely visited by travelers, is one of the most important wildlife sanctuaries in Asia . . . There are more than a hundred species of birds; and among the many types of monkeys we see are the crab-eating Macaque, the Sunda Island leaf monkey and the gray gibbon . . ."[3]

If you are like us, you want to go, on all three tours, one right after the other, never mind the expense. Yet we picked these almost at random out of the 181 tours summarized for you in this book. Their range is incredible, from tracking the colorful Old Squaw Duck 250 miles south of the North Pole, to birding the Magellanic Penguin off the tip of Argentina at Tierra del Fuego.

What is it that lures us, in contrast to other living things, away from the familiar? There's the shot-in-the-arm our systems get on discovering the new—new friends, new facts, new customs and, of course, new birds. But also, as Massachusetts Audubon says in its Natural History Tours brochure:

[1] From Mountain Travel's Kenya Natural History Safari brochure.

[2] From Questers' Directory of Worldwide Nature Tours.

[3] From Hanns Ebensten's River Safari in Borneo brochure.

"The Eiffel Tower will stand for years to come, but we cannot be as optimistic about the rain forests of Peru, or the wetlands of Mexico or the sea off California. [Many people] are just gearing up to begin plundering in earnest. Wouldn't it be wise to see some of the magnificent natural specialties this planet still contains?"

"We believe," states Questers' Directory of Worldwide Nature Tours, "that international and domestic travel to wildlife sanctuaries and nature reserves can help encourage further conservation efforts."

Choosing a Tour

Whether boredom, or conservationist's zeal, or the wish simply to add birds to your own life list prods you to get up and go, you'll find a lot of tours to choose from. How do you decide which probably will satisfy you most? A good way is to talk to other bird watchers who've gone. Another is to find a travel agent specializing in nature tours. A third is to peruse the information blocks

that follow (keeping in mind that dates and prices change), pick an area of the world that intrigues you, and ask the organizations listed to send you current brochures.

Remember that most tour operators use the "good news, bad news" means of signing you up. Brochures contain the good news, the 'sell'. Once you send your deposit, you get a long typed list of what's called "Travel Preparation Information." It's here you learn how to lather yourself twice daily with foam repellent to keep chiggers and ticks from inflaming your flesh, here that you realize the brochure's phrase, "First class hotel when available" translates into "For all but one night, bring ground cloth, sleeping bag, and lots of mosquito netting."

In other words, when you've been turned rhapsodic by brochures, know that Travel Preparation Information will follow.

You can, however, use the brochures to do a lot of weeding. Ask yourself these questions:

1. What's the status of my health (to what altitudes can I safely go, how long can I hike over frozen tundra)?

2. How much money can I spend so that, if I have a good time, I can afford another tour next year? (Be sure to scrutinize the brochures' fine print to determine what the 'all-inclusive' price includes. Does it include all tips? Doubtful. Does it include all meals? Doubtful. Liquor? Doubtful again. What we're saying is, be realistic about how much the trip will cost, and then add 15%.)

3. With how much discomfort am I willing to put up in order to see the birds I want to see? (Is violent sea-sickness a small price to pay for a glimpse of the Yellow-nosed Albatross? What about the Black Fly's maddening itch—am I willing to trade that for a month in order to add the Bright-rumped Attila—*Attila spadiceus*—to my life list?)

When you know the answers to these questions, you'll find you can toss away many of the brochures without studying them further.

From the brochures remaining you'll want to learn more. Here are some suggestions.

1. Discover how much actual birding gets done, then ask yourself how much birding you wish to do. It may be that you prefer to swim and read as well as peer through binoculars.

2. In how large a group will you be traveling? The small group can move faster, perhaps see more birds, but the large group has its advantage if moving fast is precisely not what you are on vacation to do. Be cautious about joining groups of more than 25 enthusiasts; they may frighten the wildlife into hiding.

3. Discover how much time you'll have to spend accumulating gear, a passport, vaccinations. If you exhaust yourself before the tour gets started, you'll have no energy left for birding.

4. Be sure that your tour leader is both a naturalist who knows the birds where you are going as well as the birds back home. There is no point in him or her being an expert on water birds in the heart of the Gobi Desert. Nor is there point in having a herpetologist as leader when it's motmots and toucans you want to learn more about, not the red-eyed tree frog. The best way to guess how knowledgeable your leader is about birds at the destination is to find out how many tours he's already led there, and what emphasis the brochure puts on birds.

We talked a bit about the 'Travel Preparation Information' sent after you mail your deposit. Some of that information is bad news, true, yet all of it is helpful. The Massachusetts Audubon Society, for instance, offers these hints about Mexico: "A flashlight and a *quiet* wind-up alarm clock are useful. Conversely, ear plugs are a must for light sleepers, for Mexico is one of the liveliest countries in the world at night—and we often get up early." When you receive your Travel Preparation Information sheets, do everything you're told. Remember that hints contained therein are the result of experience rather than someone's fancy.

How to Use the Listings

To make choosing easier for you we've grouped the tours geographically, not by organization. Everything fit under the headings assigned except the Seychelles, 92 islands in the Indian Ocean 600 miles from Madagascar. You'll find the Seychelles tour following the tour to Rwanda/Zaire, under "Africa." Tours to the British Isles, by the way, come under the heading, "Europe."

Most of the tours are run by United States and Canadian firms who do nothing else. The rest are organized by Audubon societies, an ornithological club, an observatory, the UCLA Department of Biology, and by individuals.

A number of the tours you'll read about include archeology and all of nature as subjects to which time will be given. Some tours even offer college credit for what you learn. As dedicated a bird watcher as Frank Farran told us, "My own interest in birds is just part of my interest in nature, but birds are one of her more evident forms." You, the reader, are the one to decide if you are a naturalist first or a birder first, and choose your tour on that basis.

Because of space limitations, after "Probable Birds" within each tour we list up to six species. You're going to see more species than that. Even remote Arctic Outpost Camps, 250 miles south of the Magnetic North Pole, lists 45 nesting species alone. It's a good idea, by the way, when you write for a tour brochure, to ask that a list of probable birds be included.

One way to tell how popular an area is for birding, is to see how many tours are heading into that area. Our survey shows that, with 14 different tours, the Galapagos Islands off the coast of Ecuador wins hands down. With 12 tours, Africa's Kenya comes in second. When you consider, however, that the Galapagos Archipelago is 74 times smaller than Kenya (3,029 square miles of mostly ocean, versus 224,960 square miles of mostly land) you wonder if birding the Galapagos may not be a bit like birding downtown New York.

We could only list those tours whose operators completed our questionnaires. We wish to mention, however, two other organizations whose birding tour reputations are excellent. These are Bird Bonanzas, Inc. (12550 Biscayne Blvd., North Miami, FL 33181, president Ira Joel Abramson—phone 305/895-0606) and Flying Carpet Tours, Inc. (6220 So. Orange Blossom Trail, Orlando, FL 32809, president C. Russell Mason—phone 305/859-7142).

Here is a final tip before you move into the information blocks themselves. If you have never been on a tour before, memorize this piece of etiquette: no matter how anxious you are to see your first South American Thick-knee (*Burhinus oedicnemus*) or Philippine Trogon (*Harpactes ardeus*), it is considered poor form to dash out in front of your group, binoculars at the ready, scaring all birds away before others have the chance to see them.

Tours and Expeditions

Africa

Cameroons: Carrier: Air France. Depart from: New York. Season/Dates: April 10. Duration: 3 weeks. Locale: coastal area, jungle, dry semi-desert. Features: rare birds. Requirements: 6 participants. Cost/Person: $3,195. Includes: all expenses from, and return to New York. Organizer: World Nature Tours, Inc., P.O. Box 693, Silver Spring MD 20901. Contact: Donald H. Messersmith (301) 593-2522.

Kenya: Depart from: Nairobi. Season/Dates: August, 1979. Duration: 21 days in Africa. Locale: savannah, woodlands, tropical rain forest, fresh and soda lakes, ocean coast, desert. Features: Masai Mara Game Reserve, Tsavo National Park, Amboseli N.P. Mzima Springs. Snorkle in Indian Ocean. Probable birds: previous groups recorded 200 species. Group size: 10 to 18 persons. Cost/Person: $1,772. Includes: all land transportation, boats, guides, necessary equipment, meals. Organizer: Adventures International, 4421 Albert St., Oakland CA 94619. Contact: Brad Goodhart (415) 531-6564.

Kenya: Carrier: British Airways, Pan Am Airlines. Depart from: Los Angeles, New York, Miami. Season/Dates: June 12, 1978. Duration: 18 days. Locale: arid, tropical. Features: tour Kenya in minibuses, see Lake Nakuru Sanctuary, bird watching at Lake Baringo, tours of tea estates, explore Meru Game Reserve. Probable birds: flamingoes, Goliath Heron, many species of waterfowl, waders, shorebirds. Cost/Person: $1,955 (New York). Includes: all meals, airfares, all transportation, transfers, excursions and accommodations based on double occupancy (offers best of lodging in variety of lodges, hotels). Organizer: Aventura Natural History Tours, 508 North Sierra Drive, Beverly Hills CA 90210. Contact: Pamela Axelson (213) 276-6081.

Kenya: Depart from: Los Angeles CA. Season/Dates: July 12, 1978. Duration: 22 days. Features: visit famous national parks and game reserves including Nairobi, Mt. Kenya, Samburu, Meru, Lakes Nakuru and Naivasha, Masai Mara, Amboseli, Tsavo, coastal towns of Mombasa/Malindi; provides in depth study of biology and behavior of East African wildlife; emphasis on mammals and birds. College credit available. Cost/Person: $2,720. Includes: tuition/instructional materials, transportation, meals, accommodations. Organizer:

Dept. of Biological and Physical Sciences, UCIA Extension, P.O. Box 24902, Los Angeles CA 90024. Contact: Sakura Berry (213) 825-7093.

Kenya: Carrier: British Airways. Depart from: London. Season/Dates: Jan./Mar.—Jun/Dec. Duration: 17 days. Features: guest lecturer accompanies each departure; transportation by 7-seater Safari coaches with 5 passengers per coach. Probable birds: Red-billed Hornbill, Layard's Black-headed Waver, flamingos, Red and White Barbet, African Hoope, Lilac-breasted Roller. Requirements: visas for Kenya; valid certificates of smallpox, yellow fever, cholera inoculations. Group size: not to exceed 30. Cost/Person: $1,702. Includes: air travel to and from Nairobi from London, travel/game viewing by Safari coach, all hotel accommodations, meals, gratuities, taxes, Flying Doctor Service. Organizer: Esplanade Tours, W.F. & R.K. Swan (Hellenic) Ltd., 38 Newbury St., Boston MA 02116. Contact: Jacqueline R. Keith (617) 266-7465. Cable: Esplatrav, Telex 940421.

Kenya: Carrier: British Airways. Depart from: New York NY. Season/Dates: March, October. Duration: 17 days. Features: visit Northern Frontier District of Kenya on foot, with camel support, to see Africa as did the early explorers. Group size: 12 participants. Cost/Person: $2,450. Includes: all luggage transfers, sightseeing, leader and staff, local guides, meals, taxes, necessary items of equipment. Organizer: Hanns Ebensten Travel, Inc., 55 West 42 St., New York, NY 10036. Contact: Hanns Ebensten (212) 354-6634. Cable: HANEBTRAVL.

Kenya, Tanzania—East Africa: Carriers: IATA Jet International, micro-buses, land rovers. Depart from: New York (flexible). Season/Dates: Jan. through Aug. Duration: 21 days. Locale: flatlands, warm. Features: scientific leaders, experts in birding, wildlife, flora. Visit Kenya and Tanzania, or just Kenya. Itineraries arranged for special needs. Visit out-of-the-way places rather than tourist centers. Requirements: valid passport, visas; smallpox, yellow fever, cholera vaccinations. Suggested reading list provided. Group size: 20 to 60 (divided into smaller groups). Cost/Person: $2,157 to $2,347. Includes: all expenses (meals, first class hotels, lodges, airfare, tips, taxes, entrance fees, transportation within East Africa, sightseeing). Organizer: Holbrook Travel, Inc., 3520 NW 13th St., Gainsville FL 32601. Contact: Mary Ann Graudon (904) 377-7111.

Kenya: Depart from: New York City. Season/Dates: fall. Duration: 32 days. Features: leisurely and comprehensive wild-life study. Group size: 20 participants. Cost/Person: $3,900. Includes: hotel (first class), meals and gratuities, guide service, luggage tipping. Organizer: Massachusetts Audubon Society, South Great Road, Lincoln MA 01773. (617) 259-9500.

Kenya by Horseback: Carrier: TWA. Depart from: New York. Season/Dates: Nov. 18-Dec. 10, 1978; June 19-July 11, 1979; Dec. 11-Jan 2, 1979. Duration: 22 days. Locale: Savannah, forest, rivers. Features: Viewing birds and big game of Africa on horseback is unique in that birds and animals allow a horse a much closer approach than they would a landrover. Probable birds: flamingoes, cormorants, many more. Requirements: prior knowledge of horseback riding is helpful. Group size: 12 persons maximum. Cost/Person: $1,995. Includes: all costs, except airfare to Nairobi (NY-Nairobi-NY fair via TWA: $951). Organizer: Mountain Travel, 1398 Solano Ave., Albany CA 94706. Contact: Pam Shandrick (415) 527-8100.

Kenya: Depart from: New York. Season/Dates: June 19 to July 11, 1979. Duration: 22 days. Features: expert naturalist will accompany this safari; safari will cover Kenya's major game parks and many little-known lakes and forests. Probable birds: flocks of vulturine, Guinea Fowl, Sand Grouse. Requirements: hiking experience helpful. Group size: maximum 12 people. Cost/Person: $1,950. Includes: all costs but airfare to Nairobi (NY-Nairobi-NY airfare $951). Organizer: Mountain Travel, 1398 Solano Ave., Albany CA 94706. Contact: Pam Shandrick (415) 527-8100.

Kenya: Carrier: British Airways. Depart from: San Francisco/New York/others available. Season/Dates: June, Aug., each year. Duration: 21 days. Locale: African savannah. Features: safari led by expert naturalist/ornithologist; several hundred species birds to be seen in game parks. Group size: maximum 20 persons. Cost/Person: $1,790. Includes: all land transportation and transfers, all accommodations (first class hotel in Nairobi; deluxe tenting in field), all meals except in Nairobi, park entrance fees, instruction. Organizer: Nature Expeditions International, 599 College Ave., Palo Alto CA 94306. Phone (415) 328-6572.

Kenya: Depart from: New York City on

Sabena Airlines. Season/Dates: Jan. 27, April 14, July 28, Oct. 19, 1979; Duration: 23 days. Features: arrive Nairobi, drive to Samburu Game Reserve to see extensive bird life including Tufted and Vulturine Guinea Fowl; two days at Lake Baringo, see largest nesting colony of Goliath Herons in East Africa; safari visits to game reserves, including Lake Nakuru, East Africa's only national park intended primarily for birds (over 400 species recorded); excellent views of Kilimanjaro en route. Cost/Person: $2,713. Includes: land costs and airfare NY/NY. Organizer: Questers Worldwide Nature Tours, 257 Park Ave., South, New York, NY 10010. Contact: Michael Parkin (212) 673-3120.

Kenya: Carrier: Pan Am Airlines. Depart from: New York City NY. Season/Dates: June 3-25, 1978. Duration: 23 days. Locale: Kakamega Forest, Lake Victoria, Lake Nakuru, Masai Mara, Kenya coast. Features: over 400 species birds; see many big game mammal species. Group size: maximum 10 participants. Cost/Person: $2,920. Includes: all accommodations, meals; all land transportation, air charters; all national park entrance fees; hotel and baggage tipping; professional services of D.A. Turner as local ornithological guide. Organizer: Victor Emanuel Nature Tours, 1603 W. Clay, Houston TX 77019. Contact: Victor Emanuel: (713) 528-3725.

Madagascar: Depart from: New York NY. Season/Dates: Nov. 11-27, 1978. Duration: 16 days. Features: bird watching; tour leader and local tour guides. Cost/Person: $4,395. Includes: airfare and surface arrangements, meals, tips, entrance fees. Organizer: Bird Bonanzas, Inc., 12550 Biscayne Blvd., Suite 501, North Miami FL 33179. Contact: Carol Poloniecki (305) 895-0607.

Rwanda/Zaire: Depart from: Nairobi, Kenya. Season/Dates: July, 1979. Duration: 18 days in Africa. Locale: African plains, woodlands, tropical rain forests; elevation up to 10,000 feet. Features: fascinating bird-life of old Congo; all wild game typical of East Africa; Virunga Nature Preserve; rare opportunity to observe and photograph gorillas at close range. Requirement: able to walk as much as 6 hours on two different days. Group size: 6 to 18 persons. Cost/Person: $1,880. Includes: all land transportation, boats, guides, necessary equipment, meals (also includes 2 charter air flights within Zaire and Rwanda). Organizer: Adventures International, 4421 Albert St., Oakland CA 94619. Contact: Brad Goodhart (415) 531-6564.

The Seychelles: Carrier: British Airways. Depart from: London. Season/Dates: May, Oct., April. Duration: 17 days. Features: guest lecturer accompanying each

departure, bibliography provided for each passenger. Probable birds: Seychelles Kestrel, Lesser Vasa Parrot, Praslin, Seychelles Paradise Flycatcher, Seychelles Sunbird, Seychelles White-eye. Requirements: smallpox and cholera inoculations. Group size: not to exceed 30. Cost/Person: $1,614. Includes: air travel economy class, all travel, sightseeing, all accommodaitons, all gratuities, all taxes. Organizer: Esplanade Tours, W.F. & R.K. Swan (Hellenic) Ltd., 38 Newbury St., Boston MA 02116. Contact: Jacqueline R. Keith (617) 266-7465. Cable: Esplatrav, Telex 940421.

Zambia: Carrier: British Airways, Zambia Airways. Depart from: London. Season/Dates: June, July, Aug., Sept. Duration: 22 days. Features: guest lecturer accompanying each departure, game viewing by safari coach and land rover, bibiography provided for each passenger prior to departure. Probable birds: Skimmer, Domesticated Eland, Red Lechwe, White-breasted Cormorant, White Pelican, Hammerhead. Requirements: visa; inoculations for smallpox, cholera and yellow fever. Group size: not to exceed 30. Cost/Person: $2,259. Includes: travel by economy jet service London/Lusaka/Dar-es-Salaam and within Zambia and Tanzania; private motor coach land travel; first class rail travel Fuga/Dar-es-Salaam; all accommodaitons; all meals; all gratuities; all taxes. Organizer: Esplanade Tours, 38 Newbury St., Boston Ma 02116. Contact: Jacqueline R. Keith (617) 266-7465. (Cable: Esplatrav Telex 940421).

Antarctica

Antarctica: Carrier: Aerolineas Argentinas. Depart from: Miami, Los Angeles, New York. Season/Dates: Nov., Feb.

Duration: 24 days. Features: cruise Antarctic Peninsula. Probable birds: penguins, albatrosses, petrels. Requirements: bring water-proof pants and boots, plus warm clothing. Group size: 128 passengers. Cost/Person: $2,575. Includes: land arrangements—Buenos Aires, all services on board cruise, lecturers, etc. Organizer: W. David Campbell Travel, Ltd., 527 Madison Ave., Suite 1207, New York NY 10022. Contact: David Campbell (212) 752-8908.

Antarctica: Carrier: Braniff Airlines. Depart from: Los Angeles/Miami/New York. Season/Dates: Jan. 29, 1979. Duration: 24 days. Locale: Antarctic and Sub-Antarctic waters. Features: Twenty-four-day cruise on MS World Discoverer, expert lectures during landings at scientific stations (including Falkland Islands). Probable birds: Black-browed Albatross, Gentoo, Adelie, Rockhopper, Magellanic, and Macaroni Penguin, Arctic Terns, Falkland Goose. Cost/Person: from $2,575, depending on cabin. Includes: all costs, except air transportation USA/Buenos Aires/USA; also includes deluxe hotel accommodations/Buenos Aires, and all special clothing equipment needed. Organizer: Society Expeditions, P.O. Box 5088, University Station, Seattle WA 98105. Contact: T.C. Swart (206) 324-9400. Cable: Society Seattle. Telex: 910-444-1381.

Asia

India: Carrier: British Airways, Air India. Depart from: London. Season/Dates: Apr., Feb. Duration: 23 days. Features: guest lecturer accompanying each departure, bibliography provided each passenger. Probable birds: Black-necked Stork, Ring-tailed Fish Eagle, Peacock, Green Pigeon,

Crested Serpent Eagle, Black Ibis. Group size: not to exceed 30. Cost/Person: $2,062. Includes: all airfare London/London, and within the tour, all land travel and sightseeing, all accommodations, all meals, gratuities and taxes. Organizer: Esplanade Tours, W.F. & R.K. Swan (Hellenic) Ltd., 38 Newbury St., Boston MA 02116. Contact: Jacqueline R. Keith (617) 226-7465. Cable: Esplatrav, Telex 940421.

Northern India: Carrier: British Airways. Depart from: New York. Season/Dates: November. Duration 21 days. Locale: jungle and sandstone desert of Northern India. Features: visits to the Pushkar Fair, Ghana Bird Sanctuary, Tiger Haven. Probable birds: storks, wild ducks, geese, pelicans. Group size: 16 participants. Cost/Person: $1,985. Includes: luggage transfers, sightseeing, leader/staff, local guides, meals, taxes, items of equipment as may be needed. Organizer: Hanns Ebensten Travel, Inc., 55 West 42 St., New York NY 10036. Contact: Hanns Ebensten (212) 354-6634.

India (Northern India/Nepal): Depart from: New York City. Season/Dates: Feb. 23, Oct. 5, 1979. Duration: 36 days. Features: leisurely paced tour, sightseeing in New Delhi and Jaipur; see Amber Fort on elephant back, observe water birds at Keoladeo Ghana Bird Sanctuary, watch sun rise and set at the Taj Mahal; visit Buddhist temples and take early-morning boat ride on Ganges; fly to Napal, two nights spent in Chitawan National Park at Tiger Tops, view Mt. Everest; fly to Calcutta, field trips taken again via elephant; visit Darjeeling and Bombay, view Ellora and Ajanta Caves. Cost/Person: $3,788. Includes: air fare NY/NY, land costs. Organizer: Questers Worldwide Nature Tours, 257 Park Avenue South, New York NY 10010.

Contact: Michael Parkin (212) 673-3120.

India (Southern India): Depart from: New York City. Season/Dates: Nov. 10, 1978; Jan. 26, Nov. 9, 1979. Duration: 17 days. Features: arrive in Bombay; sightsee in nearby cities, visit various wildlife sanctuaries en route; field trips in coastal areas via foot and launch — view water birds and elephants; see Indian temples. Cost/Person: $2,131. Includes: land costs, and air fare NY/NY. Organizer: Questers Worldwide Nature Tours, 257 Park Ave. South, New York NY 10010. Contact: Michael Parkin (212) 673-3120.

India/Bhutan/Nepal: Carrier: Air India. Depart from: New York. Season/Dates: 1978: Nov. 3-26; Dec. 1-24; 1979: Jan. 5-28; Feb. 2-25; Mar. 2-25; Apr. 6-29; Nov. 2-25; Nov. 30-Dec. 23. Duration: 24 days. Locale: Himalayan lowland jungle (terai), central Indian plains, riverine environment, the sal forests of central India. Features: bird watching from elephant back in Kaziranga National Park, by canoe on the Manas River in Bhutan; 3-day river rafting trip to Tiger Tops Jungle Lodge in Nepal; stay on naturalist's ranch near Nepal; stay in tented camp accommodations in Kanha National Park in India. Probable birds: Racket-tailed Drongo, Paradise Flycatcher, Painted Stork, Purple Sunbird, Tree-pie, Pheasant-tailed Jacana; see over 20 species Asian birds. Group size: maxium 12 people. Requirements: recommend 1) bring binoculars, light hiking shoes, small day pack and 2) some experience in camping/"roughing it". Cost/Person: $1,775. Includes: all costs, except airfare New York-India. Organizer: Mountain Travel, 1398 Solano Ave., Albany CA 94706. Contact: Pam Shandrick (415) 527-8100.

India/Sir Lanka/Nepal: Carrier: Air India. Depart from: New York City. Season/

Dates: Nov. 6, 1978; Feb. 6, Nov. 6, 1979. Duration: 23 days. Features: view numerous species of wildlife, gain appreciation of Buddhist tradition to preserve wildlife. Probable birds: Indian Pond Heron, Black Kite, Indian Roller, Asian Pied Myna. Cost/Person: $2,653. Includes: air fare NY/NY, twin bedded rooms, three meals/day, overland transportation throughout, airport/hotel/tour transfers, guest lectures. Option: Burma extension: $793. 7 days. Organizer: Explorer Tours, 640 Cathcart St., Suite #307, Montreal, Canada H3B 1M3. Contact: Karen Zimmer (514) 861-676. Cable: ACALIAISON.

Indonesia: Carrier: UTA French Airlines. Depart from: Los Angeles. Season/Dates: April, September. Duration: 23 days. Locale: tropical jungle, coastal marshland, one week on Mahakam River. Features: carefully surveyed foray to remote parts of Indonesia — Western Java and Boreno (Kalimantan) — to view wildlife; river safari in Borneo. Probable birds: peacocks, more than 100 other species. Group size: 18 participants. Organizer: Hanns Ebensten Travel, Inc., 55 West 42 St., New York NY 10036. Contact: Hanns Ebensten (212) 354-6634.

Indonesia (Sumatra, Java, Bali): Depart from: Los Angeles. Season/Dates: Apr. 14, Jun. 30, Sept. 8, 1979. Duration: 24 days. Features: overnight in Hong Kong and Singapore on way to Sumatra where see Lake Toba and various islands; fly to Java, visit celebrated Botanical Gardens in Bogor, field trips to see rare forms of wildlife including Javan rhinoceros; visit island of Bali; tour western portion of Java to observe additional wilflife and birds. Cost/Person: $3,414. Includes: air fare Los Angeles/Los Angeles and land costs. Organizer: Questers Worldwide Nature Tours, 257 Park Av. South, New York NY 10010. Contact: Michael Parkin (212) 673-3120.

Kashmir (Valley of Ladakh): Depart from: New York City. Season/Dates: Jul. 6, Aug. 3, Sept. 7, 1979. Duration: 23 days. Features: visit Moghul monuments, including Taj Mahal, visit Keoladeo Ghana Bird Sanctuary (one of world's best breeding places for water birds); visit Sariska Game Sanctuary; fly to Srinagar to begin expedition to Leh in Valley of Ladakh, visit monasteries, cross the Indus River, visit Shey Palace and Monastary; take various field trips to wildlife sanctuaries, see the rare Kashmir stag. Cost/Person: $2,449. Includes: air fare NY/NY, land costs. Organizer: Questers Worldwide Nature Tours, 257 Park Av. South, New York NY 10010. Contact: Michael Parkin (212) 673-3120.

Malaysia/Hong Kong: Depart from: San Francisco. Season/Dates: Aug. 31. Duration: 26 days. Locale: tropical jungles, oriental cities. Features: visit Borneo and Taman Negara. Requirements: 10 participants. Cost/Person: $3,395. Includes: all expenses, from and return to San Francisco. Organizer: World Nature Tours, Inc., P.O. Box 693, Silver Springs, MD 20901. Contact: Donald H. Messersmith (301) 593-2522.

Malaysia, Singapore, Brunei: Depart from: Los Angeles. Season/Dates: Jan. 27, May 5, Jul. 21, Sept. 29, 1979. Duration: 23 days. Features: arrive Hong Kong, visit Penang Island and Kuala Lumpur, capital of Malaysia; travel via riverboat to see one of the largest national parks in the world, abundant in bird life; spend three days in Singapore, cross South China Sea to Sarawak; fly to Sabah for three nights stay in Kinabalu National Park to view many species of flora and fauna; visit an orangutan reserve in Sandaken; fly to Manila for return to L.A. Cost/Person: $3,520. Includes: air fare LA/LA, and land costs. Organizer: Questers Worldwide Nature Tours, 257 Park Av. South, New York NY 10010. Contact: Michael Parkin (212) 673-3120.

Nepal: Carrier: Pam Am/Air India airlines. Depart from: New York. Season/Dates: Mar. 31-Apr. 26, 1979. Duration: 28 days. Locale: Himalayan foothills, altitudes from 5,000-11,000 ft. Features: exceptional number of birds to be seen (migration and nesting season); 60-ft tall rhododendron forest in full bloom; mountain travel trip leader and expert local naturalist as escorts. Probable birds: suggest reading Robert Fleming's BIRDS OF NEPAL. Requirements: hiking/camping ability. Group size: approx. 10-15 persons. Cost/Person: $1,575. Excludes: NY/India/NY airfare. Organizer: Mountain Travel 1398 Solano Av., Albany CA 94706. Contact: Pam Shandrick (415) 527-8100.

Nepal Trek: Depart from: New York via Air India. Season/Dates: Mar. 23, Oct. 12, 1979. Duration: 23 days. Features: arrive Delhi: explore Kathmandu Valley (includes air excursion with view of Mt. Everest); view rhododendron forests out of city of Gorkha and see trees covered with hanging moss and immense orchids, all seen on 11-day trek covering from five to eight miles per day, all camping chores handled by Sherpa leader and staff; stay in jungle foothills out of Meghauli, field trips taken to view abundant bird life. Cost/Person: $2,563. Includes: air fare NY/NY, land costs. Organizer: Questers Worldwide Nature Tours, 257 Park Av. South, New York NY 10010. Contact: Michael Parkin (212) 673-3120.

Sri Lanka: Depart from: New York City. Season/Dates: Feb. 9, Nov. 23, 1979. Duration: 18 days. Features: visit Wilpattu National Park to explore inland lakes and great variety of water birds; spend two days observing sculpture and architectural remains of Sri Lanka's two principal ancient cities, birding and picnicking along the way; view fifth-century frescoes at Sigiriya; visit Royal Botanic Gardens; visit Temple of the Tooth — attend evening ceremonies; visit coral reef, in glass-bottomed boat, of coastal area; visit Sinharaja Forest, country's richest birding area — see Red-faced Malkoha, Malabar Trogon, Ceylon Magpie. Cost/Person: $1,981. Includes: land costs and air fare NY/NY. Organizer: Questers Worldwide Nature Tours, 257 Park Ave. South, New York NY 10010. Contact: Michael Parkin (212) 673-3120.

Canada

Alberta: Depart from: Calgary. Season/Dates: May to September. Duration: 12 days. Locale: Canadian Rocky Mountains, foothills, prairies. Features: observe native flora, fauna (alpine and prairie bird species), camping, leisurely day hiking, lots of time for enjoying and photographing surroundings. Requirements: be physically fit for short hikes/camping. Cost/Person: $675 Canadian currency. Includes: transportation from Calgary, 2 nights motel accommodations, food, tent, sleeping bag, foamie, pillow, liner, all eating/cooking equipment. Organizer: Photographic Nature Tours, Box 250, Canmore, Alberta, Canada T0L 0M0. Contact: Halle Flygare (403) 678-4236.

Alberta/Yukon/Northwest Territories: Depart from: Edmonton, Alberta. Season/Dates: June 16, July 7, Aug. 11, 1979. Duration: 15 days. Features: Field trip to Elk Island National Park, sanctuary for much wildlife (Edmonton, Alberta); visit Whitehorse in the Yukon, Dawson City and the Klondike; field trips along Dempster Highway—only road penetrating remote mountain reaches of Yukon; visit Eskimo community and Hudson Bay Company supply point at Tuktoyaktuk, Northwest Territories; view coastal bird life of Yukon; lake cruise on Great Slave Lake, Yellowknife, capital of NWT; stay at Ptarmigan Inn and take field trip to Lady Evelyn and Alexander Falls. Probable birds: Peregrine Falcon, Gyrfalcon, Whooping Crane. Cost/Person: $1,485. Includes: air and land costs. Organizer: Questers Worldwide Nature Tours, 257 Park Ave. South, New York, NY 10010. Contact: Michael Parkin (212) 673-3120.

Manitoba: Depart from: Winnipeg. Season/Dates: June. Duration: 12 days. Features: bird watching. Watch for: Hudsonian Godwit, Whistling Swan, Arctic Plover. Group size: 20 persons. Cost/Person: $850. Includes: hotel (first class), transportation during tour, guide services, luggage tipping. Organizer: Massachusetts Audubon Society, South Great Road, Lincoln MA 01773. Phone (617) 259-9500.

Manitoba: Depart from: Winnipeg, Manitoba. Season/Dates: August. Duration: 7 days. Locale: tundra. Features: visit remote and beautiful region notable for lack of human activity. Probable birds: shore birds, water fowl. Other wildlife: polar bear, caribou moose, whales. Group size: 15 participants. Cost/Person: $1,850. Includes: luggage transfers, leader and staff, sightseeing costs, meals, taxes, necessary items of equipment. Organizer: Hanns Ebensten Travel, Inc., 55 West 42 St., New York NY 10036. Contact: Hanns Ebensten (212) 354-6634.

Manitoba: Carrier: scheduled air carrier and rental automobile. Depart from: Winnipeg. Season/Dates: early July. Duration: 8 days. Locale: tundra, boreal forest, shore of Hudson Bay. Features: breeding shorebirds with young, Beluga whales, tundra landbirds and flowers. Cost/Person: $750 (approx.). Includes: leadership, transportation, lodging. Organizer: Northeast Birding, Seal Harbor, Main 04675. Contact: Will Russell (207) 276-3963.

Northwest Territories: Depart from: Yellow Knife NWT. Season/Dates: May to Sept. 15. Duration: 12 days minimum. Locale: Canada's Arctic wilderness. Features: wilderness camping and travel by canoe, wildlife photography, fishing; cater to special interests. Probable birds: Whistling Swan, Gyrfalcon, Golden Eagle, Bald Eagle, Peregrine Falcon. Rough-legged Hawk. Requirements: good health. Cost/Person: from $850. Includes: all costs from Yellow Knife NWT and return—includes food, equipment, guide air charter fees. Organizer: Canoe Arctic, Inc., 9 John Beck Cres., Brampton, Ontario, Canada L6W 2T2. Contact: Alex Hull (416) 451-0290.

Northwest Territories: Carrier: PWA, Edmonton, Cambridge Bay; fly twin otter from Cambay to camp (land at our own airstrip). Depart from: Edmonton, Alberta. Season/Dates: July & Aug. (July 1-8, bird watchers only.) Duration: 7 days. Locale: arctic tundra, 250 miles above arctic circle. Features: Eskimo guides. Probable birds: Arctic Loon, Snowy Owl, Whistling Swan, Red Phalarope, Hudsonian Godwit, Pomerine Jaeger. Requirements: warm clothing, good footwear. Group size: 24 persons (approx.). Cost/Person: $1,300. Includes: all costs, except liquor/commissary. Sleep accommodaitons are tentframe cabins, with main lodge. Organizer: Arctic Outpost Camps 1976 Ltd., P.O. Box 1104, Edmonton, Alberta, Canada T5J 2M1. Contact: Vicki Grell (403) 453-2920.

Northwest Territories: Carrier: float

plane charter. Depart from: Watson Lake, Yukon. Season/Dates: June 24-July 7; July 10-July 23. Duration: 14 days. Locale: mountain wilderness. Features: tour entire length of Nahanni National Park—see geothermal hot springs, spectacular canyons, cave exploration. Probable birds: eagles, Peregrine Falcon, northern ducks and loons. Group size: maximum 15 persons. Cost/Person: $1,320. Includes: transportation to and return from Watson Lake, all meals, all camping equipment. Organizer: North-West Expeditions, Ltd., P.O. Box 1551, Edmonton, Alberta, Canada T5J 2N7. Contact: David Rowe (403) 452-4433.

Northwest Territories: Carrier: charter float planes. Depart from: Yellowknife NWT. Season/Dates: July 31-Aug. 13. Duration: 14 days. Locale: tundra, river valley, boreal forest, barren lands. Features: descent of Coppermine River to Arctic Ocean; view wildlife, excellent fishing. Group size: maximum 15 persons. Requirements: physical fitness. Cost/Person: $1,452. Includes: transportation costs from and return to Yellowknife, all meals on river, all camping boating equipment. Organizer: North-West Expeditions Limited, P.O. Box 1551, Edmonton, Alberta, Canada T5J 2N7. Contact: David Rowe (403) 452-4433.

Central America

Costa Rica: Carrier: IATA International, busses, outboard dugout canoes, land rovers. Depart from: New York (flexible). Season/Dates: January (flexible). Duration: 15 days. Locale: mountains, tropical savannah, marshes, rain forests.Comfortable temperatures. Guided by excellent ornithologists. Group size: limited. Probable birds: Resplendant Quetzal, Three-wattled Bellbird, tinamous, guans, antbirds. Requirements: Good health. Suggest background reading. Cost/Person: $992. Includes: all accommodations, meals, all transportation costs, taxes, entrance fees. Organizer: Holbrook Travel, Inc., 3520 NW 13th St., Gainesville FL 32601. Contact: Mary Ann Graudon 904/377-7111.

Costa Rica: Depart from: Miami FL. Season/Dates: winter. Duration: 15 days. Features: rain forest living in field stations. Probable birds: Quetzal, Bellbird. Group size: maximum 13 persons. Cost/Person: $1,450. Includes: hotel (first class), guide services, meals and gratuities, luggage tipping, transportation during tour. Organizer: Massachusettes Audubon Society, South Great Road, Lincoln MA 01773. Tel: (617) 259-9500.

Guatamala: Carrier: no air fare provided. Depart from: Flores, Guatamala. Season/

Dates: March 9, 1979. Duration: 14 days. Locale: Usumacinta River. Features: raft trip; pre-trip tour of Tikal; layover stops at Mayan ruins — Yaxchilan and Piedras Negras. Probable birds: Scarlet Macaw, toucans, kingfishers. Requirements: Good health. No experience necessary. Bring sleeping bag and light tent. Group limited to 20. Cost/Person: $800. (approx.). Includes: transportation to Tikal from Flores for pre-trip 1-day tour; transportation to river from Flores; all meals; transportation from river to Palenque, Mexico on 14th day. Organizer: Wilderness World, 1342 Jewell Av., Pacific Grove CA 93950. Contact: Nada Kovalik (408) 373-5882.

Guatemala: Carrier: Aviateca; rented vans. Depart from: Guatemala City or Miami. Season/Dates: February 2-19, 1979. Locale: desert, Caribbean, cloud forest, jungle, lava beds, mountain highlands. Features: American leaders, local guides. Probable birds: motmots, toucans, parrots, Ocellated Turkey, trogons, the elusive Quetzal. Requirements: no experience required, not especially strenuous. Group size: 8-12. Cost/Person: $1,000. Includes: transportation within country, tips, taxes, food, lodging. Organizer: Wilderness Southeast, Inc., Rt. 3, Box 619, Savannah GA 31406. Contact: Joyce Murlless (912) 355-8008.

Guatemala: Depart from: Miami FL. Season/Dates: August. Duration: 10 days. Features: visit Tikal — Mayan ceremonial site, rain forests. Three tour leaders: archeologist, ecologist and experienced field ornithologist. Cost/Person: $950. Includes: twin-bedded accommodations, meals and gratuities, guide services, transportation during tour. Organizer: Massachusetts Audubon Society, South Great Road, Lincoln MA 01773. Phone: (617) 259-9500.

Guatemala: Depart from: Miami FL. Season/Dates: March. Duration: 15 days. Features: Tikal-site of Mayan ceremonial civiliation; Lake Axtlan. Probable birds: resplendent Quetzal. Group size: maximum 20 persons. Cost/Person: $1,250. Includes: hotel (first class), meals and gratuities, guide services, luggage tipping, transportation during tour. Organizer: Massachusetts Audubon Society, South Great Road, Lincoln MA 01773. Phone: (617) 259-9500

Guatemala/Panama: Depart from: Miami. Season/Dates: July 27. Duration: 19 days. Locale: tropical forests/mountains/beaches. Probable birds: resplendent Quetzal, other rare birds. Requirements: 8 participants. Cost/Person: $2,096. Includes: all expenses (first class hotels) from and return to Miami. Organizer: World Nature Tours, Inc., P.O. Box 693, Silver Spring MD 20901. Contact: Donald H. Messersmith (301) 593-2522.

Guatemala/Honduras/Belize: Depart from: Miami, Florida. Season/Dates: Dec. 16, 1978; Jan. 27, Feb. 17, Mar. 17, Nov. 3, Dec. 22, 1979. Duration: 19 days. Features: arrive in Guatemala City, drive to Chichicastenango, drive to Lake Atitlan (field trip searches for the endemic Atitlan Grebe); drive to the mountainous Baja Verapaz province to search for the resplendent Quetzal in the cloud forest; continue to Honduras to observe lowland tropical birds; visit Tikal, explore jungle and Mayan ruins, also, remarkably rich bird life found here; visit Seibal and view excavated Mayan ceremonial center found in the lush rain forest; field trip on Belize River; field trip off Belize coast to world's second largest barrier reef. Probable birds: toucans, trogons, hummingbirds, macaws (the species sacred to the Mayans). Cost/Person: $1,678 from Miami. Includes all land and air fare costs. Organizer: Questers Worldwide Nature Tours, 257 Park Av., New York NY 10010. Contact: Michael Parkin (212) 673-3120.

Panama: Depart from: Miami FL. Season/Dates: winter. Duration: 15 days. Features: bird watching. Probable birds: toucans, trogons, manakins, cotingas, resplendent Quetzal. Group size: 10-15 persons. Cost/Person: $1,665. Includes: twin-bedded accommodations, meals and gratuities, guide services, luggage tipping, Miami/Panama City round trip airfare. Organizer: Massachusettes Audubon Society, South Great Road, Lincoln MA 01773. Phone: (617) 259-9500.

Panama: Depart from: Miami FL. Season/Dates: summer, 1979. Duration: 1 week. Locale: Panamanian highlands and lowlands. Features: personal birding tour with guide Warren D. Harden; small group. Cost/Person: $950 (aprox.). Includes: accommodations and transportation. Organizer: Warren D. Harden, 2409 Butler Drive, Norman OK 73069. Phone: (405) 364-2575.

Europe

England/France: Carrier: commercial airlines/rental autos. Depart from: London, England. Season/Dates: mid-May. Duration: 14 days. Locale: marshes, sea bird cliffs, coastal woodlands. Features: see flamingos at the Canargue, thousands of sea birds at Fair Isle, spring migrants on the north Norfolk coast. Cost/Person: $1,000 (approx.). Includes: lodging, food, transportation, leadership. Organizer: Northeast Birding, Seal Harbor, Maine 04675. Contact: Will Russell (207) 276-3963.

England, Wales, The Scottish Lowlands: Depart from: New York City. Season: May 25, Jun. 22, Jul. 13, Aug. 3, 1979. Duration: 23 days. Features: British

Airways flight to London, local sightseeing; visit Havergate Island and Minsmere reserve, home for 100 of Britain's 210 breeding birds; visit Royal Society for the Protection of Birds and Old Winchester Hill Nature Reserve; full day field trip to refuge for Britain's reptiles; see 160 different species of birds in natural surroundings at Wildlife Trust at Slimbridge; arrive in Carmarthen, Wales, for a boat trip to see 10,000 pairs of breeding grey seals on Skomer Island, visit national nature reserve. Tour includes field trip to Farne Islands and Lindisfarne Reserve, a favorite migration watchpoint. Two nights at Edinburgh, visit the Castle and Palace of Holyroodhouse, boat trip to Bass Rock to view large gannetry. Cost/Person: $1,942. Includes: air fare New York/New York and land costs. Organizer: Questers Worldwide Nature Tours, 257 Park Av. South, New York NY 10010. Contact: Michael Parkin (212) 673-3120.

Germany, Austria, Switzerland: Carrier: Charter flight/and private coach. Depart from: New York or Washington. Season/Dates: May 20. Duration: 2 weeks. Locale: Alps. Features: overnights in old castle and inns. Requirements: 15 participants. Cost/Person: $959. Includes: hotels, continental breakfasts, coach, trip across Lake Lucerne, all sightseeing, entrance fees, transfers, leaders, taxes, tips, and service charges. Organizer: World Nature Tours, Inc., P.O. Box 693, Silver Spring MD 20901. Contact: Donald H. Messersmith (301) 593-2522.

Greenland: Depart from: New York City. Season/Dates: Jun. 19, Jul. 1, Jul. 31, 1979. Duration: 11 days. Features: explore national parks, field trips by boat and by foot, view icebergs and Arctic fauna, visit the site where Eric the Red settled in 985. Probable birds: Common Eider, Great Black-backed, Iceland Gull, Arctic Tern. Cost/Person: 1,541. Includes: air fares New York/New York, all in-tour air fares and land costs. Organizer: Questers Worldwide Nature Tours, 257 Park Av. South, New York NY 10010. Contact: Michael Parkin (212) 673-3120.

Iceland: Depart from: New York City. Season/Dates: Jun. 8, Jun. 29, July 20, Aug. 10, 1979. Duration: 16 days. Features: field trips to Thingvellir National Park, Skaftafell National Park; view Europe's largest glacier, observe plants and animals existing in conditions similar to those existing during the Ice Age; visit Lake Myvatn with its many islands of rich flora and large bird populations; boat trip to view puffin colonies; drive to see Iceland's largest breeding colony of Arctic Tern; excursion to Westman Islands (recently recovered from volcanic activity). Other probable birds: Kittiwake, Fulmar, guillemots, petrels. Cost/Person: $1,942. Includes: air fare New York/New York and

land costs. Organizer: Questers Worldwide Nature Tours, 257 Park Av. South, New York NY 10010. Contact: Michael Parkin (212) 673-3120.

Norway: Depart from: New York City. Season/Dates: June 8, Jul. 6, 1979. Duration: 24 days. Features: arrive Oslo via Scandinavian Airlines; visit home of one of Norway's leading naturalists, visit Natural History Museum, Botanical Gardens, train to Flam, visit museum housing the Kon Tike raft and exploratory ship Flam; ferry and motorcoach to Laerdal, time provided for afternoon birding; visit Geiranger Fjord Alesund, bird island of Runde; coastal steamer north from Trondheim; tour national parks, visit North Cape to see the midnight sun. Probable birds: puffins, gannets, Kittiwake, guillemots, razorbills, nesting Arctic Skua. Cost/Person: $3,173. Includes: air fare New York/New York, land costs. Organizer: Questers Worldwide Nature Tours, 257 Park Av. South, New York NY 10010. Contact: Michael Parkin (212) 673-3120.

Norway: Carrier: Scandinavian Airways. Depart from: Oslo, Norway. Season/Dates: June 14. Duration: 3 weeks. Locale: mountainous. Requirements: 10 participants. Cost/Person: $1,150. Includes: all expenses (first-class hotel), except meals. Organizer: World Nature Tours, Inc., P.O. Box 693, Silver Spring MD 20901. Contact: Donald H. Messersmith (301) 593-2522.

Scotland: Carrier: British Airways. Depart from: San Francisco, New York (others available). Season/Dates: Jun-Jul each year. Duration: 21 days. Locale: highlands and isles. Features: tour led by two expert naturalists/ornithologists, will visit very remote and scenic areas. Watch for:

guillemots, razorbills, puffins, Great Skua, gannets, Peregrine Falcon. Group size: maximum 20 people. Cost/Person: $1,390. Includes: all land/sea transportation and transfers, all accommodations, all meals except in Edinburgh, all entrance fees, all tips. Organizer: Nature Expeditions International, 599 College Avenue, Palo Alto CA 94306. Phone (415) 328-6572. Cable: Naturetour.

Scotland: Depart from: New York City. Season/Dates: June to Sept. Duration: 10 days. Locale: the inaccessible islands off Scotland's spectacular West Coast. Features: unhurried cruise for people who enjoy outdoor pleasures, hiking beaches to see sea birds. Probable birds: auks, shearwaters, fulmars, petrels. Group size: 6 participants. Cost/Person: $985. Includes: accommodations, luggage transfers, sightseeing, leader and staff, local guides, meals, taxes, necessary items of equipment. Organizer: Hanns Ebensten Travel, Inc., 55 West 42 St., New York NY 10036. Contact: Hanns Ebensten (212) 354-6634.

Scotland: Carrier: British Airways. Depart from: New York City. Season/Dates: May and September. Duration: 17 days. Locale: Scottish Highlands — moors, pine forests, coastal areas, mountains. Features: hike unspoiled countryside, observe wildlife. Probable birds: gulls, cormorants, swans, Golden Eagle, osprey. Group size: 12 participants. Cost/Person: $1,645. Includes: accommodations, luggage transfers, sightseeing, leader and staff, local guides, meals, taxes, necessary items of equipment. Organizer: Hanns Ebensten Travel, Inc., 55 West 42 St., New York NY 10036. Contact: Hanns Ebensten (212) 354-6634.

Scotland: Depart from: New York City.

Season/Dates: May 25, Jun. 15, Jul. 13, Aug. 24, 1979. Duration: 23 days. Features: arrive in Glasgow to visit the outer islands and highlands of Scotland, observe the largest remaining colony of Greylag Geese in Britain, tour castle at Dunvegan, home of the Clan MacLeod; visit Britain's largest nature reserve, Cairngorms; fly to the Orkneys to view Stone Age excavations; excursions made from the Shetlands to visit nature reserve (see breeding pair of Snowy Owls). Cost/Person: $2,106 (May); $2,219 (June, July, Aug.). Includes: air fare New York/New York, and land costs and in-tour air fare. Organizer: Questers Worldwide Nature Tours, 257 Park Av. South, New York NY 10010. Contact: Michael Parkin (212) 673-3120.

Spain/Portugal: Depart from: Boston MA. Season/Dates: May. Duration: 21 days. Features: bird watching, wildflowers, castles. Group size: 20 persons. Cost/Person: $2,140. Includes: hotel (first class), meals and gratuities, guide services, luggage tipping, entrance fees to wildlife refuges. Organizer: Massachusetts Audubon Society, South Great Road, Lincoln MA 01773. Phone: (617) 259-9500.

Switzerland: Depart from: New York City. Season/Dates: June 15, Jul. 20, Aug. 17, 1979. Duration: 17 days. Features: tour Lake Geneva area and surrounding mountainous countryside; visit Linnaean Garden planted in 1889 containing 2500 Alpine plants; return to the valley and drive along Rhone, then by rail to Zermatt; view the Matterhorn, visit the Brissag Islands and its botanical garden; explore Swiss National Park, with birding before breakfast; excursion via electric rack railway to the highest railway station in Europe; sightsee in Basel; boat trip to Lake Lucerne; farewell candlelight dinner. Cost/Person: $2,216. Includes: air fare New York/New York, land costs. Organizer: Questers Worldwide Nature Tours, 257 Park Av. South, New York NY 10010. Contact: Michael Parkin (212) 673-3120.

Mexico

Baja: Carrier: cruise ship H&M Landing. Depart from: San Diego CA. Season/Dates: Dec. to June. Duration: varies from 3½ to 10 days. Locale: wilderness islands and seacoasts. Features: staff of experienced naturalists; scheduled trip or design your own to fit particular interests. Probable birds: shore, pelagic and marsh birds, including California Brown Pelican. Group size: up to 32 persons. Cost/Person: 3½ day $250; 7½ day $510. Includes: meals, accommodations, transportation. Organizer: H&M Landing, 2803 Emerson St., San Diego CA 92106. Contact: Catherine Miller (712) 222-1144 or (213) 626-8005.

Baja: Depart from: San Diego. Season/Dates: Feb. 1, 1979. Duration: 9 days. Features: San Diego Zoo; board the Royal Polaris to sail off-shore islands; two days spent observing migratory grey whales. Cost/Person: $695 (land and cruise costs). Organizer: Questers Worldwide Nature Tours, 257 Park Av. South, New York NY 10010. Contact: Michael Parkin (212) 673-3120.

Baja: Depart from: San Diego. Season/Dates: April 1979. Duration: 9 days. Features: cruise Sea of Cortez from San Felipe to La Paz, stopping at islands/bays to explore, photograph and observe nesting birds. Probable birds: Nesting boobies, pelicans, Elegant Tern. Group size: 20 persons (approx.). Cost/Person: $610. Includes: all land transportation, boats, guides, necessary equipment, meals. Organizer: Adventures International, 4421 Albert St., Oakland CA 94619. Contact: Brad Goodhart (415) 531-6564.

Baja: Depart from: San Diego. Season/Dates: Feb. and Mar. (departs each Saturday). Duration: 8 days. Locale: beach; mangrove areas nearby. Features: beach camping in Magdalena Bay, out of La Paz; observe grey whales during mating season; observations of birds and whales from small skiffs. Probable birds: Yellow-crowned Heron, Little Blue Heron, White Ibis, Louisana Heron, Caracara, Mangrove Warbler. Group size: 20, or less. Cost/Person: $530. Includes: all land

transportation, boats, guides, necessary equipment, meals and preparation by camp staff, air transportation from San Diego to La Paz and return. Organizer: Adventures International, 4421 Albert St., Oakland CA 94619. Contact: Brad Goodhart (415) 531-6564.

Baja: Depart from: San Diego. Season/Dates: Dec/March. Duration: 8,9 days. Locale: desert wilderness. Features: natural history study led by expert naturalists; excellent whale-watching; bird watching in mangrove swamp at San Ignacio Lagoon and at sea. Group size: maximum 32 persons. Cost/Person: $590. Includes: accommodations, meals (except San Diego), fishing license fee, instruction and educational materials. Organizer: Nature Expeditions International, 599 College Av., Palo Alto CA 94306. Contact: Margaret Betchart (415) 328-6572. Cable: Naturetour.

Baja: Depart from: San Diego/Los Angeles. Season/Dates: Feb. 24-Mar. 8, 1978. Duration: 10 days. Features: exploration of the natural history of Sea of Cortez led by expert naturalist/ornithologist. Watch for: boobies, Frigate Birds, Osprey, petrels, loons, Brown Pelican. Group size: maximum 18 persons. Cost/Person: $650. Includes: ship transportation and land transfers; hotel/ship accommodations; all meals except San Diego; park fees, fishing license fee. Organizer: Nature Expeditions International, 599 College Avenue, Palo Alto CA 94306. Contact: Margaret Betchart (415) 328-6572. Cable: Naturetour.

Baja: Carrier: Baja Expeditions. Depart from: San Diego CA. Season/Dates: Nov. 11, 1978. Duration: 7 days. Features: natural history study cruise visiting remote islands and mainland habitats; see many species of tropical marine birds including boobies, tropic birds, Magnificent Frigatebirds; includes live collecting of small mammals, reptiles, marine organisms for observations and study. Cost/Person: $675. Includes: tuition (credit available), instruction, all cruise expenses, all air/bus transportation from San Diego (does not include accommodations in San Diego). Organizer: Department of Biological and Physical Sciences, UCLA Extension, P.O. Box 24902, Los Angeles CA 90024. Contact: Sakura Berry (213) 825-7093.

Colima: Carrier: Mexicana Airlines Aeromexico. Depart from: Dallas, Houston. Season/Dates: May 13-22, 1978. Duration: 11 days. Locale: tropical, mountain, coastal. Features: access to variety of bird habitats. Probable birds: parakeets, Squirrel Cuckoo, motmots, oropendolas, woodcreepers, Roseate Spoonbill. Requirements: group limit, 25. Cost/Person: $440. Includes: room, board; travel in Colima. Organizer: Hacienda El Colbano, 1700 ASP, Norman OK 73037. Contact: Richard

Hancock, (405) 325-1941.

Colima: Depart from: Dallas TX, or Guadalajara. Season/Dates: Dec. 26-Jan. 4. Duration: 10 days. Features: bird watching, with field trip to Volcan de Fuego and pacific coast under direction of experienced guide Dr. William Carter. Watch for: Chestnut-sided Shrike, Vireo, Thick-billed Parrot, Cinnamon Flower Piercer, Orange-breasted Bunting. Cost/Person: $440 from Guadalajara. Includes: board, room, and transportation. Organizer: Warren D. Harden, 2409 Butler Drive, Norman OK 73069. Contact: Warren D. Harden, (405) 364-2575.

Chihuahua: Carrier: Mexicana Airlines, Aeromexico. Depart from: Dallas, Houston. Season/Dates: May 22-31; Dec. 26-Jan. 6. Locale: Tropical-mountain, coastal. Features: travel on Chihuahua Pacific Railroad. Probable birds: Lilac-crowned Parrot, Brown-backed Solitaire, Squirrel Cuckoo, Coppery-tailed Trogon, Violet-crowned Hummingbird, Elegant Quail. Group size: 25. Cost/Person: $600. Includes: room, board; round trip from El Paso TX. Organizer: Hacienda El Cobano, 1700 ASP, Norman OK 73037. Contact: Richard Hancock, (405) 325-1941.

Eastern Mexico: Depart from: Mexico City. Season/Dates: Winter (Jan.). Duration: 15 days. Features: bird watching. Watch for: Red Warbler, Gray Silky Flycatcher, Russet Nightingale. Group size: 10-15 persons. Cost/Person: $1,100. Includes: first-class hotel accommodations, guide services, luggage tipping, transportation during tour. Organizer: Massachusetts Audubon Society, South Great Road, Lincoln MA 01773. Phone: (617) 259-9500.

Eastern Mexico: Depart from: Mexico City. Season/Dates: Jan., Feb., Mar. Duration: approx. 12 days. Features: detail itinerary provided for each tour with list of birds to be seen. Watch for: Lesser Yellow-headed Vulture, Plumbeous Kite, Ornate Hawk-Eagle, Laughing Falcon, Crested Caracara, Bat Falcon, Purple Gallinule, Bee Hummingbird. Group size: maximum 20 persons. Cost/Person: upon request. Organizer: Massachusetts Audubon Society, Dept. of Natural History Services, Lincoln MA 01773. Contact: James Baird. Phone: (617) 259-9500.

Eastern Mexico: Carrier: rental vans. Depart from: Brownsville Texas. Season/Dates: early March, 1979. Duration: 8 days. Locale: mountains, rivers, lowland forest. Features: Mexican species and wintering North American birds. Cost/Person: $550. Includes: transportation, lodging, food and leadership from Brownsville. Organizer: Northeast Birding, Seal Harbor, Maine 04675. Contact: Will Russell (207) 276-3963.

Southern Mexico: Depart from: Mexico City. Season/Dates: Dec. 17, 1978; Jan. 14, Feb. 4, Mar. 4, Oct. 21, Dec. 23, 1979. Duration: 14 days. Features: visit Oaxaca, explore site of ancient Zapotec city and Mixtec burial ground; visit valley of Hueyzacatlan in Chiapas, field trips to Lagunas de Montebello National Park near Guatemalan border — view many varieties of birds and orchids; take field trip by charter aircraft deep into Chiapas jungle, see Mayan murals; visit La Venta Museum in Villahermosa; drive to Campeche, and on to Uxmal, first stop in Yucatan, then to Merida for return connections. Cost/Person: $1,166 (excludes round trip hometown air fare; otherwise, includes all land and in-tour air fare costs). Organizer: Questers Worldwide Tours, 257 Park Av. South, New York NY 10010. Contact: Michael Parkin, (212) 673-3120.

Tamaulipas: Carrier: participants' private cars to Gomez Farias, Tamps., Mexico. Depart from: Brownsville TX (private cars in caravan). Dates: post Christmas, but always including Jan. 1st. Duration: 5 days (approx.). Locale: cloud forest, tropical evergreen, humid pine. Features: participants encouraged to help with Jan. 1 Audubon count. Group size: 18-24 participants. Requirements: age level 18 and over; bring cameras, binoculars, hiking gear for Karst topography; clothing for 30°-60° F. temperatures. Cost/Person: $185 (approx.). Includes: four-wheel drive vehicle transportation to and from Gomez Farias, with provisions made for parking private cars in Gomez Farias; board/room at biological field station (bring sheets/towels, etc.); exellent meals provided. Organizer: Gorgas Science Society, Texas Southmost College, Brownsville TX 78520. Contact: Barbara Warburton (512) 541-1241 X289.

Western Mexico: Carrier: rented VW buses, charter boats. Depart from: Mazatlan. Season/Dates: February, 1979. Duration: 11 days. Locale: mountains to 7000 ft, forests, marsh, ocean. Features: three boat trips, deep canyons of Sierra Madre. See neotropical bird species and wintering North American birds. Group size: 15 persons maximum. Cost/Person: $625. Includes: transportation, food, lodging and leadership from Mazatlan. Organizer: Northeast Birding, Seal Harbor, Maine 04675. Contact: Will Russell (207) 276-3963.

Western Mexico: Depart from: Los Angeles (others available). Season/Dates: Apr. 13-22/1979. Duration: 10 days. Locale: tropical coastal areas, including thorn forests, mangrove swamps, palm jungles, pine-oak forests. Features: bird watching, flora observations. Watch for: Tufted Jay, Purplish-backed Jay, trogons, Military Macaw. Group size: maximum 16 participants. Cost/Person: $590. Includes: boat/ vehicle transportation, hotels, meals except Mazatlan, park fees, service/handling charges, tips. Organizer: Nature Expeditions International, 599 College Avenue, Palo Alto CA 94306. Contact: Margaret Betchart (415) 328-6572. Cable: Naturetour.

Western Mexico: Depart from: Dallas TX. Season/Dates: May, 1979. Duration: 10 days. Locale: mountains, coastal lowlands, and Gulf of California. Features: bird watching field trips around and into Copper Canyon in Chihuahua; boat trip to Farallon Rock in Gulf of California; plane excursion over Copper Canyon area. Cost/Person: $600. Includes: board, room, and transportation. Organizer: Warren D. Harden, 2409 Butler Drive, Norman OK 73069. Contact: Warren D. Harden (405) 364-2575.

Western Mexico: Depart from: Mazatlan. Season/Dates: March. Duration: 12 days. Features: bird watching. Watch for: Russet-crowned Motmot, Lilac-crowned Parrot, Military Macaw. Group size: 15 persons. Cost/Person: $845. Includes: hotels, meals, guide service, transportation during tour. Organizer: Massachusetts Audubon Society, South Great Road, Lincoln MA 01773. Phone: (617) 259-9500.

Yucatan: Depart from: Mexico City. Season/Dates: Fall. Duration: 15 days. Locale: Chiapas highlands, Palenque rain forests, Yucatan arid areas, Maya ruins. Features: bird watching. Group size: 13-15 persons. Cost/Person: $1,250. Includes: first-class hotel accommodations, meals and gratuities, guide service. Organizer: Massachusetts Audubon Society, South Great Road, Lincoln MA 01773. Phone: (617) 259-9500.

Yucatan: Depart from: New Orleans LA. Season/Dates: Dec. 26-Jan. 6. Duration: 12 days. Locale: rain forest out of Merida and Villahermosa. Features: bird watching and Mayan history; guides will be Warren Harden and a Mayan ruin specialist; also, a professional painter will accompany group. Cost/Person: $1,073. Includes: board, room, and transportation. Organizer: Warren D. Harden, 2409 Butler Drive, Norman OK 73069. Contact: Warren D. Harden (405) 364-2575.

South America

Argentina: Carrier: Avianca Airlines. Depart from: Los Angeles. Season/Dates: December 9, 1978. Duration: 21 days. Locale: pampas. Features: will bird Argentina from pampas to Tiera del Fuego, with special flight to Falkland Islands. Leader of group will be Arnold Small, president of the American Birding Association. Probable birds: many inland birds; Antarctic species; penguins and albatrosses. Cost/Person: $3,000 (approx.). Includes: all costs. Organizer: Aventura Natural History Tours, 508 North Sierra Drive, Beverly Hills CA 90210. Contact: Pamela. Axelson (213) 276-6081.

Agrentina: Depart from: New York, Miami. Season/Dates: Nov., Dec., Jan. Duration: 21/22 days. Features: see penguins, seals on Valdez Peninsula, see albatrosses on Falkland Islands; local naturalist guides. Requirements: bring light weight parkas, good walking shoes. Group size: 16·persons. Cost/Person: $1,875. Includes: hotels, most meals, sightseeing excursions, escorts. Organizer: W. David Campbell Travel Ltd., 527 Madison Av., Suite 1207, New York NY 10022. Contact: David Campbell (212) 752-8908.

Agrentina: Depart from: Miami FL. Season/Dates: Nov. 9, 1978; Feb. 8, Nov. 8, 1979. Duration: 29 days. Features: early-morning birding out of Buenos Aires, explore penguin rookery, watch sea elephants, visit sea colonies on Isla de los Pajaros, see the Black-browed Albatross; explore glaciers at La Glaciares National Park; travel to Tierra del Fuego, visit Lapataia Bay on the Beagle Channel — look for sea lions and the Upland Goose; explore Lake Nahuel Huapi and Lanin National Parks and Laguna Blanca (created specifically to preserve its bird life). Cost/Person: $3,157. Includes: land costs, in-tour air costs, and Miami/Miami air fare. Organizer: Questers Worldwide Nature Tours, 257 Park Av. South, New York NY 10010. Contact: Michael Parkin (212) 673-3130.

Argentina: Depart from: New York/Miami. Season/Dates: monthly, from Oct. through Mar. Duration: 15-31 days, depending on options. Locale: Patagonia, Tierra del Fuego, Andean Lake region. Features: expert nature escort/guide; optional extension to Easter Island or the Galapagos. Probable birds: Antarctic Penguin, Black-necked Swan, flamingoes, storks, Megellanic Penguin. Group size: maximum 20 ·persons. Cost/Person: $1,550 to $2,050, depending on options. Includes: all costs, except air fare USA/South America/USA. Organizer: Society Expeditions, P.O. Box 5088, University Station, Seattle WA 98105. Contact: T.C. Swartz (206) 324-9400. Cable: Society Seattle.

Argentina/Ecuador: Carrier: Braniff Airlines. Depart from: Miami FL. Season/Dates: Jan. 4 to Feb. 5, 1979. Duration: 33 days. Locale: windswept, remote Falklands; barren sheep ranching country; Tierra del Fuego; fjords; glaciers; Magellan beech forests; Galapagos; volcanic archipelago. Features: Ian Strange, Falklands naturalist, will accompany trip; Natalie Goodall, expert naturalist, will be visited in Tierra del Fuego; 2-week Galapagos cruise; some all-day hikes. Group size: 15 people maximum. Cost/Person: $1,875. Includes: all expenses except air fare from Miami to Quito/Buenos Aires $1,105/Braniff. Organizer: Mountain Travel, 1398 Solano Av., Albany CA 94706. Contact: Pam Shandrick (415) 527-8100

Brazil/Peru: Depart from: New York, Miami. Season/Dates: Feb., Mar., Oct, Nov. Duration: 18 days. Locale: tropical. Features: excursions on Amazon River, visit to Amazon jungle; rich areas of bird life; local naturalist guides. Group size: approx. 16 persons. Cost/Person: $1,450. Includes: hotel accommodations, most meals, sightseeing excursions, plus escort. Organizer: W. David Campbell Travel Ltd., 527 Madison Av., Suite #1207, New York NY 10022. Contact: David Campbell (212) 752-8908.

Colombia: Carrier: Avianca Airlines. Depart from: Miami FL. Season/Dates: Jul. 9 to Jul. 30 (1978). Duration: 21 days. Features: bird watching with tour leader and additional local tour guides; small group of enthusiastic birders. Cost/Person: $1,995. Includes: air fare and surface arrangements, meals, tips, entrance fees. Organizer: Bird Bonanzas, Inc., 12550 Biscayne Blvd. Suite 501, North Miami FL 33179. Contact: Carol Poloniecki. Phone: (305) 895-0607.

Ecuador: Carrier: Avianca Airlines. Depart from: Los Angeles, New York, Miami. Season/Dates: April 6, 1978. Duration: 17 days. Locale: temperate, sub-tropical areas. Features: this special Birds-of-Ecuador tour visits Mt. Pichincha, Volcan Cotopaxi, Lake San Pablo, Cuicocha Lake cruise, Tinalandia, overnight at Jaguar Hotel (deep in the Amazonas). Probable birds: Andean Condor, Hummingbirds. Over 1,400 species of birds inhabit/visit Ecuador. Cost/Person: $1,261 (from New York). Includes all costs. Organizer: Aventura Natural ·History Tours, 508 North Sierra Drive, Beverly Hills CA 90210. Contact: Pam Axelson (213) 276-6081.

Ecuador: Carrier: Avianca Airlines. Depart from: Los Angeles, New York, Miami. Season/Dates: 1978: Jun. 22-Jul. 6, Jul. 6-20, Jul. 27-Aug. 10, Aug. 17-31. Duration: 17 days. Locale: tropical. Features: explore upper Amazon on Flotel Orellana, a 180-ton first-class floating hotel built especially for this tour; side trips made on motor canoes; visit Yumbo Indians and Monkey Island. Probable birds: many, many species tropical birds. Cost/Person: $1,128 from Miami. Includes: all costs. Organizer: Aventura Natural History Tours, 508 North Sierra Drive, Beverly Hills CA 90110. Contact: Pam Axelson (213) 276-6081.

Ecuador: Depart from: Miami FL. Season/Dates: March. Duration: 16 days. Features: bird watching;. see volcanes, Andean lakes and Indian villages amidst cloud forests and tropical jungle. Group size: 20 persons. Cost/Person: $1,825. Includes: twin-bedded accommodations (first class), meals and gratuities, guide services, transportation during tour, entrance to wildlife refuges. Organizer: Massachusetts Audubon Society, South Great Road, Lincoln MA 01773. Phone: (617) 259-9500.

Ecuador/Galapagos: Carrier: Ecuatoriana Airlines. Depart from: Los Angeles; New York; Miami. Season/Dates: year-around departures. Duration: 15 days. Features: one-week Galapagos cruise; expert nature guide. Probable birds: Frigate Bird, Galapagos Albatross, penguins, boobies, Flightless Cormorant, thirteen species Darwin's Finches. Requirements: bring good rubber-soled walking shoes. Group size: 16 persons. Cost/Person: $1,595. Includes: all costs, except air fare USA/Ecuador/USA and $184 charter air fare Ecuador/Galapagos/Ecuador. Organizer: Society Expeditions, P.O. Box 5088, University Station, Seattle WA 98105. Contact: T.C. Swartz (206) 324-9400/ Cable: Society Seattle/Telex: 910-444-1381.

Ecuador/Galapagos: Depart from: Miami, FL. Season/Dates: Mar. 2, May 4, Jul. 6, Oct. 19, 1978; Feb. 22, Apr. 26, Jul. 19, Oct. 11, 1979. Duration: 15 days. Features: night flight from Miami to Quito, visit various museums in nearby cities; descend Andes via narrow guage railway to coastal plains, visit city of Guayaquil; travel on motor vessel Buccaneer to Galapagos, visiting all of the major islands, much bird watching and general nature study, observe one of the world's most active volcanoes. Leave from Taltra by air for Quito. Probable birds: Darwin's Finches, Vermilion Flycatchers, Waved Albatross, petrels, shearwaters, flamingos. Cost/Person: $1,704 Miami/ Miami. Includes: all land and air costs. Organizer: Questers Worldwide Nature Tours, 257 Park Av. South, New York NY 10010. Contact: Michael Parkin (212) 673-3120.

Ecuador/Galapagos: Carrier: Braniff International. Depart from: New York, Miami. Season/Dates: Feb., Jul., Aug., Nov. Duration: 17 days. Locale: Galapagos Islands. Features: adventurous cruises to remote areas of the islands for travelers who wish maximum exposure to wildlife and scenery (tour title: The Great Galapagos Hiking Adventure). Probable birds: Waved Albatross, mockingbirds, boobies, Swallow-tailed Gull, Darwin's Finches, flamingos. Group size: 14 participants. Cost/Person: $2,465. Includes: luggage transfers, sightseeing, leader and staff, local guides, meals, taxes, necessary items of equipment. Organizer: Hanns Ebensten Travel, Inc., 55 West 42 St., New York NY 10036. Contact: Hanns Ebensten (212) 354-6634.

Ecuador/Galapagos: Carrier: Braniff Airlines. Depart from: Miami FL. Season/Dates: Aug. 7-30, 1978; Aug. 6-29, 1979. Duration: 24 days. Locale: Amazon rain forest, high altitude Andean plateau, volcanic island archipelago. Features: local birders and naturalist will accompany tour. Probable birds: penguins, Blue-footed Booby. Requirements: physical agility, ability to "rough it". Group size: maximum 15 people. Cost/Person: $1,575. Includes: all costs, except air fare Miami-Quito-Miami $317. Organizer: Mountain Travel, 1398 Solano Av., Albany CA 94706. Contact: Pam Shandrick (415) 527-8100.

Ecuador/Galapagos: Carrier: Ecuatoriana Airlines. Depart from: New York/Miami. Season/Dates: Mar., Oct., 1979. Duration: 17 days. Locale: Galapagos Islands. Features: cruise for budget-minded travelers interested in ecology and wildlife of the islands; tour accompanied by naturalist leader and physician, as well as government-trained guides. Probable birds: Waved Albatross, mockingbirds, boobies, Swallow-tailed Gull, Lava Gull, Darwin's Finches, flamingos, Flightless Cormorant, pelicans. Group size: 66 persons. Cost/Person: $1,065 minimum. Includes: luggage transfers, leader and staff, local guides, meals, taxes, necessary items of equipment. Organizer: Hanns Ebensten Travel, Inc., 55 West 42 St., New York NY 10036. Contact: Hanns Ebensten (212) 354-6634.

Ecuador/Galapagos: Depart from: Miami FL. Season/Dates: Summer, 1979. Duration: 2 weeks. Locale: Galapagos Archipelago in Pacific Ocean, Ecuadorian Andes. Features: 11-day yacht cruise in Galapagos Islands, with personal guide Warren D. Harden and Galapagos naturalist. Watch for: Darwin's Finches, boobies, petrels, shearwaters. Cost/Person: $2,000 (approx.). Includes: room, transportation, most meals. Organizer: Warren D. Harden, 2409 Butler Drive, Norman OK 73069. Phone: (405) 364-2575.

Ecuador/Galapagos: Depart from: Miami FL. Season/Dates: March. Duration: 9 days. Features: bird watching; visit Charles Darwin Research Station. Watch for: Flightless Cormorant. Group size: 20 persons. Cost/Person: $1,735. Includes: hotel, meals and gratuities, guide services, transportation during tour. Organizer: Massachusetts Audubon Society, South Great Road, Lincoln MA 01773. Phone: (617) 259-9500.

Ecuador/Galapagos: Carrier: Braniff Airlines. Depart from: Los Angeles/Miami/others available. Season/Dates: 4-6 expeditions a year, usually Dec., Apr., Jun., Aug. Duration: 20 days. Features: observe wildlife, study natural history of Galapagos by travel on sailing craft; expert naturalist accompanies tour. Probable birds: Frigate

Bird, boobies, albatrosses, Galapagos Dove. Group size: maximum 16 persons. Cost/Person: $1,390. Includes: all ship/vehicle transportation; all accommodations (including sailing vessel), all meals except in Quito, park fees, tips, instruction. Organizer: Nature Expeditions International, 599 College Avenue, Palo Alto CA 94306. Phone: (415) 328-6572.

Ecuador/Galapagos: Carrier: Avianca Airlines. Depart from: Los Angeles, New York, Miami. Season/Dates: throughout year, with special charters during Summer months. Duration: 15 days. Locale: coastal islands, mainland beach areas, lowlands, travel 13,000 ft. Andean pass. Features: Galapagos Islands via cruise ship, the Neptuno (air conditioned cabins); Darwin Research Station; island hiking; beach swimming; cruise Guayas River via privately chartered yachts; ride "Devil's Nose" railroad; attend Ballet Folklorico performance; visit Pululahua volcano. Cost/Person: $1,450 double cabin from Miami. Includes: all costs. Organizer: Aventura Natural History Tours, 508 North Sierra Drive, Beverly Hills CA 90210. Contact: Pam Axelson (213) 276-6081.

Ecuador/Galapagos: Carrier: Baniff. Depart from: Miami FL. Season/Dates: Jul. 1-18, 1979; Dec. 16-Jan. 2, 1980. Duration: 17 days. Locale: volcanic archipelago, equatorial Pacific waters. Features: trained naturalist and mountain travel leader will accompany. Probable birds: Blue-footed Booby, Flightless Cormorant, albatrosses, Darwin's Finches. Group size: 10 people maximum. Cost/Person: $1,580. Includes: all costs, except air fare to Quito (Braniff round-trip fare from Miami FL, $317). Organizer: Mountain Travel, 1398 Solano Av., Albany CA 94706. Contact: Pam Shandrick (415) 527-8100.

Ecuador/Galapagos: Carrier: Ecuatoriana Airlines. Depart from: Miami. Season/Dates: June 18. Duration: 3 weeks. Locale: jungles/tropical islands. Probable birds: Darwin's Finches, other rare tropical birds. Requirements: 14 participants. Cost/Person: $2,638. Includes: all expenses (first-class hotel reservations) from, and return to, Miami. Organizer: World Nature Tours, Inc., P.O. Box 693, Silver Spring MD 20901. Contact: Donald H. Messersmith (301) 593-2522.

Ecuador/Galapagos: Carriers: IATA International, U.S. Safety Standard expedition ships. Depart from: Miami, New York. Season/Dates: April, June, July, Aug., Dec. Duration: 2-3 weeks. Locale: tropical; comfortable temperature year-round. Features: personalized group itineraries; knowledgeable leaders. Probable birds: Galapagos Hawk, Galapagos Albatross, Darwin's Finches, boobies, herons. Requirements: proof of citizenship. Group size: 16 to 68. Cost/Person: $1,597-$2,197. Includes: all costs. Organizer: Holbrook Travel, Inc., 3520 NW 13th St., Gainesville FL 32601. Contact: Mary Ann Graudon. Phone (904) 377-7111.

Equador/Galapagos/Panama: Carrier: air and staysail schooner. Depart from: Oklahoma City OK. Season/Dates: July 31-Aug. 13. Duration: 2 weeks. Features: bird watching — see rare species, Darwin's Finches, many ocean species. Group size: 10 persons. Cost/Person: $2,250. Includes: transportation, meals on boat, all lodging, all park fees. Organizer: Warren Harden, 2409 Butler Drive, Norman OK 73069. Phone: (405) 364-2575.

Ecuador/Galapagos/Peru: Carrier: Braniff. Depart from: New York City NY. Season/Dates: December 12-25, 1978.

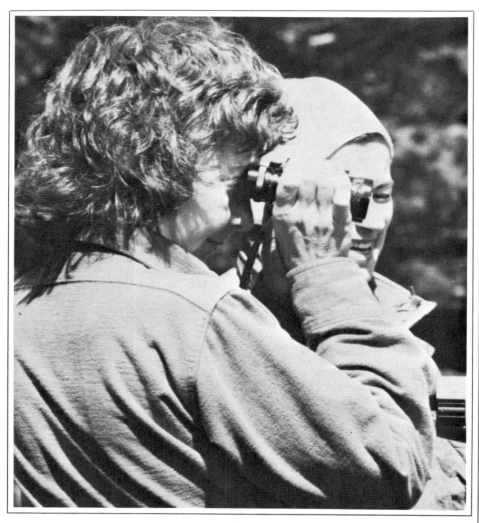

Duration: 13 days with optional 7 day extension. Features: escort from N.Y. Zoological Society. Requirements: membership in New York Zoological Society. Cost/Person: $2,075. Includes: air/land costs, all tips. Organizer: New York Zoological Society, Animal Kingdom Tours, Box 108, Bronx NY 10460. Contact: Iris Freed (212) 220-5085.

Peru: Carrier: IATA Jet International, busses, train. Depart from: New York, Miami. Season/Dates: June. Duration: 15 days (approx.). Locale: very high altitude; temperature comfortable to cool. Features: Inti Raymi Festival, hiking Inca trail, expert guide, porters to carry packs. Requirements: passport, excellent health, experience in hiking. Bring sleeping bag, small tent, backpack. Group size: limited to 21. Cost/Person: $1,257. Includes: International air; food, sightseeing, transportation within Peru, tips, taxes, porterage, first-class hotel when available. Organizer: Holbrook Travel, Inc., 3520 NW 13th St., Gainesville FL 32601. Contact: Mary Ann Graudon (904) 377-7111.

Peru: Carrier: Braniff Airlines. Depart from:

Miami FL. Season/Dates: July 8-27, 1978. Duration: 20 days. Locale: Andes, Amazon rain forest, seacoast. Probable birds: over 550 species, including toucans, Andean Condor, Torrent Duck, shearwaters, 7 species macaws, 17 species parrots. Group size: maximum 10 persons. Cost/Person: $2,328. Includes: food, lodging, ground transportation, internal flights, tips, baggage handling, guide services (3). Organizer: Victor Emanuel Nature Tours, 1603 W. Clay, Houston TX 77019. Contact: Victor Emanuel (713) 528-3725.

Peru: Carrier: Braniff/Lufthansa. Depart from: New York, Miami. Season/Dates: July to September. Duration: 16 days. Locale: Andes. Features: trekking on foot along ancient Inca trail from Cuzco, high above Urubamba Valley, to Machu Picchu; see the Andean Condor, largest flying bird in the world. Group size: 10 participants. Cost/Person: $1,950. Includes: all luggage transfers, sightseeing, leader and staff, local guides, meals, taxes, necessary items of equipment. Contact: Hanns Ebensten Travel, Inc., 55 West 42 St., New York NY 10036. Contact: Hanns Ebensten (212) 354-6634.

Peru: Depart from: Los Angeles CA. Season/Dates: June 20, 1978. Duration: 19 days. Locale: tropical rain forest. Features: explore and study natural history and ecology of the Amazon by chartered double-deck riverboat; exploration at camps is on foot and by small boats and canoes; designed for the adventurous traveler. Cost/Person: $1,615. Includes: tuition (credit available), instruction, instructional materials, transportation, meals, accommodations. Organizer: Department of Biological and Physical Sciences, UCLA Extension, P.O. Box 24902, Los Angeles, CA 90024. Contact: Sakura Berry (213) 825-7093.

Peru: Depart from Miami, FL. Season/Dates: Apr. 7, Jun. 9, Jul. 21, Nov. 1979. Duration: 23 days. Features: arrive Lima, orientation tour; drive to Paracas, visit Inca ruins, national parks, national reserve areas, number of museums; fly across Andes to Amazon basin, proceed by canoe to jungle outpost in a wildlife preserve (field trips into rain forest, visit Huarayo Indians); spend one week in high Andes observing Inca ruins, museums; travel by rail to Lake Titicaca, take field trips to floating islands of the Uru Indians and the Sillustani Chullpas — full-day excursion by chartered hydrofoil to Islands of the Sun and Moon in Bolivia. Cost/Person: $2,619 (includes land costs and air fare Miami/Miami). Organizer: Questers Worldwide Nature Tours, 257 Park Av. South, New York NY 10010. Contact: Michael Parkin (212) 673-3120.

Venezuela: Carrier: Avianca Airlines. Depart from: Los Angeles, New York, Miami. Season/Dates: January 4. Duration: 18 days. Locale: lowlands, mountains. Features: bird-oriented trip via bus throughout Venezuela; visit number of national parks, enjoy overnight visits at picturesque lodges, hotels. Probable birds: Quetzal, toucans, woodcreepers, tanagers, tree ducks, storks. Cost/Person: $1,454 (from New York). Includes: all costs (accommodations based double occupancy). Organizer: Aventura Natural History Tours, 508 North Sierra Dr., Beverly Hills CA 90210. Contact: Pam Axelson (213) 276-6081.

Venezuela: Depart from: Caracas. Season/Dates: February. Duration: 18 days. Probable birds: Hatzin, Sunbittern, Golden-headed Quetzal, Beryl-spangled Tanager. Group size: 20 people. Cost/Person: $1,785. Includes: hotel accommodations, meals and gratuities, guide services, transportation during tour. Organizer: Massachusetts Audubon Society, South Great Road, Lincoln MA 01773. (617) 259-9500.

Venezuela: Depart from: Miami FL. Season/Dates: Dec. 20/Jan. 3 (1978).

Duration: 14 days. Locale: high mountain, tropical jungle. Features: bird watching; tour leader with local tour guides. Cost/Person: $1,495. Includes: air fare and surface arrangements, meals, tips, entrance fees. Organizer: Bird Bonanzas, Inc., 12550 Biscayne Blvd. Suite 501, North Miami FL 33179. Contact: Carol Poloniecki (305) 895-0607.

South Pacific

Australia: Carrier: Qantas Airlines. Depart from: Los Angeles. Season/Dates: October 23. Duration: 4 weeks. Locale: sub-tropical plains and forests. Probable birds: parrots, Fairy Wren, other endemic species. Requirements: 10 participants. Includes: all expenses from Los Angeles, and return. Organizer: World Nature Tours, Inc., P.O. Box 693, Silver Spring MD 20901. Contact: Donald H. Messersmith. (301) 593-2522.

Australia: Depart from: Los Angeles CA. Season/Dates: Sept. 12 to Oct. 11. Duration: 27 days. Features: local tour guides. Cost/Person: $3,695. Includes: air fare and surface arrangements, meals, tips, entrance fees. Organizer: Bird Bonanzas, Inc., 12550 Biscayne Blvd., Suite 501, North Miami FL 33179. Contact: Carol Poloniecki (305) 895-0607.

Australia/New Zealand: Carrier: Pam Am, Qantas. Depart from: Los Angeles. Season/Dates: May 4, Nov. 6, 1979. Duration: 25 days. Locale: island, desert, mountain. Features: observe unusual wildlife. Cost/Person: $4,148. Includes: air fare Los Angeles/Los Angeles, twin bedded room, three meals day, overland transportation, airport/hotel/tour event transfers, guest lecturers. Organizer: Explorer Tours, 640 Cathcart St., Suite #307, Montreal, Canada H3B 1M3. Contact: Karen Zimmer (514) 861-6763. Cable: ACALIAISON.

Australia/New Zealand: Depart from: Los Angeles via Air New Zealand. Season/Dates: Feb. 3, Jul. 21, Sept. 22, 1979. Duration: 30 days. Features: arrive Sydney, visit local national park and wildlife sanctuary, see the koala; Brisbane area includes visit to Great Barrier Reef and field trip to island's numerous bird colonies; visit Northern Territory, field trip by boat along a billabong to look for crocodiles, water buffalos and birds; visit Melbourne, and Philip Island; fly to New Zealand where sightseeing includes glacier viewing, geothermal areas, national parks. Cost/Person: $4,640. Includes: land costs and air fare LA/LA. Organizer: Questers Worldwide Nature Tours, 257 Park Av. South, New York NY 10010. Contact: Michael Parkin (212) 673-3120.

Fiji/New Guinea/Papua/Solomon Islands: Depart from: Los Angeles via Air New Zealand. Season/Dates: Jun. 29, Oct. 19, 1979. Duration: 25 days. Features: explore coral reef, exciting native flora and fauna, see orchid gardens and tea and coffee plantations; seven-day river expedition, local native tribal rituals; visit wildlife and bird sanctuaries. Probable birds: many varieties of birds of paradise; also, Torres Strait Pigeon, cassowaries, ibises, Magnificent Rifle Bird. Cost/Person: $3,581. Includes: land costs, and air fare LA/LA. Organizer: Questers Worldwide Nature Tours, 257 Park Av. South, New York NY 10010. Contact: Michael Parkin (212) 673-3120.

Micronesia: Carrier: Air Micronesia. Depart from: Honolulu, Los Angeles. Season/Dates: June 9 (Honolulu); June 8 (Los Angeles). Duration: 3 weeks. Locale: tropical islands and atolls. Features: first known birding trip to these islands. Probable birds: rare endemic birds on Ponape, Turk, Guam, Saipan, Tinian, Yap, Peleliu, Palau. Group size: 15 participants. Cost/Person: $2,090. Includes: all expenses from, and return to, Honlulu, except meals. Organizer: World Nature Tours, Inc., P.O. Box 693, Silver Spring MD 20901. Contact: Donald H. Messersmith. Phone: (301) 593-2522.

New Guinea: Depart from: San Francisco. Season/Dates: Aug. 18 to Sept. 10 (1978). Duration: 21 days. Locale: mountain ranges with snow covered peaks, altitude to 16,500 ft.; also, swampy plains. Features: bird watching in small groups with tour leader and local tour guides. Watch for: birds of paradise, cassowaries, kingfishers, flycatchers. Cost/Person: $3,295. Includes: air fare and surface arrangements, meals, tips, entrance fees. Organizer: Bird Bonanzas, Inc., 12550 Biscayne Blvd. Suite 501, North Miami FL 33179. Contact: Carol Poloniecki (305) 895-0607.

New Zealand: Carrier: Air New Zealand. Depart from: Los Angeles. Season/Dates: February of each year. Duration: 24 days. Features: New Zealand's most lovely natural areas will be explored primarily on foot, including famous Milford Sound trek; expert naturalist/ornithologist leads trip. Group size: maximum 16 persons. Cost/Person: $1,390. Includes: all land transportation and transfers, all accommodations (first class hotels; cabins; camping — gear provided), all meals except Auckland and Christchurch, entrance fees, tips, instruction. Organizer: Nature Expeditions International, 599 College Avenue, Palo Alto CA 94306. Phone: (415) 328-6572.

New Zealand/Society Islands: Depart from: Los Angeles via UTA French Airlines. Season/Dates: Feb. 23, Nov. 16, 1979. Duration: 23 days. Features: arrive Auckland, New Zealand, visit surrounding countryside, observe geothermal areas; on to Christchurch and flight next day to Te Anau, cross lake to begin what has been called the "finest walk in the world" — five days (33 miles) walking Milford Track (overnight stops at comfortable hotels), explore Fiordland habitats; visit Mt. Cook National Park, excursion to Tasman Glacier. Visit Tahiti and Moorea (Society Islands), magnificent views of Pacific Ocean, eat wild boar and freshwater fish. Cost/Person: $2,827. Includes: land costs and air fare LA/LA. Organizer: Questers Worldwide Nature Tours, 257 Park Av. South, New York NY 10010. Contact: Michael Parkin (212) 673-3120.

Soloman Islands: Carrier: UTA and Pan Am Airlines. Depart from: Los Angeles. Season/Dates: August 1978. Duration: 15 days. Locale: tropical. Features: explore secluded lagoons/coves, coral reefs under and above water; hike jungle trails, swim, snorkel; possible sighting of the Cagou (nearly extinct bird) and fruit bats; visit botanical gardens, participate in native feast on Hideway Island. Cost/Person: $1,925. Includes: all costs (deluxe and first class hotel accommodations). Organizer: Aventura Natural History Tours, 508 North Sierra Drive, Beverly Hills CA 90210. Contact: Pamela Axelson (213) 276-6081.

United States

Alaska: Carrier: Alaska Airlines. Depart from: Juneau. Season/Dates: June 23-July 14, 1979. Duration: 24 days. Locale: Alaskan coastal rain forest, volcanic desert, arctic island. Features: one week spent circling Nunivak Island by boat and on foot. Probable birds: Black-legged Kittiwake, Horned and Tufted Puffin, Parakeet and Crested Auklet, Pigeon Guillemot. Group size: maximum 12 persons. Cost/Person: $1,600. Includes: all costs except air fare to Juneau and certain meals in the non-camping portion of trip. Organizer: Mountain Travel, 1398 Solano Av., Albany CA 94706. Contact: Pam Shandrick (415) 527-8100.

Alaska: Carrier: scheduled air carriers, rental automobiles, Alaska State Ferry. Depart from: Anchorage. Season/Dates: late June/July. Duration: 18 days. Locale: tundra, mountains, forest, ocean. Features: Alaskan breeding birds, spectacular scenery, flowers. Cost/Person: $2,400 (approx.). Includes: lodging, transportation, leadership. Organizer: Northeast Birding, Seal Harbor, Maine 04675. Contact: Will Russell (207) 276-3963.

Alaska: Carrier: commercial air craft, vans, boat, bus. Depart from: Anchorage. Season/Dates: May/June. Duration: 19 days. Locale: coast, tundra, mountains. Features: See Asiatic birds, breeding shorebirds; spectacular scenery. Requirements: sleep on cot in Eskimo house; this is a moderately rigorous trip. Group size: maximum 15 persons. Cost/Person: $2,500. Includes: lodging, transportation, leadership, some food costs. Organizer: Northeast Birding, Seal Harbor, Maine 04675. Contact: Will Russel (207) 276-3963.

Alaska/Aleutians: Carrier: commercial airlines departing from Anchorage. Season/Dates: May/June. Duration: 19 days. Locale: tundra, ocean edge. Features: unusual bird watching — observe Asian strays. Requirements: willing to camp; a rigorous trip. Group size: maximum 15 persons. Cost/Person: $2,300. Includes: food, transportation, lodging (hotel one night, otherwise Eskimo-style housing). Organizer: Will Russell (207) 276-3963.

Alaska/Pribilofs: Carrier: Alaska Airlines. Depart from: Fairbanks, Juneau. Season/Dates: July 14-Aug. 4; Aug. 11-Sept. 1, 1979. Locale: McKinley National Park, Arctic National Wildlife Range, Pribilof Islands. Group size: 12. Cost/Person: $2,490. Includes: all costs (except certain meals when not camping), air fare to Juneau, plus some intra-Alaska charters. Organizer: Mountain Travel, 1398 Solano Av., Albany CA 94706. Contact: Pam Shandrick (415) 527-8100.

Alaska: Carrier: Alaska Airlines. Depart from: Seattle WA. Season/Dates: Jun. 9, Jun. 30, Jul. 21, Aug. 11, 1979. Duration: 17 days. Features: arrive in Ketchikan, collection of totem poles in Saxman Park; fly to Sitka for field trip by launch to Lazaria Island National Wildlife Refuge; stay at Glacier Bay Lodge, take boat trip to observe Muir and John Hopkins glaciers; visit Whitehorse in the Yukon; train to Mt. McKinley National Park, explore arctic terrain, on to Anchorage to explore Katmai National Monument; visit Valley of the Ten Thousand Smokes. Cost/Person: $2,064. Includes: land and air costs from Seattle. Organizer: Questers Worldwide Nature Tours, 257 Park Av. South, New York NY 10010. Contact: Michael Parkin (212) 673-3120.

Alaska/Pribilofs: Depart from: Anchorage. Season/Dates: Jun. 25, July 16, Aug. 6, Aug. 27, 1979. Duration: 4 days. (Note: This tour is usually taken as an extension to the tour of Alaska.) Features: field trip via cruise on Kachemak Bay, observe Gull Island, home of 13 species of nesting sea birds; stay on St. Paul Island, Pribilofs, see breeding grounds for largest fur seal herd in the world, also found here is sanctuary for more than 180 varieties of birds; visit Aleut community, one of the last in existence; visit bird rookeries. Cost/Person: $645. Includes: land and air costs. Organizer: Questers Worldwide Nature

Tours, 257 Park Av. South, New York NY 10010. Contact: Michael Parkin (212) 673-3120.

Alaska/Pribilofs: Carrier: Alaska Airlines. Depart from: Seattle WA. Season/Dates: June, Sept, each year. Duration: 18 days. Locale: wilderness. Features: natural history study led by expert naturalist/ ornithologist. Watch for: eagles, puffins, cormorants, guillemots, oystercatchers, kittiwakes. Cost/Person: $1,390. Includes: all land/water transportation, all transfers, first-class hotel accommodations (cabins/ Mt. McKinley; 2 nights on ship/Glacier Bay), meals at Glacier Bay and Mt. McKinley, entrance fees, instruction. Organizer: Nature Expeditions International, 599 College Avenue, Palo Alto CA 94306. Contact: Margaret Betchart (415) 328-6572. Cable: Naturetour.

Arizona: Carrier: rented vehicles. Depart from: Tucson. Season/Dates: April 26. Duration: 2 weeks. Locale: mountains and desert. Requirements: 9 participants. Cost/ Person: $585. Includes: all expenses except meals. Organizer: World Nature Tours, Inc. P.O. Box 693, Silver Spring MD 20901. Contact: Donald H. Messersmith (301) 593-2522.

Arizona: Season/Dates: summer, 1978. Duration: 6 days. Features: emphasis on identification and ecology of birds ranging from desert grassland through pine-oak woodland to fir forest and mountain meadow; see birds typical of Rocky Mountains, the highlands and Chichuahuan and Sonoran Deserts of Mexico; striking scenery, numerous species of plants, reptiles, mammals. Cost/Person: $200. Includes: tuition (credit available) and room and board at Southwestern Research Station of American Museum of Natural History. Organizer: Department of Biological and Physical Sciences, UCLA Extension, P.O. Box 24902, Los Angeles CA 90024. Contact: Sakura Berry (213) 825-7093.

Arizona: Depart from: Tucson AZ. Season/Dates: May. Duration: 10 days. Watch for: Coppery-tailed Trogon, Red-faced Warbler, Five-striped Sparrow. Group size: 14 participants. Cost/Person: $845. Includes: first-class hotel accommodations, meals, gratuities, guide services, land transportation during tour, wildlife refuge entrance fees. Organizer: Massachusetts Audubon Society, South Great Road, Lincoln MA 01773. Phone: (617) 259-9500

Arizona: Carrier: Mercedes-Benz tour bus. Depart from: Tucson. Season/Dates: May 7-14. Duration: 8 days. Locale: desert, forest areas. Probable birds: Elegant Trogon, Montezuma (Harlequin) Quail, Arizona Woodpecker, Red-faced Warbler, Five-

striped Sparrow, Black hawk. Group size: maximum 15 people. Cost/Person: $600. Includes: all food, lodging, ground transportation, tips, baggage handling, guide service. Organizer: Victor Emanuel Nature Tours, 1603 W. Clay, Houston TX 77019. Contact: Victor Emanuel (713) 528-3725.

California: Depart from: San Diego, San Francisco, Monterey, Bodega Bay CA. Season/Dates: year-round. Duration: 1 day. Features: Pacific Ocean bird studies; expert leaders. Organizer: Western Field Ornithologists, 376 Greenwood Beach Rd., Tiburon CA 94920. Contact: Phil Schaeffer (415) 388-2524.

California: Depart from: San Diego. Season/Dates: fall. Duration: 15 days. Features: bird watching tour ending in San Francisco. Watch for: California Condor, Black-footed Albatross, Yellow-billed Magpie, Wrentit. Group size: 20 participants. Cost/Person: $1,025. Includes: twin-bedded first-class accommodations, meals and gratuities, guide services, land transportation during tour, entrance fees to wildlife refuges. Organizer: Massachusetts Audubon Society, South Great Road, Lincoln MA 01773. Phone: (617) 259-9500.

California: Carriers: rental automobiles, charter boat. Depart from: San Francisco. Season/Dates: mid-September. Duration: 12 days. Locale: coast, mountains, desert. Probable birds: Pelagic birds off Monterey, mountain birds near Yosemite, possibly California Condor. Cost/Person: $675 (approx.). Includes: leadership, transportation, lodging. Organizer: Northeast Birding Seal Harbor, Maine 04675. Contact: Will Russell (207) 276-3963.

California/Nevada: Depart from: Palm Springs CA. Season/Dates: April 21, Oct. 6, 1979. Duration: 9 days. Features: cross Mojave Desert to Valley National Monument; visit Scotty's Castle and Furnace Creek Ranch; visit Park Service and Borax Museums; visit Zabriskie Point; magnificent view of Death Valley; overnight camping in Panamint Mountains, and various other places en route. Good opportunities for birding. Cost/Person: $635. Includes: all costs. Organizer: Questors Worldwide Nature Tours, 257 Park Av. South, New York NY 10010. Contact: Michael Parkin (212) 673-3120.

Colorado: Depart from: Denver CO. Season/Dates: July. Duration: 13 days. Features: bird watching, wildflowers. Watch for: McCown's and Chestnut-collared Longspur on Pawnee grasslands. Group size: 20 persons. Cost/Person: $835. Includes: first-class hotel accommodations, meals and gratuities, guide service, land transportation, wildlife refuge entrance fees. Organizer: Massachusetts Audubon

Society, South Great Road, Lincoln, MA 01773. Phone: (617) 259-9500.

Florida: Backpacking, camping trip departing from St. Marys, GA. Season/Dates: Oct. 20-26, 1978. Locale: coastal island—beach, dunes, ponds, maritime forest, marshes. Probable birds: Painted Bunting, roosting herons, egrets, Glossy Ibis, Anhinga, Wood Stork, Peregrine Falcons on migration, terns, skimmers, Brown Pelican. Requirements: sleeping bag (can rent, if necessary); experience in backpacking. Group size: 16. Cost/Person: $140. Includes: natural history teachers, food tents, backpacks, boat transportation. Organizer: Wilderness Southeast, Inc. Rt. 3, Box 619, Savannah, GA 31406. Contact: Joyce Murlless (912) 355-8008.

Florida: Depart from: Miami, FL. Season/Dates: May. Duration: 7 days. Features: bird watching; visit Sanibel Island, Corkscrew Swamp. Watch for: Magnificent Frigatebird, Everglade Kite, Roseate Spoonbill, Sooty and Noddy Terns. Group size: 17 persons. Cost/Person: $685. Includes: first-class accommodations, meals, gratuities, guide service, transportation. Organizer: Massachusetts Audubon Society, South Great Road, Lincoln, MA 01773. Phone: (617) 259-9500.

Florida: Depart from: Lake Placid, Florida. Season/Dates: spring. Duration: 1 day. Locale: scrub, prairie, cypress swamp, oak hammock (South Florida—Glades County). Features: guides are experienced, practicing wildlife biologists; tour customized to your needs, if desired. Probable birds: Burrowing Owl, Sandhill Crane, Bald Eagle, Turkey, Caracara, Short-tailed Hawk. Requirements: provide own binoculars, camera, rain gear. Cost/Person: $75 (and up, for custom tours). Includes: light breakfast, lunch, transportation. Organizer: Lykes Florida Nature Tours, c/o Wildlife Research Laboratory, 4005 S. Main St., Gainesville, FL 32601. Contact: Stephen Nesbitt (904) 376-6481.

Florida: Carriers: rented houseboats, canoes. Season/Dates: year-around. Duration: 7 days. Locale: Everglades. Features: two experienced teacher/leaders. Probable birds: Roseate Spoonbills, nesting Bald Eagle, Brown and White Pelicans, Osprey, Swallow-tail Kite, Wood Ibis, Great White Heron. Requirements: activity-oriented people. Group size: 8-14 people. Cost/Person: $240. Includes: all expenses (except transfer from Miami airport). Organizer: Wilderness Southeast, Inc., Rt. 3, Box 619, Savannah, GA 31406. Phone: (912) 355-8008.

Florida: Depart from: Miami, FL. Season/Dates: Mar. 29, Nov. 8, 1979. Duration: 11 days. Locale: Everglades, and southwest Florida. Features: visit John Pennekamp Coral Reef State Park (swim, take cruise over reef in glass-bottomed boat, explore

mangrove swamp), boat trip into Ten Thousand Islands; spend full day at National Audubon Society's Corkscrew Swamp Sanctuary; also, shelling opportunities on island beaches. Probable birds: herons, egrets, ibises, Roseate Spoonbill, Reddish Egret. Cost/Person: $695. Includes: all costs. Organizer: Questers Worldwide Nature Tours, 257 Park Ave. South, New York, NY 10010. Contact: Michael Parkin (212) 673-3120.

Florida Keys: Carrier: rental van, charter boat. Depart from: Miami. Season/Dates: early May, 1979. Duration: 5 days. Probable birds: Audubon's Shearwater, Blue-faced Booby, Brown Booby, Sooty Tern, Noddy Tern. Cost/Person: $300 from Miami (approx.). Includes: lodging, transportation, leadership from Miami. Organizer: Northeast Birding, Seal Harbor, Maine 04675. Contact: Will Russell (207) 276-3963.

Georgia: Depart from: Savannah. Season/Dates: June 17-23. Locale: coastal islands of Georgia, salt marshes, beaches, estuary. Probable birds: photograph nesting Night Herons, American and Snowy Egret, Little Blue and Louisiana Heron, Osprey, skimmers, terns, oystercatchers. Requirements: camera, 35mm, plus desire to learn photography; group limit, 12. Cost/Person: $225, plus $40 lab. fee. Includes: all meals, tents, boat transportation, instruction, developing and printing. Organizer: Wilderness Southeast, Inc., Rt. 3, Box 619, Savannah, GA 31406. Phone: (912) 355-8008.

Georgia: Carrier: canoes. Depart from: Folkston, GA. Season/Dates: Apr. 4-9. Locale: Okefenokee Swamp. Features: two knowledgable leader/teachers (teach you to canoe, also). Probable birds: White Ibis, Woodstork, Red-shouldered Hawk, Barred Owl, Prothonotary Warbler, Red-cockaded Woodpecker. Requirements: be active learner. Group size: 6-18. Cost/Person: $140. Includes: food, tents, canoes, paddles, lifejackets, cooking equipment, permits, camping fees. Organizer: Wilderness Southeast, Inc., Rt. 3, Box 619, Savannah, GA 31406. Contact: Joyce Murlless, (912) 355-8008.

Hawaii: Depart from: Los Angeles/ San Francisco. Season/Dates: March, each year. Duration: 10 days. Features: leisurely explore three outstanding natural areas—Volcanoes National Park, Maui, and Kauai, with expert naturalist leaders; excellent birding and whale observation. Group size: maximum 20 persons. Cost/Person: $590. Includes: land/sea transportation, first-class hotel accommodations, park fees, tips. Organizer: Nature Expeditions International, 599 College Avenue, Palo Alto, CA 94306. Contact: Margaret Betchart: (415) 328-6572. Cable: Naturetour.

Hawaii: Carrier: air and rented vehicles. Depart from: Los Angeles. Season/Dates:

May 23. Duration: 2 weeks. Locale: tropical beaches and forests, mountains. Features: endemic species of birds, including several endangered species. Requirements: 9 participants. Cost/Person: $1,195. Includes: all expenses from, return to Los Angeles, except meals. Organizer: World Nature Tours, Inc., P.O. Box 693, Silver Spring, MD 20901. Contact: Donald H. Messersmith. Phone: (301) 593-2522.

Hawaii: Carrier: United Airlines. Depart from: Los Angeles. Season/Dates: Feb. 11, Apr. 8, July 15, Oct. 7, Dec. 23, 1979. Duration: 15 days. Features: visit Hawaiian Volcanoes National Park on Hawaii (explore volcanic highlands, tropical rain forests by motor vehicle, foot), spend two nights at Kona; visit Haleakala National Park, Maui—see Haleakala Crater; spend four nights at Hanalei Colony Resort, Kauai (includes field trip to Pacific Tropical Botanical Garden), chartered helicopter visit to Alakai Swamp and Kalalau Beach on otherwise inaccessible Na Pali coast. Cost/Person: $1,762. Includes: land and air costs. Organizer: Questers Worldwide Nature Tours, 257 Park Avenue South, New York, NY 10010. Contact: Michael Parkin (212) 673-3120.

Idaho: Depart from: Boise, Idaho. Season/Dates: July 25, 1979. Duration: 14 days. Locale: Idaho Primitive Area—rugged peaks, heavy forests land, deep rock canyons. Features: this is a raft trip which floats the Middle Fork of the Salmon River to the confluence of the main branch of the Salmon; day begins with early-morning birding in the vicinity of overnight camping area; skilled raftsmen guide rafts and run the rapids. Probable birds: Golden Eagle, Bald Eagle, Osprey, hawks. Cost/Person: $1,085. Includes: all costs (accommodations are provided under canvas). Organizer: Questers Worldwide Nature Tours, 257 Park Avenue South, New York, NY 10010. Contact: Michael Parkin (212) 673-3120.

Maine: Depart from: Rockland, Maine. Season/Dates: late Sept/early Oct. Duration: 7 days. Locale: small forested island off Maine coast. Features: relaxed birding on foot with large numbers of migrant birds. Cost/Person: $400 (approx.). Includes: lodging, transportation, food, leadership. Organizer: Northeast Birding, Seal Harbor, Maine 04675. Contact: Will Russell (207) 276-3963.

Maryland: Depart from: Ocean City, MD. Season/Dates: Sept. 9, Sept. 17, Oct. 21, Nov. 25, Dec. 30. Duration: 1 day. Features: spend day on open ocean in chartered fishing boats observing pelagic birds, whales, dolphins. Trip can be rigorous. Children/pets not appropriate. Requirements: bring foul weather gear. Watch for (depending on season): Manx Shearwater, Black-capped Petrel, White-tailed Tropicbird, Wilson's Storm Petrel,

Red Phalarope, Dovekie, Atlantic Puffin, Yellow-nosed Albatross. Cost/Person: $35. Organizer: Richard A. Rowlett, 715 Main St., #5 Laurel, MD 20810. Phone: (301) 498-6091.

Minnesota: Carrier: canoes. Depart from: Ely, Minnesota. Season/Dates: July 14, Aug. 18, 1979. Duration: 9 days. Features: base camp on Moose Lake; visit Quetico Provincial Park of Canada, unique canoe country (no public roads, travel possible only by canoe/water craft), five day canoe exploration of this area, thousands of crystal-clear lakes, park abounds in wildlife; end of each day's canoeing, dinner and conversation around the campfire. Probable birds: over 130 species, including loon, Pileated Woodpecker, Yellow Warbler, White-throated Sparrow, mergansers and flycatchers; breeding area of Bald Eagle. Cost/Person: $545. Includes: all meals, camping equipment, tents, sleeping bags, etc. Organizer: Questers Worldwide Nature Tours, 257 Park Avenue South, New York, NY 10010. Contact: Michael Parkin (212) 673-3120.

New Jersey: Depart from: Layton, NJ. Season/Dates: May/Sept. Duration: 1, 2 or 3 days. Locale: Delaware Water Gap National Recreation Area. Features: canoe trip to observe bird life. Watch for: Bald Eagle, Golden Eagle, Great Blue Heron, Green Heron, Mute Swan, Pileated Woodpecker. Requirements: club membership—R.R.B.O.; ability to swim and canoe. Group size: 6-8 people. Cost/Person: $40 per day. Includes: guide, overnight accommodation, meals, canoes with life jackets. Organizer: Raccoon-Ridge Bird Observatory, Box 81, Layton, NJ 07851. Contact: Dorothy Hughes (201) 948-6102.

New Jersey: Hainesville. Season/Dates: Sept. and Oct. Duration: 1, 2 or 3 days. Locale: Delaware Water Gap National Recreation Area. Features: hiking tour to observe migrating hawks on Kittitany Ridge and Delaware River. Watch for: Turkey Vulture, Goshawk, Sharpshin Hawk, Golden Eagle, Osprey, Merlin, American Kestrel. Requirements: club membership R.R.B.O., over 18 years of age. Group size: 6-8 persons. Cost/Person: $30 per day. Includes: R.R.B.O. guide, overnight accommodations, meals, transportation to and from Linwood/Appalachian Trail. Organizer: Raccoon-Ridge Bird Observatory, Box 81, Lyton, NY 07851. Contact: Dorothy Hughes (201) 948-6102.

North Carolina: Carrier: charter boat. Depart from: Kitty Hawk, NC. Season/Dates: Aug. 27. Duration: 2 days. Locale: outer banks of North Carolina, National Wildlife Refuges, and open ocean. Features: sea birds in Gulf Stream. Probable birds: Audubon's Shearwater, Bridled Tern. Requirements: none. Group size: 40-60. Cost/Person: $55 (approx.). Includes:

boat, leadership, evening program. Organizer: Will Russell/ABA Weekends, Box 631, Bar Harbor, ME 04609. Contact: Will Russell (207) 276-3963.

North Carolina: Hiking. Depart from: Cataloochee Cove, NC. Season/Dates: Apr. 21-24. Duration: 3 days. Locale: Smokey Mountains. Features: field teachers. Height of warbler migration. Quiet and secluded. Requirements: be active learner. Cost/Person: $60. Includes: two teachers/leaders, tents, all food and preparation equipment (not sleeping bags or transfer from airport) and camping fees. Organizer: Wilderness Southeast, Inc., Rt. 3, Box 619, Savannah, GA 31406. Contact: Joyce Murlless (912) 355-8008.

Oregon: River trip. Owyhee River, Oregon. Depart from Rome, Oregon (drive cars to Rome, cars then shuttled to end of trip take-out site). Season/Dates: May, 1978. Duration: 5 days. Locale: colorful canyon in remote Southeastern Oregon. Features: habitat for many types of birds: waterfowl, Chukar, eagles. Requirements: good health. No previous experience necessary. Cost/Person: $260 (approx.). Includes: all meals and guide service—all special rafting equipment. Organizer: Wilderness World, 1342 Jewell Ave., Pacific Grove, CA 93950. Contact: Nada Kovalik (408) 373-5882.

Texas: Carrier: multi-passenger vans. Depart from: Houston, TX. Season/Dates: Apr. 24 - May 7, 1978. Duration: 14 days. Locale: Texas coast, hill country and Big Bend area. Probable birds: expect over 300 species, including Colima Warbler, Brown Jay, Ringed Kingfisher, Golden-cheeked Warbler, Black-capped Vireo. Group size: 16 persons maximum. Cost/Person: $695 (double occupancy). Includes: all food, lodging, ground transportation, tips, baggage, handling and guide services (two group leaders). Organizer: Victor Emanuel Nature Tours, 1603 W. Clay, Houston, TX 77019. Contact: Victor Emanuel (713) 528-3725.

Texas: Carrier: multi-passenger vans. Depart from: Midland, TX. Season/Dates: May 7-14. Duration: 7 days. Locale: Big Bend National Park (desert, mountains). Probable birds: Colima Warbler, Lucifer Hummingbird (last tour added new bird to U.S. list—Aztec Thrush). Group size: limited to 8 persons. Cost/Person: $495 (double occupancy). Includes: all food, lodging, ground transportation, tips, baggage handling, guide service. Organizer: Victor Emanual Nature Tours, 1603 W. Clay, Houston, TX 77019. Contact: Victor Emanuel (713) 528-3725.

Texas: Depart from: Corpus Christi, TX. Season/Dates: April. Duration: 15 days. Watch for: White Pelican, Reddish Egret, Black-bellied Tree Duck, White-tailed Hawk. Group size: 20 persons. Cost/Person: $935. Includes: first-class hotel

accommodations, meals and gratuities, guide services, land transportation during tour, wildlife refuge entrance fees. Organizer: Massachusetts Audubon Society, South Great Road, Lincoln, MA 01773. Phone: (617) 259-9500.

Texas: Carrier: rented vehicles. Depart from: Beaumont, TX. Season/Dates: April 1. Duration: 2 weeks. Locale: coastal. Probable birds: Whooping Crane, other rare birds. Requirements: 9 participants; bring binoculars. Cost/Person: $698. Includes: accommodations, transportation, leadership, boats, entrance fees. Organizer: World Nature Tours, Inc., P.O. Box 693, Silver Spring, MD 20901. Contact: Donald H. Messersmith (301) 593-2522.

Texas: Carrier: rented vehicles. Depart from: Odessa, TX. Season/Dates: April 16. Duration: 9 days. Locale: semi-desert. Probable birds: Colima Warbler. Requirements: 9 participants; bring binoculars. Cost/Person: $334. Includes: all expenses except meals. Organizer: World Nature Tours, Inc., P.O. Box 693, Silver Spring, MD 20901. Contact: Donald H. Messersmith (301) 593-2522.

Washington: Season/Dates: September. Duration: 13 days. Features: bird watching. Group size: 20 participants. Cost/Person: $975. Includes: twin-bedded, first-class hotel accommodations, meals and gratuities, guide services, land transportation, wildlife refuge entrance fees. Organizer: Massachusetts Audubon Society, South Great Road, Lincoln, MA 01773. Phone: (617) 259-9500.

West Indies

Bermuda: Depart from: Boston, MA. Season/Dates: fall (Sept., Oct.). Duration: 7 days. Features: bird watching, beaches, shops. Watch for: White-tailed Tropic-bird. Group size: maximum 20 persons. Cost/Person: $810. Includes: round trip fares from Boston, twin-bedded accommodations (first-class). Organizer: Massachusetts Audubon Society, South Great Road, Lincoln, MA 01773. Phone: (617) 259-9500.

Cayman Islands: Depart from: St. Pete, Key West/Miami, FL. Season/Dates: year-around. Duration: 4, 5 or 8 days. Locale: reef-sheltered beaches, towering cliffs, lush woods on high plateau. Features: bird watching, nature study, photography, snorkeling, shelling on a unique island (mostly uninhabited). Stay in conventional motel units in unforgettable tropical setting. Watch for: Vitelline Warbler (found only in Caymans). Group size: 4 to 20 persons. Cost/Person: $251 up (tours guided by John Edscorn begin at $355 for 4-day, 3-night visit). Includes: all air transportation to and from Cayman Brac, all meals and gratuities.

Organizer: John B. Edscorn, 5620 N. Galloway Rd., Lakeland, FL 33801. Contact: John B. Edscorn, (813) 858-2068.

Jamaica: Depart from: Miami. Season/Dates: July 11. Duration: 2 weeks. Locale: tropical beaches, lakes, mountains/forests. Probable birds: Palmchat, todies, other Caribbean birds. Group size: 10 participants. Cost/Person: not yet known; will include all expenses from and return to Miami. Organizer: World Nature Tours, Inc., P.O. Box 693, Silver Spring, MD 20901. Contact: Donald H. Messersmith (301) 593-2522.

Puerto Rico/Virgin Islands: Depart from: Miami. Season/Dates: June 25, 1979. Duration: 2 weeks. Locale: tropical forests/beaches. Features: rare birds. Requirements: 10 participants. Cost/Person: not yet known. Includes: all expenses from and return to Miami. Organizer: World Nature Tours, Inc., P.O. Box 693, Silver Spring, MD 20901. Contact: Donald H. Messersmith (301) 593-2522.

Trinidad: Depart from: New York/Miami/Toronto. Season/Dates: year-round. Duration: 15 days (less can be arranged). Locale: tropical rain forest. Features: birding tours daily with local experts, transportation and box lunch. Tobago extention optional. Probable birds: Blue-headed Parrot, Great Antshrike, Bearded Bellbird. Group size: average 16 people. Requirements: bring binoculars. Cost/Person: $843. Includes: round-trip air fare from New York; overnight accommodations at Asa Wright Nature Center, and all other accommodations. Organizer: Wonder Bird Tours, 500 Fifth Ave., New York, NY 10036. Contact: Manny Arias (212) 279-7301.

Trinidad/French Guiana: Carrier: BWIA, Air France. Depart from: New York, Miami. Season/Dates: Aug. and Oct. Duration: 11 days. Locale: tropical rain forest, savannah. Features: observe and study wildlife. Probable birds: hummingbirds, ibis, parrots, toucans, White Egret, macaws. Group size: 18 participants. Cost/Person: $965. Includes: luggage transfers, sightseeing, leader and staff, meals, taxes, all necessary items of equipment. Organizer: Hanns Ebensten Travel, Inc., 55 West 42nd St., New York, NY 10036. Contact: Hanns Ebensten (212) 354-6634.

Trinidad/Tobago: Carrier: British West Indies Airlines. Depart from: New York, Miami. Season/Dates: Oct. 27. Duration: 2 weeks. Locale: tropical jungle/swamps. Features: South American/Caribbean birds. Requirements: 10 participants. Cost/Person: $995. Includes: all expenses from New York, (and return). Organizer: World Nature Tours, Inc., P.O. Box 693, Silver Spring, MD 20901. Contact: Donald H. Messersmith. Phone: (301) 593-2522.

Trinidad/Tobago: Depart from: New York. Season/Dates: Mar. 13, Nov. 20, 1979. Duration: 11 days. Features: arrive in Port of Spain, five days spent at Spring Hills Estate Nature Center (northern mountain range of Trinidad), visit swamp areas, see breeding colony of nocturnal Oilbird or Guacharo; fly to Tobago, five days spent here enjoying traditional Caribbean pleasures such as swimming and snorkeling, also field trip by boat to Little Tobago, visit to undersea garden of Buccoo Reef; early morning field trips with naturalist. Cost/Person: $997 (spring), $867 (fall). Includes: air fare New York/New York, land costs. Organizer: Questers Worldwide Nature Tours, 257 Park Ave., South, New York, NY 10010. Contact: Michael Parkin (212) 673-3120.

Trinidad/Tobago: Carrier: British West Indies Airlines. Depart from: New York. Season/Dates: Nov. 9-21, 1978. Duration: 12 days. Locale: tropical rain forest, beach areas. Features: unusual birds; escorted by curator of New York Zoological Society. Requirements: membership in New York Zoological Society. Cost/Person: $1,000. Includes: air/land costs. Organizer: New York Zoological Society, Animal Kingdom Tours, Box 108, Bronx, NY 10460. Contact: Iris Freed (212) 220-5085.

Trinidad/Tobago: Carrier: National Airlines, British West Indies Airlines. Depart from Los Angeles, New York, Miami. Season/Dates: September 5. Duration: 15 days. Locale: tropical. Features: visit Dunston Caves (Oilbirds nest here), boat excursion to Little Tobago Island, visit private bird sanctuary of Grafton Estate, observe coral gardens/rainbow-hued fish from glass bottom boat; group leader is an ornithologist and entomologist. Probable birds: Rufous-tailed Jacamar, Orange-billed Nightingale, Yellow-legged Trush, Scarlet Ibis, Red-billed Tropicbird, possibly Bird-of-Paradise. Cost/Person: $1,023 (from New York). Includes all costs. Organizer: Aventura Natural History Tours, 508 North Sierra Drive, Beverly Hills, CA 90210. Contact: Pam Axelson (213) 276-6081.

Trinidad/Tobago: Depart from: Miami. Season/Dates: winter (Feb.). Duration: 10 days. Features: Asa Wright Nature Center at Springhill Estate. Probable birds: Bearded Bellbird, Oilbird, Tufted Coquette. Group size: maximum 13 participants. Cost/Person: $1,050. Includes: hotel (first class), meals and gratuities, guide services, luggage tipping, transportation during tour. Organizer: Massachusetts Audubon Society, South Great Road, Lincoln, MA 01773. Phone: (617) 259-9500.

Appendix A

Zoos and Natural History Museums

What follow are the 159 zoos and natural history museums in the United States and Canada where you have the best chance to see birds. In the museums you see them stuffed and mounted in their simulated habitats. But you might ask the curator if he has a collection of skins (birds stuffed with cotton and placed in drawers for the use of ornithologists). If the answer is yes, he may let you take a peek. It's a wonderful way to see differences in coloration and markings.

A zoo offers you two kinds of birdlife. The first are the caged birds, brought mostly from out of the area. But in cages you won't see insect-eating birds; they kill themselves against the glass or wire.

The second kind of birdlife you find at zoos are the pond birds and natives who come for a free meal. With so many visitors buying dainties like hot dogs, cotton candy, and caramel corn, the local birds know their zoo is the best bird restaurant in town.

You'll note we've added the founding date for both zoos and museums. The older the institution is, the more likely you are to find spacious grounds with the large trees and dense undergrowth that birds delight in.

United States

ALABAMA

ANNISTON MUSEUM OF NATURAL HISTORY.
McClellan Blvd., Anniston, AL 36201. Phone (205) 236-8806. Tues.-Sat. 10 to 5; Sun. 2 to 5. Free. Founded 1930.

BIRMINGHAM ZOO.
2630 Cahaba Rd., Birmingham, AL 35118. Phone (205) 879-0408. Daily 9:30 to 5. Admission charge. Founded 1955.

UNIVERSITY OF ALABAMA MUSEUM OF NATURAL HISTORY.
P.O. Box 5897, University, AL 35486. Phone (205) 348-5061. Daily 8 to 5. Free. Founded 1848.

ALASKA

HOMER MUSEUM.
P.O. Box 682, Homer, AK 99603. Phone (907) 235-8635. Memorial Day-Labor Day Daily 10 to 5. Free. Founded 1968.

MT. McKINLEY NATIONAL PARK.
Box 73, Kotzebue, AK 99752. Phone (907) 683-2294. Daily 8 to 4:30. Free. Founded 1917.

ARKANSAS

ARKANSAS STATE UNIVERSITY MUSEUM.
Drawer HH, State University, AR 72467. Phone (501) 927-2074. Mon-Fri. 8 to 5; Sun. 2 to 6. Free. Founded 1936.

LITTLE ROCK ZOOLOGICAL GARDENS.
Little Rock, AR 72201. Phone (501) 663-4733. Daily 9:30 to 5:30. Free. Founded 1926.

MUSEUM OF SCIENCE AND HISTORY.
MacArthur Park, Little Rock, AR 72202. Phone (501) 376-4321. Mon.-Sat. 9 to 5; Sun. 1 to 5. Free. Founded 1924.

ARIZONA

ARIZONA-SONORA DESERT MUSEUM.
P.O. Box 5607, Tucson, AZ 85703. Phone (602) 792-1530. Daily 8:30 to

sundown. Admission charge. Founded 1952.

MUSEUM OF NORTHERN ARIZONA.
Fort Valley Road, Route 4, P.O. Box 720, Flagstaff, AZ 86001. Phone (602) 774-5211. Mon.-Sat. 9 to 5; Sun. 1:30 to 5. Free. Founded 1928.

CALIFORNIA

LOS ANGELES ZOO.
5333 Zoo Drive, Los Angeles, CA 90027. Phone (213) 666-4650. Winter daily 9 to 5; Summer 9 to 6. Admission charge. Founded 1912.

SAN DIEGO ZOOLOGICAL GARDEN.
P.O. Box 551, San Diego, CA 92112. Phone (714) 234-5151. Daily 9 to dusk. Admission charge. Founded 1916.

SAN FRANCISCO ZOOLOGICAL GARDENS.
Zoo Rd. & Skyline Blvd. San Francisco, CA 94132. Phone (415) 661-2023. Daily 10 to 5:30. Admission charge. Founded 1930.

COLORADO

CHEYENNE MOUNTAIN ZOOLOGICAL PARK.
P.O. Box 158, Colorado Springs, CO 80901. Phone (303) 475-9555. Summer daily 9 to 6; Winter daily 9 to 5. Admission charge. Founded 1926.

DENVER ZOOLOGICAL GARDENS.
City Park, Denver, CO 80205. Phone (303) 297-2754. Summer daily 10 to 6; Winter daily 10 to 5. Admission charge. Founded 1896.

UNIVERSITY OF COLORADO MUSEUM.
Broadway, between 15th and 16th Sts., Boulder, CO 80309. Phone (303) 492-6165. Mon.-Fri. 9 to 5; Sat. 9 to 4. Free. Founded 1902.

CONNECTICUT

AUDUBON SOCIETY OF THE STATE OF CONNECTICUT.
2325 Burr St., Fairfield, CT 06430. Phone (203) 259-6305. Tues.-Sat. 10 to 5; Sun. 12 to 5. Admission charge. Founded 1898.

THE ENVIRONMENTAL CENTERS, INC.
950 Trout Brook Dr., West Hartford, CT 06119. Phone (203) 236-2961. Tues.-Fri. 8:30 to 4:30; Sun. 1 to 5. Admission charge. Founded 1927.

PEABODY MUSEUM OF NATURAL HISTORY.

170 Whitney Ave., New Haven, CT 06520. Phone (203) 432-4044. Mon.-Sat. 9 to 5; Sun. 1 to 5. Admission charge. Founded 1867.

DELAWARE

DELAWARE MUSEUM OF NATURAL HISTORY.
Kennett Pike, Route 52, Box 3937, Greenville, DE 19807. Phone (302) 658-9111. Wed.-Sat. 9 to 4; Sun. 1 to 5. Admission charge. Founded 1957.

DISTRICT OF COLUMBIA

NATIONAL MUSEUM OF NATURAL HISTORY.
10th St. and Constitution Ave., N.W., Washington, DC 20560. Phone (202) 381-5954. Daily 10 to 5:30, extended summer hours. Free. Founded 1846.

NATIONAL ZOOLOGICAL PARK.
Rock Creek Valley, N.W., Washington, DC 20009. Phone (202) 381-7217. Apr.-Sept. buildings-9 to 6:30, grounds-6 to 8; Oct.-Mar. buildings-9 to 4:30, grounds-6 to 5:30. Admission charge. Founded 1889.

FLORIDA

CRANDON PARK ZOOLOGICAL GARDENS.
4000 Crandon Blvd., Miami, FL 33149. Phone (305) 361-2515. Daily 9:30 to 5. Admission charge. Founded 1948.

FLORIDA STATE MUSEUM.
University of Florida, Gainesville, FL 32611. Phone (904) 392-1721. Mon.-Sat. 9 to 4:30; Sun. 1 to 4:30. Free. Founded 1917.

MUSEUM OF SCIENCE.
3280 S. Miami Ave., Miami, FL 33129. Phone (305) 854-4242. Mon.-Sat. 9 to 5; Sun. 1:30 to 10. Free. Founded 1949.

GEORGIA

ATLANTA ZOOLOGICAL PARK.
518 Atlanta Ave., S.E., Atlanta, GA 30315. Phone (404) 622-4839. Daily 9 to 5. Admission charge. Founded 1889.

FERNBANK SCIENCE CENTER.
156 Heaton Park Dr., N.E., Atlanta, GA 30307. Phone (404) 378-4311. Mon., Sat. 8:30 to 5; Tues.-Fri. 8:30 to 10; Sun. 1:30 to 5. Free. Founded 1967.

GEORGIA STATE MUSEUM OF SCIENCE AND INDUSTRY.
Room 431, Georgia State Capitol,

Atlanta, GA 30334. Phone (404) 656-2846. Mon.-Fri. 8:30 to 4:30. Free. Founded 1895.

HAWAII

BERNICE P. BISHOP MUSEUM.
1355 Kalihi St., Honolulu, HI 96818 (808) 847-3511. Mon.-Sat. 9-5, Sun. 12-5. Admission charge. Founded 1889.

HONOLULU ZOO.
151 Kapahulu Ave., Honolulu, HI 96815. Phone (808) 923-7723. Daily 9 to 5. Free. Founded 1914.

THOMAS A. JAGGAR MEMORIAL MUSEUM.
Hawaii Volcanoes National Park, HI 96718. Phone (808) 967-7311. Mon.-Fri. 7:30 to 5; Sat.-Sun. 9 to 5. Free. Founded 1953.

IDAHO

IDAHO STATE UNIVERSITY MUSEUM.
Box 8096, ISU Campus, Pocatello, ID 83209. Phone (208) 236-3209. Mon.-Fri. 8 to 5. Free. Founded 1934.

ST. GERTRUDE'S MUSEUM.
College of St. Gertrude, Cotton-wood, ID 83522. Phone (208) 962-3531. By appointment only. Free. Founded 1931.

ILLINOIS

CHICAGO ZOOLOGICAL PARK (BROOKFIELD ZOO).
8400 W. 31st St., Brookfield IL 60513. Phone (312) 485-0263. Summer daily 10 to 6; Winter daily 10 to 5. Admission charge. Founded 1934.

FIELD MUSEUM OF NATURAL HISTORY.
Roosevelt Rd. at Lake Shore Dr., Chicago IL 60605. Phone (312) 922-9410. Daily 9 to 4, 5 to 6; Fri. 9 to 9. Admission charge. Founded 1893.

LINCOLN PARK ZOO. 100 W. Webster, Chicago, IL 60614. Phone (312) 294-4660. Daily 9 to 5. Free. Founded 1868.

INDIANA

INDIANA UNIVERSITY MUSEUM.
Student Building 107, Indiana University, Bloomington, IN 47401. Phone (812) 337-7224. Mon.-Sat. 9 to 12, 1 to 5; Sun. 1 to 5. Free. Founded 1973.

JOSEPH MOORE MUSEUM.
Earlham College, Richmond, IN 47374. Phone (317) 962-6561. Sept.-June Mon.-Fri. 9 to 5; Sun. 1 to 5.

July-Aug. Sun. 1 to 5. Free. Founded 1887.

MESKER PARK ZOO.
Bement Ave., Evansville, IN 47712. Phone (812) 426-5610. Summer daily 9 to 5; Winter daily 9 to 4. Admission charge. Founded 1926.

IOWA

CHILDREN'S ZOO.
Fejervary Park, 12 and Wilkes Sts., Davenport, IA 52803. Phone (319) 326-7811. Summer daily, Holidays 10 to 6. Admission charge. Founded 1952.

MUSEUM OF NATURAL HISTORY.
The University of Iowa; Iowa City, IA 52240. Phone (319) 353-5893. Mon.-Sat. 8 to 5; Sun. 1 to 4:30. Free. Founded 1858.

UNIVERSITY OF NORTHERN IOWA MUSEUM.
31st and Hudson Rd., Cedar Falls, IA 50613. Phone (319) 273-2188. Daily 9 to 12; closed school vacations. Free. Founded 1890.

KANSAS

BIOLOGY DEPT. MUSEUM.
Emporia Kansas State College, 1200 Commercial St., Emporia, KS 66801. Phone (316) 343-1200. Mon.-Fri. 8 to 5; Sat. 8 to 12. Free. Founded 1959.

SYSTEMATICS MUSEUMS UNIVERSITY OF KANSAS.
Dyche Hall, University of Kansas, Lawrence, KS 66044. Phone (913) 864-4541. Mon.-Sat. 8 to 5; Sun. 1:30 to 5. Free. Founded 1866.

WICHITA MUNICIPAL ZOO.
Nims at Murdock, Wichita, KS 67202. Phone (316) 363-2811. Daily 9 to 5. Free. Founded 1909.

KENTUCKY

EXPERIMENTAL GAME FARM.
Route 2, Box 11, Frankfort, KY 40601. Phone (502) 223-8211. Daily sunup-sundown; tours Mon.-Fri, by appointment. Founded 1945.

KENTUCKY MUSEUM.
Western Kentucky University, Bowling Green, KY 42101. Phone (502) 745-2592. Mon.-Fri. 9 to 4:30; Sat. 11 to 3; Sun. 2 to 4. Free. Founded 1930.

TRANSYLVANIA MUSEUM.
300 N. Broadway, Lexington, KY 40508. Phone (606) 233-8223. By appointment. Free. Founded 1882.

LOUISIANA

AUDUBON PARK AND ZOOLOGICAL GARDENS.
Audubon Park, New Orleans, LA 70118. Phone (504) 861-2537. Daily 9 to 5. Admission charge. Founded 1884.

MUSEUM OF NATURAL SCIENCE.
Louisiana State University, Baton Rouge, LA 70803. Phone (504) 388-2855. Mon.-Fri. 8 to 5; Sat. 8 to 12; Sun. 2 to 5. Free. Founded 1936.

THE ZIGLER MUSEUM.
411 Clara St., Jennings, LA 70546. Phone (318) 824-0114. Tues.-Fri. 10 to 12, 2 to 5; Sat.-Sun. 2 to 5. Free. Founded 1963.

MAINE

MAINE STATE MUSEUM.
State House, Augusta, ME 04333. Phone (207) 289-2301. Daily 9 to 5. Free. Founded 1965.

STANTON MUSEUM.
Bates College, Department of Biology, Carnegie Hall, Lewiston, ME 04240. Phone (207) 784-8333. By appointment only. Free. Founded 1864.

YORK INSTITUTE MUSEUM.
375 Main St., Saco, ME 04072. Phone (207) 282-3031. Winter: Wed.-Sat. 1 to 4; Summer: Wed.-Sun. 1 to 4. Free. Founded 1867.

MARYLAND

CABIN JOHN REGIONAL PARK — NOAH'S ARK.
7400 Lux Court, Rockville, MD 20854. Phone (301) 299-4555. Daily 10 to sunset. Free. Founded 1967.

CYLBURN MUSEUM.
Cylburn Mansion, 4915 Greenspring Ave., Baltimore, MD 21209. Phone (301) 396-0180. Mon.-Fri. 8 to 3:30, Sat.-Sun. as announced. Free. Founded 1954.

MASSACHUSETTS

BERKSHIRE MUSEUM.
39 South St., Pittsfield, MA 01201. Phone (413) 442-6373. Tues.-Sat. 10 to 5; Sun. 2 to 5. Admission charge. Founded 1903.

MUSEUM OF COMPARATIVE ZOOLOGY.
Oxford St., Cambridge, MA 02138. Phone (617) 495-2467. Mon.-Sat. 9 to 4:30; Sun. 1 to 4:30. Free. Founded 1859.

SPRINGFIELD SCIENCE MUSEUM.
236 State St., Springfield, MA 01103. Phone (413) 732-4317. Tues.-Sat. 1 to 5; Sun. 2 to 5. Free. Founded 1859.

MICHIGAN

DETROIT ZOOLOGICAL PARK.
8450 W. 10 Mile Rd., Royal Oak, MI 48068. Phone (313) 398-0900. Mid-May-mid-Sept. Mon.-Sat. 10 to 5, Sun. 9 to 6; mid-Sept.-mid-May Wed.-Sun. 10 to 4. Admission charge. Founded 1928.

KINGMAN MUSEUM OF NATURAL HISTORY.
Leila Arboretum, Battle Creek, MI 49017. Phone (616) 965-5117. Tues.-Sat. 9 to 5; Sun. 1 to 5. Admission charge. Founded 1869.

WAYNE STATE UNIVERSITY MUSEUM OF NATURAL HISTORY.
Cass and Warren, Detroit, MI 48202. Phone (313) 577-2555. Mon.-Fri. 1:30 to 4:30. Free. Founded 1972.

MINNESOTA

JAMES FORD BELL MUSEUM OF NATURAL HISTORY.
17th and University Aves., S.E., Minneapolis, MN 55455. Phone (612) 373-2423. Mon.-Tues., Thurs.-Sat. 9 to 5, Wed. 9 to 9; Sun. 2 to 5. Free. Founded 1872.

MINNEAPOLIS PUBLIC LIBRARY SCIENCE MUSEUM AND PLANETARIUM.
300 Nicollet Mall, Minneapolis, MN 55407. Phone (412) 372-6543. Oct.-May, Mon.-Sat. 9 to 5, Sun. 2 to 5; June-Sept., Mon.-Fri. 9 to 5, Sat.-Sun. 2 to 5. Free. Founded 1872.

ST. PAUL'S COMO ZOO.
Midway Parkway and Kaufman Dr., St. Paul, MN 55103. Phone (612) 488-3221. Summer: daily 8 to 8, Winter: daily 8 to 4:30. Free. Founded 1897.

MISSISSIPPI

JACKSON ZOOLOGICAL PARK.
2918 W. Capitol St., Jackson, MS 39209. Phone (601) 354-5211. Fall, Winter: daily 9 to 5:30; Spring, Summer: daily 9 to 6:30. Admission charge. Founded 1919.

MISSISSIPPI MUSEUM OF NATURAL SCIENCE.
111 N. Jefferson St., Jackson, MS 39202. Phone (601) 354-7303. Mon.-Sat. 8 to 4:30. Free. Founded 1934.

MISSOURI

MISSOURI STATE MUSEUM.
State Capitol, Jefferson City, MO 65101. Phone (314) 751-2854. Daily 8 to 5. Free. Founded 1920.

MUSEUM OF SCIENCE AND NATURAL HISTORY.
Oak Knoll Park, St. Louis MO 63105. Phone (314) 726-2888. Tues.-Sat. 9 to 5; Sun. 1 to 5. Free. Founded 1959.

ST. LOUIS ZOOLOGICAL PARK.
Forest Park, St. Louis, MO 63110. Phone (314) 781-0900. Daily 9 to 5. Free. Founded 1913.

MONTANA

RED LODGE ZOO.
Box 826, Red Lodge, MT 59068. April 15-Oct. 15 daily 7 to 9. Admission charge. Founded 1928.

RICKETTS MEMORIAL MUSEUM.
Hamilton, MT 59840. Phone (706) 363-2207. June-Sept. Mon.-Fri. 10 to 5. Free. Founded 1966.

SCRIVER MUSEUM OF MONTANA WILDLIFE.
P.O. Box 172, Browning, MT 59417. Phone (406) 338-4525. Easter to Thanksgiving daily 7 to 8. Admission charge. Founded 1953.

NEBRASKA

CHADRON STATE COLLEGE MUSEUM.
Main St., Chadron, NE 69337. Phone (308) 432-5571. Mon.-Fri. 8 to 5. Closed school holidays. Free. Founded 1939.

HENRY DOORLY ZOO.
River View Park, Omaha, NE 68107. Phone (402) 733-8401. April 1-Nov. 1; Mon.-Sat. 10 to 5; Sun., Holidays 10 to 6. Admission charge. Founded 1965.

LINCOLN'S CHILDREN'S ZOO.
2800 A St., Lincoln, NE 68502. Phone (402) 475-6741. Tues.-Sat. 10 to 5; Wed. 11:30 to 8:30; Sun. 10 to 6. Admission charge. Founded 1959.

NEVADA

LEHMAN CAVES NATIONAL MONUMENT.
Baker, NV 89311. Phone (702) Lehman Caves Toll Sta. 1. Daily, Winter 8 to 4:30; Memorial Weekend-Labor Day 8 to 5:30. Admission charge. Founded 1933.

MUSEUM OF NATURAL HISTORY.
University of Nevada, Las Vegas, NV 89154. Phone (702) 739-3381. Mon.-Fri. 8 to 5. Free. Founded 1967.

NEVADA STATE MUSEUM.
Carson City, NV 89710. Phone (702) 885-4810. Daily 8:30 to 4:30. Free. Founded 1939.

NEW HAMPSHIRE

FOX STATE FOREST.
Hillsboro, NH 03244. Phone (603) 464-3453. By appointment. Free. Founded 1930.

N.H. AUDUBON NATURE CENTER.
Bear Brook State Park, Suncook, NH 03275. Phone (603) 485-3782. Late June thru Labor Day Tues.-Sun. 10 to 5. Free. Founded 1961.

SQUAM LAKES SCIENCE CENTER.
Box 146, Holderness, NH 03245. Phone (603) 968-7194. Summer: Mon.-Sat. 10 to 5. Admission charge. Founded 1966.

NEW JERSEY

PRINCETON UNIVERSITY MUSEUM OF NATURAL HISTORY.
Princeton University, Guyot Hall, Princeton, NJ 08540. Phone (609) 452-4102. Mon.-Sat. 9 to 5; Sun., Holidays 2 to 5. Free. Founded 1856.

SPACE FARMS ZOOLOGICAL PARK AND MUSEUM.
Beemerville Rd., Sussex, NJ 07461. Phone (201) 875-5800. May 1-Nov. 1 Daily 9 to 6. Free. Founded 1927.

TRAILSIDE NATURE AND SCIENCE CENTER.
Coles Ave. and New Providence Rd., Mountainside, NJ 07092. Phone (201) 232-5930. Mon.-Thurs. 3 to 5; Sat.-Sun. 1 to 5. Free. Founded 1941.

NEW MEXICO

RIO GRANDE ZOOLOGICAL PARK.
903 Tenth St. S.W., Alburquerque, NM 87102. Phone (505) 766-7823. Winter: daily 10 to 5; Summer: daily 10 to 7. Admission charge. Founded 1927.

SPRING RIVER PARK AND ZOO.
City Hall, Roswell, NM 88201. Phone (505) 622-5811. Daily 1 to sunset. Free. Founded 1966.

UNIVERSITY OF NEW MEXICO BIOLOGY DEPARTMENT.
Alburquerque, NM 87131. Phone (505) 277-3411. Daily 9 to 5. Free. Founded 1890.

NEW YORK

AMERICAN MUSEUM OF NATURAL HISTORY.
79th St. and Central Park West, New York, NY 10024. Phone (212) 873-1300. Mon.-Sat. 10 to 4:45; Sun., Holidays 11 to 5. Discretionary admission charge. Founded 1869.

BUFFALO ZOOLOGICAL GARDENS.
Delaware Park, Buffalo, NY 14214. Phone (716) 837-3900. Winter: daily 10 to 4:30; Summer: daily 10 to 5:30. Admission charge. Founded 1870.

173

NEW YORK ZOOLOGICAL PARK.
185 5th Street and Southern Blvd., Bronx, NY 10460. Phone (212) 933-1500. Nov.-Jan. Daily 10 to 4:30; Feb.-Oct. Daily 10 to 5. Admission charge. Founded 1895.

NORTH CAROLINA

NATURE SCIENCE PARK.
Museum Dr., Winston-Salem, NC 27105. Phone (919) 767-6642. Daily 9 to 5; Sun. 1 to 6. Free. Founded 1964.

SCHIELE MUSEUM OF NATURAL HISTORY AND PLANETARIUM.
P.O. Box 953, 1500 E. Garrison Blvd., Gastonia, NC 28052. Phone (704) 864-3962. Tues.-Fri. 9 to 5; Sat.-Sun. 2 to 5. Free. Founded 1961.

WEYMOUTH WOODS-SAND-HILLS NATURE PRESERVE MUSEUM.
Aberdeen Rd., Raleigh, NC 27611. Phone (919) 692-2167. Oct.-March Tues.-Sun. 8 to 6; April-May and Sept. Tues.-Sun. 8 to 8; June-Aug. Tues.-Sun. 8 to 9. Free. Founded 1968.

NORTH DAKOTA

THEODORE ROOSEVELT NATIONAL MEMORIAL PARK-VISITOR CENTER.
Medora, ND 58645. Phone (701) 623-4466. Memorial Day-Labor Day Daily 8 to 8; Labor Day-Memorial Day Daily 8 to 4:30. Free. Founded 1959.

UNIVERSITY OF NORTH DAKOTA ZOOLOGY MUSEUM.
Grand Forks, ND 58201. Phone (701) 777-2621. Mon.-Fri. 9 to 6; Sat. 9 to 5. Free. Founded 1883.

OHIO

AKRON MUSEUM OF NATURAL HISTORY AND THE CHILDREN'S ZOO.
500 Edgewood Ave., Akron, OH 44307. Phone (216) 535-1011. Mon.-Sat. 10 to 5; sun. 10 to 6. Admission charge. Founded 1950.

CINCINNATI MUSEUM OF NATURAL HISTORY.
1720 Gilbert Ave., Cincinnati, OH 45202. Phone (513) 621-3889. Tues.-Sat. 9 to 4:30; Sun. 12:30 to 5. Admission charge. Founded 1835.

CLEVELAND METRO PARKS ZOOLOGICAL PARK.
P.O. Box 09040, Cleveland, OH 44109. Phone (216) 661-6500. Daily 10 to 5; Summer Sundays, Holidays 10 to 7. Admission charge. Founded 1882.

OKLAHOMA

EAST CENTRAL STATE UNIVERSITY MUSEUM.
Ada, OK 74820. Phone (405) 332-8000. Mon.-Fri. 8 to 5; Sat.-Sun. by appointment. Closed college vacations. Free. Founded 1955.

NORTHWESTERN STATE COLLEGE MUSEUM.
Jesse Dunn Hall, Alva, OK 73717. Phone (405) 327-1700. Mon.-Fri. 9 to 5. Free. Founded 1902.

STOVALL MUSEUM OF SCIENCE AND HISTORY.
University of Oklahoma, 1335 Asp St., Norman, OK 73069. Phone (405) 325-4711. Mon.-Fri. 9 to 5; Sat.-Sun. 1 to 5. Founded 1899.

OREGON

MUSEUM OF NATURAL HISTORY.
University of Oregon, Eugene, OR 97403. Phone (503) 686-3033. Mon.-Fri. 8 to 4:30; Sat.-Sun. 1 to 4:30. Free. Founded 1936.

OREGON STATE UNIVERSITY

MUSEUM OF NATURAL HISTORY.
Zoology Dept., Corvallis, OR 97331. Phone (503) 754-1105. Mon.-Fri. 8 to 5; Sat. by appt. Free. Founded 1948.

SOUTHERN OREGON STATE COLLEGE MUSEUM OF VERTE—BRATE NATURAL HISTORY.
1250 Siskiyou Blvd., Ashland, OR 97520. Phone (503) 482-6341. Founded 1969.

PENNSYLVANIA

ACADEMY OF NATURAL SCIENCES OF PHILADELPHIA.
19th and Parkway, Philadelphia, PA 19103. Phone (215) 567-3700. Mon.-Sat. 10 to 5; Sun. 1 to 5. Admission charge. Founded 1812.

CONSERVATORY AVIARY.
Ridge Ave. and Arch St., Pittsburgh, PA 15212. Phone (412) 322-7855. Daily 9 to 4:30. Admission charge. Founded 1952.

PHILADELPHIA ZOOLOGICAL GARDEN.
34th St. and Girard Ave., Philadelphia, PA 19104. Phone (215) 243-1100. Mon.-Fri. 9:30 to 5; May-Oct. Sat., Sun., Holidays 9:30 to 6. Admission charge. Founded 859.

RHODE ISLAND

ROGER WILLIAMS PARK MUSEUM.
Roger Williams Park, Providence, RI 02905. Phone (401) 941-5640. Mon.-Sat. 8:30 to 4:30; Sun., Holidays 2 to 5. Free. Founded 1896.

SOUTH CAROLINA

CHARLESTON MUSEUM.
121 Rutledge Ave., Charleston, SC 29401. Phone (803) 722-2996. Mon.-Sat. 9 to 5; Sun., Holidays 1 to 5. Admission charge. Founded 1773.

GREENVILLE ZOO.
Cleveland Park Dr., Greenville, SC 29602. Phone (803) 232-8079. Daily 9:30 to 5. Free. Founded 1957.

THE MUSEUM.
Phoenix St., Greenwood, SC 29646. Phone (803) 229-7093. Mon.-Fri. 9 to 5; Sun. 2 to 5. Free. Founded 1968.

SOUTH DAKOTA

GREAT PLAINS ZOO.
224 West Ninth St., City Hall, Sioux Falls, SD 57102. Phone (605) 339-7059. Daily 10 to 5; Labor Day-Memorial Day Daily 10 to 8. Admission charge. Founded 1957.

PETTIGREW MUSEUM.
131 N. Duluth, Sioux Falls, SD 57104. Phone (605) 336-6272. Mon.-Sat. 9 to 12 and 1:30 to 5; Sun. 2 to 5. Free. Founded 1926.

TENNESSEE

OVERTON PARK ZOO AND AQUARIUM.
Memphis, TN 38112. Phone (901) 2887. Summer: Daily 10 to 6; Winter: Daily 10 to 5. Admission charge. Founded 1905.

STUDENTS' MUSEUM, INC. 516 Beaman, Chilhowee Park, Knoxville, TN 37914. Phone (615) 637-1121. Mon.-Sat. 9 to 5; Tues. 7 to 9; Sun. 1 to 5. Admission charge. Founded 1960.

SUGARLANDS VISITOR CENTER.
Great Smoky Mountains National Park.
Gatlinburg, TN 37738. Phone (615) 436-5616, ext 70. May-Oct. daily 8 to 9, Nov.-Apr. daily 8 to 4:30. Free. Founded 1961.

TEXAS

ABILENE ZOOLOGICAL GARDENS.
Hwy. 36 at Loop 322. Abilene, TX

79604. Phone (915) 672-9771. Summer: Daily 10 to 7; Winter; Daily 10 to 5. Admission charge. Founded 1965.

DALLAS ZOO.
621 E. Claredon Dr., Dallas, TX 75203. Phone (214) 946-5155. Oct.-April Daily 9 to 5; May-Sept. Daily 9 to 6; Mon.-Fri., Sun., Holidays. Admission charge. Founded 1904.

SAN ANTONIO ZOOLOGICAL GARDENS AND AQUARIUM.
3903 N. St. Mary's St., San Antonio, TX 78212. Phone (512) 734-7183. Summer: Daily 9:30 to 6:30; Winter: Daily 9:30 to 5. Admission charge. Founded 1914.

UTAH

HOGLE ZOOLOGICAL GARDEN.
2600 E. Sunnywide Ave., P.O. Box 8475, Salt Lake City, UT 84108. Phone (801) 582-1631. Summer: Daily 9:30 to 6; Winter: Daily 9:30 to 4:30. Admission charge. Founded 1933.

NATURAL HISTORY STATE MUSEUM.
235 E. Main St., P.O. Box 396, Vernal, UT 84116. Phone (801) 789-3799. Daily June-Sept. 8 a.m. to 9 p.m.; Sept.-May 8 to 5. Free. Founded 1946.

VERMONT

DISCOVERY MUSEUM.
51 Park St., Essex Jct., VT 05452. Phone (802) 878-8687. Daily 1-4:30. Free. Founded 1975.

FAIRBANKS MUSEUM OF NATURAL SCIENCE.
83 Main St., St. Johnsbury, VT 05819. Phone (802) 748-3413. Mon.-sat. 9 to 4:30; Sun. 1 to 5. Free. Founded 1889.

VIRGINIA

D. RALPH HOSTETTER MUSEUM OF NATURAL HISTORY.
Harrisonburg, VA 22801. Phone (703) 433-2771. Sept.-May Sat.-Sun. 2 to 4; June-July, Sun. 2 to 4; other times by appointment. Free. Founded 1968.

PEAKS OF OTTER VISITOR CENTER.
Blue Ridge Pkwy., Milepost 86, Bedford, VA 24523. Apr.-Nov. daily 9 to 5; Dec.-Mar. Sat.-Sun. 9 to 5. Free. Founded 1958.

PENINSULA NATURE AND SCIENCE CENTER.
524 J. Clyde Morris Blvd., Newport News, VA 23601. Phone (804) 595-1900. Mon.-Sat. 10 to 5; Sun. 1 to 5; Thurs. 7 to 9. Admission charge. Founded 1964.

WASHINGTON

CATHERINE MONTGOMERY INTERPRETIVE CENTER.
Federal Forest State Park, Enumclaw, WA 98022. Phone (206) 753-2025. Daily 9 to 5. Free. Founded 1967.

THOMAS BURKE MEMORIAL WASHINGTON STATE MUSEUM.
University of Washington, Seattle, WA 98195. Phone (206) 543-5590. Tues.-Sat. 10 to 4:30; Sun. 1 to 4:30. Free. Founded 1885.

WOODLAND PARK ZOO-LOGICAL GARDENS.
5500 Phinney Ave., N., Seattle, WA 98103. Phone (206) 782-5046. Daily 8:30 to dusk. Free. Founded 1909.

WEST VIRGINIA

FRENCH CREEK GAME FARM.
Rte. 1, Box 210, French Creek, WV 26218. Phone (304) 924-6211. Daily dawn to dusk. Free. Founded 1923.

SUNRISE FOUNDATION, INC..
755 Myrtle Rs., Charleston, WV 25314. Phone (304) 344-8035. Tues.-

Sat. 10 to 5; Sun. 2 to 5. Free. Founded 1960.

WISCONSIN

MILWAUKEE COUNTY ZOOLOGICAL PARK.
10001 W. Bluemound Rd., Milwaukee, WI 53226. Phone (414) 771-3040. Nov.-Feb. daily 9:30 to 4:30; March-May, Sept.-Oct. daily 9:30 to 4:50; June-Aug. Mon.-Sat. 9:30 to 5:50; Sun. 9:30 to 6:50. Admission charge. Founded 1958.

THE MUSEUM OF NATURAL HISTORY.
University of Wisconsin, Stevens Point, WI 54481. Phone (715) 346-2858. Daily and every evening except Sat. Free. Founded 1968.

VITERBO COLLEGE MUSEUM.
815 S. 9th St., La Crosse, WI 54601. Phone (608) 784-0040. Daily 2 to 5. Admission charge. Founded 1890.

WYOMING

GUERNSEY STATE MUSEUM.
Guernsey State Park, Guernsey, WY 82214. Mon.-Tues., Thurs.-Sat. 10 to 5, Sun. 8 to 6:30. Free. Founded 1958.

LANDER CONSERVATION CENTER.
863 Sweetwater St., Lander, WY 82520. Phone (307) 332-4644. Mon.-Fri. 8 to 4:30. Free. Founded 1968.

YELLOWSTONE NATIONAL PARK.
Yellowstone Park, WY 82190. Phone (307) 344-7381. Mid-May to Mid-Sept. daily 8 to 8. Free. Founded 1872.

Canada

ALBERTA

BANFF PARK NATURAL HISTORY MUSEUM.
Banff Ave., Banff, AB, CAN. Phone Phone (403) 762-3324. Summer: Daily 11 to 8; Winter: Thurs.-Mon. 10 to 6. Free. Founded 1904.

CALGARY ZOO, BOTANICAL GARDENS AND NATURAL HISTORY PARK.
St. George's Island, Calgary, AB, CAN. Phone (403) 265-9310. May-Sept. Daily 8 to dusk. Admission charge. Founded 1918.

STORYLAND VALLEY ZOO.
132 St. and Buena Vista Rd., Edmonton, AB., CAN. Phone (403) 488-8115. May-Oct. Daily 12 to 8. Admission charge. Founded 1958.

BRITISH COLUMBIA

BRITISH COLUMBIA PROVINCIAL MUSEUM.
Heritage Court, 601 Belleville St., Victoria, BC., CAN. Phone (604) 387-3701. April-Sept. Daily 10 to 8:30; Oct.-March Daily 10 to 5:30. Free. Founded 1886.

COWAN VERTEBRATE MUSEUM.
University of B.C. Dept. of Zoology, Vancouver, BC., CAN. Phone (604) 228-4665. Mon.-Fri. 9 to 5. Free. Founded 1944.

GRAND MANAN MUSEUM.
Grand Harbor, Grand Manan, BC., CAN. June 15-Sept. 15 Mon.-Wed., Fri.-Sat. 2 to 5, Thurs. 2 to 5, 7 to 9. Closed Sept. 16-June 14. Founded 1962.

MANITOBA

ASSINIBOINE PARK ZOO.
2355 Corydon Ave., Winnipeg, MB., CAN. Phone (204) 888-3634. Daily, Holidays 10 to sunset. Free. Founded 1904.

B.J. HALES MUSEUM OF NATURAL HISTORY.

Grandon University, Brandon, MB., CAN. Phone (204) 728-4029. Daily 2 to 5. Free. Founded 1915.

MANITOBA MUSEUM OF MAN AND NATURE.
190 Rupert Ave., Winnipeg, MB., CAN. Phone (204) 947-5794. Mid-May-mid-Sept. Mon.-Sat., Holidays 10 to 9, Sun. 12 to 9; mid-Sept.-mid-May Mon. 10 to 4; Tues.-Sat. 10 to 9; Sundays, Holidays 12 to 6. Admission charge. Founded 1965.

NEW BRUNSWICK

NEW BRUNSWICK MUSEUM.
277 Douglas Ave., Saint John, NB, CAN. Phone (506) 693-1196. Winter: daily 2 to 5, Summer: daily 10 to 9. admission charge. Founded 1842.

SUNBURY SHORES ARTS AND NATURE CENTER.
139 Water St., St. Andrews, NB., CAN. Phone (506) 529-3386. Mon.-Fri. 10 to 4; Sat.-Sun. 2 to 4:30. Free. Founded 1964.

NOVA SCOTIA

NOVA SCOTIA MUSEUM.
1747 Summer St., Halifax, NS., CAN. Phone (902) 429-4610. Winter: Daily 9 to 5, Wed. 9 to 5; Summer: Mon.-Fri. 9 to 8; Sat.-Sun. 9 to 5. Free. Founded 1831.

ONTARIO

NIAGARA PARKS COMMISSION SCHOOL OF HORTICULTURE.
Niagara Parks Blvd. N., Niagara Falls ON., CAN. Phone (416) 356-8554. Daily sunrise-sunset. Free. Founded 1936.

ONTARIO SCIENCE CENTRE.
770 Don Mills Rd., Toronto, ON., CAN. Phone (416) 978-3692. Mon. 10 to 5; Tues.-Sat. 10 to 9; Sun. 1 to 9. Admission charge. Founded 1964.

WYE MARSH WILDLIFE CENTRE.
Box 100, R.R. 1, Midland, ON., CAN. Phone (705) 526-7809. Mid May-Sept. Daily 10 to 6; Sept.-Oct. 10 to 5. Admission charge. Founded 1968.

QUEBEC

JARDIN ZOOLOGIQUE DE QUEBEC.
8191 Ave. du Zoo, Charlesbourg, PQ., CAN. Phone (418) 642-2310. Daily 10 to 8. Admission charge. Founded 1932.

MONTREAL ZOO.
La Ronde, St. Helen's Island, Montreal, PQ., CAN. Phone (514) 872-2815. May-Sept. daily 10 to dusk. Sept.-May Sat., Sun., Holidays 12 to 6. Admission charge. Founded 1921.

SOCIETE ZOOLOGIQUE DE ST. FELICIEN.
St.-Felicien, PQ., CAN. Phone (418) 679-0543. Daily 9 to 7. Admission charge. Founded 1961.

SASKATCHEWAN

GRAND COTEAU MUSEUM.
Center St., Shaunavon, SON 2MO, SK, CAN. Phone (306) 297-2644. Mar.-Oct. 31 Wed., Sat. 2 to 4. Closed Nov.-Feb. Free. Founded 1932.

MUSEUM OF NATURAL HISTORY, DEPARTMENT OF TOURISM AND RENEWABLE RESOURCES.
Wascana Park, Regian, SK., CAN. Phone (306) 565-2809. May-Sept. Daily, Holidays 9 to 9; Oct.-April Mon.-Fri. 9 to 5 Sat., Sun., Holidays 10 to 6. Free. Founded 1913.

SWIFT CURRENT MUSEUM.
105 Chaplin E., Swift Current, SK, CAN. Phone (306) 773-9888. Jul.-Aug. daily2 to 4, 7 to 9. Sept., Oct., June Mon., Sat.-Sun 2 to 5. Nov.-May 31 Sun.-Mon. 2 to 5. Free. Founded 1937.

Appendix B

How To Ask Birds To Your Home (And How To Suggest They Leave)

The art of inviting birds to one's home is, for many, a lifetime pursuit. It involves providing special plantings, water, dust baths (the birds need the dust to rid their skins of parasites, of which there are about 1,300 species), feeders, storm shelters, man-made perches (or the shoring up of dead trees), and bird houses. In the Publications sections of this book we review four books that deal with nothing but enticing birds hither. A fifth book, and one of the best, is unfortunately out of print; you may be able to pick up a used copy. That's the 1974 *Attracting Birds to Your Garden* by Cristine Russell and Philip Edinger, Sunset Books, Menlo Park, CA 94025.

Since bird houses are usually what beginners think of when they take an interest in watching birds at home, here is a chart giving basic facts about how to build, and how high to place, houses (sometimes called nesting boxes) for 26 kinds of birds. The information comes from the U.S. Department of Interior's Fish and Wildlife Service.

Dimensions of bird houses for species of birds that use them, and the height at which they should be placed above the ground.

Species	Floor of Cavity	Depth of Cavity	Entrance above Floor	Diameter of Entrance	Height above Ground
	Inches	*Inches*	*Inches*	*Inches*	*Feet*
Bluebird	5x5	8	6	1½	5—10
Robin	6x8	8	(1)	(1)	6—15
Chickadee	4x4	8—10	6—8	1⅛	6—15
Titmouse	4x4	8—10	6—8	1¼	6—15
Nuthatch	4x4	8—10	6—8	1¼	12—20
House Wren	4x4	6—8	1—6	1—1¼	6—10
Bewick's Wren	4x4	6—8	1—6	1—1¼	6—10
Carolina Wren	4x4	6—8	1—6	1½	6—10
Violet-green Swallow	5x5	6	1—5	1½	10—15
Tree Swallow	5x5	6	1—5	1½	10—15
Barn Swallow	6x6	6	(1)	(1)	8—12
Purple Martin	6x6	6	1	2½	15—20
Prothonotary Warbler	6x6	6	4	1½	2—4
Starling	6x6	16—18	14—16	2	10—25
Phoebe	6x6	6	(1)	(1)	8—12
Crested Flycatcher	6x6	8—10	6—8	2	8—20
Flicker	7x7	16—18	14—16	2½	6—20
Golden-fronted Woodpecker	6x6	12—15	9—12	2	12—20
Red-headed Woodpecker	6x6	12—15	9—12	2	12—20
Downy Woodpecker	4x4	9—12	6—8	1¼	6—20
Hairy Woodpecker	6x6	12—15	9—12	1½	12—20
Screech Owl	8x8	12—15	9—12	3	10—30
Saw-whet Owl	6x6	10—12	8—10	2½	12—20
Barn Owl	10x18	15—18	4	6	12—18
Sparrow Hawk	8x8	12—15	9—12	3	10—30
Wood Duck	10x18	10—24	12—16	4	10—20*

(1) Leave one or more sides open.

It may be that you aren't handy with tools — you prefer to buy a bird house ready-made. Or perhaps you'd like an overview of who is offering what for garden birds. A list of mail-order suppliers follows. Most of them sell houses and feeders, some sell seeds, some sell baths and heaters. Write for their free catalogs.

1. Ardsley Woodcraft Products, 263 Douglas Road, Staten Island, NY 10304.
2. Audubon Workshop, 1501 Paddock Drive, Northbrook, IL 60062.
3. Ben Smith Martin Houses, Bailey's Harbor, WI 40202.
4. Bird Furniture, Box 781, Torrington, CONN 06790.
5. The Bird Tree, 5 Swallow Lane, North Oaks, St. Paul, MN 55110.
6. Bower Manufacturing Company, 1021 South 10th Street, Goshen, IND 46526.
7. Colebrook Specialties, Colebrook, CONN 06790.
8. Dina Dee, Box 6101, San Antonio, TX 78209.
9. Droll Yankees, Mill Road, Roster, RI 02825.
10. Duncraft, 25 South Main Street, Penacook, NH 03301.
11. Frye Feeders, 5301 Ocean Terrace, Marathon, FL 33050.
12. Hummingbird Heaven, 10726 Samoa Avenue, Tujunga, CA 91042.
13. Hyde Bird Feeder, 56 Felton Street, Waltham, MASS 02154.
14. Jae Jae Industries, 3121 Oak Street, Santa Ana, CA 92707.
15. Libner Grain, 25 Commerce Street, Norwalk, CONN 06850.
16. Long Life Dial-A-Bird Home, Box 449, Westwood, NJ 07675.
17. Massachusetts Audubon Society, South Great Road, Lincoln, MASS 01773.
18. Nature House, Griggsville, IL 62340.
19. Nelson Manufacturing Company, Box 636, Cedar Rapids, IOWA 52406.
20. Pecano Bird Feed Company, 110 West Street, Albany, GA 31701.
21. Smelser and Family, Route 2, Paoli, IND 06032.
22. Swift Redwood Playhouses, Rt 4, Box 206, Terrell, TX 75160.
23. Tucker Wild Bird Sanctuary, 29322A Modjeska Canyon Road, Orange, CA 92667.
24. Valley Bird Shoppe, 4870 Lander Road, Chagrin Falls, OH 44022.
25. James R. Waite, Box 78, Manhasset, NY 11030.
26. Wildlife Refuge, Box 987, East Lansing, MI 48823.
27. Woodland Specialties, Box 395, Hempstead, NY 11951.
28. Yield House, North Conway, NH 03860.

If you plan to landscape a barren plot for birds, or to rearrange your garden, the main thing to keep in mind is that an ecotone, or edge, attracts the maximum variety of birds. What's an ecotone? Where two types of vegetation meet, such as grassland and woods. Thus it's best to surround a lawn with shrubs or trees. The following list of plantings gives ideas for food, shelter, and places to build nests. The list comprises the favorites of most birds.

Birds' Favorite Plants

FOR SEEDS (FLOWERS)

Amaranthus
Aster
Bachelor's Button
Bellflower
Black-eyed Susan
Calendula
Campanula
Cardium
Chrysanthemum
Columbine
Coreopsis
Dianthus
Forget-me-not
Four-o-clock
Larkspur
Marigold
Petunia
Pink
Poppy (California)
Portulaca
Phlox
Sorghum
Sunflower
Sweet William
Verbena
Zinnia
Alder
Ash
Birch
Maple
Spindle tree (Euonymus)

FOR INSECTS

Birch
Elm
Maple
Sycamore
Willow

FOR FRUITS (WINTER)

American Holly
Amur Cork Tree
Amur Honeysuckle
Common Hackberry
American Cranberry
Bayberry
Eastern Red Cedar
Japanese Rose
Russian Olive
Sargent Crabapple
Staghorn Sumac
Tulip Tree
Washington Thorn

FOR FRUITS (SUMMER)

Bayberry
Blackberry
Blueberry
Cherry
Crabapple
Dogwood
Firethorn
  (Pyracantha)
Hawthorn
Holly
Honeysuckle
Mountain Ash
Plum
Raspberry
Shadbush
Toyon
Viburnum

FOR NESTS

Arrowwood
Autumn Eleagnus
Barberry
Blue Beech
Buckthorn
Cornelian Cherry
Crabapple
Dogwood
Eastern Red Cedar
Elderberry
Hawthorn
Hemlock
Holly
Matrimony Vine
Mulberry
Nannyberry
Pine
Spruce

FOR SHELTER

Arrowwood
Barberry
Buckthorn
Elderberry
Fir
Greenbrier
Juniper
Matrimony Vine
Mulberry
Pine
Privet
Spruce
Tatarian Honeysuckle
Virginia Creeper

You will also want, especially in winter, to put out homemade fare. Small birds have more heat-losing surface in relation to their weight than large birds. You would hardly expect a California Condor to settle in your garden — it's the small birds you'll see, and the small birds you'll have to keep fed. The English or House Sparrow survives only a few hours after its alimentary canal empties (the California Condor can fast for a week). No matter what food you put out, keep it coming, that's the important rule. In winter if you tire, the birds may die.

All garden-variety birds except hummingbirds will eat seeds, even those who prefer insects. Sunflower and millet seeds are favorites. Supermarkets, nurseries, and mail-order houses sell wild-bird seed mixes. Our advice: put out a mix, keep tabs on which seeds disappear first, and tabs on which birds are eating what. Soon you can custom-make your own seed mix depending on the birds you want to attract.

If you'd just as soon not provide the insect-lovers, the tanagers and wrens, with bugs, try peanut butter or suet mixed with seeds. Some say that adding corn meal stops the mix from clogging the birds' throats, others say that clogging is no problem. Take your choice. You can get suet (the hard fat about the kidneys and loins in beef) from your butcher — ask for the so-called 'short', not the stringy kind. What you do is spread the peanut butter-and-seeds or suet-and-seeds (both with a little salt added) on a dead branch. Or pack a gob in a dish or wire cage where the birds can reach it. To save money, for peanut butter or suet substitute discarded kitchen fat. You can collect it in a tin can.

Here is a species count of the birds found to like the different foods you can prepare.

Beef Suet — 57 species
Sunflower Seeds — 46 species
White Bread Crumbs — 44 species
Peanut Butter — 38 species
Doughnuts (suspended or crumbled) — 34 species
Millet Seeds — 29 species
Pecan Meats — 24 species
Corn Bread Crumbs — 22 species
Walnut Meats — 21 species
Grapes — 19 species
Oats — 16 species
Hemp Seeds — 15 species
Sliced Raw Apple — 13 species
Corn — 13 species
Sliced Bananas — 11 species
Dog Biscuit Crumbs — 11 species
Orange Halves — 10 species
Pie Crust Crumbs — 10 species
Mashed Potatoes — 7 species
Pumpkin Seeds — 5 species

Let's talk now about how to ask certain birds to leave. Why are some folks such foes of English (House) Sparrows (*Passer domesticus*) and Starlings (*Sturnus vulgaris*, a dark, short-tailed bird) brought from England by home-sick immigrants in the 19th century? For one thing, both will take nests from other birds, sometimes going so far as to peck holes in their eggs or even in their young. For another, they often gang feeders, stopping other species from getting the seeds you've put out. For a third, many find the House Sparrow's repeated chirp as annoying as the Starling's squeak.

What can you do?
1. Don't leave perches on your bird houses or vertical feeders; most native birds don't need them, the English Sparrows and Starlings use them to intimidate the other birds.
2. Scatter cheap feed like bread crumbs away from your feeder. Since English Sparrows and Starlings prefer to feed off the ground, you may lure them from the main repast (this trick lures away jays as well.
3 If you are a Purple Martin (*Progne subis*, a type of swallow)

lover, keep your Purple Martin houses boarded up until the martins come home from South America in the spring.
4. It's legal to trap English Sparrows and Starlings if you release them elsewhere (it is not legal to trap any other bird except the Rock Dove — *Columbia livia*, domestic pigeon — unless you have a permit).
5. Tie ropes around the branches where Starlings have been roosting. Shake the branches every evening. The Starlings won't roost there long.
6. Put up an imitation owl or, better, a real one that's been stuffed.

You may, of course, be one of those who likes English Sparrows and Starlings. If you're a city dweller and bed-ridden, the sparrow's chirp may not annoy you at all — it may be the only bird you hear. And if the Japanese beetle has infested your fruit trees, every Starling's squeak is music to your ears.

What about fruit by the way? How do you save your cherries, apples, plums and berries from avian marauders? Here are four ways:

1. Cover the trees or vines with cheesecloth or nylon netting (available at nurseries).
2. Post a stuffed fox or owl nearby (we don't want you to stuff them, but you'd be surprised what treasures lurk in the shadows of secondhand stores).
3. Cut a life-size hawk from black posterboard (the silhouettes in Roger Tory Peterson's *A Field Guide to the Birds*, published by Houghton Mifflin, are great for starters). Suspend it from a pole with fishing line. Chances are he'll swirl in the wind.
4. Install the farmer's classic, a scarecrow. But be sure to give him lots of clothes and streamers that flap. Change them often; if you don't the birds will ignore him in a few days.

Suppose you fail to discourage unwanted birds, what then? Or suppose, all birds being your friends, your garden becomes such an uncaged aviary of chirrups, warbles, trills and twitters, whistles, peeps, and squawks that the neighbors threaten citizen's arrest?

In such circumstances the best we can recommend, though it pains us to do so, is to move to a different neighborhood or bring in a truckload of cats.

Appendix C

The 50 Official State Birds

Alabama . . . . Flicker, Common *Colaptes auratus*
Alaska . . . . Ptarmigan, Willow *Lapopus lagopus*
Arizona . . . . . . Wren, Cactus *Campylorhynchus brunneicapillus*
Arkansas . . . . Mockingbird *Mimus polyglottos*
California . . . . Quail, California *Lophortyz californicus*
Connecticut . . . . Grosbeak, Rose-breasted *Pheucticus
ludovicianus*
Delaware . . . . Cardinal *Cardinalis cardinalis*
District of Columbia . . . . . . Thrush, Wood *Hylocichla mustelina*
Florida . . . . Mockingbird *Mimus polyglottos*
Georgia . . . . Thrasher, Brown *Toxostoma rufum*
Hawaii . . . . Goose, Nene *Branta sandvicensis*
Idaho . . . . Bluebird, Mountain *Sialia currucoides*
Illinois . . . . Cardinal *Cardinalis cardinalis*
Indiana . . . . Cardinal *Cardinalis cardinalis*
Iowa . . . . Goldfinch, American *Spinus tristis*
Kansas . . . . Meadowlark Western *Sturnella neglecta*
Kentucky . . . . Cardinal *Cardinalis cardinalis*
Louisiana . . . . Pelican, Brown *Pelecanus occidentalis*
Maine . . . . Chickadees, Black-capped *Parus atricapillus*
Maryland . . . . Oriole, Northern (Baltimore) *Icterus galbula*
Massachusetts . . . . Veery *Catharus fuscescens*
Michigan . . . . Robin, American *Turdus migratorius*
Minnesota . . . . Goldfinch, American *Spinus tristis*
Mississippi . . . . Mockingbird *Mimus polyglottos*
Missouri . . . . Bluebird, Eastern *Sialia sialis*

Montana . . . . Meadowlark, Western *Sturnella neglecta*
Nebraska . . . . Meadowlark, Western *Sturnella neglecta*
Nevada . . . . Bluebird, Mountain *Sialia currucoides*
New Hampshire . . . . Finch, Purple *Carpodactus purpureus*
New Jersey . . . . Goldfinch, American *Spinus tristis*
New Mexico . . . . Roadrunner *Geococcyx californianus*
New York . . . . Bluebird, Eastern *Sialia sialis*
North Carolina . . . . Chickadee, Carolina *Parus carolinensis*
North Dakota . . . . Meadowlark, Western *Sturnella neglecta*
Ohio . . . . Wren, House *Troglodytes aedon*
Oklahoma . . . . Bobwhite *Colinus virginianus*
Oregon . . . . Meadowlark, Western *Sturnella neglecta*
Pennsylvania . . . . Grouse, Ruffed *Bonasa umbellus*
Rhode Island . . . . Bobwhite *Colinus virginianus*
South Carolina . . . . . Wren, Carolina *Thryothorus ludovicianus*
South Dakota . . . . Meadowlark, Western *Sturnella neglecta*
Tennessee . . . . Mockingbird *Mimus polyglottos*
Texas . . . . Mockingbird *Mimus polyglottos*
Utah . . . . Gull, California *Larus californicus*
Vermont . . . . Thrush, Hermit *Catharus guttata*
Virginia . . . . Robin, American *Turdus migratorius*
Washington . . . . Goldfinch, American *Spinus tristis*
West Virginia . . . . Cardinal *Cardinalis cardinalis*
Wisconsin . . . . Robin, American *Turdus migratorius*
Wyoming . . . . Meadowlark, Western *Sturnella neglecta*

Appendix D

Rare Bird Phone Numbers

If you dial (415) 843-2211, you will hear something like the following:

"This is your Northern California Rare Bird Alert for Wednesday the 5th, sponsored by the Golden Gate Audubon Society. A Red-eyed Vireo was found yesterday at Audubon Canyon Ranch. To get to the ranch you . . . If you spot an unusual bird, call the following number. This recorded message will be updated in two weeks."

You can dial 24 Rare Bird Alerts in the United States, and three in Canada. Each 24-hour recorded message tells you when and what unusual birds have been identified in the area, and gives precise directions on how to get to the places the birds were seen. Because these directions become complicated, you may want to have your own tape recorder ready to record the recorded message. If you are calling long distance, remember that rates are lowest between 11 p.m. and 8 a.m. weekdays, and 11 p.m. Friday until 5 p.m. Sunday.

U.S.A.

ALASKA	Anchorage	(907) 344-9168
CALIFORNIA (Northern)	Berkeley (San Francisco)	(415) 843-2211
CALIFORNIA (Southern)	Los Angeles	(213) 847-1318
	Santa Barbara	(805) 964-8240
GEORGIA	Atlanta	(404) 634-5497
ILLINOIS	Chicago	(312) 283-2144
MAINE	Lincoln Center	(207) 794-6761
MARYLAND		(301) 652-3295
MASSACHUSETTS (Eastern)	Lincoln	(617) 259-8805
MASSACHUSETTS (Western)	Springfield	(413) 566-3590
MICHIGAN-ONTARIO	Detroit, Windsor	(313) 545-2224
MINNESOTA	Deluth	(218) 525-1617
MISSISSIPPI	Jackson	(601) 353-0012
NEW YORK	Buffalo	(716) 896-1271
	Schenectady	(518) 377-9600
	New York	(212) 832-6523
OHIO	Cleveland	(216) 861-2447
	Columbus	(614) 221-9736
PENNSYLVANIA	Delaware Valley — Philadelphia	(215) 236-2473
	Western Pennsylvania	(412) 486-2090
VERMONT	Woodstock	(802) 457-2779
WASHINGTON	Seattle	(206) 455-9722
WASHINGTON, D.C.		(202) 652-3295
WEST VIRGINIA	Triadelphia	(304) 547-1053

CANADA

BRITISH COLUMBIA	Clearwater	(604) 674-3660
ONTARIO	Port Hope and Cobourg	(418) 885-6068
NEW BRUNSWICK	Sackville	(506) 536-3025

Appendix E

The 718 Species of North American Birds

The following birds are those listed in the American Ornithologists' Union's *Check-List of North American Birds,* fifth edition, (a sixth edition is being prepared as this book goes to press). You can see or hear these birds in the United States and Canada. Representing one-twelfth of all known species of birds in the world, they do not include hybrids or accidentals.

The bird are listed alphabetically by common (English) name,

according to the Linnaean system of taxonomy. Thus the first entry is Albatross, Black-browed. Other types of albatrosses are indented alphabetically underneath. Where birds are known by names other than their official common names, the other names are set in parentheses.

The line following each entry is for your convenience, allowing you to write in the date you see that particular species.

Albatross, Black-browed	_____	Caracara	_____	Dotterel	_____	Flycatcher, Acadian	_____
Black-footed	_____	Cardinal	_____	Dove, Ground	_____	Alder	_____
Laysan	_____	Catbird, Gray	_____	Inca	_____	Ash-throated	_____
Short-tailed	_____	Chachalaca	_____	Mourning	_____	Beardless	_____
White-capped	_____	Chat, Yellow-breasted or		Ringed Turtle	_____	Buff-breasted	_____
Yellow-nosed	_____	Long-tailed	_____	Rock	_____	Coues'	_____
Anhinga	_____	Chickadee, Black-capped	_____	Spotted	_____	Dusky	_____
Ani, Groove-billed	_____	Boreal	_____	White-fronted	_____	Fork-tailed	_____
Smooth-billed	_____	Carolina	_____	White-winged	_____	Gray	_____
Auklet, Cassin's	_____	Chestnut-backed	_____	Dovekie	_____	Great Crested	_____
Crested	_____	Gray-headed	_____	Dowitcher, Long-billed	_____	Hammond's	_____
Least	_____	Mexican	_____	Short-billed	_____	Kiskadee	_____
Parakeet	_____	Mountain	_____	Duck, Black	_____	Least	_____
Rhinoceros	_____	Chicken, Greater Prairie	_____	Black-bellied Tree	_____	Olivaceous	_____
Whiskered	_____	Lesser Prairie	_____	Fulvous Tree	_____	Olive-sided	_____
Avocet, American	_____	Chuck-will's-widow	_____	Gray	_____	Sissor-tailed	_____
Bananaquit (Bahama		Chukar	_____	Harlequin	_____	Sulphur-bellied	_____
Honeycreeper)	_____	Condor, California	_____	Labrador	_____	Traill's	_____
Becard, Rose-throated	_____	Coot, American	_____	Masked	_____	Vermillion	_____
Bittern, American	_____	Cormorant, Brandt's	_____	Mexican	_____	Western	_____
Least	_____	Double-crested	_____	Mottled	_____	Wied's Crested	_____
Blackbird, Brewer's	_____	Great	_____	Ring-necked	_____	Willow	_____
Red-winged	_____	Olivaceous	_____	Ruddy	_____	Yellow-bellied	_____
Rusty	_____	Pelagic	_____	Whistling	_____	Frigatebird	_____
Tricolored	_____	Red-faced	_____	Wood	_____	Fulmar, Northern	_____
Yellow-headed	_____	Corn Crake	_____	Dunlin	_____	Gadwal	_____
Bluebird, Eastern	_____	Cowbird, Brown-headed or		Eagle, Bald	_____	Gallinule, Common	_____
Mountain	_____	Common	_____	Golden	_____	Purple	_____
Western	_____	Bronzed or Red-eyed	_____	Egret, Cattle	_____	Gannet	_____
Bluethroat	_____	Crane, Sandhill	_____	Great	_____	Gnatcatcher, Black-tailed	_____
Bobolink	_____	Whooping	_____	Reddish	_____	Blue-gray	_____
Bobwhite	_____	Creeper, Brown	_____	Snowy	_____	Godwit, Bar-tailed	_____
Booby, Blue-faced	_____	Crossbill, Red	_____	Eider, Common	_____	Hudsonian	_____
Blue-footed	_____	White-winged	_____	King	_____	Marbled	_____
Brown	_____	Crow, Common	_____	Spectacled	_____	Goldeneye, Barrow's	_____
Brant	_____	Fish	_____	Steller's	_____	Common	_____
Black	_____	Northwestern	_____	Falcon, Aplomado	_____	Goldfinch, American	_____
Bufflehead	_____	Cuckoo, Black-billed	_____	Peregrine	_____	Lawrence's	_____
Bulbul, Red-whiskered	_____	Black-eared or Mangrove	_____	Prairie	_____	Lesser	_____
Bunting, Indigo	_____	Yellow-billed	_____	Finch, Black Rosy	_____	Goose, Barnacle	_____
Lark	_____	Ground	_____	Brown-capped Rosy	_____	Cackling	_____
Lazuli	_____	Curlew, Bristle-thighed	_____	Cassin's	_____	Canada	_____
McKay's	_____	Eskimo	_____	Gray-crowned Rosy	_____	Emperor	_____
Painted	_____	Hudsonian	_____	House	_____	Ross'	_____
Snow	_____	Long-billed	_____	Purple	_____	Snow	_____
Varied	_____	Spanish	_____	Flamingo, American	_____	White-fronted	_____
Bushtit	_____	Dickcissel	_____	Flicker, Common (Gilded, Red-		Goshawk	_____
Canvasback	_____	Dipper	_____	shafted, Yellow-shafted)	_____	Mexican	_____

Grackle, Boat-tailed _____

  Bronzed see Common

  Common _____

  Great-tailed _____

  Purple see Common

Grebe, Eared _____

  Horned _____

  Least (Mexican) _____

  Pied-billed _____

  Red-necked (Holboell's) _____

  Western _____

Grosbeak, Black-headed _____

  Blue _____

  Evening _____

  Pine _____

  Rose-breasted _____

Ground-chat _____

Grouse, Blue _____

  Ruffed _____

  Sage _____

  Sharp-tailed _____

  Spruce _____

Guillemot, Black _____

  Pigeon _____

Gull, Black-headed _____

  Bonaparte's _____

  California _____

  Franklin's _____

  Glaucous _____

  Glaucous-winged _____

  Great Black-backed _____

  Heermann's _____

  Herring _____

  Iceland _____

  Laughing _____

  Little _____

  Mew _____

  Ring-billed _____

  Ross' _____

  Sabine's _____

  Thayer's _____

  Western _____

Gyrfalcon _____

Hawk, Black _____

Broad-winged _____

  Cooper's _____

  Duck see Falcon, Peregrine

  Fish see Osprey

  Gray _____

  Harlan's see Red-tailed

  Harris' _____

  Marsh (Harrier) _____

  Red-shouldered _____

  Red-tailed _____

  (Harlan's) _____

  Rough-legged _____

  Sharp-shinned _____

  Short-tailed _____

  Sparrow see Kestrel,

  American _____

  Swainson's _____

  White-tailed _____

  Zone-tailed _____

Heron, Black-crowned Night _____

  Great Blue _____

  Great (White) _____

  Green _____

  Little Blue _____

  Louisiana _____

  Yellow-crowned Night _____

Honeycreeper, Bahama see

  Bananaquit

Hummingbird, Allen's _____

  Anna's _____

  Black-chinned _____

  Blue-throated _____

  Broad-billed _____

  Broad-tailed _____

  Buff-bellied _____

  Calliope _____

  Costa's _____

  Lucifer _____

  Rivoli's _____

  Ruby-throated _____

  Rufous _____

  Violet-crowned _____

  White-eared _____

Ibis, Glossy _____

  Scarlet _____

  White _____

  White-faced _____

  Wood see Stork

Jacana _____

Jaeger, Long-tailed _____

  Parasitic _____

  Pomarine _____

Jay, Arizona (Mexican) _____

  Blue _____

  California see Scrub

  Canada see Gray

  Florida see Scrub

  Gray (Canada) _____

  Green _____

  Pinon _____

  Scrub (Florida, California) _____

  Steller's _____

Junco, Dark-eyed _____

  (Slate-colored) _____

  Dark-eyed (Oregon) _____

  Dark-eyed (White-winged) _____

  Gray-headed _____

  Mexican _____

  Oregon see Dark-eyed

  Pink-sided see Dark-eyed

  (Oregon)

  Red-backed _____

  Slate-colored see Dark-eyed

  White-winged see Dark-eyed

  Yellow-eyed _____

Kestrel, American _____

Killdeer _____

Kingbird, Cassin's _____

  Eastern _____

  Gray _____

  Tropical _____

  Western _____

Kingfisher, Belted _____

  Green _____

  Ringed (Texas) _____

Kinglet, Golden-crowned _____

  Ruby-crowned _____

Kite, Everglade (Snail) _____

  Mississippi _____

  Swallow-tailed _____

  White-tailed _____

Kittiwake, Black-legged _____

  Red-legged _____

Knot, Red _____

Lapwing _____

Lark, Horned _____

Limpkin _____

Linnet _____

Longspur, Chestnut-collared _____

  Lapland _____

  McCown's _____

  Smith's _____

Loon, Arctic _____

  Common _____

  Red-throated _____

  Yellow-billed _____

Magnificent Frigate bird see

  Frigatebird

Magpie, Black-billed _____

  Yellow-billed _____

Mallard _____

"Man-o'-war Bird" See

  Frigatebird

Martin, Purple _____

Meadowlark, Eastern _____

  Western _____

Merganser, Common _____

  Hooded _____

  Red-breasted _____

Merlin _____

Mockingbird _____

Murre, Common _____

  Thick-billed _____

Murrelet, Ancient _____

  Craveri's _____

  Kittlitz's _____

  Marbled _____

  Xantus' _____

Nighthawk, Common _____

  Lesser _____

Nightjar see Whip-poor-will

Nutcracker, Clark's _____

Nuthatch, Brown-headed _____

  Pigmy _____

  Red-breasted _____

  White-breasted _____

Oldsquaw _____

Oriole, Baltimore see Northern

  Black-headed _____

  Bullock's see Northern

  Hooded _____

  Lichtenstein's _____

  Northern (Baltimore) _____

  Northern (Bullock's) _____

  Orchard _____

  Scott's _____

  Spotted-breasted _____

Osprey _____

Ouzel _____

Ovenbird _____

Owl, Barn _____

  Barred _____

  Boreal _____

  Burrowing _____

  Elf _____

  Ferruginous _____

  Flammulated _____

  Great Gray _____

  Great Horned _____

  Hawk _____

  Long-eared _____

  Pygmy _____

  Saw-whet _____

  Screech _____

  Short-eared _____

  Snowy _____

  Spotted _____

  Whiskered _____

Oystercatcher, American _____

  Black _____

Parakeet, Carolina _____

  Monk _____

Parrot, Thick-billed _____

Partridge, Gray _____

Pauraque _____

Pelican, Brown _____

  White _____

Petrel see also Storm-Petrel

  Black-capped _____

  Cape _____

  Scaled _____

Pewee, Eastern Wood _____

  Western Wood _____

Phainopepla _____

Phalarope, Northern _____

  Red _____

  Wilson's _____

Pheasant, Ring-necked _____

Phoebe, Black _____

  Eastern _____

  Say's _____

Pigeon, Band-tailed _____

  Domestic see Dove, Rock

  Red-billed _____

  White-crowned _____

Pintail _____

Pipit, Sprague's _____

  Water (American) _____

Plover, American Golden _____

  Black-bellied (Grey) _____

  Mountain _____

  Piping _____

  Ringed _____

  Semipalmated _____

  Snowy _____

  Upland see Sandpiper, Upland

  Wilson's _____

Poor-will _____

Ptarmigan, Rock _____

  White-tailed _____

  Willow _____

Puffin, Common _____

  Horned _____

  Tufted _____

Pyrrhuloxia _____

Quail, California _____

  Gambel's _____

  Montezuma (Harlequin) _____

  Mountain _____

  Scaled _____

Rail, Black _____

  Clapper _____

  King _____

  Virginia _____

  Yellow _____

Raven, Common _____

  White-necked _____

Razorbill _____

Redhead _____

Redpoll, Common _____

  Hoary _____

Redstart, American _____

Painted _____
Roadrunner _____
Robin, American _____
Ruff _____
Sanderling _____
Sandpiper, Buff-breasted _____
Curlew _____
Least _____
Pectoral _____
Purple _____
Red-backed see Dunlin _____
Rock _____
Semipalmated _____
Sharp-tailed _____
Solitary _____
Spoon-bill _____
Spotted _____
Stilt _____
Upland _____
Western _____
White-rumped _____
Sapsucker, Yellow-bellied _____
Williamson's _____
Scaup, Greater _____
Lesser _____
Scoter, Black (Common) _____
Surf _____
Velvet _____
White-winged _____
Seedeater, White-collared _____
Shearwater, Audubon's _____
Black-tailed _____
Cory's _____
Flesh-footed _____
Greater _____
Little _____
Manx _____
New Zealand _____
Pink-footed _____
Short-tailed _____
Sooty _____
Shoveler _____
Shrike, Loggerhead _____
Northern _____
Siskin, Pine _____
Skimmer, Black _____
Skua _____
Skylark _____
Snipe, Common (Wilson's) _____
Solitaire, Townsend's _____
Sora _____
Sparrow, Bachman's _____
Baird's _____
Black-chinned _____
Black-throated _____
Botteri's _____
Brewer's _____
Cassin's _____
Chipping _____
Clay-colored _____
European Tree _____
Field _____
Fox _____
Golden-crowned _____
Grasshopper _____
Harris' _____
Henslow's _____
House (English) _____
Lark _____

Le Conte's _____
Lincoln's _____
Olive _____
Rufous-crowned _____
Rufous-winged _____
Sage _____
Savannah _____
Savannah (Ipswich) _____
Seaside _____
Seaside, Cape Sable _____
Seaside, Dusky _____
Sharp-tailed _____
Song _____
Swamp _____
Tree _____
Vesper _____
White-crowned _____
White-throated _____
Spoonbill, Roseate _____
Starling _____
Stilt, Black-necked _____
Stork, Wood (Ibis) _____
Ashy _____
Black _____
Black-bellied _____
Fork-tailed _____
Galapagos _____
Harcourt's _____
Leach's _____
Least _____
White-faced _____
Wilson's _____
Surfbird _____
Swallow, Bank _____
Barn _____
Cave _____
Cliff _____
Rough-winged _____
Tree _____
Violet-green _____
Swan, Mute _____
Trumpeter _____
Whistling _____
Swift, Black _____
Chimney _____
Vaux's _____
White-throated _____
Tanager, Hepatic _____
Scarlet _____
Summer _____
Western _____
Tattler, Wandering _____
Teal, Baikal _____
Blue-winged _____
Cinnamon _____
Green-winged _____
Tern, Aleutian _____
Arctic _____
Black _____
Black Noddy _____
Bridled _____
Caspian _____
Blue-winged _____
Canada _____
Cape May _____
Cerulean _____
Chestnut-sided _____
Colima _____
Connecticut _____

Common _____
Elegant _____
Forster's _____
Gull-billed _____
Least _____
Noddy _____
Roseate _____
Royal _____
Sandwich (Cabot's) _____
Sooty _____
Trudeau's _____
Thrasher, Bendire's _____
Brown _____
California _____
Crissal _____
Curve-billed _____
Le Conte's _____
Long-billed _____
Sage _____
Thrush, Gray-cheeked _____
Hermit _____
Swainson's (Olive-backed) _____
Varied _____
Wood _____
Titmouse, Black-crested _____
Bridled _____
Plain _____
Tufted _____
Towhee, Abert's _____
Brown _____
Green-tailed _____
Rufous-sided _____
Trogon, Coppery-tailed _____
Tropicbird, Red-billed _____
Red-tailed _____
White-tailed _____
Turkey _____
Turnstone, Black _____
Ruddy _____
Veery (Wilson's) _____
Verdin _____
Vireo, Bell's _____
Black-capped _____
Black-whiskered _____
Gray _____
Hutton's _____
Philadelphia _____
Red-eyed _____
Solitary _____
Warbling _____
White-eyed _____
Yellow-green _____
Yellow-throated _____
Vulture, Black _____
Turkey _____
Wagtail, Yellow _____
White _____
Warbler, Arctic _____
Bachman's _____
Bay-breasted _____
Black-and-white _____
Blackburnian _____
Blackpoll _____
Black-throated Blue _____
Black-throated Gray _____
Black-throated Green _____
Golden-winged _____
Grace's _____
Hermit _____

Hooded _____
Kentucky _____
Kirtland's _____
Lucy's _____
MacGillivray's _____
Magnolia _____
Mourning _____
Nashville _____
Olive _____
Olive-backed see Parula
Orange-crowned _____
Palm _____
Parula, Northern _____
Parula, Tropical (Olive-backed) _____
Pine _____
Prairie _____
Prothonotary _____
Red-faced _____
Swainson's _____
Tennessee _____
Townsend's _____
Virginia's _____
Wilson's _____
Worm-eating _____
Yellow _____
Yellow-rumped _____
Yellow-throated _____
Waterthrush, Louisiana _____
Northern _____
Waxwing, Bohemian _____
Cedar _____
Wheatear _____
Whimbrel (Hudsonian Curlew) _____
Whip-poor-will _____
Ridgway's _____
Widgeon, American _____
European _____
Willet _____
Woodcock, American _____
Woodpecker, Acorn _____
Arizona _____
Black-backed Three-toed _____
Downy _____
Gila _____
Golden-fronted _____
Hairy _____
Ivory-billed _____
Ladder-backed _____
Lewis' _____
Northern Tree-toed _____
Nuttall's _____
Pileated _____
Red-bellied _____
Red-headed _____
White-headed _____
Wren, Bewick's _____
Brown-throated _____
Cactus _____
Canyon _____
Carolina _____
House _____
Long-billed Marsh _____
Rock _____
Short-billed Marsh _____
Winter _____
Wrentit _____
Yellowlegs, Greater _____
Yellowthroat, Common _____

Appendix F

Equipment Manufacturers

AIC PHOTO, INC.
Carle Place, NY 11514. (Soligor telephoto lenses)

AUDIO-TECHNICA U.S., INC.
33 Shiawassee Ave., Fairlawn, OH
44313. (Audio-technica microphones)

BERKEY MARKETING
COMPANIES
25-20 Brooklyn-Queens Expwy West,
Woodside, NY 11377. (Tamron telephoto lenses, Silk tripods)

BURLEIGH BROOKS OPTICS,
INC.
44 Burlews Court, Hackensack, NJ
07601. (Novoflex telephoto lenses)

BUSHNELL OPTICAL CO.
2828 East Foothill Blvd.
Pasadena, CA 91107. (Bushnell,
Bausch & Lomb binoculars, spotting
scopes, tripods)

CANON USA, INC.
10 Nevada Drive, Lake Success, NY
11040. (Canon telephoto lenses)

CELESTRON INTERNATIONAL
2835 Columbia, Torrance, CA 90503.
(Celestron binoculars, spotting
scopes, telephoto lenses)

CHINON CORP. OF AMERICA, INC.
43 Fadem Road, Springfield, NJ
07081. (Chinon telephoto lenses)

CRAIG CORP.
921 W. Artesia Blvd., Compton, CA
90220. (Craig tape recorders)

DAVIS & SANFORD CO., INC.
24 Pleasant St., New Rochelle, NY
10802. (Davis & Sanford tripods)

ELECTRO-VOICE, INC.
656 Cecil St., Buchanan, MI 49107.
(Electro-Voice microphones)

FUJI PHOTO FLIM USA, INC.
350 Fifth Ave., New York, NY 10001.
(Fujica telephoto lenses)

GENERAL ELECTRIC CO.
3135 Easton Turnpike, Fairfield, CT
06430. (G.E. tape recorders)

HANIMEX, INC.
1801 Touhy Ave., Elk Grove Village,
IL 60007. (Hanimex binoculars and
telephoto lenses)

KARL HEITZ, INC.
979 Third Ave., New York, NY 10022.
(Gitzo tripods)

JVC AMERICA COMPANY
58-75 Queens Midtown Expressway,
Maspeth, NY 11378. (JVC tape
recorders and microphones)

E. LEITZ CO.
Rockleigh, NJ 07647. (Leitz binoculars)

MINOLTA CORP.
101 Williams Dr., Ramsey, NJ 07446.
(Rokkor telephoto lenses)

NAKAMICHI RESEARCH (USA)
INC.
220 Westbury Ave., Carle Place, NY
11514. (Nakamichi tape recorders
and microphones)

NIKON, INC.
623 Stewart Ave., Garden City, NY
11530. (Nikon binoculars, Nikkor
telephoto lenses)

OLYMPUS CAMERA CORP.
Crossways Park, Woodbury, NY
11797. (Zuico telephoto lenses)

OLYMPUS CORP. OF AMERICA
2 Nevada Dr., New Hyde Park, NY
11040. (Pearlcorder tape recorders)

PANASONIC CO.
1 Panasonic Way, Secaucus, NJ
07094. (Panasonic tape recorders and
microphones)

PIONEER ELECTRONICS OF
AMERICA
1925 E. Dominguez St., Long Beach,
CA 90810. (Pioneer tape recorders)

QUESTAR CORP.
Box 700, New Hope, PA 18938.
(Questar spotting scopes and tele-
photo lenses)

R.D. SYSTEMS OF CANADA LTD.
116 Wheeler Ave., Toronto, Ontario,
M4L 3V2 Canada. U.S.A. Distribu-
tors: A.V. Explorations, Inc., 2000
Eggert Rd., Amherst, NY 14226. (Dan
Gibson Parabolic Microphone)

ROLLEI OF AMERICA
5501 South Broadway, Littletown,
CO 80121. (Rolleinar telephoto
lenses)

SENNHEISER ELECTRONIC
CORP.
10 West 37th St., New York, NY
10018. (Sennheiser microphones)

SHURE BROTHERS, INC.
222 Hartrey Ave., Evanston, IL 60204.
(Shure microphones)

SONY CORPORATION OF
AMERICA
9 West 57th St., New York, NY

10019. (Sony cassette tape recorders
and microphones)

SUPERSCOPE, INC.
20525 Nordhoff St., Chatsworth, CA
91311. (Sony open reel tape
recorders, Superscope tape recorders and microphones)

SWIFT INSTRUMENTS, INC.
952 Dorchester Ave., Boston, MA
02125. (Swift binoculars, spotting
scopes, tripods)

TASCO SALES, INC.
1075 N.W. 71st St., Miami, FL 33138.
(Tasco binoculars, spotting scopes,
tripods)

UHER CORP.
612 South Hindry Ave., Inglewood,
CA 90301. (Uher tape recorders and
microphones)

UNITRON INSTRUMENTS, INC.
101 Crossways Park West, Woodbury, NY 11797. (Unitron spotting
scopes)

VELBON INTERNATIONAL
CORP.
2433 Moreton St., Torrance, CA
90505. (Velbon tripods)

VIVITAR CORP.
1630 Stewart St., Santa Monica, CA
90406. (Vivitar telephoto lenses)

YASHICA, INC.
411 Sette Dr., Paramus, NJ 07652.
(Contax telephoto lenses)

CARL ZEISS, INC.
444 Fifth Ave., New York, NY 10018.
(Zeiss binoculars)

Glossary

Accidental: An accidental is a bird that does not breed regularly or occur annually in any given geographical territory.

Avian: Relating to, or derived from, birds.

Aviary: A place for keeping birds confined. The terms BIRD WATCHER and BIRDER do not usually imply looking at birds in aviaries.

Aviculture: The raising and care of birds, especially wild birds in captivity as opposed to barnyard birds.

Angle of View: If you multiply this by the magic constant, 52.5, you get FIELD OF VIEW—the number of feet across you can see through your lens, binoculars, or scope at 1,000 yards.

Banding: The act of wrapping an aluminum band around the leg of a bird so that the same bird can be identified later. The practice was started by a Dane in 1899. In England the word used is Ringing. In the United States all banding is controlled by the U.S. Fish and Wildlife Service's Office of Migratory Bird Management, Laurel, MD 20811.

Big Day: A BIRDER'S term, used to describe any 24-hour period, usually midnight to midnight, during which one counts as many species of birds (usually by sight, but sometimes by sound) as possible. The American Birding Association allows a group of four to pool the birds they find; its record is 204 species counted within 24 hours.

Bioacoustics: The science of listening to, recording, and analyzing animal sounds.

Biotic Community: A natural neighborhood of living things, like a prairie, or chaparral.

Bird (noun): A warm-blooded vertebrate whose body is covered with feathers and whose forelimbs are modified as wings.

Bird (verb): To bird is to seek out birds away from one's home in order to watch or listen to them.

Birder: One who seeks out uncaged birds to watch or listen to. A birder's skill lies primarily in identification. He or she often keeps a list of the birds identified.

Bird Watcher: Same as BIRDER except implies less aggression. A bird watcher may watch (or listen to) birds in his or her garden; no birder ever would.

Blind: A device used to keep the birds, usually birds close by, from seeing you. A blind can be made of brush, wood, cloth, or even a large umbrella with proper camou-flage. In England a blind is called a hide.

Calls: All those squawks, peeps, hisses, and grunts a bird makes to communicate with other birds, or to express alarm.

Cassette: A 2½″ x 4″ sealed plastic cart-ridge containing magnetic tape with the tape on one reel passing to the other. A cassette tape recorder is one which uses cassettes.

Car Mount: Device to hold a SPOTTING SCOPE or TELEPHOTO LENS steady in the open window of a car.

Central Focus: Means binoculars can be focused by revolving a dial between the two barrels, once you have focused the right barrel for your own particular eye. Speeds process of focusing first on a bird close by, then on one far away. For contrast, see INDIVIDUAL FOCUS.

Check List: A printed list of all the birds in a region, ranging in area from a city to the world. The list is used by bird watchers to check off the birds they see. Compare with the handwritten LIST.

Chum (Verb): Term coined to describe vocal means of bringing birds closer. Methods include PISHING, sucking back of hand, and playing a recorded bird sound out in the field.

Condenser Microphone: Works by the action of two closely-placed metalized plates, one of which vibrates with sound. Requires a PRE-AMPLIFIER. Modern, more sensitive version is the Electret Con-denser microphone. See also MICRO-PHONE and, for contrast, DYNAMIC MICROPHONE.

Count: A method of trying to evaluate how many birds are in a given area. The most famous count is the National Audubon Society's Christmas Count, where mem-bers of local chapters across the United States spend 12 hours on Christmas Day counting birds out in the field. The results are published in the Society's bimonthly, *American Birds.*

Dynamic Microphone: Here the current is produced by sound moving a coil of wire past a permanent magnet. Also called a Moving Coil microphone. See also MICRO-PHONE and, for contrast, CONDENSER MICROPHONE.

Ecotone: Sometimes called an edge, it is a transition area between two adjacent BIOTIC COMMUNITIES, such as where a lawn and hedge meet, or forest and grass-land.

Exit Pupil: This is the little circle of light you see in the middle of the eyepiece lens (the lens you put close to your eye) when you hold binoculars or scope a foot away from you. Its diameter is that of the beam of light reaching your eye.

External Jacks: Jack is another term for socket. How many 'external' jacks a tape recorder has tells how many external MICROPHONES and HEADPHONES you can plug in.

Eyecups: Rubber or plastic cylinders placed at the end of eyepiece lenses on binoculars. They can be rolled or screwed out or in. When in, manufacturers claim people who wear eyeglasses get same, maxi-mum FIELD OF VIEW that non-eyeglass-wearers get when eyecups are fully extended.

f/Stop: An optical ratio designated by a number. This number tells the amount of light a camera lens will let in. If the f/stop number is low, like f/4, the lens can let in a lot of light. If it's high, like f/32, the lens lets in little light. Most camera lenses have a range of f/stop numbers.

Falconry: The sport of hunting small game by the use of trained falcons. Often frowned-on by bird watchers, falconry got its start in China over 2,000 years ago.

Field: Term "in the field" means out in the open, away from home. A BIRDER goes in the field to seek out birds.

Field Glasses: The predecessor of binocu-lars, they use only lenses, no prisms. Thus field glasses cannot magnify with as much power as binoculars. Field glasses called opera glasses, with a magnification of 2X or 3X, are still used for indoor performances.

Field Guide: A pocket-size, usually paper-bound book with illustrations and descrip-tions, used to identify birds out in the open. The two field guides used most for North American birds are *Birds of North America by Robbins, Bruun, and Zim, and Roger Tory Peterson's A Field Guide to the Birds* (east of the Mississippi), and *A Field Guide to Western Birds* (west of the Mississippi).

Field Marks: The visible parts of birds that distinguish one SPECIES from another.

Field Notes: Notes written down or vocally recorded out in the open, upon seeing a bird. Should include date, weather, habitat, who you were with, FIELD MARKS, what the bird was doing, description of its sounds. Useful for later identification or data for research.

Field of View: Tells how wide an area in feet you can see through binoculars at distance of 1,000 yards.

Field Ornithology: The scientific study of live birds, uncaged and out of doors. ORNITHOLOGY by itself connotes either the scientific study of live birds, or of dead birds in the laboratory.

Filter Size: Gives the diameter, in MILLI—METERS, of various colored filters that attach to camera lenses in order to modify the photographic image.

Finder Scope: Low, usually 5X, power tele-scope mounted on top of the SPOTTING SCOPE proper, to help you locate the bird before increasing the scope's magnification further.

Fixed Power: Only one magnification possible, unless you unscrew the eyepiece and replace it with another. Term used with binoculars, scopes, and telephoto lenses. For contrast, see ZOOM.

Fledge: To acquire the feathers necessary for flight. A fledging is a young bird that has these feathers but still depends on his parents for food.

Flyway: An established air route of migra-tory birds. The United States has four main flyways, the Pacific, the Rocky Mountains, the Mississippi, and the Atlantic. see MIGRATION.

Focal Length: The distance between the OBJECTIVE LENS and the point where the image comes into focus. Used with TELE-PHOTO LENSES and SPOTTING SCOPES, it also implies magnification. As a rule of thumb, a focal length of 50mm (see MILLIMETERS) equals 1X.

Frequency Response: The range of sound frequencies which a tape recorder can pick up or transmit. Frequency response is measured in a unit called a Hertz.

Game Bird: A bird that can be hunted legal-ly. Term is used mostly for ducks, geese, pheasants, and grouse.

Genus: A term used in TAXONOMY to link SPECIES that have common character-istics. In the system invented by Carl Linnaeus (1707-1778), all living things are described in Latin, first by their genus, then by their species. Thus the English Sparrow is *Passer domesticus*, where *Passer* is its genus, and *domesticus* is its species.

Head: The top platform on a TRIPOD or MONOPOD, to which the scope or camera attaches. The head tilts up and down, and usually revolves in a 360° circle.

Headphones: Also called earphones, and sometimes available for one ear only instead of two, these devices allow you to hear only the sound you are recording or transmitting, nothing extraneous except internal machine noise.

High-Resolution: The ability of an optical device — such as a SPOTTING SCOPE or TELEPHOTO LENS — to keep the neigh-boring parts of a distant object clear.

Hybrid: The offspring of two different SPECIES of birds; less often, of two different genera (see GENUS).

Impedance Rating: Microphones always have an impedance rating. So do tape recorders, but it often is harder to find. The ratings should be compatible, else one or the other, your microphone or your tape recorder, won't work well. Impedance measures resistance to alternating current. It is expressed in a unit called an ohm.

Individual Focus: Means left barrel of a pair of binoculars has to be focused each time you focus right barrel. Changing over-all focus takes more time than with binocu-lars that have CENTRAL FOCUS.

Information Block: Term coined to describe the boiled-down units of informa-tion presented in this book for fast compre-hension. Pages of information blocks appear after the introductory material of each chapter.

Life History Study: A scientific study of a single individual's life from its birth to its death. The most famous bird life history study is Margaret Morse Nice's *Life History of the Song Sparrow.*

Linnaean: Following the methods of the Swedish Botanist Carl von Linne (1707-78), often called Linnaeus, who put all living things in a TAXONOMIC system that names them first by GENUS, then by SPECIES.

List: A written record of the number of birds seen. A Life List has all the birds seen during one's lifetime. A Backyard List has all the birds seen in one's backyard, and so forth. The types of lists are endless.

Lister: A person who keeps a written record of birds seen. A Life Lister is one who keeps a LIST of the birds seen during his or her lifetime.

Macro Lens: Also called a close focus lens, this special feature makes ZOOM lens capable of focusing on a bird inches from your nose. For most TELEPHOTO LENSES, zooms included, the MINIMUM FOCUSING DISTANCE is 8 feet or longer.

Microphone: A device causing sound waves to generate an electric current in order to broadcast or record sounds.

Migration: Moving periodically from one region to another (twice a year for birds) in order to find food or to breed. The Arctic Tern is the world champ of migration, travel-ling from Labrador to southeastern Africa back, 11,000 miles each way.

Mike: Slang for MICROPHONE.

Millimeter (mm): The term used to measure dimension in many bird watching equipment components. 1mm equals 0.04 inch; 25mm equals 1 inch.

Minimum Aperture: The f/STOP number that designates the tiniest space a TELE-

PHOTO LENS can make to let light through.

Minimum Focusing Distance: Tells the closest distance at which a TELEPHOTO LENS can bring an object into focus.

Mirror Lens: See REFLECTIVE SCOPE.

Mist Net: A fine-mesh, black or green, nylon netting used to trap birds so that they can be BANDED.

Monograph: A scientific paper, usually lengthy, that sets out to enlarge a small area of knowledge.

Monopod: A metal or plastic "stick" designed to hold a SPOTTING SCOPE or TELEPHONE LENS steady where there is not much space. See TRIPOD.

Native: A native bird is one that breeds regularly or occurs annually in a given geographical territory. For contrast, see ACCIDENTAL.

Natural History: The study of the objects of nature (as opposed to man-made objects), especially in the FIELD, from an amateur or popular point of view.

Naturalist: A student of NATURAL HISTORY.

Nature Center: An organized place where one can observe nature. Usually includes trails, restroom facilities, a building housing exhibits, and attendants to answer questions.

Nest Box: A bird house.

Objective Lens: The largest lens in binoculars and scopes. It is the one located furthest from your eye.

Observatory: A bird observatory is a natural area set aside strictly to study birds. It is manned by one or more FIELD ORNITHOLOGISTS. SPOTTING SCOPES are a staple of bird observatories.

Offset Binoculars: Binoculars whose two eyepiece lenses are closer together than the OBJECTIVE LENSES. Often called 'conventional' binoculars because they were developed prior to STRAIGHTLINE BINOCULARS.

Omni-Directional: Refers to the type of microphone that can pick up sound from all directions. When recording bird sounds, requires a PARABOLIC REFLECTOR. See also MICROPHONE, CONDENSER MICROPHONE, and DYNAMIC MICROPHONE.

Open Reel: 5" or 7" spool wound with magnetic tape, not enclosed in a cartridge. An open reel tape recorder is one which uses open reels. For contrast, see CASSETTE.

Optics: The science that deals with the phenomena of light, and how light can be used. Word often used as a synonym for lens or lens systems.

Ornithology: The scientific study of birds.

Often used interchangeably with BIRD WATCHING, but the latter is more recreational. See FIELD ORNITHOLOGY.

Output Level: This figure tells how strong a signal your microphone can impart to your tape recorder. It is measured in minus decibels, expressed — dB.

Pan: Term used in photography and television. It means to revolve. If a TRIPOD'S HEAD pans 360º, that means it revolves 360º.

Parabolic Reflector: A dish-shaped device of aluminum or plastic, 18" to 24" across, that both reflects and focuses sound waves into a microphone. Often used for recording bird sounds.

Passerine: A bird of the order *Passeriforms*, which contains over 5,000 species or 60% of all species. Passerines are generally small to medium-sized perching birds. Most of the passerines are SONGBIRDS, that is, they sing as well as make other noises.

Pause Control: This tape-recorder button or switch allows you to stop the tape from running without turning the machine all the way off. This control helps you cut down on WOW AND FLUTTER.

Pelagic: Means of the open seas. Pelagic birds, such as the albatross, live most of their lives beyond the continental shelf. All true pelagic species belong to the order *Procellariiformes*.

Pishing: The technique of repeating "Pssssst" without the "t" on the end, used for CHUMMING birds closer to you.

Portable Tape Recorder: A tape recorder that can be powered by batteries, thus allowing it to be taken into the FIELD.

Pre-Amplifier: Amplifies the sound after it has gone into the microphone but before it is amplified in the tape recorder. It is a separate unit.

Race: Synonymous with subspecies, race is a term used in TAXONOMY to classify local populations of birds with characteristics differing from other populations of the same SPECIES.

Radial Braces: Those braces on a TRIPOD that reach horizontally from leg to leg, increasing the tripod's strength and steadiness.

Raptor: A bird of prey (one which eats flesh). Eagles, hawks, vultures, and owls are raptors.

Recording Level Control: Device that controls the strength of the sound that gets recorded on tape recorders. It can be automatic or manual. For recording bird sounds, you are better off with manual

Reel-To-Reel: See OPEN REEL.

Reflective Scope: Uses same principle employed in high-power astronomy telescopes. Incoming light rays are folded twice,

by two mirrors, before reaching your eye. Can be used as a TELEPHOTO LENS (also called a catadioptric lens, a mirror lens, or a mirror reflex lens). For contrast, see REFRACTIVE SCOPE.

Refractive Scope: It employs lenses, and sometimes prisms, to gather light and to magnify. This is the principle used in binoculars, and in most TELEPHOTO LENSES. For contrast, see REFLECTIVE SCOPE.

Rifle Stock: The wooden stock manufactured to hold a rifle barrel, but often modified by bird watchers to hold a SPOTTING SCOPE or TELEPHOTO LENS.

Rookery: The nests or breeding place of a colony of birds.

Scope: Abbreviated term for SPOTTING SCOPE or telescope. 'Scoper' is slang for someone who uses a scope.

Shorebird: A special term covering 17 families of birds whose toes are usually webbed. Includes gulls, terns, auks, plovers, snipes, and avocets.

Signal-To-Noise Ratio: Signal means the bird's voice or your voice. Noise is the internal noise made by all tape recorders. The higher the ratio, the more clearly the signal will record.

Single Lens Reflex Camera: Often abbreviated SLR, this is the most popular type of camera, distinguished by focusing and composing your picture through a single, fully-open lens. It's the type of camera for which TELEPHOTO LENSES are mostly made.

Skin: The term skin, or bird skin, is used to describe a disemboweled corpse which has been stuffed with cotton for preservation and ORNITHOLOGICAL study.

Songbird: A species belonging to the order *Passeriformes*. See PASSERINE.

Species: A term used in TAXONOMY to describe a population of living things that have common characteristics distinguishing them from other populations. All species within the next higher classification, a GENUS, can interbreed but usually don't. If they do, the offspring is called a HYBRID.

Specimen: Often used specifically to describe an individual bird killed for laboratory study.

Spotting Scope: A telescope, usually 15X to 40X in magnification, used to locate and study wild birds. Most spotting scopes are mounted on rifle stocks or tripods to steady them.

Straightline Binoculars: Binoculars whose two eyepiece lenses are the same distance from each other as the two OBJECTIVE LENSES. Often called H-shape binoculars, they were developed more recently than OFFSET BINOCULARS.

Suet: The hard fat about the kidneys and loins in beef (and mutton) that yields tallow. Beef suet is one of the most popular foods for birds.

Systematics: The science of classification, or a particular system of classification. See TAXONOMY. For the Linnaean system, the one used for living things today, see GENUS and SPECIES.

T-Mount: A device for turning a SPOTTING SCOPE into a TELEPHOTO LENS.

Tape Counter: Numbers or a window that tell you how far along on a tape you are when recording or listening to bird sounds. This way you can tell when you are about to run out of tape. You also tell how to locate a recorded sound quickly.

Taxonomy: The orderly classification of plants and animals according to their supposed natural relationships. Today such classification is based on the evolutionary history of a SPECIES or a group of species.

Teleconverter: A special lens that doubles or triples the FOCAL LENGTH (magnification) of an existing lens without adding much to its length or weight.

Telephoto Lens: A lens designed to give a large image of a distant object, utilizing mirrors, lens elements, prisms, or all three. Telephoto lenses for bird watching are usually 200mm and up.

Transformer: Used with some microphone/tape recorder combinations to equalize the IMPEDANCE RATING.

Travel Preparation Information: The mimeographed or typed sheets of paper sent you by a tour operator after you have mailed in your deposit. These sheets of paper give you practical hints for getting the most out of your tour — what clothes to wear, what hazards to expect, what the weather is likely to be, what handy items to bring along.

Tripod: A three-legged object made to support and keep steady a SPOTTING SCOPE or a camera with a TELEPHOTO LENS.

Tubular Legs: Some tripods have tubular, or hollow-cylinder, legs. These are often stronger, less susceptible to buckling, than tripod legs square or rectangular in cross section. But see RADIAL BRACES.

Uni-Directional: Refers to the type of microphone that picks up sound from a 180^0 or less radius, rather from 360^0. A uni-directional microphone called a shotgun mike is most specific about where it picks up sound. See also MICROPHONE, CONDENSER MICROPHONE, and DYNAMIC MICROPHONE.

Waterfowl: A special term denoting ducks, swans, and geese only.

Wildlife: Members of the animal kingdom that are neither human nor domesticated, especially mammals, fishes, and birds.

Wow and Flutter: Expressed as a single percentage in tape recorder terminology, wow and flutter express speed waverings. You don't want these waverings; the lower the percentage the better.

X: Symbol used to denote magnfication in binoculars and SCOPES. Thus a pair of binoculars rated 8X has a magnification of 8 power, meaning it can seem to bring the bird 8 times closer (make it 8 times larger). See FOCAL LENGTH.

Zoom: Term used to describe certain binoculars, SCOPES, and TELEPHOTO LENSES which have ability to change magnification upon the turn of a dial.

Notes